Children and
the Environment

Human Behavior and Environment

ADVANCES IN THEORY AND RESEARCH

Volume 3: Children and the Environment

Children and the Environment

EDITED BY

IRWIN ALTMAN
University of Utah
Salt Lake City, Utah

AND

JOACHIM F. WOHLWILL
The Pennsylvania State University
University Park, Pennsylvania

PLENUM PRESS · NEW YORK AND LONDON

Library of Congress Cataloging in Publication Data

Main entry under title:

Children and the environment.

(Human behavior and environment; v. 3)
Includes bibliographies and index.
1. Child psychology — Addresses, essays, lectures. 2. Environmental psychology —
Addresses, essays, lectures. I. Altman, Irwin. II. Wohlwill, Joachim F.
BF353.H85 vol. 3   301.31s [155.4′18]   78-13511
ISBN 0-306-40090-1

© 1978 Plenum Press, New York
A Division of Plenum Publishing Corporation
227 West 17th Street, New York, N.Y. 10011

Articles Planned for Volume 4
CULTURE AND ENVIRONMENT
Editors: Irwin Altman, Joachim F. Wohlwill, and Amos Rapoport

Personal Space, Crowding and Spatial Behavior in a Cultural Context

JOHN R. AIELLO

Human Ecology as Human Behavior: A Normative Anthropology of Resource Use and Abuse

JOHN W. BENNETT

Cultural Ecology and Individual Behavior

JOHN W. BERRY

Cross-Cultural Research Methods: Strategies, Problems, Applications

RICHARD W. BRISLIN

Territory in Urban Settings

SIDNEY BROWER

Cross-Cultural Aspects of Environmental Design

AMOS RAPOPORT

Cultural Change and Urban Form

MILES RICHARDSON

Culture, Ecology, and Development

IGNACY SACHS

Cross-Cultural Differences in Human Response to Natural Hazards

GILBERT WHITE AND JOHN SORENSON

Contributors

JOHN C. BAIRD · Department of Psychology, Dartmouth College, Hanover, New Hampshire

PAUL V. GUMP · Department of Psychology, University of Kansas, Lawrence, Kansas

ROBERT V. KAIL, JR. · Psychology Department, University of Pittsburgh, Pittsburgh, Pennsylvania

KATHLEEN C. KIRASIC · Psychology Department, University of Pittsburgh, Pittsburgh, Pennsylvania

ROBIN MOORE · The People Environment Group, San Francisco, California

JILL N. NAGY · Department of Psychology, Loyola University, Chicago, Illinois

ROSS D. PARKE · Department of Psychology, University of Illinois, Champaign-Urbana, Illinois

ALEXANDER W. SIEGEL · Psychology Department, University of Pittsburgh, Pittsburgh, Pennsylvania

YI-FU TUAN · Department of Geography, University of Minnesota, Minneapolis, Minnesota

MAXINE WOLFE · Environmental Psychology Program, City University of New York Graduate School, New York, New York

DONALD YOUNG · Berkeley, California

Preface

In the first two volumes of the series we elected to cover a broad spectrum of topics in the environment and behavior field, ranging from theoretical to applied, and including disciplinary, interdisciplinary, and professionally related topics. Chapters in these earlier volumes dealt with leisure and recreation, the elderly, personal space, aesthetics, energy, behavioral approaches to environmental problems, methodological issues, social indicators, industrial settings, and the like. Chapters were written by psychologists, sociologists, geographers, and other social scientists, and by authors from professional design fields such as urban planning, operations research, landscape architecture, and so on. Our goal in these first two volumes was to present a sampling of areas in the emerging environment and behavior field and to give readers some insight into the diversity of research and theoretical perspectives that characterize the field.

Beginning with the present volume, our efforts will be directed at a series of thematic volumes. The present collection of chapters is focused on children and the environment, and, as much as possible, we invited contributions that reflect a variety of theoretical and empirical perspectives on this topic.

The next volume in the series, now in preparation, will address the area of "culture and the environment." Suggestions for possible future topics are welcome.

Irwin Altman
Joachim F. Wohlwill

Contents

CHAPTER 2

CHILDREN'S HOME ENVIRONMENTS: SOCIAL AND COGNITIVE EFFECTS

ROSS D. PARKE

CHAPTER 3

CHILDHOOD OUTDOORS: TOWARD A SOCIAL ECOLOGY OF THE LANDSCAPE

ROBIN MOORE
DONALD YOUNG

CHAPTER 4

SCHOOL ENVIRONMENTS

PAUL V. GUMP

CHAPTER 5

CHILDHOOD AND PRIVACY

MAXINE WOLFE

CHAPTER 6

STALKING THE ELUSIVE COGNITIVE MAP: THE DEVELOPMENT OF CHILDREN'S REPRESENTATIONS OF GEOGRAPHIC SPACE

ALEXANDER W. SIEGEL
KATHLEEN C. KIRASIC
ROBERT V. KAIL, JR.

CHAPTER 7

CHILDREN AS ENVIRONMENTAL PLANNERS

JILL N. NAGY
JOHN C. BAIRD

Introduction

THE CONFLUENCE OF DEVELOPMENTAL AND ENVIRONMENTAL PSYCHOLOGY

This, the third volume in the *Human Behavior and Environment* series, brings together contributors identified with the field of environment and behavior with developmental psychologists who have become interested in particular facets of the role of the physical and spatial environment in child behavior. The convergence of these two endeavors is a natural one in several respects. First, the major role of environmental influences on child behavior and development has been stressed consistently in the history of child psychology over the past several decades, as the history of the heredity–environment controversy illustrates. Partly owing to the pervasive influence of S-R reinforcement theory in child psychology in the 1930s and 1940s, which conceptualized environmental influences largely in terms of reward and punishment, and partly because of the natural inclination of social scientists to focus on the influences of parents, peers, school, and culture, the environment was considered almost exclusively in interpersonal and social terms. However, in more recent years there has been a counteracting trend, deriving from theories concerned with the role of exteroceptive stimulation on behavioral development, as reflected in the work of Hebb (1949) and his colleagues, Hunt (1961), Fiske and Maddi (1961), and others, along with a growing concern over possible sources of distraction and overstimulation originating in the physical as well as the social environment. These have led to a broader conception of relationships between environmental and behavioral variables as they affect the development of the child. Further reinforcing this trend, though from an entirely different direction, is the growing influence

1

of the behavioral-ecology view in developmental psychology, represented by the work of Barker, Wright, and their associates, which focuses attention on the role of behavior settings, defined in physical, spatial, or institutional terms (cf. Gump, 1975).

From the environmental side, children have proven to be popular subjects of study, as well as being of social concern, for behavioral scientists and professionals who have entered the field of environment and behavior. This may be the case, in part, because children often respond more immediately to environmental conditions, freer of the overlay of symbolic, cultural, and past experiences that may obscure or distort adult reactions. In addition, children may be more subject to adverse impacts of particular environmental problems and to be in need of protection from them. Indeed, if we compare the evidence on effects of environmental stressors, such as noise and crowding, on children with those found in adults, it appears that the most deleterious effects may be reserved for the young, perhaps because they have not had an opportunity to adapt. Conversely, the opportunity for achieving a positive impact on their development through suitable design of the environment may be correspondingly greater in the case of a young child.

Thus, historically as well as substantively, an overview of research and thinking on the environment and child behavior appears timely. Inevitably the papers assembled in a volume such as this relate in different ways and to varying degrees to the themes cited above. Yet it is interesting to find a very real convergence between the developmental and the environmental domains, as exemplified by the papers of Parke and Wolfe. As a developmental psychologist, Parke examines an array of problems relating to child behavior in the home environment (from physical stimulation to social interaction to television) and treats the issue of privacy as only one of a number of diverse phenomena relating to the home as a modulator of child behavior. Wolfe, on the other hand, focuses on the concept of privacy and children's interpretation of what privacy means and how it is achieved at different ages. She treats the problem from a broader concern with the issue of privacy *per se* as an aspect of the individual's self-regulation of the use of space and interpersonal contact and examines this phenomenon in children so as to obtain insights into the origins and dimensions of this aspect of behavior.

The papers by Gump (an ecological psychologist), Moore and Young (landscape architects), and Parke (a developmental psychologist) also complement one another in their ecological orientation. Moore and Young contribute an ecological analysis of children's environments outside the home, with particular emphasis on play and other unstructured activities. Parke, as noted above, examines the home as a complex environment within which the child develops. Gump's chapter provides an excellent illustration of the behavioral ecologist's perspective to another important environmental domain, the school. We had hoped in addition to include a chapter on experimental research on children's play and exploratory behavior, in recognition of the theoretical as well as practical significance of play as a mode of relating to the environment, and to examine the function of environmental stimuli in exploratory and curiosity-derived behaviors. Unfortunately, the paper originally planned on this topic was not forthcoming.

A complementary relationship also applies to the chapter by Siegel, Kirasic, and Kail, and that of Nagy and Baird. In the former case, we see a team of cognitive-development specialists tackling one of the favorite topics of environmental psychology, namely, spatial representation and mental mapping. The Siegel *et al.* chapter places these processes within the framework of broader aspects of cognitive development and also examines them by means of controlled experimental research of a kind that has been relatively lacking heretofore. In this respect, Nagy and Baird are kindred spirits to Siegel *et al.*; yet the problem they deal with has a Piagetian flavor, as they attempt to describe age changes in children's representations of ideal and actual geographic environments. Nagy and Baird's subjects are studied as the budding town-planners a few of them may indeed grow up to be some day. Few topics are better calculated to bring home the possibilities for a real amalgamation of developmental and environmental perspectives.

Finally, occupying a place somewhat apart from the others is the first chapter of this volume, Tuan's essay on children and nature. His contribution encompasses within it the various perspectives of the geographer, anthropologist, child-psychologist, and, last but not least, humanist. It reminds us that our understanding of the relation between children and the environment can profitably be approached from a broad perspective that encompasses a diversity of disciplines.

The papers in this volume and those in other volumes, such as McGurk (1977), indicate that the conjunction of environmental and developmental disciplines is already well underway and is a flourishing area of research. It is highly likely that we will see further expansion of such efforts at an accelerating rate. We must express, however, the hope that some of this research be deployed in a more truly developmental direction, in the sense of examining the differential modes of children's relations to the physical environment as they grow to maturity. We know as yet very little, for instance, about how the child's response to the world of nature or to the built environment evolves. More fundamentally, we lack information on the process of adaptation to environmental conditions at different ages, and thus the ability to assess the effects of various environmental stressors on children. And we know little about responses to change in the environment (through migration, or alteration of the environment itself), at successive periods of a child's development.

Clarke and Clarke (1976) and Kagan (1976), among others, have recently challenged persuasively the view of children's development as essentially frozen into a fixed mold once the child has reached the early childhood years, or as being impervious to the influence of subsequent events and changes in the child's life. These writers confined themselves for the most part to the role of educational and interpersonal agents. A similar longitudinal attack on adaptation to environmental stimulation and on the effects of cumulative environmental experiences should provide a better understanding of the complex relationship between developmental and environmental domains. Such an attack presupposes a true bridging of the disciplines interested in children and their environments. We trust that the chapters presented in this volume will constitute a beginning toward the realization of that goal.

REFERENCES

Clarke, A. M., & Clarke, A. D. B. The formative years? Overview and implications. In A. M. Clarke & A. D. B. Clarke (Eds.), *Early experience: Myth and evidence*. New York: The Free Press, 1976. Pp. 3–26; 259–274.

Fiske, D. W., & Maddi, S. (Eds.), *Functions of varied experience*. Homewood, Ill.: Dorsey Press, 1961.

Gump, P. V. Ecological psychology and children. *In* E. Hetherington (Ed.), *Review of child development research*. Chicago: University of Chicago Press, 1975.

Hebb, D. O. *The organization of behavior*. New York: Wiley, 1949.

Hunt, J. McV. *Intelligence and experience*. New York: Ronald, 1961.

Kagan, J. *Resilience and continuity in psychological development. In* A. M. Clarke & A. D. B. Clarke (Eds.), *Early experience: Myth and evidence*. New York: The Free Press, 1976. Pp. 97–121.

McGurk, H. (Ed.) *Ecological factors in human development*. Amsterdam: North-Holland, 1977.

Children and the Natural Environment

YI-FU TUAN

INTRODUCTION

Children are prepubertal human beings. The definition seems clear-cut. But what is the natural environment? And when we use the expression "children and the natural environment," what kinds of relationships do we postulate? These appear to be straightforward questions but are not because the key terms have meanings that are elusive and laden with culturally biased values of which we may not be aware. It is necessary that we be aware of them and of our culturally conditioned categories of thought before we attempt detailed descriptive analyses.

CHILDREN: A HISTORICAL NOTE

When does a child become a youth, or a youth an adult? Society defines these categories, and the definitions are subject to change. What is a child's nature? That has also changed strikingly in the course of Western thought. From classical antiquity to the beginning of the modern period, it was common to look upon infants and small children as subhuman (deMause, 1975). The rate of infant mortality was high.

YI-FU TUAN · Department of Geography, University of Minnesota, Minneapolis, Minnesota.

Adults viewed the death of the very young with an apparent indifference that shocks the sensibility of modern man and woman. The child's nature was regarded as wild, needing to be tamed. The child behaved naturally and hence badly. Christian doctrine insinuated that infants were easily possessed by the devil. Their tantrums and, by adult standard, misshapen bodies suggested animality and, worse, possession: the idea that infants were on the verge of turning into evil beings was one of the reasons why they were tied up, or swaddled, so long and so tightly.

In the seventeenth century the idea of childlike innocence emerged in Western Europe (Ariès, 1965, p. 110). The idea affected attitude and behavior toward the child in two ways: one way led to guarding him against pollution from adult sexuality, the other to developing his character and capacity for reasoning. The school was about to become a major social institution. The school taught "reason," that is to say, self-control, rationality, and seriousness (Ariès, 1965, p. 119).

NATURAL ENVIRONMENT

What is the relation between reason and nature? In the late seventeenth and in the eighteenth centuries the two terms were interchangeable. To philosophers and educators of the period, the laws of nature were the laws of reason; they were always and everywhere the same (Willey, 1962, p. 10). Nature and reason both displayed the characteristics of order, proportion, and harmony. Man-made environments, insofar as they showed these characteristics, were natural. It was possible to see society and its architectural shells (towns and cities) as products of reason and of nature. No necessary dichotomy existed between human artifacts and the natural; hence, the idea that children would benefit from exposure to an entity called "natural environment" distinct from one constructed by human beings could not arise.

In the eighteenth century, although philosophers saw no necessary dichotomy between the human world and nature, they were aware of its existence in fact; they often described the European society they knew in somber epithets of superstition and tyranny while painting in rosy hues the peoples and lands in distant parts of the world (Willey, 1962, pp. 19–21). It was, however, in the nineteenth century that more and more Europeans spoke in terms of two irreconcilable environments—man-made and natural. A major reason for this trend is clear: cities grew rapidly and sprawled over the countryside; some were badly polluted by new industries. Human reason and energy created the cities, the worlds of industry and commerce, yet it was obvious to more and more observers that cities often lacked order and harmony. A consequence of this awareness was that the meaning of nature progressively excluded artifacts—human works. Today, if people are asked for a definition of nature, they are likely to say that "nature" or "the natural" is whatever has not been made by human beings. Acceptance of this definition, combined with a conscious awareness of urban decay, makes it possible for us to speak of "natural environment" as though it were a self-evident phenomenal category rather than a mixed concept with a long and complicated history behind it.

Although we may give a restrictive definition of nature, we seldom stand by it in casual judgment. For example, when psychologists speak of the child's "natural environment," they may not be thinking of trees and grass, but rather of the classroom as distinct from an experimental laboratory. People still regard some man-made landscapes as natural because they look harmonious. The suburb, with its lawns and curved streets, looks natural—at least in comparison with the inner city. Farm lands are "natural," although they are clearly humanized landscapes. Thus, the old notion that even human works can belong to the realm of nature still lingers.

MAN-ENVIRONMENT RELATIONSHIPS

Environmentalism is the belief that nature (particularly climate) affects human beings and their institutions. It has been a favorite theme in Western thought since the time of Hippocrates (Glacken, 1967). In the United States few ideas are as popular as the belief that life is healthier and more virtuous in the country than in the city. Every spring *The New York Times* begins a campaign for funds to send the city's underprivileged children to summer camps, as though a week or two among the trees will somehow restore the children's health and enliven their spirit. How does the natural environment affect children's health? Posed in this general way the question is largely meaningless. Children's health depends more on the quality of parental care, nutrition, medical services, and the socioeconomic environment in which the children are raised than on whether they live surrounded by buildings or by woods. In romanticizing nature we choose to forget the commonplace fact that the infant mortality rate is much higher in New Guinea than in a modern metropolis such as Sydney, Austrailia. Yet it is reasonable to assume that the natural environment does have an impact on human well-being, including that of children. What this impact might be—its nature and extent—has not been subjected to systematic scientific study except within the narrower compass of medical climatology. American medical science has tended to relegate medical climatology to the past, seeing it as an approach of only historical interest. In Europe, climatotherapy, particularly as it applies to sick children, is still an active front of research (Menger, 1964). To evaluate its methods and findings requires detailed physiological knowledge. Such an undertaking is well worthwhile but it will divert us from another, more manageable and in some ways more important, aspect of the child–environment relationship.

COGNITION AND BEHAVIOR

Instead of asking, "How does the natural environment affect children?" we may ask the following questions which treat children as active, goal-oriented, and highly educable beings. How do children perceive nature? What aspects of the natural environment do they respond to and how do they adapt to it in feeling, ideas, and outward behavior?

The helplessness of the human infant and its long road to maturity are well known. The child has few instinctual skills that he can use to survive alone. At birth he is exposed to the values and practices of a human group. Very early in life he becomes a cultural being by learning the ways of his people. Dorothea Leighton and Clyde Kluckhohn (1947) say of the Navaho child that when he attains the age of six months "typically Navaho conceptions of life have begun to permeate and to attain a sway which will last forever" (p. 40). Anthropological literature is rich in examples of how culture affects a young child's perception, values, and behavior.

To speak of *the* child as distinct from a Japanese boy or a Mexican girl is to speak at a high level of abstraction. But it is a meaningful level of abstraction. Culture cannot suppress the imperatives of biology. All children go through similar stages of maturation. They can be toilet-trained only at a certain age. Complicated acts and ideas can be taught only at a certain age and not earlier. Facts like these are well established in developmental psychology. In discussing children we need to be aware of the dual roles of nature and culture: they are inextricably bound. The biological given allows us to speak of children in general. Young human beings have common innate capacities; how these develop and the degree to which they are developed vary widely from individual to individual and from group to group.

CHILDHOOD AND NATURE

Newborn infants already have a rudimentary sense of location and direction (Haith and Campos, 1977, p. 258). Babies soon learn to babble, and the sounds they make eventually cohere into language under the encouragement of adults. These competencies are a part of our biological heritage. What others do we have? A question of special importance to our theme is whether children can be said to have an innate sense of kinship with nature, one that becomes manifest by the time they reach a certain age. An opinion that exerts considerable influence among educators is that of Edith Cobb (1969). She wrote:

> There is a special period, the little-understood, prepubertal, halcyon, middle age of childhood, approximately from five or six to eleven or twelve—between the strivings of animal infancy and the storms of adolescence—when the natural world is experienced in some highly evocative way, producing in the child a sense of some profound continuity with natural processes and presenting overt evidence of a biological basis of intuition. (pp. 123–124)

Is this halcyon period of childhood universal? In Western society, well-educated adults of middle-class background appear to believe in it. Burdened with the trials and responsibilities of adult life, they look back to a golden age in their own past when, as Thomas Traherne (1636–1674) put it, "The corn was orient and immortal wheat which never should be reaped nor was ever sown." The beauty of childhood emerged as a prominent theme in Western art in the early modern period (Ariès, 1965, pp. 33–49). Although the sentiment is not shared by preliterate and Oriental peoples, it remains possible that prepubertal children everywhere feel, in varying degree, a love of nature. The idea needs to be explored, but in the exploration we should be wary of the influence of our own subconsciously held values.

THE WILD CHILD

Can a child abandoned at a tender age survive the rigors of nature and grow up apart from human society? What will his world be like—a world that culture has not made intelligible? Will his senses be keen and unspoilt, or will they simply be undeveloped? In a state of nature and living in the midst of nature, can he know happiness? These questions enthrall Western scholars who are intent on resolving the nativist–empiricist debate. An answer might be possible if a true wild child can be found. Many reports on wild children exist. Of these the most reliable—and certainly the best written—is that of the French educator and medical scientist Jean-Marc-Gaspard Itard (1962).

In 1799 a wild boy, ten to twelve years old, was captured in the woods of southern France. He was eventually placed under the care of Itard, who recorded his observations in 1801 and 1806. Itard (1962, p. 15) noted that the child's sense organs were keenly developed in some directions and wholly undeveloped in others. The child had an obstinate habit of smelling at anything that was given to him, even the things which normal people consider devoid of smell; yet when snuff was put in his nose he did not sneeze. Of all his senses, the ear appeared the least sensitive. Nevertheless, the sound of a cracking walnut or other favorite eatable never failed to make him turn around.

Despite the boy's fine velvety skin, he appeared wholly insensitive to heat and cold, wind and rain. Before capture he tolerated the cold winter of the broad plateau in the department of Aveyron. He was seen "swimming in streams, climbing trees, running at great speed on all fours, digging for roots; and when the wind blew from the Midi, turning toward the sky he rendered up deep cries and great bursts of laughter" (Lane, 1976, p. 7). After capture, when inclement weather drove everyone indoors, that was the moment he chose to go out. Itard (1962) gave several touching descriptions of the boy's longing for sun, wind, and freedom:

> When watched inside his own room he was seen swaying with a tiresome monotony, turning his eyes constantly towards the window, looking sadly over the airy plains outside. If at such a time a stormy wind chanced to blow, if the sun behind the clouds showed itself suddenly illuminating the atmosphere more brightly, there would be an almost convulsive joy. (p. 12)

The boy was also capable of displaying a contemplative attitude toward nature:

> During the night by the beautiful light of the moon, when the rays of this heavenly body penetrated into his room, he rarely failed to waken and place himself before the window. He stayed there . . . for part of the night, standing motionless, his neck bent, his eyes fixed upon the moonlit fields giving himself up to a sort of contemplative ecstasy, the silence and immobility of which were only interrupted at long intervals by deep inspirations nearly always accompanied by a plaintive little sound. (p. 13)

The human body evolved in close adaptation to the forces of nature. It is built to respond sympathetically to weather's less extreme buffetings, to the sensory stimuli of rock, water, and vegetation, and to nature's diurnal and seasonal rhythms. The wild child's delight in open spaces, sun, and moon seems to confirm Cobb's idea that the prepubertal child has "a sense of some profound continuity with natural processes" (Cobb, 1969, p. 124). It also supports many educated people's belief in the existence of a sympathetic bond between children and nature—a belief that has its roots in the European Romantic tradition.

Itard's wild boy, although he acquired many social skills, never learned more than a few phrases of speech despite his mentor's dedicated and imaginative teaching. Was the boy feeble-minded and hence abandoned, or was he a normal child lost in the woods who could not be taught human speech because he did not enjoy human companionship in the critical years of his life? This question remains unresolved. It is not, however, central to our concern. Central is the question of whether the child did survive alone with nature over a number of years. This would seem to have been the case. Central also is the question of whether Itard was right in attributing happiness and joy to the boy whenever the boy was surrounded by nature. Itard might have allowed sentiment to color his description, but we have no reason to doubt its essential correctness.

INNER-CITY CHILDREN AND NATURE

If human beings have an innate capacity to appreciate nature, it can nonetheless be rendered ineffectual. Cultural conditioning is often all important. Consider the case of children brought up in urban slums. They do not yearn for the fresh air of summer camps. To adults of middle-class background, certain parts of Brooklyn are a "concrete jungle." To children raised there, however, they are not so much a jungle as their *turf*, borrowing a term that suggests ordered space. In comparison with the known turf, the world of summer camps seems alien and threatening. Here is a vivid description of how a teenaged gang from Brooklyn responded to the natural environment. Vincent Riccio, a social worker, took the youngsters to a park in New Jersey that was under 25 miles from Times Square. Riccio and Slocum (1962) wrote:

> Adventure was not long in coming. They had asked endlessly about the presence of wild animals, and I had assured them that there was nothing wild within a thousand miles. Then the headlights picked up a strange beast on the road. They screamed in terror. "It's a lion! A goddam lion!" one shouted. It was a baby doe. It took a lot of talking to quiet them. Yeah, they knew what a fawn was. "It's a baby deer. And their fathers have got horns ten feet long. Two of 'em. They could kill you with them fuckin' horns." (p. 100)

Riccio and his tough young charges arrived at the camp and started to build a fire. The fire proved to be a problem because the youngsters were petrified by the dark and the woods. They refused to gather kindling in the thin forest surrounding the camp. Daylight diminished their terror, though not completely. They went fishing. Riccio continued:

> I had to bait their hooks. They had seen worms, but they were afraid to put them on a hook. Baldie caught a sunfish smaller than his hand and screamed in terror as it flipped at his feet.
> "Take him off the hook," I said. "He's good eating."
> "I wouldn't touch that sonofabitch for nothin," Baldie yelled.
> "Get him away from me."
> So I unhooked a two-ounce sunfish for a seventeen-year-old boy who I knew had the courage to lead his friends into gang war where the kids fought with bats, knives and even guns. (p. 101)

NATURAL ENVIRONMENT AND LEARNING

Inner-city children are disadvantaged; their capacity to enjoy and benefit from nature has been warped into indifference and fear. The example of the Brooklyn teenagers shows how extreme this warping can be as a result of living in an impoverished social and physical environment.

A belief once popular among educators holds that children are naturally creative and imaginative, but that these powers tend to be curtailed by formal instruction. If adults would only provide nurture and affection to their offspring, and allow them to play freely in a stimulating physical setting, then the children will of themselves develop their imaginative faculties; they will organize games, invent stories, imitate adult behavior, and so in these and other ways broaden their world. Associated with this belief is another: the notion that the natural environment is more stimulating than the man-made one. The Bushman infant plays with twigs, leaves, and pebbles; the Western infant plays with toys of relatively simple geometric design. The New Guinea child roams in the intricate world of sea and land, while the Western child is restricted to the school grounds, the footpaths, and play areas of a largely man-made world. Does the Western child's imaginative faculty suffer because he does not live in the midst of nature?

Margaret Mead, in an early work first published in 1930, took up these beliefs and challenged them. Her skepticism is based on her knowledge of the Manus children of the Admiralty Islands, north of New Guinea. Manus children are free to play all day long. Adults shower them with care and attention but offer only minimal schooling. The physical environment is ideal, a safe shallow lagoon, its monotony broken only by the change of tide and driving rains. The children have plenty of material to play with, including palm leaves, raffia, rattan, bark, seeds, red hibiscus flowers, coconut shells, pandanus leaves, aromatic herbs, pliant reeds and rushes. They have their own canoes. They have the wherewithal to imitate any province of adult life. Do their activities and games show evidence of exceptional imagination? Mead wrote:

> Alas for the theorists, their play is like that of young puppies or kittens. Unaided by the rich hints for play which children of other societies take from the admired adult traditions, they have a dull, uninteresting child life, romping good humouredly until they are tired, then lying inert and breathless until rested sufficiently to romp again. (p. 8)

TYPEWRITER AND LEARNING: A CONTRAST

Itard's wild boy may have a deep sense of kinship with nature, but he lacks knowledge of a formal and progressive kind that is characteristic of human beings. Manus children romp good humoredly in nature, but their imagination is little developed and they make only minimal use of the resources of their environment. The child's world does not automatically expand because he is well fed and has peers to play with, even when the setting itself is rich in possibilities. The idea that nature offers more intricate and stimulating playthings to children than can be found in the built environment is also of doubtful validity. In specific cases the idea is obviously false. Consider an increasingly common object in the man-made world—the portable electric typewriter. What single object in nature compares with this machine in its ability to stimulate the young child's senses, muscular coordination and, above all, mind? To the little boy or girl the typewriter is, first of all, a machine that moves, whirls, and makes all kinds of interesting sounds. Over this machine the child feels he has control: he moves, it moves. John Holt perceptively described the ways a child relates to the typewriter. Even an infant can have fun with it. Lisa, only sixteen months old, sat on Holt's lap in front of the machine. Holt (1970) wrote: "Having seen me poke at the keys, one finger at a time, she did the same, and seemed pleased by what happened—something flew through the air and made a sharp click, and there was a general impression of activity and motion, and mysterious things going on inside the machine, things that she was making happen" (p. 15).

Older children, three or four years of age, soon become curious over the letters on the keys. They recognize a few; they have their favorites and begin to punch them. They then notice the marks on the paper. Fascination with the machine changes character: it is not just something that moves, it can be made to say something. Holt reported:

> Elsie (aged five-and-a-half;, sister of Charlie (four), had a turn. She can read and spell. She wrote, without help, "DEAR DADDY, I LOVE YOU AND YOUR ROOM." This excited and aroused Matt (four). He wanted to write something to his father. I showed him what keys to hit to make DEAR DADDY. He wrote DDEAR DDADDY. But this was all he could think of to say. Perhaps the slowness of having to hunt for the letters made his thinking freeze up. He was torn between his desire to make the machine go lickety-split, and his desire to make it say something. (p. 37)

EXPANDING WORLD

The newborn infant's world is tiny and largely undifferentiated. In the course of time and under human care this world expands and becomes increasingly differentiated. The curve of growth, organic and intellectual, shows certain general characteristics that transcend environmental and cultural variations. An American lives in a very different sort of world from that of a New Guinean, but being an American baby feels much the same as being a New Guinean baby. Whether an infant is raised on the Arctic coast or in the humid tropics, his microclimate is warm and subject to little change. The infant has no geography, no more than does the world traveler who always stays in Holiday Inns. The adult traveler can, however, *see* geographical differences from behind the window of a jetliner or hotel room. This is not true of the infant. What the Eskimo baby sees is much the same as what the Pygmy baby sees in his quite dissimilar environment. The reason is that the infant's attention span is short and his field of vision highly limited. Experiments show that the duration of visual fixation on objects by infants aged 6 to 20 weeks varies as a function of object distance between one and three feet. Fixation times decline in a linear fashion within this short span (McKenzie & Day, 1972, p. 1108).

The man-made environment is inanimate. The natural environment is both animate and inanimate. Little children do not distinguish between natural and man-made objects at the conceptual level. Are they aware of the difference between animate and inanimate? Mahler

(1958) believes that as early as the first day of extrauterine life the infant has the ability to discriminate in a sensorimotor way between living and lifeless matter. But that he may not do so visually is suggested by Spitz's experiments on the smiling response (Spitz, 1965, pp. 90–94). This response begins to appear when the child is about three months old. It is elicited by a nodding human face; however, he also smiles at a nodding mask. The smile acknowledges a visual configuration rather than the object's animate quality.

If we accept the human body as a part of nature, then nature is the first environment the infant actively explores. A feeding baby explores his mother's breast with his mouth and his busy fingers. Left alone in the crib, he may grasp and play with his feet. Is the baby aware of his own body schema? Awareness is fragmentary at first and gradually becomes integrated. Only around the sixth month does the child begin to attend his own hands and use one to manipulate the other experimentally. Does the child perceive other persons as integral beings? Probably not in the first few months. The earliest attempts at observation of others consist in fixations on parts of the body. The child looks at the feet, the mouth, the hand; he does not look at the person. The French philosopher Maurice Merleau-Ponty (1964) noted: "At six months, at last, the child looks the other child in the face, and one has the impression that here, for the first time, he is perceiving another" (p. 125).

The little child's world is fragmented and consists of small specific objects close by. Toddlers one-and-a-half to two-and-a-half years old play with objects around their feet. Occasionally they stand up straight and point to things at a distance that have attracted their attention. Adults can rarely be sure what these are (Anderson, 1972, p. 205). Power to perceive and conceptualize progresses through stages. Culture decides in large measure the kinds of objects and concepts to which the growing child attends. In Western society a two-year-old can appreciate the moon. A three-year-old displays a new interest in landmarks, recognizing and anticipating them when he is away from home, out for a walk or a ride. At four he begins to grasp large concepts like the world, the sky, and the ocean. Collective nouns and generalizing phrases emerge in his speech. At five or six the child shows solicitous interest in young animals like puppies and kittens, and in growing things. He may become passionately fond of flowers; picking them is a favorite activity. He displays some sensitiveness to the beauties of nature, to sunsets, clouds, and rainbows (Gesell, Ilg, & Bullis, 1950, pp. 113–138). However, picturesque scenes and landscapes have as yet little appeal. They are too static. Their appreciation is beyond the small child because it calls for a contemplative mood and because it relies on memory as well as on acquired awareness of landscape elements, their spatial disposition and meaning.

ANIMISM, ARTIFICIALISM, AND SCALE

The modern adult lives in a world of objects and abstractions: even people can be counted and filed away as though they were things. In contrast, the children's world is colorful, vibrant, and alive. Children are natural animists. These beliefs are widely held. Though true as broad generalizations, they can also be very misleading. Even educated adults behave like animists on many occasions. We swear involuntarily at the table that we bump into, and we say "the sun is trying to break through the mist" as though they are engaged in conflict. In many ways the adult's world is more animated than that of a small child. Landscapes, to us, have moods. A spring scene full of budding plants is "happy." A broken mirror or an abandoned tricycle looks "sad." Children four to five years old are known to be baffled by these animistic adult responses. Speaking like matter-of-fact scientists they ask: "How can a scene, with no people in it, look happy or sad?" (Honkavaara, 1961, pp. 41–42). Dudley Kidd (1906) wrote: "I can remember as a child feeling sorry for stones, thinking that they must get very tired of looking at the same objects every day; so I used to turn them over or throw them over a hedge so that they might get a new outlook" (p. 147). Young Dudley Kidd must have been an exceptional child. Little children do not normally attribute sentience and perception to immobile objects. Only when they are intensely absorbed in a game do they do so. The ability to contemplate a landscape or an object and discern mood or animation in it has to be cultivated: it is characteristic of educated adults.

Children's tendency toward animism is enforced by their egocentric and functional view of things. A mountain, they would say, is "for climbing up." A countryside is "for traveling in." The sun is "for warming us." A child will endow objects with consciousness when he sees a necessity for them to fulfill their respective functions. Piaget (1969) observed: "A child of seven will refuse to admit that the sun can see in the room . . . but he will maintain that it can go with us when we are walking because it has to accompany us 'to make us warm'" (p. 222). Objects that provoke pain or fear are regarded as acting delib-

Children and the Natural Environment

17

erately. We have just noted that even adults turn into animists when objects frustrate them and cause pain. In pain, fear, or frustration adults become egocentric like children and lose their power of impersonal judgment.

According to Piaget, children tend to take for granted that things are human products. Things are made by parents and other adults. The word for this tendency is *artificialism*. Artificialism and animism together permit the child to comprehend his world and see it as essentially friendly. The child experiences a sense of participation, not so much between himself and things as between adults (his parents in particular) and the world of matter (Piaget, 1969, p. 263).

From the eighteenth century onward, adults have progressively learned to appreciate Switzerland's natural beauty (Zeller, 1936). Do Swiss children also admire it? If artificialism characterizes the thought of the very young, then the idea of *natural* beauty necessarily escapes them. The city of Geneva is man-made, as are the cultivated fields with which the Swiss children are familiar. So far the judgment is sound, perhaps even sounder than that of an adult who is tempted to see Geneva as artifactual but to see the plowed fields as "natural." To the children, however, even clouds, lakes, and mountains are human works. Boys and girls four to six years old look at the clouds and think of them as smoke that has come out of chimneys. They look at lakes and rivers and see that they are bordered by man-made quays and roads and that their beds are cleaned by dredges. Children, says Piaget, show a tendency to concentrate on signs of human activity. They look at Lake Geneva and what impresses them is not its size but the fact that quays border it (Piaget, 1969, pp. 352–353).

A child's notion of relative size, distance, and time are crude; hence artificialism is a possible stance for him. To an adult Swiss, natural scenery is sublime because it is almost inconceivably greater and older than anything that human beings can make. But to the little child, the city of Geneva is older than the lake it borders and quite as large. Clouds and the moon are not far away, and even the sky (made by man or God) is close, being situated somewhere near the height of the roofs or mountains. Notice that the adult, although he can be stirred by the vast size of mountains and oceans, seldom responds emotionally to distances and objects of astronomical dimensions. He may know that the sun is 93 million miles from the earth, but it is an abstract kind of knowledge that has little bearing on the familiar world of direct experience. It is therefore possible, even natural, for him to speak of "the sun struggling to break through the mist."

PLAY AND PLAYTHINGS

Natural and artificial environments differ in the kinds of play-things they offer to children. Can we say that natural play objects are superior to those that can be found in schools and artificial play-grounds? Belief in the superiority of natural playthings exists. For example, concerning Bushmen infants in southwest Africa, M. J. Kon-ner (1972) wrote: "When they begin to crawl the entire natural world is open to them—sticks, grass, rocks, nutshells, insects, dung and the ubiquitous sand—and they exploit it just as Western infants use toys, with the difference that nature never gets boring, and yet is somehow orderable" (p. 292). Nature may indeed be prodigal of play objects, but it is not inevitable that children become aware of them and know what to do with them. Margaret Mead has shown that Manus children make little use of their natural environment for lack of adult guidance; they romp like puppies. On the other hand, John Holt has shown how, under adult guidance, a typewriter can fascinate and reward children, even infants.

WATER, SAND, CLAY, AND MUD

The infant's primary environment is the mother; hence, geography (the varying character of the earth's surface) has little significance for him. Wherever water is available children seem drawn to it and like to play with this accommodating and exciting medium. But water is too scarce and valuable a commodity to be a plaything for the Bushman child living in the Kalahari desert. In the People's Republic of China, small children are rarely seen to play with water within the school compounds; water is not abundantly available and its play tends to be disorderly (Kessen, 1975, p. 78). Snow fascinates many children. Not only can snow be molded into exciting shapes but it may change into water, miraculously as it were, right before the child's eyes. Snow, however, is not ubiquitous. Nature's toys vary from one place to another. Nevertheless, children almost everywhere have access to certain kinds of natural play materials, including water, sand, clay, and mud.

Robert Kates and Cindy Katz (1977) observed: "Water is a special part of the play world of the child" (p. 58). In the child's play, water is an object of curiosity, exploration, appraisal, and use. Children imitate adult activities; they recreate the worlds of kitchen and nature (mountains and rivers) so as to understand them. There exists also an element of simple delight, one which adults retain in water sports and recreation. Kates and Katz wrote: "Watch a child trail her or his hands through a tub of water, intently pour water from container to container, frolic through an early morning snowfall, or splash in a summer wading pool. Are these not the forerunners of a quiet morning's fishing, of sitting by a waterfall, of skiing on fresh powder, or of riding the waves on an ocean shore? The most joyful of adult play resonates to the spontaneous joy of our youthful years" (p. 60).

The fun and usefulness of water are greatly increased when the water can be mixed with sand and mud: the child then has the where-withal to create a world—from pies to volcanoes and castles. The child takes simple pleasure in *making*, which mud and water permit. Anyone watching a small child rounding out the edges of a mud pie, or a bigger one putting on the crenelation of a sandcastle, must be impressed by the human dedication to workmanship. On the other hand, these common substances also give scope to the child's destructive impulses. The anger that cannot be directed against adults can be directed against mud and water; both making things and destroying them give the child a sense of power. Joan Cass (1971) put it thus:

> All these substances [water, sand, clay, and mud] can be maltreated in all sorts of ways: pounded, banged, pummeled, moulded . . . yet nothing has been destroyed that cannot be put right again . . . . So when putting bits of clay or dough through a mincing machine, jumping on a sandcastle or slapping or moulding a mud pie, children are enabled in phantasy to identify these objects and acts with people and things that have angered and frustrated them. (pp. 27–28)

Climbing Trees

Children like to climb trees. This action has been observed in many parts of the world. The postural repertoire of a dignified adult is extremely limited: he sits, stands, or lies down. In contrast, when a youngster reads a book he may have his feet up on the chair and his head on the floor. Small children fight against stiff and static positions. They like to swing and to be swung around. The tree provides ample opportunity for the active child to engage in postural acrobatics, to use his muscles and feel the thrill of temporary disorientation. Climbing a tree also means bodily contact; it requires one to hug the tree's limbs. D. H. Lawrence (1960, p. 100) described the deep satisfaction of clasping the silvery birch trunk against one's breast and sensing its smoothness and hardness, its vital knots and ridges. The West Indian writer V. S. Naipaul (1967, pp. 120–121) suggested that home is the body's memory of climbing up the smooth trunk of the poui tree as a child. One may emigrate to England as an adult, but England can never feel like home because there one learns abstractly: "this is an elm," "that is an oak." To the young child, moreover, the tree offers the excitement, the vastly expanded horizon, and the status of height. On top of a branch he is no longer a dwarf among giants; he is a giant himself and commands a world. The popularity of trees among children is commonly noted in the ethnographic literature on children. Here is one account from New Guinea:

> Instruction in climbing the tall almond trees is unnecessary, for, like European children, these boys go scrambling about in the branches when they are only four or five years old. At seven or eight they begin to accompany their fathers to the nut groves, though for a time they are dissuaded from attempting to reach too great a height. Some children, however, are as expert as their elders, and I often saw Sabwakai picking nuts on a limb nearly a hundred feet above the ground. (Hogbin, 1970, p. 149)

SLIDING

Every modern playground for children has a slide. Children in all parts of the world appear to enjoy rolling or sliding down a slope. Where an aluminum surface designed for the purpose is absent, children are ingenious in discovering other means. In East Africa, Idakho youngsters (western Kenya) slide down a slope while seated on the slippery portions of the banana plant (Lijembe, 1967, p. 11). Chaga children (Tanzania) use the hard fruits of the *kigelia* tree, which are the shape of a large cucumber. The boys cut seats into them and ride down steep grass-covered inclines (Raum, 1940, p. 265). Eskimo children have no difficulty finding slippery slopes; they use their fur coats to protect their backsides, much to the distress of mothers and grandmothers, who fear irreparable damage to the fur. Peter Feuchen (1965) reported:

> Once, on a summer day, I was busy in the shop, and Mequsaq and Pipaluk were playing outside with their little friends. Their game was to crawl up on a big slanting rock and slide down its smooth side. Up and down they went in one wild tumble. Then I heard their grandmother, Kasalum, come out and shout to them: "Oh no, dear children, don't do that! Think of your poor father who has to drive long stretches in the cold and dark to get skins for your pants. Now you are wearing off the fur. It is unreasonable, you must not do it!"
>
> Then she went back inside, and the children resumed their sliding down the rock, a wonderful game in any latitude! (p. 83)

Nooks and Play Houses

Children like to get into or make small places. Small corners and shelters are scaled to their size. In them the children feel in control and can allow their imaginations to fly. Small dark places are exciting—one can imagine all sorts of phantoms in them—and yet they are also womblike and secure. Infants are known to explore the shadow under the chair and they may sometimes be found under the grand piano in an apparent state of bliss. Children like to hide in cupboards and, fatally, in abandoned ice boxes. Vladimir Nabokov (1966, p. 23) recalls how as a child he derived fantastic pleasure creeping through the dark tunnel behind a couch roofed with cushions. Pearl Buck (1954) notes in her autobiography that her early memories are not of parents but of places. "Thus our big, white-washed, bricked bungalow, encircled by deep, arched verandas for coolness, was honeycombed with places that I loved. Under the verandas the beaten earth was cool and dry, and I had my haunts there" (p. 17). The tree house is doubly exciting to the imaginative child: the shelter is cozy but it is located up in the air and is accessible only to the intrepid one who dares to climb.

Does the natural environment provide as many places for children to hide and play in as the carpentered world of civilized societies? Probably not. For lack of cupboards, the abandoned car, the upturned couch, the dark area under the stairs or the veranda, primitive children have to create their own spaces. Making toy houses is a game but also training for an activity that they shall engage in when they grow up. Of the Chaga children in east Africa, O. F. Raum (1940) wrote:

> One of the favorite themes of mimicry play is the building of a hut. Any person strolling over the pastures or through the groves cannot but notice the many and varied miniature dwellings built by children. Some are made of sticks and grass, others of dracaenas rammed into the ground, others, again, of clay mixed with water. The huts are usually not destroyed at once and often serve as a center of imitative play activities for a long period. (p. 199)

CHILDREN, ANIMALS, AND PLANTS

Human beings identify with animals more closely than with any other aspect of nature. Attachment to rock, water, and plants is derivative because their appeal depends on the degree we see them in animate or anthropomorphic terms. We rely on animals for our sense of self, for our livelihood, and as sentimental outlets.

IDENTITY

Who are we? The human sense of identity, especially among the young, is insecure: it becomes more secure when "self" and "others"— the personal pronouns that are a language universal—can be linked to external objects. What objects in nature best serve as human self-images? Answer: animals. It is the contention of anthropologists such as James Fernandez (1974) and Claude Lévi-Strauss (1966) that animals are the natural predicates of human subjects: without them our sense of self remains inchoate. Prehistoric peoples, hunters and gatherers, pastoral nomads, all have the closest association with animals. It is surprising how the relationship—though in diluted form—persists in modern society. Infants play with stuffed animals. College stores sell stuffed animals to coeds. Sports teams often use animal emblems. Fond parents pretend to eat their small children up, and offer them piggyback rides. Children play at being animals, at being animals and man (hunters and hunted) in perhaps all societies. In the course of such play they learn group distinctions between "us" and "them"; they learn personality traits in their roles as chicken or hawk, and they gain a sense of self through the recognition that they transcend the roles they play. Fernandez wrote: "Children who have identified with animals come to act out their mastery over them. They fully become subjects, that is themselves, by becoming master of animals" (p. 122).

LIVELIHOOD AND HUNTING

Human beings were hunters and gatherers through most of the course of their biological evolution. The human body and mind are well adapted to chasing down and killing game. Sherwood Washburn and C. S. Lancaster (1968) noted:

> The extent to which the biological bases for killing have been incorporated into human psychology may be measured by the ease with which boys can be interested in hunting, fishing, fighting, and games of war. It is not that these behaviors are inevitable, but they are easily learned, satisfying, and have been socially rewarded in most cultures. The skills for killing and the pleasures of killing are normally developed in *play*, and the patterns of play prepare the children for their adult roles. (p. 300)

In Western society hunters have guns. The power of hunters lies in their implements, and their skill is manifest in the precision of their aim. Teaching a child how to hunt is primarily a matter of teaching him how to aim and shoot. The natural environment is reduced to an abstract space with two critical points, that of the hunter and that of his victim. Primitive hunters do not have powerful implements, nor, contrary to popular belief, do they put much stress on the accuracy of aim. What, then, accounts for their remarkable success? The answer lies in their detailed knowledge of the natural environment and of animal behavior. William Laughlin (1968) observed:

> Children were taught to close the distance between themselves and their quarry by sophisticated stalking methods that depended more upon comprehensive observation, detailed ethological knowledge and an equally detailed system of interpretation and action, than upon the improvement of their equipment and the addition of ten or twenty yards to its effective range. In fact, one may . . . suggest that the very slow improvement in technology, clubs, spears, throwing boards, bows and arrows, as indicated by the archaeological record, was contingent upon success in learning animal behavior. It was easier or more effective to instruct children in ethology, to take up the slack by minimizing their distance from the animal prey, than to invest heavily in equipment improvement. (p. 306)

MIMICRY

Children are talented mimics. In a hunting economy, without instruction, they learn to mimic the behavior of animals and thus feel a closeness to them—an unsentimental intimacy with animate nature— that is remote from the experience of city children and, for that matter, from the habit of children raised in modern farms. Here is Elizabeth Thomas's description of two Bushman boys playing a game of hyena-mating next to a group of adults:

> Giamakwe took the part of the male hyena, Wite took the part of the female. First they walked together on all fours and rubbed faces, and then Giamakwe climbed on Wite's back, emitting a lonesome howl just like the howl we had heard. It was not meant to be funny, and the other boys watched it calmly, treating the mating of hyenas as a matter of course. All in all it was a majestic imitation, with snarls and growls, then mounting and pretending to copulate with shivering and ecstasy, then more growls, until finally the male fell away exhausted and curled up on his side, whereupon the female attacked him. (Thomas, 1965, p. 120)

Bushman adults raise no objection when their children mimic animal behavior and sexuality. This kind of knowledge is useful in an economy dependent on hunting and gathering. On the Indonesian island of Bali, however, the animal nature of human beings is suppressed. Eating is to be done in private because it is an animal function, and small children are discouraged from crawling because it is the posture of animals (Geertz, 1972, p. 7).

Affective Ties

Apart from knowing the habits of animals, do the children of simple societies also love them and want to keep them as pets? Hunters must kill to survive. They cannot afford to be sentimental toward their prey, and as a rule they are not, nor are their children. With herders the affective bond with animals is more ambivalent. The shepherd, in the Western world, is the archetypal image of selfless care, yet the relationship is ultimately one of exploitation (Passmore, 1974, p. 9). Cattle herders in east Africa appear to be intensely attached to their stock and identify with its members individually. Children share the enthusiasm. Raum (1940) noted: "Goats and sheep early lend themselves to being looked after by children. The woolly sweetness of a lamb stirs the heart of a Chaga boy as it did of Blake" (p. 199). On the other hand, Robert and Barbara LeVine (1963) offer contrary evidence from what they know of a Gusii community (Nyansongo) in Kenya. According to the LeVines,

> Nyansongo children view animals more in terms of fear and aggression than as objects of nurturance and warmth . . . . In herding, boys sometimes beat the rump of a cow more than is necessary to make her move, and they also throw stones at cows to herd them from a distance. No particularly close relationship between children and cattle, sheep, goats or even dogs and cats, was observed. Boys of about four or five occasionally beat dogs, particularly puppies with sticks, much as they would an animal in herding, and the cries of the puppies elicit no negative reaction from adults, some of whom find it amusing. (p. 181)

Plants

Plants stir the human emotions less than do animals. Interest in plants, other than in sophisticated societies, is almost exclusively utilitarian. Children know about the vegetation in their environment, and take pride in the knowledge, as part of their cultural heritage. Of the Wogeo children in New Guinea, Ian Hogbin (1970) observed: "They identified themselves with their culture . . . . The little boys of Dap used to make a point on our walks together of indicating the different trees and shrubs and explaining that 'we' make such and such from this one, 'we' eat the fruit of that one, and so forth" (p. 141). Meyer Fortes (1970) reported that Tallensi children in northern Ghana, by the age of nine or ten, become thoroughly familiar with the ecological environment of their clan settlements. "They know the economically important trees, grasses, and herbs, e.g., a girl of about nine once

named and showed me nine varieties of herbs used for making soup"
(pp. 39–40).

LEARNING ABOUT THE NATURAL ENVIRONMENT

The natural environment, however varied and stimulating, does
not in itself inspire the children to learn. Nature is an inarticulate
teacher—or one might say that its messages are too subtle to be understood by the immature mind. Children have to be taught by adult
human beings. They show a natural curiosity about the world, but this
curiosity is easily repressed when adults fail to nurture it. To children's
questions, adults in primitive societies may give answers which are
unsatisfactory both because they tend to be curt and also because they
are often incorrect. Chaga children ask the following kinds of questions
and get the following kinds of answers. "Where does the sun go?"
"Into the mountain." "When we burn the weeds in the fields, where
does the smoke go?" "Into the sky." "If I shoot an arrow into the sky,
what happens?" "Water comes out" (Raum, 1940, pp. 247–248). Sometimes children puzzle a little as to how plants and animals grow bigger,
but the problem is too difficult and adults are not much help. As a
Bantu child said plaintively to Dudley Kidd, "What is the use of puz-
zling about such things? The trees will grow as well without my trou-
bling about the way they grow" (Kidd, 1906, p. 152).

In primitive societies, children's more theoretical questions tend
to be shunted aside, or given replies that are wrong from a scientific
viewpoint. But children do acquire a rich store of taxonomic and applied knowledge of the natural environment by observing and participating in the adults' business of making a living. Children are also
explicitly taught. A primitive child is blessed with personal tutelage
from a grown-up, and the classroom is the field. Here is Raum's account
of pedagogic technique among the Chaga in east Africa:

> In teaching his son the differences in the various species, a father uses the
> following criteria: the shape of the leaves, the form of the fruit, and the
> colour of the bark. When these marks are not distinctive enough, the smell
> of wood or leaf is examined. Another guiding principle is that of locality.
> This may be mechanically applied, as when a boy is advised to obtain
> fodder where his father got it for years. But occasionally attention is paid
> to general geographical features. (Raum, 1940, p. 198)

A Sioux Indian recalls how his uncle, who was a strict discipli-
narian, taught him when he was a boy living in Minnesota in the 1870s:

> When I left the teepee in the morning, he would say: "Hakadah, look
> closely to everything you see"; and at the evening, on my return, he used
> often to catechize me for an hour.
>   "On which side of the trees is the lighter-colored bark? On which side
> do they have most regular branches?"
>   It was his custom to let me name all the new birds that I had seen
> during the day. I would name them according to the color or the shape of
> the bill or their song or the appearance and locality of the nest . . . . I made
> many ridiculous errors, I must admit. He then usually informed me of the
> correct name. Occasionally I made a hit and this he would warmly com-
> mend. (Eastman, 1971, pp. 43–44)

Learning occurs at several levels, from informal observation and
mimicry, to explicit teaching of useful knowledge in the field, to the
transference of the lores and traditions of a people. The latter would
include ideas concerning natural phenomena: the cosmos, the heavens,
and the earth. Although traditional lores may have relatively little
bearing on daily and practical life, they tend to have high prestige.
This tendency is probably enhanced through contact with Europeans
who accord exceptional value to school learning. Margaret Read (1960)
noted:

> In talking with Ngoni (of Nyasaland) about the way in which they were
> handling their traditional knowledge to the younger generations, they often
> distinguished between two kinds of knowledge: one a wide range of per-
> ceptions and information necessary to carry out daily and occasional activ-
> ities in the household and village; and in the other, a corpus of traditional
> lore about natural phenomena, and about their history and law . . . . The
> Ngoni were often apt to stress the importance of this second kind of knowl-
> edge because they resented the attitude of many Europeans that the Ngoni,
> and other African peoples, were "ignorant" until the schools came. (p. 122)

AMERICAN CHILDREN AND THE NATURAL ENVIRONMENT

In the United States an adult's perception of the child's world
tends to be colored by a myth of boyhood enshrined in such literary
creations as Huckleberry Finn and Tom Sawyer. The red-blooded
American boy is an undomesticated being who thrives in the open
spaces, close to nature and away from the importuning of solicitous
aunts. Water is a powerful symbol of childhood freedom. "In its classic
form," Page Smith (1973) notes

> it is the old swimming hole or the broad Mississippi of Tom Sawyer or
> Huck Finn. It is the symbol for freedom and also for mystery and perhaps
> for something deeper. In the swimming hole, clothes and the conventions
> of the town are discarded. The adult world is rejected in this unique arena

which custom has allowed as the American boy's special preserve. The pond, the lake, the river, the swamp, the stream; it is as though here the small-town boy is dimly aware that he touches the source of life—dangerous, strangely loving and enfolding. (p. 219)

In the antebellum South the slave child enjoyed freedom in the midst of nature no less than the white child did. They were often playmates, and together they roamed the plantation or went hunting, fishing, berry picking, or raiding watermelon and potato patches (Blassingame, 1972, p. 95).

As farms are mechanized and people abandon agriculture for city life, fewer and fewer American children experience the kind of intimacy with nature that is captured in the childhood reminiscences and literature of an earlier period. That young fictional hero of the 1950s, Holden Caulfield, escaped not into the wilderness but into New York City (Salinger, 1951). To the middle-class child raised under the influence of metropolitan values, nature is a trip to the zoo or museum, a special project on ecology or a summer camp, and not the womb and antagonist of day-to-day living. Children might take a course on "environment(al) appreciation," just as they take a course on "music appreciation" (P. W. Porter, personal communication, 1977). Nature becomes a field of study and a place for recreation rather than one's daily world.

Perhaps only in the poorer parts of rural America do children still grow up with nature woven into the texture of their lives. The works of Robert Coles contain many perceptive and detailed observations of the way children in the rural South and in Appalachia are raised to respond to their natural environment. Contact with nature begins at the tenderest age in the hollows of Appalachia. Coles (1971) wrote:

One morning I watched Mrs. Allen come out from the cabin in order, presumably, to enjoy the sun and the warm, clear air of a May day. Her boy has just been breast-fed and was in her arms. Suddenly the mother put the child down on the ground, and gently fondled him and moved him a bit with her bare feet . . . . The child did not cry. The mother seemed to have almost exquisite control over her toes. It all seemed very nice, but I had no idea what Mrs. Allen really had in mind until she leaned over and spoke very gravely to her child: "This is your land, and it's about time you started getting to know it." (p. 204)

At three Danny had been all over his father's land, and up and down the hollow. He would roam about with his older brother or sister . . . . He knew about spiders and butterflies and nuts and minnows . . . . He went after caterpillars. He collected rocks of all sizes and shapes; they were in fact his toys . . . . At three he had been learning all that for about a year. (p. 216)

At a later age the child acquires a conscious sense of pride in the natural beauties of his home. Eight-year-old Billy from Logan County, West Virginia, boasted:

> For me, this is the best place in the whole world. I've not been to other places, I know; but if you have the best place right around you, before your eyes, you don't have to go looking. Mrs. Scott says they come from all over the country to look at the mountains we have, and Daddy says he wouldn't let one of them, with the cameras and all, into the creek, because they just want to stare and stare, and they don't know what to look for. He says they'll look at a hill, and they won't even stop to think what's on it—the different trees and the animals and birds. The first thing he taught us was what to call the different trees and bushes and vines. He takes us walking and he'll see more than anyone else. (Coles, 1971, p. 242)

Children model themselves after adults; they adopt the attitudes and values of the adult world. In Wisconsin, Frank and Elizabeth Estvan (1959) studied the environmental values of first- and sixth-grade children in both rural and city schools. The Estvans showed these grade-school pupils pictures of four physical settings: farm, village, city, and factory. They asked the children, "What story does this picture tell?" From the replies it is clear that the farm is the most preferred in the series while the village shares last place with the factory. Both city and rural children prefer the farm to the city and both groups have more to say about farm life than about city life. The environments in which they live seem to have less impact than what they learn from adults at home and in the school. Boys, on the whole, identify more with the farm than do girls, who see it primarily as a man's world. The relative unpopularity of the village is surprising. Many first graders fail to recognize it as an entity. To the younger children the farm presents a fairly clear idea and image and so does the city, but not the village, while the factory is farthest removed from their experience.

The children, especially the first graders, are far more interested in the people and their activities than they are in the physical setting. The farm has special appeal to boys because they see it as a place where they are most free to do what they like. It offers more opportunities for play and for the kind of work that might be fun (such as helping to drive a tractor) than do other environments. Pleasurable activity rather than aesthetic quality or any idea of virtuous living seems to be foremost in the children's mind. With regard to the physical setting, the younger pupils tend to see only the individual components such as a tree or a church rather than the total unit. In time they learn to see the larger entity and to place it within a regional context. Sixth graders introduce time elements in their interpretations of the different places; they are also able to say how a farm or factory functions. In general, children's feeling toward the physical world becomes more positive as they know more and gain greater confidence in themselves.

SUMMARY AND CONCLUSION

To the Western scientist the study of "children and the natural environment" presents a special challenge in objectivity. The social scientist, whether he is aware of it or not, is embedded in the dominant values of his culture. In the Western world, "nature" is such a value. For centuries thinkers have argued over the meaning of "nature" and of "the natural." Nature at one time implied reason and order, and hence the idea did not exclude human society and the man-made world. Increasingly, however, nature was contrasted with society, to the latter's detriment. By the eighteenth century, deism and romanticism had elevated nature to a cult. The cities, meanwhile, suffered from overcrowding, and those which acquired industries at the time of the Industrial Revolution became badly polluted. It is easy to associate nature with health and happiness, and to think of children raised in cities as leading warped, unnatural lives.

Except in the very rare case of the wild child surviving alone or under the care of other animals, a child's world is never nature. It is nature ordered by society, and this is true even where man-made things are of the simplest kind. A child's imagination must be constantly stimulated by the world of adults; it does not develop of itself in free play. In primitive societies adults encourage their offspring to imitate the gestures of practical life. Children are taught the lores of nature. The knowledge they gain is necessary to survival, but it is also a source of pride.

Perception and culture-bound values apart, it remains true that the human body evolved biologically in close association with nature's animate and inanimate elements. Human beings are predisposed in their favor. A sense of kinship with nature is universal. Children can easily be taught to appreciate hunting, and to develop a close, if not sentimental, relationship with animals and growing things. Children the world over seem to enjoy playing with such basic earth substances as water, clay, and sand; they like to climb trees and slide down slopes. Nature has few "do" and "don't" signs posted by adults. It is a relatively unstructured environment in which children's carefree vigor can be allowed full play.

Is such exuberance possible in the small and "manicured" spaces of the modern city and suburb? Adults are concerned; hence the question "children and the natural environment" is raised. The issues are complex and little understood. In what ways can a natural setting speed the recovery of children suffering from certain kinds of disease? Medical and environmental sciences need to join forces in answering this question. In what ways can a natural setting affect the perceptual and conceptual development of the child? How does such a setting compare in educational effectiveness with the toys and books to be found in a man-made environment? It will not do to imply an answer by comparing children raised in an ideal society and natural environment with those brought up haphazardly in an urban slum. To answer these questions, significant progress along four fronts is necessary: (1) a historical understanding of the meaning of nature, the natural, and children in the researcher's own culture so as to guard against one's unperceived biases; (2) detailed observation of how children in primitive and rural societies are raised to respond to nature; (3) the relative importance of applied and conceptual knowledge in different cultures and, if conceptual knowledge has high value, the most efficacious means to attain it; (4) the application of learning theories to the study of children living in natural environments.

REFERENCES

Anderson, J. W. Attachment behavior out of doors. In N. Blurton Jones (Ed.), Ethological studies of child behavior. Cambridge: Cambridge University Press, 1972.
Ariès, P. Centuries of childhood. New York: Vintage, 1965.
Blassingame, J. W. The slave community. New York: Oxford University Press, 1972.
Buck, P. My several worlds. New York: John Day, 1954.
Cass, J. The significance of children's play. London: Batsford, 1971.
Cobb, E. The ecology of imagination in childhood. In P. Shepard & D. McKinley (Eds.), The subversive science: Essays toward an ecology of man. Boston: Houghton Mifflin, 1969.
Coles, R. Migrants, sharecroppers, mountaineers. Boston: Little, Brown & Co., 1971.
deMause, L. The evolution of childhood. In L. deMause (Ed.), The history of childhood. New York: Harper Torchbook, 1975.
Eastman, C. A. Indian boyhood. New York: Dover, 1971. First published in 1902.
Estvan, F. J., & Estvan, E. W. The child's world: His social perception. New York: Putnam, 1959.
Fernandez, J. The mission of metaphor in expressive culture. Current Anthropology, 1974, 15 (2), 119–145.
Feuchen, P. Book of the Eskimos. New York: Fawcet, 1965.
Fortes, M. Social and psychological aspects of education in Taleland. In J. Middleton (Ed.), From child to adult: Studies in anthropology and education. Austin: University of Texas Press, 1970.
Geertz, C. Deep play: notes on the Balinese cockfight. Daedalus, 1972, 101 (1), 1–37.

Gesell, A., Ilg, F. L., & Bullis, G. E. *Vision: Its development in infant and child.* New York: Paul B. Hoeber, 1950.

Glacken, C. *Traces on the Rhodian shore.* Berkeley and Los Angeles: University of California Press, 1967.

Haith, M. M., & Campos, J. J. Human infancy. *Annual Review of Psychology,* 1977, *28,* 251–293.

Hogbin, H. I. A New Guinea childhood: from weaning till the eighth year in Wogeo. *In* J. Middleton (Ed.), *From child to adult: Studies in anthropology and education.* Austin: University of Texas Press, 1970.

Holt, J. *How children learn.* New York: Dell, 1970.

Honkavaara, S. The psychology of expression. *British Journal of Psychology Monograph Supplements,* 1961, no. 32, 41–42.

Itard, J. M. G. *The wild boy of Aveyron.* New York: Appleton-Century-Crofts, 1962.

Kates, R. W., & Katz, C. The hydrologic cycle and the wisdom of the child. *Geographical Review,* 1977, *67* (1), 51–62.

Kessen, W. *Childhood in China.* New Haven: Yale University Press, 1975.

Kidd, D. *Savage childhood: A study of Kafir children.* London: Adam & Charles Black, 1906.

Konner, M. J. Aspects of the developmental ethology of a foraging people. *In* N. Blurton Jones (Ed.), *Ethological studies of child behavior.* Cambridge: Cambridge University Press, 1972.

Lane, H. *The wild boy of Aveyron.* Cambridge: Harvard University Press, 1976.

Laughlin, W. S. An integrating biobehavior system and its evolutionary importance. *In* R. B. Lee and I. de Vore (Eds.), *Man the hunter.* Chicago: Aldine, 1968.

Lawrence, D. H. *Women in love.* New York: Viking Compass, 1960. p. 100.

Leighton, D., & Kluckhohn, C. *Children of the people: The Navaho individual and his development.* Cambridge: Harvard University Press, 1947.

Lévi-Strauss, C. *The savage mind.* London: Weidenfeld & Nicolson, 1966.

LeVine, R. A., & LeVine, B. B. Nyansongo: a Gusii community in Kenya. *In* B. B. Whiting (Ed.), *Six cultures: Studies in child rearing.* New York: Wiley, 1963.

Lijembe, J. A. The valley between: a Muluyia's story. In L. K. Fox (Ed.), *East African childhood.* Nairobi: Oxford University Press, 1967.

McKenzie, B. E., & Day, R. H. Object distance as a determinant of visual fixation in early infancy. *Science,* 1972, *178,* 1108–1110.

Mahler, M. S. Autism and symbiosis, two extreme disturbances of identity. *International Journal of Psychoanalysis,* 1958, *39,* 77–83.

Mead, M. *Growing up in New Guinea.* New York: Blue Ribbon Books, 1930.

Menger, W. Climatotherapy in children. *In* S. Licht (Ed.), *Medical climatology.* Baltimore: Waverly Press, 1964.

Merleau-Ponty, M. *The primacy of perception.* Evanston: Northwestern University Press, 1964.

Nabokov, V. *Speak memory: An autobiography revisited.* New York: Putnam, 1966.

Naipaul, V. S. *The mimic men.* London: Andre Deutsch, 1967.

Passmore, J. *Man's responsibility for nature.* London: Duckworth, 1974.

Piaget, J. *The child's conception of the world.* Totowa, N. J.: Littlefield, Adams & Co., 1969.

Raum, O. F. *Chaga childhood.* London: Oxford University Press, 1940.

Read, M. *Children of their fathers: Growing up among the Ngoni of Nyasaland.* New Haven: Yale University Press, 1960.

Riccio, V., & Slocum, B. *All the way down: The violent underworld of street gangs.* New York: Simon and Schuster, 1962.

Salinger, J. D. *The catcher in the rye.* Boston: Little Brown, 1951.

Smith, P. *As a city upon a hill: The town in American history.* Cambridge: MIT Press, 1973. P. 219.

Spitz, R. *The first year of life.* New York: International Universities Press, 1965.

Thomas, E. M. *The harmless people.* New York: Vintage, 1965.

Washburn, S. L., & Lancaster, C. S. The evolution of hunting. *In* R. B. Lee & I. de Vore (Eds.), *Man the hunter.* Chicago: Aldine, 1968.

Willey, B. *The eighteenth century background.* Harmondsworth, Middlesex: Penguin, 1962.

Zeller, R. The development of "Alpinism" in Switzerland. *Geographical Magazine,* 1936, 4 (2), 126–142.

2

Children's Home Environments: Social and Cognitive Effects

ROSS D. PARKE

INTRODUCTION

What is a home?

> "Home—the nursery of the infinite."—W.E. Channing,
> *Notebook: Children*

> "Home interprets heaven. Home is heaven for beginners."
> —Charles Parkhurst, *Sermons: The Perfect Place*

> "No place is more delightful than one's own fireside."
> —Cicero, *Epistolae ad Familiares*

Nor is it merely poets, authors, and philosophers, but parents and children have answered this question as well. . .

> "A home is where my children play and make much noise throughout the day."
> —An anonymous harrassed mother

> "A place where my toys and TV and I all live."
> —Timothy, age $4\frac{1}{2}$

ROSS D. PARKE · Department of Psychology, University of Illinois, Champaign-Urbana, Illinois. Preparation of this chapter was supported by the following grants: NICHD Training Grant HD-00244, Office of Child Development Grant OHD 90-C-900.

It is one of the ironies of the history of psychology that so little attention has been paid to one of the most important settings for the developing child—the home. In fact, until recently more was known about orphanages, institutions, hospital wards, preschools, and playgrounds than home environments. Two trends have led to an increasing interest in children's home settings. First, a major concern of the past decade has been the effects of early experience on children's social and cognitive development (Horowitz & Paden, 1973); as a result of the central role that home environments play in early development, there has been a reawakened interest in describing this principal environment of children. Second, there has been a general concern in both social and developmental psychology about the limited ecological validity of our laboratory-derived information about the development and regulation of social behavior (Bronfenbrenner, 1977; McGuire, 1973; Parke, 1976). As a result, there has been more research concerned with the study of children in naturalistic settings, including home environments.

The aims of the chapter are to review and integrate this diverse and burgeoning literature and to demonstrate that variations in the organization, structure, and content of home environments can affect children's socioemotional and cognitive development in significant ways. A developmental perspective guides the review; from this viewpoint the child is seen as an active information-processing organism who selectively perceives and conceptualizes the physical and social environment of the home differently at different developmental levels and for different functions (play, work tasks, etc.). Second, the term "environment" is viewed broadly to include both social and physical variables; it is further assumed that these two sets of variables generally function in an interdependent fashion in affecting children's behavior. Consistent with this assumption is the view that environmental influences are not limited to direct effects; rather a model that recognizes two types of environmental influence—direct and indirect—guides our analysis (Parke, Power, & Gottman, 1978). *Direct influence* is defined as the process by which a social agent or physical event influences another by directly acting on the child, while *indirect influence* refers to the process whereby agents or physical events influence another through the mediation of either another person or object. Fourth, it is assumed that a multilevel analysis is necessary, which recognizes the impact of the social and physical features of the immediate home environment as well as the wider physical and social context in which the home environment is embedded, including the neighborhood and the community (Brim, 1975; Bronfenbrenner, 1977). Finally, it is assumed that multiple methodological strategies are useful in understanding home environments, including naturalistic observational approaches, questionnaires, and interviews as well as more traditional experimental methods (Parke, 1978a,b).

HOME AS A SOURCE OF STIMULATION

In spite of the recent increase in child-care environments outside the home for infants and young children, the home environment remains a principal setting in which the child's early social and cognitive development takes place. The early social and physical environment that the home provides for the child has a marked impact on his later social and cognitive development. Although a distinction is made between the social and physical aspects of the home, the distinction is, in part, a fiction of convenience. In fact, particularly in early life, the degree of access that the child has to the physical environment and the features of the physical environment that are salient are to a large degree under social control. The physical world, in short, is very often socially mediated by parents or other social agents in the child's environment.

Therefore, in this section both direct and indirect forms of stimulation will be considered; these include social stimulation provided directly by social agents and physical stimulation provided directly by toys, books, and other physical objects, as well as indirect influences whereby the social and physical environment is mediated by the action of another social agent or alternatively the physical environment serves as a modifier of the amount and type of social stimulation in a home setting. Figure 1 outlines these two views of environmental stimulation in the home.

Two approaches have been employed in recent research—a direct-observation approach, in which actual interaction patterns are assessed and specific aspects of the physical environment are measured, and an inventory approach, in which raters evaluate a variety of aspects of the home environment, such as the involvement of the mother and the availability of toys.

SOCIAL STIMULATION IN HOME ENVIRONMENTS

Parent as Direct Stimulator

From a very early age, variations in the social environment of the home have impact on the child's cognitive and social development.

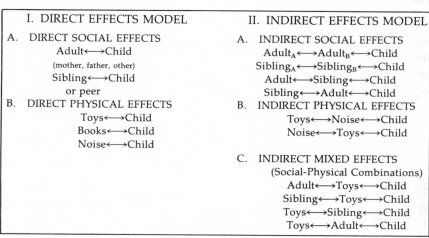

Figure 1. Models of home environmental influences.

The amount, the type, and the timing of the social stimulation provided by the social agents in a child's home are important determinants of his later development (Clarke-Stewart, 1978a; Friedlander, Sterrit, & Kirk, 1975; Lewis, 1976). However, it should be emphasized that the infant lives in a complex social environment composed, not just of mothers, but of a network of social others including fathers, siblings, peers, and relatives (Lewis & Weinraub, 1976; Parke, 1978c). All of these agents—not only the mother—play an important stimulatory role in early development. Now we turn to the evidence.

First, these effects are evident from a very early age. Recent documentation of these effects comes from an investigation by Yarrow, Rubinstein, and Pedersen (1975), who studied 5-month-old black infants in their home environments. In contrast to many earlier studies, these investigators used direct observations to assess the social interactions between mothers and their infants. Social stimulation can take a variety of forms, and the separate impact of visual, auditory, tactile, and kinesthetic input was assessed, as well as the contingency of maternal responsiveness.

Both tactile and kinesthetic–vestibular stimulation relate to infant cognitive development, but to differing degrees. Kinesthetic–vestibular stimulation, such as rocking and holding the infant in an upright or vertical position, although often not distinguished from tactile stimulation (Harlow & Harlow, 1965; Kulka, Fry, & Goldstein, 1960), has both general and specific effects. It relates not only to general measures of development—the Bayley Mental Development Index and the Psycho-motor Developmental Index—but also to five specific functions:

social responsiveness, fine motor development, goal directedness (an index of the infant's directed and persistent attempts to secure an object), problem-solving (an index which taps both cognitive abilities and the motivation to secure objects), and object permanence (an index that involves the recognition that objects exist when they are outside of immediate sensory experience). These findings are consistent with cross-cultural studies of the advanced social and cognitive development of African infants, who receive a great deal of kinesthetic stimulation (Leiderman & Leiderman, 1974; Goldberg, 1973; Konner, 1977), as well as experimental studies with institutionalized infants, which found increased alertness as a result of compensatory kinesthetic stimulation (Brossard & Decarie, 1968; White & Castle, 1964). In contrast, tactile stimulation, as indexed by patting, stroking, or caressing the infant, had only limited impact on early cognitive status. Two infant measures were positively correlated with this type of stimulation: goal directedness and secondary circular reactions—an index of the infant's repetition of a sequence aimed at producing interesting results.

Distance receptor stimulation in the form of visual and auditory input, which Walters and Parke (1965) have suggested plays a major role in early development, was related to the infant's social responsiveness and the amount of vocalization. Both visual stimulation (mutual regard between mother and infant) and auditory stimulation (vocalizations directed to the infant) were significantly related to social responsiveness. Auditory stimulation was also related to the amount of vocalization the infant showed while exploring a novel object. A number of writers have stressed the theoretical importance of contingent social stimulation (Schaffer & Emerson, 1964; Rheingold, 1969b; Gewirtz, 1961; Hunt, 1965). Yarrow et al. (1975) distinguished between maternal responsiveness that was contingent upon infant positive vocaliztion and that contingent upon response to distress. By responding contingently to their positive vocalizations in the home environment, mothers affected the amount of vocalization that the infant exhibited in an independent situation—a 10-minute period of exploration and manipulation of a toy—two weeks after the home observation. These results are consistent with other studies of the impact of the home environment. For example, Jones and Moss (1971), in a study of 3-month-old infants, found a positive relationship between the amount of infant vocalization and the frequency with which the mother's speech was contingent on the infant's vocalization in the same setting. In addition, maternal responsivity to infant vocalizations correlated significantly with the infant's manipulation of novel objects.

Maternal response to distress was positively related to a wide range of infant developmental indices, including the Bayley Mental and Motor Indices, the gross and fine motor subscales, and three measures of cognitive–motivational functions: reaching and grasping, goal directedness, and secondary circular reactions. These last two indices suggest that response to the infant's distress may facilitate the infant's motivation to interact with the environment. As Yarrow *et al.* (1975) suggest:

> It is likely that response to an infant's cries does more than reinforce crying. It reinforces active coping with the environment, reaching out to obtain feedback from people and objects. Moreover, in time, an infant whose mother is quickly responsive to his cries may come to feel that through his own actions he can have an effect on other people and his environment. (p. 86)

A similar view has been championed by Lewis and Goldberg, who report a significant relationship between maternal contingent responsiveness and the infant's habituation to a redundant visual stimulus—a likely index of cognitive status. This same theorizing has been usefully extended to aid in understanding the apathy and passivity of institutionalized infants (Lewis & Goldberg, 1969; Hetherington & Parke, 1975).

Finally, both the level (frequency and intensity of the mother's stimulation) and variety (richness and diversity of mother's input) of social stimulation was related to the infant's development. While both level and variety are related to a wide range of infant outcome variables, including the Bayley Mental Development Index, social responsiveness, goal directedness and secondary circular reactions, *variety* of social stimulation was one of the best predictors among the full set of variables in this investigation (Yarrow *et al.*, 1975).

Nor are these effects of early social stimulation restricted to the first few months of life. Clarke-Stewart (1973) found that contingent maternal social responsiveness at 12 months was highly predictive of the infant's cognitive development at 18 months.

Similarly, a recent series of studies using the Caldwell HOME Inventory have found the same general patterns of relationships, but across a 3-year period. This inventory, developed by Caldwell, Huder, and Kaplan (1966) is a combined observation–interview procedure that assesses the quality of stimulation available to the child in the home. It is composed of the following six subscales: (1) emotional and verbal responsivity of the mother; (2) avoidance of restriction and punishment; (3) organization of the environment; (4) provision of appropriate play materials; (5) maternal involvement with child; and (6) opportunities for variety in daily stimulation. Of interest here is the fact that "maternal involvement with child", assessed at 6 or 12 months, correlated highly with the child's IQ at 36 months, while the 24-month home assessment indicated that the "emotional and verbal responsivity of mother" correlated highly with the 3-year IQ score (Elardo, Bradley, & Caldwell, 1975). A follow-up study of these infants at 54 months revealed a multiple correlation between 24-month HOME assessment and the IQ measure 30 months later of .63. Maternal involvement and the mother's emotional and verbal responsivity assessed at 24 months were both significant predictors of IQ at 54 months. Similar findings, using a modified form of the Caldwell HOME inventory, have been reported by Wachs, Uzgiris, and Hunt (1971), who found that vocal and verbal stimulation of infants by their parents from seven months was consistently and positively related to cognitive development at 15, 18, and 22 months of age. However, a later study (Wachs, 1976) indicated that the amount of verbal stimulation provided by the mother related to infant cognitive development, primarily during the latter half of the second year of life. This is not surprising in view of the increasing degree of language development during this period. This serves to underline the importance of different types of stimulation at different times for different types of behavior.

In a more recent study in this series Elardo, Bradley, and Caldwell (1977) have made a significant advance over their earlier work by relating the HOME inventory, not just to IQ scores, but to specific aspects of language development. Using HOME assessments at ages 6 and 24 months, these were related to measures of the Illinois test of Psycholinguistic Abilities administered at age 3. The HOME subscales, "emotional and verbal responsivity of mother," "provision of appropriate play materials," and "maternal involvement with the child," showed the strongest overall relation to language competence. Among the psycholinguistic abilities measured, auditory reception, auditory association, visual association, and grammatical closure were most strongly associated with the quality of stimulation found in the early environment. In a related study, Tulkin and Covitz (1975) found that the length of mother–infant interactions observed when the infant was 10 months of age correlated quite highly with the Illinois Psycholinguistics instrument at age 6.

However, there appear to be sex differences. HOME scores were more frequently and strongly related to aspects of language performance for females than for males. Moore (1968) found a similar relationship: 3-year-old vocabulary scores for girls were more highly correlated with the home environment than for boys. Another recent study (Bradley, Caldwell, & Elardo, 1977) indicated similar sex differences for overall mental test performance and HOME measures. Whether these sex differences indicate "that females are more amenable to environmental events during the first three years of life . . . or whether mothers tend to be more sensitive and effective when interacting with infant girls than infant boys" (Bradley et al., 1977, p. 7) remains to be determined.

As noted earlier, mothers are not the only source of social stimulation; fathers as well as mothers contribute to early social and cognitive development. Recently, Pedersen, Rubinstein, and Yarrow (1977) reported that the absence of a father in the young infant's environment affects cognitive development. Five-month-old male infants from father-absent families were lower on the Bayley Mental Development Index than males from intact families. Similarly, these infants from father-absent homes spent less time manipulating a novel object—a measure related to later cognitive development (Yarrow, Klein, Lomonaco, & Morgan, 1975). Using a second measure—the amount of father-infant interaction—these investigators found a similar pattern of relationships. Bayley mental scores and preference for novel stimuli were both correlated positively with the amount of father contact. It is noteworthy that there were no effects for female infants. Nor were the effects due merely to the fact that an additional source of stimulation was available: Pedersen et al. found no difference between father-absent and father-present homes in the number of household members. Therefore "it appears that the father has an impact that is qualitatively different from other adults" (Pedersen et al., 1977, p. 9).

In fact, a number of recent investigations indicate that father and mother provide different types of social stimulation: mothers are more verbal, while fathers tend to be more physical in their playful interactions with their infants (Lamb, 1977; Clarke-Stewart, 1978b; Yogman, Dixon, Tronick, Als, Adamson, Lester, & Brazelton, 1977). Moreover, the father's ability to engage his child in social physical play was significantly related to the Bayley scores of 16- to 22-month-old infants, while for mothers, verbal stimulation and the expression of positive emotion were predictive of children's cognitive development (Clarke-Stewart, 1978b). A combination of a verbally stimulatory mother and a physically playful father may represent the most optimal pattern of social stimulation for promoting cognitive development.

Finally, degree of paternal stimulation in the home situation is related to infant social development as well. In their study of 8- to 9-month-old infants, Pedersen and Robson (1969) found that stimulation level of paternal play was positively related to the male infants' attachment to their fathers—as assessed by the age of onset and intensity of

greeting behavior directed to the father. As studies of maternal stimulation have found (Clarke-Stewart, 1973), quality, not quantity, of
stimulation is important, since there was no relationship between paternal availability, time spent in play and infant attachment. In addition, others (Pedersen et al., 1977) report positive relationships between
infant social responsiveness and paternal social stimulation.

Nor should peers and siblings be ignored in our analysis. As recent
studies have shown, older siblings play a potentially important role in
facilitating the social and cognitive development of younger siblings
both through direct social stimulation, feedback, and direct explanation
and by serving as social models for their sibs (Cicirelli, 1976; Lamb,
1978; Samuels, 1977). The contribution of siblings varies with a variety
of factors including the size of the family and the sex and developmental status of the sibling. Children from large families sought and
received more help in a problem-solving task than did children from
small families (Cicirelli, 1976). In both our own culture (Cicirelli, 1976)
and in other cultures such as the !Kung San of the Kalahari desert
(Konner, 1977) and the Gikuyu of Kenya (Leiderman & Leiderman,
1977), girls are more likely than boys to play an active caretaking and
helping role for their siblings. However, Leiderman and Leiderman
(1977) found the effectiveness of an older sibling or other substitute
caretaker varied with the developmental level of the sib caretaker. As
the positive relationship between age of the caretaker and infant mental
test scores among the Gikuyu tribe indicates, older caretakers are probably more effective stimulators of early cognitive growth.

Finally, peers as playmates are another important source of social
stimulation for the developing infant in the home environment. As
Hartup (1975, 1978) has documented, peers play an important role in
facilitating the development of social skills.

Together these findings provide substantial evidence that the quality of social stimulation of the home setting from a variety of social
sources during infancy and early childhood is significantly related to
the child's later social and intellectual development.

Parent as Mediator of Environmental Stimulation

Not only do social agents in the child's home environment provide
direct stimulation to support the child's emerging social and cognitive
skills, but caretakers and other socializing figures influence the child
more indirectly by serving as an organizer of the child's environment.
This is manifest in a variety of ways. In fact, this secondary role may
be even more important than the role as stimulator since the amount

of time that infants spend interacting with the inanimate environment far exceeds their social interaction time. Here are some recent estimates based on extensive home observations by White and his colleagues (White, Kaban, Shapiro, & Attonucci, 1976):

> For the 12-month-old to 15-month-old children, the figures were 89.7% for nonsocial tasks versus 10.3% for social tasks. By 18–21 months the figures are 83.8% nonsocial and 16.2% social; at 24–27 months 80.0% nonsocial and 20.0% social and at 30–33 months they were 79.1% nonsocial and 20.9% social. (p. 125)

Others (Clarke-Stewart, 1973; Wenar, 1972) report similar findings. Secondly, White *et al.* (1976) noted that over 85% of the time, 12- to 33-month-old infants *initiated* their own activities. In short, the way that the mother or other caretaker organizes the child's physical environment may be just as important as the direct social interactions between the child and his caretaker.

The level of predictability or regularity of the child's home environment—the extent to which the home is a place "where things have their time and place"—is an important way that adults affect the child's development. Wachs (1976) recently reported that regularity of the home environment was positively related to early cognitive development; other studies (Klaus & Gray, 1968) indicate a similar pattern: home environments of disadvantaged preschoolers were characterized as irregular and unpredictable. Further support comes from Bradley and Caldwell (1976b), who found that "organization of the physical and temporal environment" over the first two years—a dimension of the Caldwell HOME Inventory, which taps such aspects of the home as the regularity of substitute care, the extent to which the child routinely leaves the house, the safety of the play environment, and the availability of a special place in which the child keeps his toys—was related to IQ at age 3. However, this dimension was less strongly associated with IQ at $4\frac{1}{2}$ than at age 3, suggesting that different types of stimulation may be differentially important at various developmental points. As Bradley and Caldwell (1976b) note:

> These findings suggest that if parents assist their children during the first 2 years of life in terms of organizing the environment for them, the children may move more early from sensorimotor to preoperational thinking. Further support for this interpretation was found in a study by Bradley & Caldwell (1976a) which showed that decrease in mental test performance between 6 months and 3 years was associated with parents' failure to adequately organize the environment. Once children have made the transition to preoperational thinking and have become somewhat less dependent on parents, they may be able to organize the environment fairly adequately for themselves. (pp. 1173–74)

A second way in which the adult as organizer is evident is in their boundary-setting role. The boundaries of the home environment to which the child has access for exploration and play influences the child's cognitive development. In fact, White *et al.* (1976) argue that

> the effective child-rearer makes the living area as safe as possible for the naive newly crawling or walking child and then provides maximum access to the living area for the child. This immediately sets the process of development off in a manner that will lead naturally to the satisfaction of and the further development of the child's curiosity; the opportunity to learn much about the world at large; and the opportunity to enter into natural useful relationships with people. The child-rearer not only provides maximum access to the living area, but in addition he or she makes kitchen cabinets attractive and available and then keeps a few materials in reserve for those times when the child may become a bit bored. (pp. 150–151)

Indirect support comes from studies of differences in the home environments of lower- and middle-class infants. Tulkin (1973, 1977) and Tulkin and Kagan (1972) compared the home environments of 10-month-old girls from white middle-class and working-class families. The lower-class infants were more restricted, had less opportunity for exploration, spent less time crawling, and spent more time confined in a playpen than the middle-class infants. In turn, the working-class infants performed more poorly on laboratory measures of cognitive development. While social class differences are often problematic since so many dimensions are subsumed by this label, other evidence confirms the importance of opportunities for early home-based exploration for later development. Wachs (1976) reported that a lack of physical or visual restraints placed on the child's interactions with his environment (child can explore, see outside the house) was significantly related to cognitive development at 24 months of age.

The amount, type, and variety of inanimate stimulation that is available to the child is also directly controlled by adults. The decor and color scheme of his room, the type of mobiles and pictures, the books and toys available, are typically under the control of adults in infancy and early childhood.

Surprisingly, until recently there was little direct information concerning the contents and decorations of children's rooms. As a corrective, Rheingold and Cook (1975) documented the ways in which the contents of boys' and girls' rooms differ. These investigators canvassed the contents of the rooms of 96 children, ages 1–6 years. Boys' and girls' rooms did differ in a variety of ways. The rooms of boys contained more animal furnishings, more educational-art materials, more spatial-temporal toys (shape sorting toys, magnets, clocks, etc.), more sports equipment, more toy animals, and vastly more vehicles (cars, trucks, airplanes, trains). The rooms of girls contained more dolls, more floral furnishings and more ruffled furnishings (bedspreads, pillow, etc, with fringe, lace). There were no sex differences in the number of children's books, furniture, musical objects, and stuffed animals.

These differences in decoration are interesting in light of other reports (Bronson, 1971; Goldberg & Lewis, 1969; Jacklin, Maccoby, & Dick, 1973) that 13- to 15-month-old boys play more with mechanical and manipulative toys while girls play more with stuffed animals and "cuddly" toys in laboratory contexts.

The results clearly suggest that parents do provide very different environments for their children—depending on their sex. In short, the fashioning of the physical environment may be another way, in addition to direct instruction, reinforcement, and modeling (Mischel, 1970) that children's sex-role attitudes, behaviors, and consumer choices are shaped. In reflecting on their findings, Rheingold and Cook (1975) note:

> The rooms of children constitute a not inconsiderable part of their environment. Here they go to bed and wake up; here they spend some part of every day. Their rooms determine the things they see and find for amusement and instruction. That their rooms have an effect on their present and subsequent behavior can be assumed; a standard is set that may in part account for some differences in the behavior of girls and boys. Clear in the findings of this study was the extent to which the boys were provided objects that encouraged activities directed away from home—toward sports, cars, animals, and the military—and the girls, objects that encouraged activities directed toward the home—keeping house and caring for children. (p. 463)

However, adult influence does not end with toy selection and purchase; there is a continuing interplay between the social and physical environment. Toy play is not always a solitary affair. Rather, mothers and fathers play a continuing role as mediators of stimulation provided by the inanimate environment; a parent may make a toy available, demonstrate its unique properties, draw the infant's attention to salient features of the object or to other aspects of the child's inanimate environment, and finally serve as a playmate—using the toy as an organizer for the social interaction (Schaffer & Crook, 1978). Mothers in particular are likely to use toys as mediators in play with their infants (Clarke-Stewart, 1978b).

Nor are these effects restricted to adults: early peer-peer interaction is often centered on a shared toy or other inanimate object (Mueller & Lucas, 1975). However, both the quality and consequences of adult and peer- or sibling-mediated toy play are probably different. In a recent study of interactions between 18-month-old toddlers and their older preschool-age siblings, Lamb (1978) found that toys played an important role in sib-sib interaction, but not in the same directed and didactic fashion as in the case of parent-infant toy-mediated interaction. Instead of playing together with toys, older siblings offered toys to their younger sibs, who in turn both visually monitored the sibling's actions (rather than the sibling directly) and attempted to repeat the sibling's actions by imitation and by taking over the toys. In combination with other data (Rubinstein & Howes, 1976) which indicated that the presence of a familiar peer facilitated the level of toy play of 19-month-old infants in their home environment, sibs and peers appear most likely to impact on the child's "mastery of the object environment" (Lamb, 1978, p. 13). Since toy play is higher in the presence of peers than in the presence of the mother (Rubinstein & Howes, 1976), peers and sibs may make a unique contribution to this cognitive achievement.

In summary, parents, sibs, and peers often serve as mediators of the physical environment through organization of physical space, through selection of physical objects, and through the use of toys as mediators in social interaction. Next we turn to an evaluation of the direct impact of the physical environment on children's development.

PHYSICAL STIMULATION IN HOME ENVIRONMENTS

The Effect of Toys on Social-Cognitive Development

What impact do toys have on the child's social and cognitive development? Recent research has indicated that the properties of toys make a difference in infants' and children's attraction to and exploration and manipulation of toys. The importance of isolating the determinants of play is eloquently summarized by White (1959) in his classic article on competence and effectance motivation:

> The infant's play is indeed serious business. . . . The more closely we analyze the behavior of the human infant, the more closely do we realize that infancy is not simply a time when the nervous system matures and the muscles grow stronger. It is a time of active and continuous learning during which the basis is laid for all those processes, cognitive and motor, whereby the child becomes able to establish effective transactions with his environment and move toward a greater degree of autonomy. (p. 326)

A number of years later, Rheingold and Eckerman (1970) underlined further the importance of play in infancy:

> The infant comes in contact with an increasing number and variety of objects. Through touching them he learns their shapes, dimensions, slopes,

edges and textures. He also fingers, grasps, pushes, pulls and thus learns
the material variables of heaviness, mass and rigidity, as well as the changes
in visual and auditory stimuli that objects provide. . . . In a word, he learns
the properties of the physical world, including the principles of object
constancy and the conservation of matter. (p. 78)

What characteristics of toys determine play and exploration in the
human infant and child? McCall (1974) has recently made significant
progress in answering this question in his series of studies of 7- to 11-
month-old infants. Exploratory manipulation of objects by infants increases with the contingent responsiveness of the toys; infants played
more with toys that are relatively high in plasticity—how easily and
how much an object's shape can be changed—and high in sound
potential—the extent to which the object would produce a sound—than
toys that are rigid and noiseless. These general relationships held not
only for special experimentally designed toys but for commercially
available toys as well. Moreover, the ratings of adults—the agents who
choose toys for infants—of the complexity, sound potential, and plasticity of commercial toys were correlated highly with the infant's free
play. Similarly, there were strong relationships between the time spent
by infants exploring and playing with a set of toys and the length of
time that adults took to examine and become acquainted with the same
toys.

Play interacts with the child's level of cognitive development;
McCall (1974) found that a child would spend longer sustained periods
of time with a toy that provided feedback appropriate to the child's
contemporary level of cognitive development. This is, of course, consistent with Hunt's theory (1961), which stresses the importance of a
match between environmental stimulation and perceptual-cognitive
development.

In spite of this evidence concerning the properties of toys that
attract and sustain infant play, toy manufacturers are not always in
touch with either science or infants in their choice of toy designs. A
few years ago, a toy manufacturer produced

a whole line of aesthetically beautiful toys. The toys are made in simple
forms out of natural woods with rich grains, a very beautiful product.
However, when one examines the aesthetic behind their creation one finds
that it is not the aesthetic of the infant or young child. . . . The toy manufacturer in this instance has the aesthetic of the adult rather than the child
in mind. It is, after all, the *parent* who buys the toy for the child. (Lewis,
1971, p. 169)

Just as there have been pleas for more collaboration between architects and social scientists (Sommer, 1972, 1977; Zeisel, 1972), there clearly needs to be better interaction between toy producers and psychologists.

Do the characteristics of toys that elicit and sustain the infant's interest also affect his later cognitive functioning? A number of recent investigators have addressed this question. In their study of 5-month-old infants, Yarrow *et al.* (1975) distinguished three aspects of the infant's inanimate home environment: (1) the responsiveness of the play materials available to the infant; (2) the complexity; and (3) the variety of inanimate objects. Although these dimensions did not affect language or social development, they did relate to several aspects of cognitive and motivational development. Responsiveness of toys, for example, was related to both gross and fine motor development, cognitive motivational functions, such as reaching and grasping, goal directedness and secondary circular reactions, and a preference for visually exploring novel objects.

These correlational findings are consistent with experimental studies (Rovee & Rovee, 1969; Watson & Ramey, 1972; Finkelstein & Ramey, 1977) of the effects of contingent feedback from the physical environment. The Watson–Ramey investigation illustrates well the importance of a responsive environment for children's motivational development. Just as a responsive mother can contribute to the child's development of an attitude that he can exercise control over his social environment, so contingent feedback from the physical environment can foster this same motivational stance. In their study, Watson and Ramey (1972) compared the effects of exposure to visual stimulation that was either contingent on the 3-month-old infant's behavior or independent of his activities using a specially designed "mobile." In one case, by means of a pressure-sensitive pillow, the mobile made a 1-second turn each time the infant moved his head. In this condition, the infant had control; the movement of the mobile was contingent on the infant's behavior. During the 14 days of exposure, the infants in the other two groups were powerless to control the activity of their mobiles. In one case, during the 10-minute daily exposure period, the mobile remained stationary. In the other condition, the mobile periodically turned by itself. The movement was independent of the infant's behavior in the same way that environmental changes are often on a noncontingent basis in an institutional environment. Of central interest is the impact of experiencing such noncontingent input on later behavior. Specifically, what will happen when the infants have the opportunity to control external events at some later time? Will they remain passive as a result of their earlier failure to exercise control over their environment? To find out, Watson and Ramey exposed the infants to the mobiles again, but on this occasion all the infants could control the movement of their mobiles. In contrast to the infants who had control from the beginning and continued to successfully control the mobile, both the infants who had viewed the noncontingently turning mobile and the stationary one were unsuccessful in controlling their mobiles. Even after 6 weeks without further exposure to the mobiles, the results were the same: the infants who had experienced the uncontrollable mobiles failed to exercise control even when they had the opportunity to do so. This study provides a striking demonstration of the importance of experience with objects over which the developing child can gain control for subsequent motivational development.

Further data from the Yarrow *et al.* (1975) study indicated that the complexity of the toys available to the infants was related to variables that reflect receptivity to stimulation: reaching and grasping, secondary circular reactions, and preference for novel stimuli. In comparison to the other aspects of the inaminate environment, however, complexity was a less significant contribution to cognitive development. Variety of play materials and household objects available to the infant, in contrast, related to the *largest* number of infant outcome variables among the inanimate environmental predictors. This measure related significantly to general mental and psychomotor development as well as to cognitive motivational indices (goal directedness, reaching and grasping, secondary circular reactions, and problem solving) exploratory behavior, object permanence, and preference for novelty measures:

> The implication of these findings is that an infant's natural curiosity is strengthened by the opportunity to see and handle a wide range of objects. This is consistent with Piaget's suggestion that frequent exposure to variety in the environment results in a differentiated capacity for information processing. Both motivation and capacity to assimilate new information increase when an infant's environment is characterized by variety. (Yarrow *et al.*, 1975, p. 100)

One of the important messages of this careful investigation is the selective impact of different aspects of the social and nonsocial home environment on the infant's cognitive development. Some measures, such as social responsiveness and vocalization, were significantly related only to measures of social stimulation, while measures of exploratory behavior, preference for novel stimuli, and problem-solving were related primarily to dimensions of the inanimate environment. Still other measures of cognitive progress—object permanence and cognitive motivational measures, goal directedness, reaching and grasping, and secondary circular reactions—were influenced by both the infant's social and nonsocial home environment.

Other investigators have documented that the effects of the inanimate home environment are not restricted to early infancy. For example, Bradley and Caldwell (1976b) found that provision of appropriate play materials, assessed periodically over the first 2 years of life, was strongly related to IQ scores at 54 months. In fact, the correlation between the 24-month home assessment and the 54-month cognitive outcome index was an impressive .56. Further support comes from Wachs (1976), who found that inanimate stimulation was an important determinant of cognitive development. Wachs isolated four components that defined adequacy of stimulation, including the amount of visual and tactual-visual stimulation (availability of papers, magazines, toys, books, mobiles, etc.), the variety of inanimate objects available (e.g., the child has received new toys since the last home visit), the number of toys which produce auditory-visual feedback when activated, and finally a factor discussed above, the freedom to explore the environment. The importance of different components varied with the developmental status of the child, with amount of tactual-visual stimulation being important after 18 months and change in stimulation correlated more strongly with cognitive development before this time.

In summary, toys—significant aspect of the physical environment of the infant and the young child—can contribute to the infant's cognitive growth.

Toys can also significantly alter the child's *social* behavior in a variety of ways. First, the availability and nature of toys alter the ways in which infants interact with others in their environment. In this case, toys affect social interaction in an indirect fashion, whereby an alteration in the physical environment impacts on the interactions between social partners. Rheingold (1969a), for example, has demonstrated that availability of toys reduces children's fear when left alone in a novel environment. In addition, infants are more likely to leave their mothers voluntarily and fuss less if there are toys present than if there are no toys available (Rheingold & Eckerman, 1969). Another illustration of the way in which toys can alter social interaction patterns comes from a more recent series of studies by Corter and his colleagues (Corter, Rheingold, & Eckerman, 1972; Corter, 1977). Infants were placed in a room either with or without a toy, and the effect of the presence of the toy on the reactions of 10-month-old infants to their mother's departure was recorded. Infants who had a toy present followed the mother less quickly and following was delayed more if the toy was novel rather than familiar. The infants left with the novel toy showed less distress at being left alone. Clearly, the infant's ability to handle a strange situation is modified by nonsocial aspects of the environment. In short, toys may serve to aid the child in reducing his reliance on the mother and permit a more active and adaptive response to strange settings.

Other studies demonstrate that the nature of toys can modify the nature of social interaction patterns. Quilitch and Risley (1973) distinguished two sets of toys: "isolate" toys (e.g., gyroscope, play-dough) are play objects that require only one child at a time, in contrast to "social" toys (e.g., pick-up sticks and checkers), which require two or more children. To evaluate the impact of these two types of toys on children's play behavior, they provided groups of 7-year-old children with the two kinds of play materials and systematically observed the play patterns. Social play occurred only 16% of the time with the isolate toys, while peer interaction occurred 70% of the time when the children were provided with social toys. The implication is clear: parents and other agents in the home environment can influence the amount of social interaction not only by direct encouragement, but also by the types of toys that they make available to children.

In summary, toys play an important but underestimated role in both cognitive and social development and in the regulation of social interaction.

Television as a Physical Environmental Event

Nearly 30 years ago a major change occurred in the organization of American and European home environments—the introduction of television. Few technological advances over the past half-century have provided as suitable an opportunity to examine the impact of shifts in the physical home environment on children's behavior as this event. From the viewpoint of environmental and ecological psychology, however, this opportunity has not been fully exploited. Although TV can be viewed from a variety of perspectives, the major share of our research effort, particularly over the past 15 years, has been guided by only one perspective, namely, the role of different types of TV content in the social development and more recently the cognitive growth of children (Bandura & Walters, 1963; Liebert, Neale, & Davidson, 1973; Stein & Freidrich, 1975). Amid the debate over the potentially deleterious effects of TV violence and the potentially beneficial effects of educational innovations such as *Sesame Street* and *Mr. Rogers Neighborhood* (Ball & Bogatz, 1972; Stein & Freidrich, 1975) another perspective of interest to ecological and environmental social scientists has been relatively neglected. From this alternative viewpoint TV is conceputalized, not merely as a communicator of content, but as a major physical environmental event that potentially alters and reorganizes the allocation of time, the choice of activities, and the social interaction patterns among family members. In contrast to a view of TV as a direct effect, whereby viewer behavior is altered as a consequence of watching a particular program, TV can be treated as a social and physical factor that has an indirect *or* second-order effect on children's behavior and development. According to this alternative view, TV can be conceptualized as an environmental organizing event whose presence or availability in the home can affect children *through the modification of social interaction patterns among family members.* In contrast to a direct-effects model, this model assumes that TV has an impact as a result of changing aspects of family life. A direct-effects model might examine the impact of watching *Sesame Street* on children's cognitive development; an indirect-effects model would examine the impact of TV on cognitive development by measuring differences in the amount of verbal interaction between parents and children in TV and non-TV homes. Differences in cognitive development, then, would not be due *directly* to the effects of TV availability but to the reduced verbal interaction between parents and children in TV homes. In this case, content is of interest only to the extent that it is a determinant of the amount of time devoted to this activity. Table 1 summarizes these two models—direct and indirect—of the effects of TV. In this section the shifts in social interaction patterns among family members, and friends, the changes in community participation, and the modification of children's entertainment choices as a result of TV presence will be examined.

TV as a Family Member: The Impact on Family Interaction Patterns. TV has a major impact on the organization of children's social interaction patterns. Both the amount of time that families spend together and the quality of activities that families engage in are altered by the availability of TV. These effects were documented very early by foresightful investigators who took advantage of the fact that TV was not yet fully available in all communities. Maccoby (1951), in a pioneering study in the United States, found that TV families spend more time as a family, but TV reduces the amount of non-TV-related joint family activity. Belson (1959), in England, found a similar outcome: families with TV spent more time at home than non-TV families. The results were especially marked for small families and those in which both parents worked. TV watching in the 1970s as well as in the early days of TV has remained a family affair (Lyle, 1971), and there is a positive relationship between levels of viewing across family members: Parents

TABLE 1

DIRECT AND INDIRECT MODELS OF THE IMPACT OF TELEVISION IN HOME ENVIRONMENTS

Direct effects model: TV as a communicator of program content		Indirect effects model: TV as a physical environmental organizer of family interaction patterns		
Independent variable →	Dependent variable	Typical independent variable →	First-order dependent variable →	Second-order dependent variable
Type of program or portion of program	Laboratory-based measure of	TV availability in the home	Family-interaction patterns in and outside TV-viewing context (amount of time together, amount and type of conversation, identity of interactants)	Children's social and cognitive development
• educational	social behavior (aggression, altruism)	Number of sets in the home		
• drama (violent-nonviolent)	or	Location of sets in the home	Visitation patterns (in own home and in others' homes) Community participation, extra-home activities (type, amount of time, variety of activities)	
• commercials	cognitive development (math and verbal skills; conceptual abilities; reasoning)	Social context of TV viewing (number and identity of viewers)		
• cartoons		Amount of time spent in TV viewing	Play patterns (amount of time, type of play, play partners) Entertainment choices (movies, type of reading, hobbies)	

who are heavy viewers have children who are heavy viewers (Chafee, McLeod, & Atkin, 1970).

Most studies report that only about one-third of TV viewing is a solitary activity, whether by children (Lyle & Hoffman, 1971a) or by adults (LoSciuto, 1971). However, the extent of TV viewing with other members of the family increases with age (Ward, 1971). Among young children, siblings are more likely viewing companions while parents are more likely to share the viewing experience with older children (Lyle & Hoffman, 1971b). In spite of the fact that the comments and reactions of coviewers to TV programs can modify the reactions of children to TV fare (Hicks, 1968; Grusec, 1973), parents, it appears, often miss this opportunity for young viewers. Although parent–child viewing may be positive, the finding of Greenberg, Ericson, and Vlahos (1971), that children who viewed in the company of their parents saw more violent programs, raises some doubts.

To evaluate the quality of family interaction patterns during TV viewing, Maccoby determined the amount of conversation. Of the viewers 58% did not talk at all during a TV program, while another 20% did so on a very restricted basis. Only 11% talked frequently during a TV show. As Maccoby (1951) notes:

> It appears that the increased family contact brought about by TV is not social except in the most limited sense: that of being in the same room with the same people. . . . The television atmosphere in most households is one of quiet absorption on the part of family members who are present. The nature of the family social life during a program could be described as "parallel" rather than interactive, and the set does seem quite clearly to dominate family life when it is on. (pp. 427–428)

Across time, people have become accustomed to having TV sets available and many are able to accomplish or at least engage in other activities while watching TV; LoSciuto (1971) reported that 30% of the adults viewed programs while engaged in other activities, while 40% talked during the program. Activities include work, housework, eating, drinking, reading, or child care. The figures are even higher for children: 80% of the first graders in Lyle and Hoffman's (1971a) study reported engaging in other activities while viewing TV, such as eating, playing, and talking. Among tenth graders, almost half study while watching TV. These activities do not necessarily detract from the program, since 50% who were talking during the programs were talking about the program themselves (LoSciuto, 1971). Moreover, TV can even serve to stimulate conversation; this same investigator found that 20% of the viewers reported discussing a variety of dramatic shows, news, sports events, and other programs after seeing them. In fact, some viewers report that they viewed TV as a source of conversation (Foley, 1968). Even commercials, regardless of one's attitude toward them, stimulated family discussion (Ward, 1971).

In spite of these observations, some modern critics remain concerned:

> Like the sorcerer of old the television set casts its magic spell, freezing speech, and action, turning the living into silent statues so long as the enchantment lasts. The primary danger of the television screen lies not so much in the behavior it produces—although there is danger there—as in the behavior that it prevents: the talks, the games, the family festivities and arguments through which much of the child's learning takes place and through which his character is formed. Turning on the television set can turn off the process that transforms children into people. (Bronfenbrenner, 1970)

Family tension may also increase as a result of TV availability. Maccoby (1951) found that 20% of the families in her sample had conflicts over TV and meals while 36% of the families had a conflict regarding TV and bedtime. Television viewing and family tension cannot be understood without a consideration of the role that TV plays in the total ecology of the household.

Families with various amounts of space may use TV in different ways. In high-density homes, where there are few alternative opportunities for spatial separation, TV viewing may be a means of controlling family tension. On the other hand, in low-density homes, TV viewing is less likely to be a mechanism for controlling family tension, since other means of spatial separation are available to family members.

To evaluate this hypothesis, Rosenblatt and Cunningham (1976) interviewed families about both their level of TV watching and the level of family tension. Their results indicated that the amount of TV viewing and the level of family tension was positively related, but only in high-density homes; in low-density households the relationship was not significant. Although the results could be interpreted to support the view that TV viewing may increase family tension, additional analyses provided support for the alternative hypothesis that TV viewing is a tension-control technique in crowded households:

> If television watching is primarily a means of avoiding tense interaction, then to some extent families are held together and domestic violence is retarded by the operation of television stations. If a strike or power shortage were to put television stations off the air for a substantial amount of time, families would have higher levels of fighting, violence and break-up. (Rosenblatt & Cunningham, 1976, p. 110)

In support of this general hypothesis, Steiner (1963) presented anecdotal evidence that TV breakdowns are associated with higher tension levels. In spite of the limitations of the study, such as the sole reliance on interviews for the assessments, the investigation does indicate that the role of TV in families can be understood only in combination with other aspects of the home setting, such as available living space. Future studies could fruitfully focus directly on specific types of family conflict such as parent-child tension as well as sibling-sibling disagreements.

One modifier of the family tension-TV relationship is the presence of multiple TV sets. First, as children develop and families grow, the presence of multiple sets increases. Lyle and Hoffman (1971a) reported that 29% of their first graders reported more than one set in the house, but 61% of the sixth and tenth graders report two or more sets. By 1975 more than 60% of American families owned two or more sets. The presence of more sets is associated with more TV viewing. Robinson (1971b) noted that teenagers with three or more sets in their homes viewed more (4.2 hours) than those with two sets (3.8 hours) or one set (3.6 hours). Color has an effect on viewing time as well. Teenagers with two or more color sets watch 4.6 hours compared with 3.7 for those with one color set and 3.9 hours for those with no color set. The other main impact of multiple sets, in addition to increased viewing time, is a reduction in family conflict. There are lower levels of conflict over program selection between parents and children and children and their siblings in multiset families. This reduction in tension is probably at the price of reduced social interaction among family members, although this is not entirely clear. LoSciuto (1971), in his adult sample, reported that 91% of the viewing in multiset homes was done on the main set. More information about viewing patterns in multiple-TV households as a function of the family size, age of the children, and location of the sets is required.

Another effect on families merits mention, namely, the use of TV as an alternative to active child care. In a national survey, Steiner (1963) found that parents rated "babysitting" as one of the main advantages of TV. Nearly one-third of the parents mentioned this supervisory or babysitting capacity of TV. Some parents stressed the relief that comes from having children quietly preoccupied: "Well, it keeps them quiet, they're not apt to go running all over the place." Other parents see TV as a means of keeping their children out of trouble. Parents of younger children, especially mothers, stressed the first aspect, while parents of older children, especially fathers, viewed the second advantage as more important. The potential problem of this attitude is nicely summarized by the parent who noted that, "It takes some of the burden off me teaching them games." In short, parents may interact less with their children and specifically may feel less pressure to provide specific educational experiences for their children. TV can do it for them! Moreover, the use of TV as a "babysitter" varies with the education of the parents: 53% of the mothers and 44% of the fathers with only grade-school education mention this function of TV, in contrast to 21% and 19% of the college-educated mothers and fathers. Nevertheless, the utilization of TV clearly should not be viewed independently of other aspects of the household organization and similarly should not alone be viewed as a causative factor in accounting for social-class differences in cognitive development.

In summary, TV has a variety of effects on families, including the amount of time that they spend together, their type of interactions, and the amount of conflict among family members.

The Impact of TV on Social Interaction with Nonfamily Members. Just as families spend more time together, visiting patterns among friends are affected. In both England (Belson, 1959) and the United States (Hamilton & Lawless, 1956) non-TV families report visiting friends more frequently than TV families, while TV families invite friends to visit more frequently than non-TV families.

Nor is the curtailment of conversation evident only among families; Hamilton and Lawless (1956) report that there is less conversation among visitors in a TV household than in a non-TV home. Since these studies, TV ownership has become nearly universal in the United States and one wonders whether this has increased the degree of social isolation of families.

Children's social patterns are similar to the adult social visiting data. Children spent more time at home when TV was introduced (Belson, 1959), visited other children less, and spent less time outdoors, especially younger children (Himmelweit, Oppenheim, & Vince, 1958). Unorganized activities, such as walking and being outdoors with friends, were most affected by TV, as opposed to activities like organized sports, which suffered less from the introduction of TV.

There have been shifts across time and in amount of TV viewing since the introduction of TV. Lyle and Hoffman (1971a) compared the amount of TV viewing between 1959 and 1970. First and sixth graders were watching about one hour more per school day and about 15 minutes more on Sunday for first graders and more than $2\frac{1}{2}$ hours for sixth graders. More importantly, the amount of time that children viewed TV in the afternoon period after school increased between 1959 and 1970. In spite of this increase, Lyle and Hoffman (1971a) found that children had a higher preference for play than for TV watching during much of their free time, particularly during daylight hours. Even in evening hours when play opportunities are more restricted, play ranked only slightly lower than TV as the child's most preferred activity.

However, TV may serve as an escape for some children. Lyle and Hoffman (1971a), for example, found that children who spend most of their time with TV report the lowest frequency of play with other children after school. Similarly, Murray (1971) found that heavy TV viewers were most likely to have problems of social adjustment and be passive, bashful, and more distractable. Since these children displayed these characteristics as early as 3 years of age, TV viewing may be a symptom, not a cause. As Murray (1971) notes, "an 'electronic' peer is a more accessible playmate for a passive child" (1971, p. 365).

In summary, the presence of TV has altered the extent of outside social contacts for both adults and children. The long-term impact of this increasing social isolation on children's later social development is worthy of more attention in the future.

Community Participation and TV Availability. Few areas in North America still lack TV reception, and therefore the opportunities for assessing the impact of introducing TV are very rare. Williams and Handford (1977), however, studied a town in western Canada just prior to the introduction of TV and again 2 years later. For comparison purposes, they chose two similar towns that had either one Canadian channel for 8 years or four channels (one Canadian and three major U.S. networks) for 15 years. Using a Barker framework, they studied the availability of behavioral settings in each town and the frequency of use of these settings by the citizens. First, the absolute number of settings was similar for all towns at both time points. However, at time point one, prior to the introduction of TV the frequency of use of the settings was significantly higher in the non-TV town than in the two comparison communities. There were 25% and 37% more entries of the behavioral settings in the non-TV community than in the one and four TV-channel towns. After 2 years of TV availability, the differences between the towns were still present, although the magnitude had decreased (12% and 14% difference). In short, the availability of TV reduced the amount of community participation, as evidenced by the initial differences among the towns and by the reduction of differences between the towns after the introduction of TV.

A general picture of *reduced* social interaction as a result of TV availability emerges whether the measurement focuses on the TV setting, the home activities, visiting patterns, or community activities.

The Impact of TV on Entertainment Choices of Children. One of the most consistent findings concerns the impact of TV viewing on the choice of other types of entertainment fare, such as reading materials. Early studies in this area were executed *before* TV became common, thus permitting comparisons between communities with TV and those without. One of the earliest studies was a survey carried out by Maccoby (1951) in which she compared TV owners and non-TV owners in Cambridge. Her early results were prophetic of the findings of larger surveys, namely, that recreational readings, as well as radio listening and movie attendance, dropped with the introduction of TV. Nor did these changes represent merely a shift from one form of media to another: there was a substantial increase in the total amount of time spent in mass media activities. Maccoby indicated that the additional time came from reductions in outdoor and indoor play and in household tasks.

Two later major projects—one in England by Himmelweit *et al.* (1958) and one in North America by Schramm, Lyle, and Parker (1961) found similar evidence of the impact of TV on reading choices.

Himmelweit *et al.* (1958) utilized two designs: a before–after research design and a design matching viewers and nonviewers. These English investigators found that TV displaced a considerable amount of reading of light material such as comic books; however, the amount of reading of higher quality magazines and newspapers was not affected. Similarly, books were affected only temporarily, with no difference in book reading between viewers and nonviewers after a few years of TV exposure.

A similar picture is evident in the North American study of Schramm *et al.* (1961), who studied children in two matched groups— one TV and one non-TV community. There was a reduction in movie attendance, radio listening, and comic book consumption, although book reading was not affected. In a survey report at the same time, Bogart (1958) noted that there was a striking decrease in the amount of fiction carried by all types of publications since the advent of television. Library choices made by children provide one of the best indicators of the impact of TV on children's reading preferences. Parker (1963), using a matched-pairs before–after design with communities differing only on date of having television reception available, examined the effect of TV on library circulation. He found that television had displaced fiction circulation more than nonfiction circulation. In a more recent study, Feeley (1974) asked children to rate a series of hypothetical titles in terms of their interest value and to indicate whether they would read, watch, do both, or do nothing about each title. In addition to the interesting confirmation that children prefer to watch rather than read, she did find that boys and, to a lesser extent, girls chose reading material for informational purposes more than TV, which was more likely to be chosen for fantasy, excitement, and recreational purposes. This finding is consistent with Schramm's general thesis that children use books and other print media to satisfy informational needs and television for fantasy and entertainment purposes. Similarly, the data support the "functional similarity" principle (Himmelweit *et al.*, 1958), which states that the activities that will be given up most readily in favor of television are those that satisfy the same needs, but less effectively.

Unfortunately the impact of TV on reading may be affecting those children who can least afford any reduction in their reading. Robinson (1971) found that TV viewing interacts with grades; students with A grades watch half an hour less than C grade students. By the last 4 years of high school this differential increases to over an hour, even as the viewing among C students drops dramatically lower.

Cross-National Evidence. The effects of TV on-time are not restricted to British and American societies. Robinson (1971a) conducted a cross-national study of time allocation of TV owners and non owners across 14 survey sites in 11 different countries including the United States, Western Europe (France, Belgium, West Germany), Eastern Europe (Poland, Yugoslavia, Bulgaria), and Peru. Other media activities are affected quite clearly, including reductions in radio listening, book reading, and movie viewing. Overall, TV owners still spent almost an hour more than nonowners in contact with the mass media. Where does this extra hour come from? Both free-time and non-free-time activities are affected. First, social gatherings outside one's home, conversation, other leisure activities (mainly correspondence and knitting), decrease while entertaining in one's own home increases. Non-free-time activities affected included less sleep by TV owners and household-care decreases. The shifts are most marked for the other media activities (radio decreases 61% and movies are down 52%). In terms of secondary activities, TV owners spent more time at home with their spouse and children, but less time with friends, relatives, and neighbors. As Robinson (1971a) cautiously notes, "whether such shifts result in greater benefit or harm to the social fabric of society remains a moot point" (p. 427). He continues:

> One of the main effects of television's introduction has been that individuals receive less communication inputs from informal sources (conversation and correspondence with friends and acquaintances) and more from structured, formal and standardized sources (the mass medium of television). At the same time it has brought the family into greater proximity (even though figures indicate that they may not communicate among themselves more as

a result) perhaps at the expense of aimless visiting and low-involvement
leisure activities like knitting. (p. 577)

Interpretation of such single-assessment studies are also tempered
by the results of longitudinal studies such as the Belson (1967) and
Videotown (Cunningham & Walsh, 1959) studies, which both indicate
that television has its greatest effect on daily life during the first few
years of set ownership. In spite of these cautions, the general shifts in
increased media use do hold up across time:

> Finally it is of interest to compare television with other innovations of the
> twentieth century . . . . Cross-nationally automobile owners on the average
> spent only 6% more time in transit than non-owners. . . . The overall shift
> is pale indeed compared with the 58% increase in media usage apparently
> occasioned by the influence of television. Cross-national data also indicate
> that time spent on housework is not grossly affected by the acquisition of
> home appliances like washing machines and dryers. Thus, at least in the
> temporal sense, television appears to have had a greater influence on the
> structure of daily life than any other innovation in this century. (Robinson,
> 1971, p. 428)

Continual monitoring of the impact of TV on time allocation would be
worthwhile. In spite of the fact that monitoring secular trends has not
been given high priority in view of our search for universal laws that
transcend time boundaries (Gergen, 1973), this research on the changes
as a result of TV clearly illustrates the value of this enterprise.

In summary, the evidence discussed in this section suggests that
TV is not merely a communicator of content but an important aspect
of the physical environment in children's homes. TV can be viewed as
a major organizer and modifier of social interaction patterns both in
and outside the home environent. Continual monitoring of these effects
over time would constitute a worthwhile enterprise.

The Effects of Background Stimulation: Interior Noise

Stimulation in home settings can be conceptualized, not merely as
specific objects or events that impinge on the child, but also in terms
of the amount of nonspecific background noise. For example, does a
quiet or noisy home make a difference in the child's cognitive development?

Some suggestive evidence comes from comparisons of middle- and
working-class home environments. Tulkin and Kagan (1972), in their
study of 10-month-old female infants, found that the working-class
homes were characterized by more noise, greater crowding, more interaction with many adults, and more time in front of the TV.

More definitive evidence comes from a series of studies by Wachs and his associates (Wachs, 1973, 1976; Wachs, *et al.*, 1971) which have assessed ambient noise levels in the home and other measures of background noise such as TV and the number of people in the homes of 7- to 24-month-old infants. Across the series Wachs consistently found that a high level of noise and stimulation from which the child cannot escape (e.g., home is noisy, small, overcrowded, TV on most of the time) was *negatively* related to the infant's cognitive development. In one study Wachs, (1973) found further evidence of the possible negative impact of overstimulation. Too much social stimulation from others in the home or from visitors was correlated negatively with cognitive status. One interesting and unique finding was that the availability of a room in the home to which the child could escape from intense stimulation was positively and strongly related to a variety of cognitive measures across the second year of life. This "stimulus shelter" was one of the best predictors of later cognitive development.

Further evidence of the impact of excessive noise levels comes from Heft (cited in Wohlwill & Heft, 1977); he distinguished two types of stimulation in the home: (1) extraneous background stimulation particularly in the form of auditory noise and movement and (2) stimulus variation in the visual field. He assessed the relationship between those measures of the home environment and young children's performance on tasks of selective attention. Using an interview-based home environment inventory, a measure of background noise level was determined from a variety of indices including noise level from TV, radio, record players, appliances, and exterior sources. The level of general activity and the frequency of interruptions in the child's solitary play by other family members were used to measure general activity level in the home. To generate an overall measure of background stimulation, the noise and activity-level scales were combined with two other indices—presence of distinctive versus overlapping sounds and frequency of sudden, unexpected sounds. To assess the links between home environment measures and selective attention, 5-year-olds were presented two tasks. First, a search task that required the child to match a stimulus card with a similar card in an array of 20 cards was used. Cumulative search time in locating the target stimulus was recorded as well as incidental learning, which was indexed by the number of nontarget items the child recognized when they were interspersed among new pictures. Children from noisier homes took longer to locate the correct pictures and recognized fewer of the nontarget stimuli; in short, performance on the central task was slower and incidental learning was lower. A similar pattern is evident using the more general background stimulation index. Noisy environments appear to be related to less efficient information-processing in children. Using an auditory distraction task, these investigators showed that children from noisy environments were less affected by a noisy distractor than children from quiet home settings, although noisy environment children still performed at a lower level on the cognitive task. As Wohlwill and Heft (1977) note:

> for the children from the noisier homes, it appears that their ability to selectively attend to the relevant stimulus features in each situation was adversely affected by the high noise levels in their homes in spite of their apparent adaptation to these conditions. (p. 132)

Nor are the effects on cognitive performance of variations in the inanimate features of the home environment limited to very young children. In a study of 710 third graders, Michelson (1968) examined the impact of a wide range of physical environment variables on children's achievement—as indexed by both teacher ratings and achievement test scores. In contrast to many investigations, the effect of physical elements of the home environment on school achievement was assessed *within* categories of social environmental variables such as parental education, occupation, and income—traditional correlates of achievement. Consistent with Wachs' findings, Michelson found that high levels of noise inside the home were related to lower teacher ratings of creativity and to lower spelling and language achievement test scores. In addition, he discovered that the children who have a separate room for study, "where they can get away from either other people or possibly discordant activities" had higher achievement spelling and language scores and higher teacher ratings. While it is relatively unimportant whether or not a child shares a homework room, it is important that no other activities take place in this space concurrently with homework. Those who worked in rooms without concurrent distracting activities received higher teacher ratings than those who used rooms where other activities took place concurrently. Functional privacy is more crucial than personal privacy.

Together, these studies provide impressive support for recognition of noise levels in the home environment as an important determinant of children's cognitive development. It is also a reminder that too much stimulation can have a detrimental effect on the developing child.

The Effects of Background Stimulation: Exterior Noise

Excessive stimulation is not restricted to inside homes; the location of the home in relation to such noise sources as roadways, airports, factories, etc., can clearly affect the level of background noise that the child experiences. Just as inside noise affects children's development, exterior noise may have long-term detrimental effects on children's cognitive development. Cohen, Glass, and Singer (1973) studied children who lived in 32-floor apartment buildings located close to a heavily traveled expressway to determine if there was any relationship between the noise level in their apartment and the children's auditory discrimination skills and their reading ability.

Since noise level decreased in higher floors of the building, these investigators asked if the cognitive skills of children in the lower floors were more impaired than those of their neighbors in the higher parts of the building. The children (second through fifth graders) were given an auditory discrimination test which involved listening to pairs of words, some of which differed from each other in either initial or final sound (for example, gear-beer or cope-coke); children were simply asked to determine which pairs were different. In addition, standardized reading test scores were available from school records.

For the children living in these apartments for 4 years or more, the lower the floor level of the apartment, the poorer was their auditory discrimination. A similar relationship between floor level and reading test scores was obtained, that is, those children who lived on lower floors showed more reading defects. Moreover, these investigators demonstrated that auditory discrimination skills and reading are related, suggesting that impairments in auditory skills may, in part, be mediating the poorer reading scores.

Of course, there could be numerous alternative explanations, besides noise, for these effects. Perhaps poorer children who obtained less adequate physical care and whose parents were less educated lived on lower floors. However, the socioeconomic range was very restricted and the prices of apartments varied minimally from floor to floor. More important, the correlations between floor level and auditory discrimination were still present even when parental educational level was controlled.

What is the explanation? The authors suggest that the children who live under prolonged exposure to unwanted noise learn to "tune out" auditory cues. This problem results from overcompensating, that is, children fail to attend between relevant parts of their auditory world, such as speech, and the irrelevant aspects, such as the traffic sounds. They appear to ignore all auditory cues in their efforts to cope with the annoying and undesirable parts of their auditory environment. As a result, the ability to distinguish speech sounds is not learned as well in this type of home, as the auditory test results clearly show. As a result of this problem, learning to read becomes more difficult. In summary, children who live in a noisy environment tend to show auditory-discrimination defects. Adapting to urban noise may be a reasonable way of coping, but there seems to be a price in cognitive skills.

Although the results paralleled laboratory experiments demonstrating degradation of task performance as a direct after-effect of exposure to noise, the effects observed in the apartment study may have been mediated by shifts in the behavior of other family members, who were also affected by the street noise. As Bronfenbrenner (1977) notes:

> the impairment of the children's skills might have come about . . . because others around them were similarly affected and engaged less frequently in conversations, in reading aloud, or in correcting their child's verbal utterances . . . relevant information could have readily been obtained had the other participants in the setting been included in the research design. (p. 522)

In light of the evidence of social class differences in the amount of contingent verbal stimulation provided for infants and children, this suggestion clearly has merit (cf. Golden & Birns, 1976).

Together, these studies provide impressive support for the view that too much noise either inside or outside the home environment—which the child cannot control or escape—is negatively related to early cognitive development and later school achievement. Moreover, these studies suggest that a linear model of stimulation may be oversimplified with its implicit assumption that increasing levels of stimulation are necessarily beneficial to cognitive and social development. Rather, an optimal level of stimulation rather than merely *more* stimulation may be a more appropriate model (Fiske & Maddi, 1961; Leuba, 1955; Malmo, 1959; Cofer & Appley, 1964). Recently Wohlwill and Heft (1977) have argued that nonlinear models are appropriate for organizing developmental data:

> Behavior is more likely to vary according to an inverted U-shaped than a monotonically increasing function with stimulus parameters such as intensity, complexity, etc. While this evidence relates to the maintenance of behavior rather than to its development, it seems reasonable to suppose that the principle applies equally on the developmental side at least as far as intensity of stimulation is concerned. (p. 126)

This argument suggests that social and cognitive development can most profitably be viewed from the vantage point of a regulatory model, which suggests that for different activities, functions, and stages of development, different amounts and types of stimulation will be required. To expand this argument we next turn to a discussion of privacy, territoriality, and crowding—concepts that serve to regulate the amount and type of social interaction among family members.

SOCIAL ORGANIZATION OF HOME ENVIRONMENTS

PRIVACY REGULATION IN CHILDREN'S HOME ENVIRONMENTS

"My idea of a home is a house in which each member of the family can on the instant kindle a fire in his or her private room" (Emerson, *Journals*).

Home environments are organized by sets of social rules that aid in regulating in an orderly fashion the interactions among the occupants. Children as well as adults generally have certain areas or territories within the home that are treated as "an exclusive preserve" (Pastalan, 1970). Other home members generally recognize these areas and gain access only through the consent of the person who controls this space. Individual territories within the home environment thus permit the attainment of a degree of privacy or escape from other household members. Territoriality and privacy, in fact, can be viewed as interrelated concepts, with territoriality being one means of achieving privacy from others. In Altman's (1975) terms both concepts can be viewed as boundary-regulation processes, which serve to determine the amount and type of social and physical contact among individual family members and to limit access of outsiders.

Families do organize their home environments and these organizational patterns that serve to regulate social interaction among family members shift as the child develops. Two recent sutdies of home environment use and regulation are particularly relevant. In a pioneering investigation, Altman, Nelson, and Lett (1972) provided a descriptive overview of the organization of home environments. Using a detailed survey, they isolated clear evidence of stable patterns in a number of areas in the home setting. Family eating patterns are highly organized, with eating typically taking place in the kitchen for meals other than dinner and dinner being equally split between dining room and kitchen. Most families have fixed seating arrangements which shift only when the family is not eating together or guests are present. The usual seating pattern varies with role status of the family members, with fathers typically at the head of the table and mothers split between the opposite end to father or adjacent corner to father. Children are distributed throughout the remaining seats. Similar findings concerning family seating arrangements have been noted by Dreyer and Dreyer (1973).

The most interesting finding concerned the clear evidence of territoriality in the use of bedrooms. Among those who shared a bedroom, there were clear rules concerning the use of closets, dressers, and of course, beds. Individuals either had their own closets and dressers or they used exclusively one side of a closet or particular dresser drawers. The extent of territorial behavior appears to vary with the degree of long-term commitment, which, in turn, would determine the need for stable organization of space. Rosenblatt and Budd (1975) found that married couples were more territorial—as indexed by indicators such as separate beds or sides of the bed, separate closet areas, drawers, etc.—than unmarried cohabiting couples. In the Altman *et al.* study, another indication of the regulated nature of the home environment was the clear use of doors as privacy markers. Families respect each other's privacy by typically knocking on closed bedroom and bathroom doors before entering.

More recently, Parke and Sawin (1979), in a detailed analysis of privacy regulation in home environments, found that both developmental and situational factors play a significant role in children's use of privacy rules and markers in the regulation of family members' access to personal space areas of the home environment. Using a modified version of the Altman *et al.* (1972) questionnaire, information about the children's use of closed doors as privacy markers, use of knock rules for parents and siblings, and the degree of access to chilren's bedrooms and bathrooms permitted to other family members was secured for children ranging from 2 to 17 years of age.

Social regulation of space in homes clearly varies with the age of the child. As children grow older, their use of closed doors, knock rules, and access limitations increase, whether for the bedroom or the bathroom, and for parents as well as siblings. The greatest shift in privacy-maintaining behavior occurs during early adolescence. To evaluate the hypothesis that the increase in privacy that occurred at this time was due to shifts in physical maturity, particularly the appearance of secondary sex characteristics, Parke and Sawin examined the physical growth data for the 9- to 16-year-olds in their sample. Children were part of the Fels Research Institute's longitudinal study and semiannual physical growth data were available for these subjects. Increasing physical maturity in adolescence as measured by skeletal age, with chronological age partialed out, was significantly correlated with greater use of privacy, particularly in the bathroom. For example, while engaged in personal bathroom activities, more physically mature adolescents keep the bathroom door closed ($r = .29$) and are more likely to restrict the access of other family members (e.g., mother not allowed in bathroom while child is bathing; $r = .38$). These general developmental trends and particularly the shift toward greater privacy-maintaining behavior during adolescence are consistent with Wolfe's (Chapter 5) studies of children's cognitive conceptions of privacy.

Privacy regulation in the home varies with the sex of the child as well as the sex and age of the person seeking access. For example, for parents' knocking on their children's bedroom doors, the highest incidence of knocking is for fathers on their daughter's bedroom doors, while knocking on their sons' doors is less frequent and similar for fathers and mothers. Mothers appear to make little distinction between sons and daughters in their knocking on bedroom doors, but knock more frequently on sons' bathroom doors than on daughters'.

Access to the bathroom shows similar cross-sex interaction effects. While children are engaged in personal bathroom activities, access to their bathroom is restricted most frequently for brothers and fathers by girls and for sisters and mothers by boys. When the same sex sibling or parent is seeking access, restrictions are less prevalent. These cross-sex interaction effects showed developmental trends as well. The greatest increase in the percentage of girls reporting restricted access for fathers was in the age range from 10 to 13, while the greatest increase in the percentage of boys reporting exclusiveness occurred during the age range from 14 to 17, at which time boys become as exclusive with both parents as older girls are with their fathers.

Another modifier of children's privacy behavior is the type of activity being engaged in while privacy is being sought. The effects of this factor, too, showed age-related trends. For example, younger children (2-5 years old) appear to make few distinctions among bathroom activities in establishing bathroom access patterns for parents. In contrast, among older adolescents (14-17 years old) bathroom access restrictions are most frequently imposed during toilet use, somewhat less frequently during bathing and dressing, and most infrequently while grooming.

In general, these findings indicate that privacy is a developmental phenomenon, that the course of development is different for boys and girls, and for situations involving different activities. When the development of privacy behaviors is considered in the context of parent-child dyads, it appears that the socialization of girls' privacy habits in regard to their fathers begins quite early, and that the socialization of boys' privacy habits occurs later and is less specific to the sex of their parent. Different rates of maturation may also play a role in these sex and age interactions. Moreover, as privacy behaviors increase with age, they become more discriminating in terms of the type of personal activity involved. These developmental patterns can be viewed as a function of the ongoing socialization of children's privacy habits, of the emergence of the more obvious secondary sex characteristics, and of children's increasing awareness of other persons' awareness of them.

Several other factors proved to be determinants of children's privacy. Parke and Sawin (1979) found that the proportion of children reporting keeping their bedroom and bathroom doors closed was *positively* related to the number of rooms in the house. This association was found for other physical space variables as well. It appears, then, that less privacy is afforded children in smaller homes with fewer facilities.

Although family size failed to yield consistent associations with privacy, a variable derived from family size and home size labeled *family density* was found to be an important determinant of privacy. *Family density* was defined in the following way:

low density . . . smaller families in larger homes
moderate density . . . { smaller families in smaller homes
                         larger families in larger homes
high density . . . larger families in smaller homes

As can be seen in Figure 2, there is a U-shaped curvilinear relation between family density and children's privacy. Higher levels of restricted bathroom access were reported by children in low- and in high-density homes and fewer bathroom access restrictions were reported by the children in moderately dense homes. This relationship

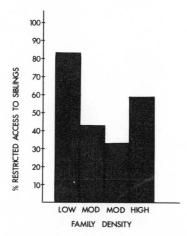

Figure 2. Restricted bathroom access × family density (square footage of home × number in household).

suggests that both the amount of space available in which one may be private *and* the psychological need for privacy in highly dense contexts contribute to higher levels of privacy use by children.

In order to determine whether privacy is related to the ongoing socialization practices in the home, Parke and Sawin examined the relation between maternal child-rearing variables and children's privacy. The Behavior Rating Scales that are based on observations of mothers with their children at regular intervals from infancy through seven years of age were used. In general, these child-rearing data yield a pattern in which it appears that restrictive and coercive mothers exercise more control over children's privacy habits, and affectionate and approving mothers have children who are less private during personal activities.

This examination of the development of privacy in childhood demonstrates the importance of considering the interactions of developmental, situational, physical space, and socialization variables in the development of children's social behavior. Finally, these findings indicate the usefulness of a multi-assessment approach including physical growth measures, situational measures, behavioral measures, and *in situ* observational measures for evaluating these interaction effects on children's development.

A word of caution is necessary. The Parke and Sawin study illustrates the fact that social organization in home environments shifts across the developmental level of the child, but the *particular* details of the family arrangements may differ across cultures and across ethnic groups. Scheflen's (1971) analysis of the organization of home space in urban Puerto Rican and Black families provides an excellent illustration. Puerto Rican families, for example, tend to cluster together in a common area such as a living room and use bedrooms only for sleeping; in contrast the Black families concentrate less in the living room and instead distribute themselves more across available rooms. The two ethnic groups divided space differently; in the Puerto Rican families, the living room might be divided into areas e.g., conversational and TV viewing, while in the Black households entire rooms were assigned to an age group with the parents in the living room and the children in a kitchen or other room. However, there were many similarities and clear illustrations of territoriality—even in shared space. Seating location was determined by a tradition of ownership, with a husband and wife seat in each room being clearly recognized. Just as door-knocking rules vary with function and identity of participants, so does territorial behavior in common or shared rooms such as the living room. While a father may assume the end of a sofa if children are present, he uses the middle if they are not present. As Scheflen notes, "even when there is a clear *a priori* pattern of site ownership, its form will depend upon the type of activity in progress. It is . . . misleading to speak of a territoriality of ownership without regard to the context" (Scheflen, 1971, p. 446).

CROWDING IN CHILDREN'S HOME ENVIRONMENTS

Crowding can be viewed as a situation that does not permit the optimal degree of privacy or social distancing between individuals in a social environment. In these terms, crowding represents a violation of the social norms that regulate social interaction and therefore can be viewed as closely linked to our earlier discussion of privacy. Crowding does not permit the appropriate degree of privacy. This view of crowding leads to a focus, not on physical or social density *per se*, but rather on the perceived violation of previously established social norms that regulate space in home environments (Altman, 1975; Loo, 1977).

The crowded home environent has often been a favorite choice of social reformers and social scientists alike as a major cause of a variety of social and psychological ills. High crime rates (Schmid, 1969), mental illness (Faris & Dunham, 1965), and juvenile delinquency (Schmitt, 1957) were all found to be correlated with population density. As Altman (1975) notes, however, not only do these correlational studies treat density in "a relatively undifferentiated fashion," but the emphasis was on outcomes with little attention paid to processes.

Although more recent studies have been more sophisticated in terms of their conceptualization of crowding, few studies have focused directly on children's home environments (see Altman, 1975; Loo, 1977 for reviews). One recent exception is a study by Murray (1974), who examined the relationship between household crowding and aggressive behavior in fourth and fifth grade children. Two measures of crowding were used: (1) persons per room and (2) family interaction density index, which is a measure of floor area by the number of personal relationships (mother–child, father–child, mother–father, etc.). Aggression was measured by a peer-nomination index (Walder, Abelson, Eron, Banta, & Laulicht, 1961). Results indicated that children from crowded homes were rated by their classmates as more aggressive than children from less crowded homes. Boys from crowded homes were also higher in extroversion and neuroticism, while girls from these types of homes were more impulsive. Although other research indicates that aggression is not necessarily an outcome of increasing spatial density (Loo, 1973; Rohe & Patterson, 1974), most of the literature is based on short-term experimental manipulations. Moreover, a distinction is necessary between behavioral indices of aggression and ratings of aggressive behavior. It is not clear that short-term shifts in aggressive behavior will be responsive to the same variables as ratings based on a long-term acquaintance with a child.

In light of the findings that parents who live in crowded homes use more punitive child-rearing practices (Roy, 1950; Newson & Newson, 1963) and the frequently reported correlation between the use of physically punitive disciplinary tactics and aggression (Becker, 1964; Martin, 1975), it may be that the greater aggression in children from crowded homes is, in part, a result of the types of discipline used by parents in crowded environments. Murray (1974) suggests that the higher use of punitive tactics may be a by-product of the greater frequency of interpersonal encounters. In fact, he argues that

> the only direct impact of crowding is on the frequency of interpersonal encounters and on the circumstances in which they occur; the members of the crowded family will experience a greater degree of mutual interference and inhibition and of agonistic encounters.

Support for this analysis comes from Mitchell's (1971) well-controlled study of high-density housing in Hong Kong. He found that there is more hostility among families who live on upper floors of high-rise apartment buildings than those who reside on lower floors. The assumption is that lower-floor dwellers can more easily escape their living conditions by their easier access to outside areas.

Finally, studies of child abuse, such as Light's (1973) analysis of the determinants of child abuse, offer further evidence for the relationship between housing conditions, frequency of interaction, and parent–child relationships.

Light found that unemployment, a condition that is likely to increase the proportion of time that a parent is in the home and thereby increase the probability of family conflict, was related to child abuse, but in interaction with housing variables:

> Abusing families where the father is unemployed are much more likely to live in an apartment than in a house relative to comparable non-abusing families where the father is unemployed . . . . Second, abusing families with an unemployed father are much more likely to "share their quarters" with other persons or families. (pp. 5, 7)

These data not only illustrate the impact of home-density variables on parent–child relations but underline the multifactor nature of social-developmental problems. It is unlikely that any single factor alone will be successful in accounting for differences in children's social behavior in home settings; rather, multiple-factor models should be the guiding rule, not the exception—as is often the case in current research.

TYPE OF HOUSING AS A DETERMINANT OF SOCIAL INTERACTION

The effects of internal crowding, defined as the amount of space inside the home, can interact with the opportunities to use outside space, such as yards or playgrounds, routinely. In turn, this opportunity for "escape to the exterior environment" is often determined by the type of building architecture. Of interest is the effect of high-rise versus low-rise buildings on social interaction patterns in homes and on children's social and cognitive development. The architecture of high- and low-rise buildings affects children both directly by affecting their opportunities for outside play and indirectly by altering interaction patterns with their parents.

In an extensive and careful study, Marcus (1974) compared low- and high-rise apartment complexes in a California urban area. Not surprisingly the low-rise site is perceived as more attractive and safer by the parents than the high-rise complex. While 73% of the respondents in the low-rise felt that their building was "a good place to bring up children," only 39% of the parents in the high-rise agreed with this view. In turn, these perceptions are reflected in the types of play opportunities that they provide for their children; 75% of the mothers in the low-rise complex indicated that they let their children out to play alone, while only 35% of the mothers in the high-rise permitted their children to play outdoors alone. Similar findings were reported by Littlewood and Sale (1972) and by Newman (1972). Although there are no directly relevant data on the impact of this restrictive play schedule, a number of outcomes are likely. First, the enforced and sustained contact between parents and their children in high-rise apartments may contribute to parental irritability and family tension which, in turn, may negatively affect the child. Just as crowded conditions may increase hostility, the inability to achieve spatial separation among family members due to building type may produce the same outcome. Peer–peer interaction is limited; this lack of interaction may, in turn, adversely affect the child's subsequent social development (Hartup, 1975, 1978). Children may not receive sufficient exercise, needed to develop their physical coordination, while the lack of sunshine could affect their health.

Support for the impact of housing types on maternal and child health comes from a study by Fanning (1967), who compared the health of both mothers and children in houses and four story flats in a British army base in Germany. Respiratory diseases were twice as high for flat-dwelling children, while the mothers who lived in flats had higher rates of psychoneurotic disorders than mothers who lived in houses. Interestingly, the rates for mothers and children increased from the first to the fourth floors of the flats. Again, it is probably the different opportunities for social interaction afforded by the two types of architectural arrangements that mediates these effects. For example, in the flats no open space for children to play was available, so children were confined more to their flats and probably to a greater degree in the higher apartments. In contrast, the houses shared a yard, which provided an arena in which mothers could interact with other parents and children could play together. This general pattern of findings is consistent with Stewart's (1970) investigation of the type of access to one's apartment on maternal ratings of loneliness. Comparisons indicated only 9% of the balcony-access apartment residents indicated loneliness, in contrast to 57% of the residents of corridor-access apartments. It would be surprising if these attitudes did not affect parent–child interaction patterns.

A systematic observational study of the interaction patterns among family members in high- and low-rise apartments is long overdue. Similarly, the long-term impact of residing in different types of housing on social and cognitive development of children at different ages would be worthwhile.

DIRECTIONS FOR FUTURE RESEARCH

Significant progress has been made in our understanding of the impact of children's home environments on their social and cognitive development. If further progress is to be made, a number of directions need to be given more attention. First, more effort should be directed toward descriptive studies of children's home environments. At present, we have only a scattered and fragmented assessment of a few aspects of children's home settings. Second, this descriptive program should be developmentally oriented, so that systematic shifts in the social, physical and intellectual spheres of the home environment can be more closely linked to shifts in the child's developmental capacities. For example, a good beginning toward a cognitive–environmental psychology has been made (Downs & Stea, 1973), but more direct attention needs to be given to children's understanding of the spatial–perceptual aspects of their home environments as well as their changing understanding of the social organization of their home settings. Third, there should be a firmer commitment to interdisciplinary research in which architects, toy manufacturers, TV programmers, and social scientists all participate in all phases of the research process from problem articulation through execution, interpretation, and eventually implementation. Fourth, more attention should be addressed to the problem of secular change and to documenting how shifts in housing designs, organization of housing projects and suburbs as well as mobility patterns alter children's behavior.

By moving in these directions, we will eventually understand home environments well enough to permit us to design homes that more adequately promote the social, affective, and cognitive development of our children.

ACKNOWLEDGMENT

The author was a Visiting Scientist at the Center for Interdisciplinary Research, University of Bielefeld, West Germany, during the preparation of this chapter and the support of Professor K. Immelmann and the staff of the center is greatly appreciated. Thanks are extended to Thomas Power for his helpful comments on the manuscript, to Mary Flowers and Steve Morice for their help in searching the literature, and to Brenda Congdon and Barbara Sackett for their preparation of the manuscript.

REFERENCES

Altman, I. *The environment and social behavior.* Monterey: Brooks/Cole, 1975.

Altman, I., Nelson, P. A., & Lett, E. E. The ecology of home environments. *Catalog of selected documents in psychology.* Washington, D.C.: American Psychological Association, Spring, 1972.

Ball, S., & Bogatz, J. Summative research of Sesame Street: Implications for the study of preschool children. *In* A. D. Pick (Ed.), *Minnesota Symposia on Child Psychology.* Vol. 6. Minneapolis: University of Minnesota Press, 1972. Pp. 3–17.

Bandura, A., & Walters, R. H. *Social learning and personality development.* New York: Holt, Rinehart & Winston, 1963.

Becker, W. C. Consequences of different kinds of parental discipline. *In* M. L. Hoffman & L. W. Hoffman (Eds.), *Review of child development research.* Vol I. New York: Russell Sage Foundation, 1964. Pp. 169–209.

Belson, W. A. *Television and the family.* London: British Broadcasting Corporation, 1959.

Belson, W. A. *The impact of television.* Hamden, Conn.: Archon Books, 1967.

Bogart, L. *The age of television.* New York: Ungar, 1958.

Bradley, R. H., & Caldwell, B. M. Early home environment and changes in mental test performance in children from 6 to 36 months. *Developmental Psychology,* 1976a, *12,* 93–97.

Bradley, R. H., & Caldwell, B. M. The relation of infants' home-environments to mental test performance at fifty-four months: A follow-up study. *Child Development,* 1976b, 47, 1172–1174.

Bradley, R., Caldwell, B., & Elardo, R. Unpublished manuscript, University of Arkansas, 1977.

Brim, O. G. Macro-structural influences on child development and the need for childhood social indicators. *American Journal of Orthopsychiatry,* 1975, 45, 516–524.

Bronfenbrenner, U. Who cares for America's children? Address presented at the conference of the National Association for the Education of Young Children, 1970.

Bronfenbrenner, U. Toward an experimental ecology of human development. *American Psychologist,* 1977, 32, 513–532.

Bronson, G. W. Exploratory behavior of 15-month-old infants in a novel situation. Paper read at the meeting of the Society for Research in Child Development, Minneapolis, 1971.

Brossard, L. M., & Decarie, T. G. Comparative reinforcing effect of eight stimulations on the smiling response of infants. *Journal of Child Psychology and Psychiatry,* 1968, 9, 51–59.

Caldwell, B. M., Huder, J., & Kaplan, B. The inventory of home stimulation. Paper presented at the meeting of the American Psychological Association, Sept. 1966.

Chaffee, S. H., McLeod, J. M., & Atkin, C. K. Parent–adolescent similarities in television use. Paper presented at the meeting of the Association for Education in Journalism, Washington, D.C., August, 1970.

Cicirelli, U. G. Siblings helping siblings. *In* V. L. Allen (Ed.), *Children as tutors.* New York: Academic Press, 1976.

Clarke-Stewart, K. A. Interactions between mothers and their young children: Characteristics and consequences. *Monographs of the Society for Research in Child Development,* 1973, 38 (6–7), Serial No. 153.

Clarke-Stewart, K. A. *Child care in the Family.* New York: Academic Press, 1978a.

Clarke-Stewart, K. A. The father's impact on mother and child. *Child Development,* 1978b, in press.

Cofer, C. N., & Appley, M. H. *Motivation: theory and research.* New York: Wiley, 1964.

Cohen, S., Glass, D. C., & Singer, J. E. Apartment noise, auditory discrimination and reading ability in children. *Journal of Experimental Social Psychology,* 1973, 9, 407–422.

Corter, C. M. Brief separation and communication between infant and mother. *In* T. Alloway, P. Pliner, & L. Krames (Eds.), *Advances in the study of communication and affect.* Vol 3. *Attachment behavior.* New York: Plenum Press, 1977.

Corter, C. M., Rheingold, H. L., & Eckerman, C. O. Toys delay the infant's following of his mother. *Developmental Psychology,* 1972, 6, 138–145.

Cunningham, J., & Walsh, F. *Videotown: 1948–1958.* New York: Cunningham and Walsh, 1959.

Downs, R. M., & Stea, D. *Image and environment: Cognitive mapping and social behavior.* Chicago: Aldine, 1973.

Dreyer, C. A., & Dreyer, A. S. Family dinner time as a unique behavior habitat. *Family Process,* 1973, 12, 291–301.

Elardo, R., Bradley, R., & Caldwell, B. The relation of infants' home environments to mental test performance from six to thirty-six months: A longitudinal analysis. *Child Development,* 1975, 46, 71–76.

Elardo, R., Bradley, R., & Caldwell, B. A longitudinal study of the relation of infants' home environments to language development at age three. *Child Development,* 1977, 48, 595–603.

Fanning, D. M. Families in flats. *British Medical Journal,* 1967, *4,* Nov. 18.

Faris, R., & Dunham, H. W. *Mental disorders in urban areas* (2nd ed.). Chicago: Phoenix Books, 1965.

Feeley, J. T. Interest patterns and media preferences of middle-grade children. *Reading World,* 1974, *13,* 224–237.

Finkelstein, N. W., & Ramey, C. T. Learning to control the environment in infancy. *Child Development,* 1977, *48,* 806–820.

Fiske, D. W., & Maddi, S. R. A conceptual framework. *In* D. W. Fiske & S. R. Maddi (Eds.), *Functions of varied experience.* Homewood, Ill.: Dorsey, 1961. Pp. 11–56.

Foley, J. M. A functional analysis of television viewing. Doctoral Dissertation, University of Iowa, 1968.

Friedlander, B. Z., Sterrit, G. M., & Kirk, G. E. (Eds.). *Exceptional infant: Assessment and intervention.* Vol 3. New York: Brunner/Mazel, 1975.

Gergen, K. Social psychology as history. *Journal of Personality and Social Psychology,* 1973, *26,* 309–320.

Gewirtz, J. L. A learning analysis of the effects of normal stimulation, privation, and deprivation on the acquisition of social motivation and attachment. *In* B. M. Foss (Ed.), *Determinants of infant behavior.* New York: Wiley, 1961.

Goldberg, S. Infant care and growth in urban Zambia. *In* F. Rebelsky & L. Dormon (Eds.), *Child development and behavior* (2nd ed.). New York: Knopf, 1973.

Goldberg, S., & Lewis, M. Play behavior in the year-old infant: Early sex differences. *Child Development,* 1969, *40,* 21–31.

Golden, M., & Birns, B. Social class and infant intelligence. In M. Lewis (Ed.), *Origins of intelligence.* New York: Plenum Press, 1976.

Greenberg, B. S., Ericson, P. M., & Vlahos, M. Children's television behaviors as perceived by mother and child. *In* E. Rubenstein, G. Comstock, & J. Murray (Eds.), *Television and social behavior.* Vol 4. Washington, D.C.: U.S. Government Printing Office, 1971. Pp. 395–410.

Grusec, J. E. Effects of co-observer evaluations on imitation: a developmental study. *Developmental Psychology,* 1973, *8* (1), 141.

Hamilton, R. V., & Lawless, R. H. Television within the social matrix. *Public Opinion Quarterly,* 1956, *20,* 393–403.

Harlow, H. F., & Harlow, M. K. The affectional systems. *In* A. M. Schrier, H. F. Harlow, & F. Stollnitz (Eds.), *Behavior of nonhuman primates.* Vol 2. New York: Academic Press, 1965.

Hartup, W. W. The origins of friendships. *In* M. Lewis & L. A. Rosenblum (Eds.), *Friendship and peer relations.* New York: Wiley, 1975.

Hartup, W. W. Children and their friends. *In* H. McGurk (Ed.), *Child social development.* London: Methuen, 1978.

Heft, H. An examination of the relationship between environmental stimulation in the home and selective attention in young children. Unpublished Ph.D. Dissertation, Pennsylvania State University, 1976.

Hetherington, E. M., & Parke, R. D. *Child psychology: A contemporary viewpoint.* New York: McGraw-Hill, 1975.

Hicks, D. J. Effects of co-observer's sanctions and adult presence on imitative aggression. *Child Development,* 1968, *38,* 303–309.

Himmelweit, H. T., Oppenheim, A. N., & Vince, P. *Television and the child.* Published for the Nuffield Foundation. New York/London/Ontario: Oxford University Press, 1958.

Horowitz, F. D., & Paden, L. Y. The effectiveness of environmental intervention programs. *In* B. Caldwell & H. Riccuiti (Eds.), *Review of child development research.* Vol 3. Chicago: The University of Chicago Press, 1973. Pp. 331–402.

Hunt, J. McV. *Intelligence and experience.* New York: Ronald Press, 1961.

Hunt, J. McV. Intrinsic motivation and its role in psychological development. *In* D. Levine (Ed.), *Nebraska symposium on motivation.* Lincoln: University of Nebraska Press, 1965.

Jacklin, C. N., Maccoby, E. E., & Dick, A. E. Barrier behavior and toy preference: Sex differences (and their absence) in the year-old child. *Child Development,* 1973, *44,* 196–200.

Jones, S. J., & Moss, H. A. Age, state and maternal behavior associated with infant vocalizations. *Child Development,* 1971, *42,* 1039–1051.

Klaus, R. A., & Gray, S. W. The early training project for disadvantaged children: A report after 5 years. *Monographs of the Society for Research in Child Development,* 1968, *33* (4), 1–66.

Konner, M. Infancy among the Kalahari Desert San. *In* P. H. Leiderman, S. R. Tulkin, & A. Rosenfeld (Eds.), *Culture and infancy.* New York: Academic Press, 1977.

Kulka, A., Fry, C., & Goldstein, F. Kinesthetic needs in infancy. *American Journal of Orthopsychiatry,* 1960, *3,* 562–571.

Lamb, M. E. Father–infant and mother–infant interaction in the first year of life. *Child Development,* 1977, *48,* 167–181.

Lamb, M. E. Interactions between 18-month-olds and their preschool-aged siblings. *Child Development,* 1978, *49,* in press.

Leiderman, P. H., & Leiderman, G. F. Familial influences on infant development in an East African agricultural community. *In* E. J. Anthony & C. Koupernik (Eds.), *The child in his family: Children at psychiatric risk, III.* New York: Wiley, 1974.

Leiderman, P. H., & Leiderman, G. F. Economic change and infant care in an East African agricultural community. *In* P. H. Leiderman, S. R. Tulkin, & A. Rosenfeld (Eds.), *Culture and infancy.* New York: Academic Press, 1977.

Liebert, R. M., Neale, J. M., & Davidson, E. S. *The early window: effects of television on children and growth.* New York: Pergamon Press, 1973.

Leuba, C. Toward some integration of learning theories: The concept of optimal stimulation. *Psychological Reports,* 1955, *1,* 27–33.

Lewis, M. Infancy and early childhood in the urban environment: Problems for the 21st century. *In Citizen and city in the year 2000.* The Netherlands: Kluwer, 1971. Pp. 167–172.

Lewis, M. *Origins of intelligence.* New York: Wiley, 1976.

Lewis, M., & Goldberg, S. Perceptual-cognitive development in infancy: A generalized expectancy model as a function of the mother–infant relationship. *Merrill-Palmer Quarterly,* 1969, *15,* 81–100.

Lewis, M., & Weinraub, M. The father's role in the infant's social network. In M. E. Lamb (Ed.), *The role of the father in child development.* New York: Wiley, 1976. Pp. 157–184.

Light, R. Abuse and neglected children in America: A study of alternative policies. *Harvard Educational Review,* 1973, *43,* 556–598.

Littlewood, J., & Sale, R. *Children at play: A look at where they play and what they do on housing estates.* London: Department of Environment, 2 Marsham St., SWL, 1972.

Loo, C. M. The effect of spatial density on the social behavior of children. *Journal of Applied Social Psychology,* 1973, *2* (4), 372–381.

Loo, C. M. Beyond the effects of crowding: Situational and individual differences. *In* D.

Stokols (Ed.), *Perspectives on environment and behavior: Theory, research and applications*. New York/London: Plenum Press, 1977. Pp. 153–169.

LoSciuto, L. A national inventory of television viewing behavior. In *Television and social behavior*. Vol 4. Washington, D.C.: U.S. Government Printing Office, 1971.

Lyle, J. Television in daily life: Patterns of use (Overview). In E. Rubinstein, G. Comstock, & J. Murray (Eds.), *Television and social behavior*. Vol 4. Washington, D.C.: U.S. Government Printing Office, 1971. Pp. 1–33.

Lyle, J., & Hoffman, H. Children's use of television and other media. In E. Rubinstein, G. Comstock, & J. Murray (Eds.), *Television and social behavior*. Vol 4. Washington, D.C.: U.S. Government Printing Office, 1971a. Pp. 129–257.

Lyle, J., & Hoffman, H. Explorations in patterns of television viewing by preschool-age children. In E. Rubinstein, G. Comstock, & J. Murray (Eds.), *Television and social behavior*. Vol 4. Washington, D.C.: U.S. Government Printing Office, 1971b. Pp. 257–274.

Maccoby, E. E. Television: Its impact on school children. *Public Opinion Quarterly*, 1951, *15*, 421–444.

Malmo, R. B. Activation: A neuropsychological dimension. *Psychological Review*, 1959, *66*, 367–386.

Marcus, C. C. Children's play behavior in a low rise inner-city housing development. In D. Carson (Ed.), *Man-environment interactions: Evaluation and applications*. Vol 12. *Childhood city*. Milwaukee, Wisc. Environmental Design Research Association, 1974.

Martin, B. Parent–child relations. In F. D. Horowitz (Ed.), *Review of child development research*. Vol IV. Chicago: The University of Chicago Press, 1975. Pp. 463–541.

McCall, R. B. Exploratory manipulation and play in the human infant. *Monographs of the Society for Research in Child Development*, 1974, 39, No. 1550.

McGuire, W. The yin and yang of progress in social psychology: Seven Koan. *Journal of Personality and Social Psychology*, 1973, *26*, 446–453.

Michelson, W. The physical environment as a mediating factor in school achievement. Paper presented at the annual meeting of the Canadian Sociology and Anthropology Association, Calgary, Alberta, June, 1968.

Mischel, W. Sex-typing and socialization. In P. H. Mussen (Ed.), *Manual of child psychology* (3rd ed.). New York: Wiley, 1970. Pp. 3–73.

Mitchell, R. E. Some social implications of high density housing. *American Sociological Review*, 1971, *36*, 18–29.

Moore, T. Language and intelligence: A longitudinal study of the first eight years, II. *Human Development*, 1968, *11*, 1–24.

Mueller, E., & Lucas, T. A developmental analysis of peer interaction among toddlers. In M. Lewis & L. A. Rosenblum (Eds.), *Friendship and peer relations*. New York: Wiley, 1975. Pp. 223–257.

Murray, J. P. Television in inner-city homes: Viewing behavior of young boys. In E. Rubinstein, G. Comstock, & J. Murray (Eds.), *Television and social behavior*. Vol 4. Washington, D.C.: U.S. Government Printing Office, 1971.

Murray, R. The influence of crowding on children's behavior. In D. Canter & T. Lee (Eds.), *Psychology and the built environment*. London: Architectural Press, 1974.

Newman, O. *Defensible space*. New York: Macmillan, 1972.

Newson, J., & Newson, E. *Infant care in an urban community*. London: Allen & Unwin, 1963.

Parke, R. D. Social cues, social control, and ecological validity. *Merrill-Palmer Quarterly*, 1976, *22*, 111–123.

Parke, R. D. Perspectives on father–infant interaction. *In* J. D. Osofsky (Ed.), *Handbook of infancy.* New York: Wiley, 1978a.

Parke, R. D. Parent–infant interaction: Progress, paradigms and problems. *In* G. P. Sackett (Ed.), *Observing behavior.* Vol 1. *Theory and applications in mental retardation.* Baltimore: University Park Press, 1978b.

Parke, R. D. Interactional designs. *In* R. B. Cairns (Ed.), *Social interactional analysis: Methods, and illustrations.* Hillsdale, N.J.: Erlbaum, 1978c.

Parke, R. D., & Sawin, D. B. Children's privacy in the home: developmental, ecological and child-rearing determinants. *Environment and Behavior,* 1979, in press.

Parke, R. D., Power, T. G., & Gottman, J. Conceptualizing and quantifying influence patterns in the family triad. *In* M. E. Lamb, S. J. Suomi, & G. R. Stephenson (Eds.), *Social interaction analysis: Methodological issues.* Madison: University of Wisconsin Press, 1978.

Parker, E. B. The effects of television on magazine and newspaper reading: A problem in methodology. *Public Opinion Quarterly,* 1963, *27,* 315–321.

Pastalan, L. A. Privacy as an expression of human territoriality. *In* L. A. Pastalan & D. H. Carson (Eds.), *Spatial behavior of older people.* Ann Arbor: University of Michigan Press, 1970.

Pedersen, F. A., Rubinstein, J., & Yarrow, L. J. Infant development in father-absent families. *Journal of Genetic Psychology,* 1978, in press.

Quilitch, H. R., & Risley, T. R. The effects of play materials on social play. *Journal of Applied Behavior Analysis,* 1973, *6,* 573–578.

Rheingold, H. L. The effect of a strange environment on the behavior of infants. *In* B. M. Foss (Ed.), *Determinants of infant behavior.* Vol 4. London: Methuen, 1969a.

Rheingold, H. L. The social and socializing infant. *In* D. Goslin (Ed.), *Handbook of socialization theory and research.* Chicago: Rand McNally, 1969b.

Rheingold, H. L., & Cook, K. V. The contents of boys' and girls' rooms as an index of parents' behavior. *Child Development,* 1975, *46,* 459–464.

Rheingold, H. L., & Eckerman, C. O. The infant's free entry into a new environment. *Journal of Experimental Child Psychology,* 1969, *8,* 271–283.

Rheingold, H. L., & Eckerman, C. O. The infant separates himself from his mother. *Science,* 1970, *168,* 78–93.

Robinson, J. P. Television's impact on everyday life: some cross-national evidence. *In* E. Rubinstein, G. Comstock, & J. Murray (Eds.), *Television and social behavior.* Vol 4. Washington, D.C.: U.S. Government Printing Office, 1971a. Pp. 410–432.

Robinson, J. P. Toward defining the functions of television. *In* E. Rubinstein, G. Comstock, & J. Murray (Eds.), *Television and social behavior.* Vol 4. Washington, D.C.: U.S. Government Printing Office, 1971b. Pp. 568–603.

Rohe, W., & Patterson, A. H. The effects of varied levels of resources and density on behavior in a day care center. Paper presented at Environmental Deisgn Research Association, Milwaukee, Wisc., 1974.

Rosenblatt, P. C., & Budd, L. G. Territoriality and privacy in married and unmarried couples. *Journal of Social Psychology,* 1975, *97,* 67–76.

Rosenblatt, P. C., & Cunningham, M. R. Television watching and family tensions. *Journal of Marriage and Family,* 1976, *38,* 105–110.

Rovee, C. K., & Rovee, D. T. Conjugate reinforcement of infant exploratory behavior. *Journal of Experimental Child Psychology,* 1969, *8,* 33–39.

Roy, K. Parents' attitudes toward their children. *Journal of Home Economics,* 1950, *42,* 652–653.

Rubinstein, J. L., & Howes, C. The effects of peers on toddler interaction with mothers and toys. *Child Development*, 1976, *47*, 597–605.

Samuels, H. R. The role of the sibling in the infant's social environment. Paper presented at the Biennial Meeting of the Society for Research in Child Development, New Orleans, March, 1977.

Schaffer, H. R., & Crook, C. K. The role of the mother in early social development. *In* H. McGurk (Ed.), *Childhood social development*. London: Methuen, 1978.

Schaffer, H. R., & Emerson, P. E. The development of social attachments in infancy. *Monographs of the Society for Research in Child Development*, 1964, *29* (3), Serial No. 94.

Scheflen, A. E. Living space in an urban ghetto. *Family Process*, 1971, *10*, 429–450.

Schmid, C. Urban crime areas: Part I. *American Sociological Review*, 1969, *25*, 527–542.

Schmitt, R. C. Density, delinquency and crime in Honolulu. *Sociology and Social Research*, 1957, *41*, 274–276.

Schramm, W., Lyle, J., & Parker, E. B. *Television in the lives of our children*. Stanford, Calif.: Stanford University Press, 1961.

Sommer, R. *Design awareness*. San Francisco: Rinehart Press, 1972.

Sommer, R. Action research. *In* D. Stokols (Ed.), *Perspectives on environment and behavior: Theory, research and applications*. New York: Plenum Press, 1977. Pp. 195–205.

Stein, A. H., & Freidrich, L. K. Impact of television on children and youth. *In* E. M. Hetherington (Ed.), *Review of child development research*. Vol 5. Chicago: University of Chicago Press, 1975.

Steiner, G. *The people look at television*. New York: Knopf, 1963.

Stewart, W. F. R. Children in flats: A family study. London: National Society for the Prevention of Cruelty to Children, 1970.

Tulkin, S. R. Social class differences in infant's reactions to mother's and stranger's voices. *Developmental Psychology*, 1973, *8* (1), 137.

Tulkin, S. R. Social class differences in maternal and infant behavior. *In* P. H. Leiderman, S. R. Tulkin, & A. Rosenfeld (Eds.), *Culture and infancy*. New York: Academic Press, 1977.

Tulkin, S. R., & Covitz, F. E. Mother–infant interaction and intellectual functioning at age six. Paper presented at meeting of the Society for Research in Child Development, Denver, April, 1975.

Tulkin, S. R., & Kagan, J. Mother–child interaction in the first year of life. *Child Development*, 1972, *43* (1), 31–41.

Wachs, T. The measurement of early intellectual functioning. *In* C. Meyers, R. Eyman, & G. Tarjan (Eds.), *Socio-behavioral studies in mental retardation*. Washington: American Association on Mental Deficiency, 1973.

Wachs, T. Utilization of a Piagetian approach in the investigation of early experience effects: A research strategy and some illustrative data. *Merrill-Palmer Quarterly*, 1976, *22* (1), 11–30.

Wachs, T. D., Uzgiris, I. C., & Hunt, J. McV. Cognitive development in infants of different age levels and from different environmental backgrounds: An exploratory investigation. *Merrill-Palmer Quarterly*, 1971, *17*, 283–317.

Walder, L. O., Abelson, R. P., Eron, L. D., Banta, T. J., & Laulicht, J. H. Development of a peer rating measure of aggression. *Psychological Reports*, 1961, *9*, 497–556.

Walters, H. R., & Parke, R. D. The role of the distance receptors in the the development of social responsiveness. *In* L. P. Lipsitt & C. C. Spiker (Eds.), *Advances in child development and behavior*. Vol 2. New York: Academic Press, 1965. Pp. 59–96.

Ward, S. Effects of television advertising on children and adolescents. *In* E. Rubinstein, G. Comstock, & J. Murray (Eds.), *Television and social behavior.* Vol 4. Washington, D.C.: U.S. Government Printing Office, 1971. Pp. 432–452.

Watson, J. S., & Ramey, C. Reactions to response-contingent stimulation in early infancy. *Merrill-Palmer Quarterly,* 1972, *18,* 219–227.

Wenar, C. Executive competence and spontaneous social behavior in one-year-olds. *Child Development,* 1972, *43,* 256–260.

White, B. L., & Castle, P. W. Visual exploratory behavior following postnatal handling of human infants. *Perceptual and Motor Skills,* 1964, *18,* 497–502.

White, B. L., Kaban, B., Shapiro, B., & Attonucci, J. Competence and experience. *In* I. C. Uzgiris & F. Weizmann (Eds.), *The structuring of experience.* New York: Plenum Press, 1976. Pp. 115–152.

White, R. W. Motivation reconsidered: The concept of competence. *Psychological Review,* 1959, *66,* 297–333.

Williams, T., & Handford, G. Television in community life. Unpublished report. University of British Columbia, 1977.

Wohlwill, J. F., & Heft, H. Environments fit for the developing child. *In* H. McGurk (Ed.), *Ecological factors in human development.* Amsterdam: North Holland, 1977.

Yarrow, L. J., Klein, R. P., Lomonaco, S., & Morgan, G. A. Cognitive and motivational development in early childhood. *In* B. Z. Friedlander, G. M. Sterrit, & G. E. Kirk (Eds.), *Exceptional infant: Assessment and intervention.* New York: Brunner/Mazel, 1975.

Yarrow, L. J., Rubinstein, J. L., & Pedersen, F. A. *Infant and environment: early cognitive and motivational development.* New York: Wiley, 1975.

Yogman, M. J., Dixon, S., Tronick, E., Als, H., Adamson, L., Lester, B., & Brazelton, T. B. Father–infant interaction. Unpublished manuscript. Harvard University, 1977.

Zeisel, J. *Sociology and architectural design.* New York: Russell Sage Foundation, 1972.

3

Childhood Outdoors: Toward a Social Ecology of the Landscape

ROBIN MOORE
AND
DONALD YOUNG

INTRODUCTION

In the urban environment, the creation of childhood places cannot be left to chance or the vagaries of pressure groups; they must be deliberately fostered by planning, design, and management to satisfy basic human needs. Our purpose therefore is to present existing empirical findings, within a behavior–environment ecological framework, to support more rational decision-making.

Under investigation is the environment actually used and experienced by children, referred to by Hart (1977) as the "phenomenal landscape" (p. 2). We present a highly simplified model of factors that control the development of the phenomenal landscape in Figure 1, which shows that a person lives simultaneously in three interdependent realms of experience: the physiological–psychological environment of body/mind; the sociological environment of interpersonal re-

ROBIN MOORE · The People Environment Group, San Francisco, California. DONALD YOUNG · Berkeley, California. Research reported in this paper was partially supported by the Farrand Endowment Fund, Department of Landscape Architecture, University of California, Berkeley, and by the National Endowment for the Arts, Washington, D.C., a Federal Agency.

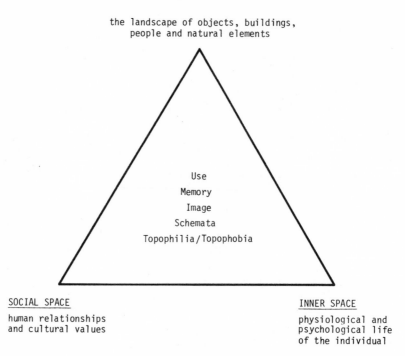

PHYSIOGRAPHIC SPACE

the landscape of objects, buildings,
people and natural elements

Use
Memory
Image
Schemata
Topophilia / Topophobia

SOCIAL SPACE   INNER SPACE
human relationships   physiological and
and cultural values   psychological life
                                                     of the individual

Figure 1. Realms of environmental experience.

lations and cultural values; and the physiographic landscape of spaces, objects, persons, and natural and built elements.

The interchange between these three realms controls use and results in what has been variously termed "image" (Boulding, 1956; Lynch, 1960); "topophilia" (Tuan 1974, emphasizing the affective domain); "cognitive map" (Downs & Stea, 1973); "mental map" (Gould & White, 1974); "schema" (defined by Bartlett, 1932, and applied by many, particularly Lee, 1968, and Abercrombie, 1969). We will use the last term to signify the cumulative content of experience. Refer to G. T. Moore and Golledge (1976) for a comprehensive review of the environmental cognition field.

Building on an earlier broad review (Cooper Marcus & Moore, 1976), we have focused upon the outdoor urban-suburban-rural environment of early-middle childhood (ages 5-12, approximately). We have focused on these years because it is the age when girls and boys are reaching out most actively to grasp and understand the natural world (Cobb, 1969).

Of the more than 50 items reviewed, 34 contained useful empirical data relating to nonsupervised outdoor settings. To summarize biases, items were classified according to spatial scale and behavioral realm (Table 1). Nearly half the studies were at residential district scale, whereas a third were at neighborhood scale and less than a sixth at play-area scale. All studies included physiographic factors (the basis of selection); of these, 24 also included physiological–psychological factors (mostly age and sex) and 17 considered social–cultural factors.

Twenty-five case study items were selected as a working collection, of which about a dozen were used as primary sources. A third of these were British works, which precede more recent American contributions by nearly a decade, reflecting early governmental research involvement in British public housing—regrettably not expanded to other children-environment contexts.

Neighborhood studies were defined as encompassing the complete territorial range of children's year-round volitional behavior. Barker and Wright's (1955) well-known study of the behavioral ecology of all 707 inhabitants of "Midwest" was a pioneering contribution, followed by Hart's (1977) study of all 86 children in the Vermont town of Inavale. A third source was Moore's unpublished Childhood Use of the Urban(izing) Landscape (CUULS) Project, with samples in Britain (BR) and America (US). CUULS : US looked at the environmental relation-

Table 1

Spatial Scale and Behavioral Realms of 34 Empirical Studies of Children's Relationships with the Outdoors

Spatial scale	Behavioral realm		
	Physiographic factors (location, element type, etc.) All 34 studies	Physiological/ psychological factors (age, sex, etc.) 24 studies	Social/cultural factors (family life style, peer relations, parental attitudes, ethnic back-ground, etc.) 17 studies
Neighborhood	12	9	9
Residential district	16	10	6
Play area	6	5	2

ships of 8- to 12-year-olds in six San Francisco Bay Area communities, across an urban–suburban–rural spectrum ($N = 265$). CUULS:BR covered three further samples ($N = 96$) from London, Stevenage New Town, and Tunstall (an older industrial town). A further significant source was Anderson and Tindall's (1972) comparison of the home range behavior of 100 urban and 100 suburban children.

Several other studies provided valuable back-up findings at neighborhood scale (Aiello, Gordon & Farrell, 1974; Auslander, Juhasz, & Carrusco, 1977; Coates & Bussard, 1974; Maurer & Baxter, 1972; Payne & Jones, 1976; Southworth, 1970). Several recent studies also served as useful methodological sources (Andrews, 1973; Ladd, 1970, 1972; Mark, 1972).

Residential-district studies included those where arbitrary study-site boundaries were drawn around a "housing project," "development" or, in Britain, an "estate." Several contributions have been made to this research area (Brower & Williamson, 1974; Cooper Marcus, 1974; Department of the Environment, 1973; Dresel, 1972; Hole, 1966; Hole & Miller, 1966). A disadvantage at this scale is that the elimination of "off-site" activity produces an inevitable bias toward what we shall later define as "habitual" range behavior. The low significance of official play areas, relative to other places used for play around the home, has been specifically indicated (Baltimore Department of Planning, 1972; Hole, 1966; Martensson, 1972; Maurer & Baxter, 1972; Sanoff & Dickerson, 1971).

Play-area studies focused specifically on playgrounds and/or other designated play areas. In this category ecologically viable research material was as sparse as the availability of ecologically viable study environments. Rare exceptions were Hayward, Rothenberg, and Beasley (1974), comparing three different types of playgrounds in New York City, and Mason, Forrester, and Hermann (1975), comparing the use of eight neighborhood parks in Berkeley. A few other studies have focused on the use of individual spaces, using interview and observation techniques (Bangs & Mahler, 1970; Byrom, 1972; Moore, 1974; Moore & Wochiler, 1974). The collected body is too small to merit extended review.

METHODS

Behavior-mapping and other systematic observation methods are the only means of recording concrete data about environmental use. Hole (1966), Coates and Sanoff (1972), Cooper Marcus (1974), and Auslander *et al.* (1977) provide typical examples. The unit of measure is an "observation," i.e., a categorized activity in space, within a given time frame. In "tracking" procedures, individual children are followed (Hayward *et al.*, 1974) to record the space-time pattern of behavior. Time-lapse photography has also been used as a recording device (G. R. Wade 1968; M. G. Wade 1977).

Simulation procedures have been used to overcome the practical difficulties of field work while still offering the subject a bridge to external reality. Compared to conventional interviewing, simulation has the advantage of introducing an artifact to stimulate the subjects' more prolonged involvement. LeVine and Taylor (1974) used "Q sort photographs"; Hart (1977) had subjects make "geographic diary" trip records on overlays on aerial photographs at the end of each day. Others have used two- or three-dimensional models (Mark, 1972; Rivlin, Rothenberg, & Justa 1974) as a response-eliciting vehicle. Brower, Gray, & Stough (1977) used a combined model–doll-play technique, involving subjects in dramatizing incidents of neighborhood life. In CUULS, subjects completed a "graphic simulation" to elicit significant elements of individual settings. Similar "mental map" methods have been used by Ladd (1970) and Maurer and Baxter (1972).

Child-guided field trips are similar to tracking, but instead of the investigator trying to maintain an unobtrusive relationship with the subject, they enter into close collusion with each other (CUULS; Gray & Brower, 1977; Hart, 1977).[1]

Assessment of factors such as age and sex are usually covered automatically in observational and simulation methods. To focus explicitly on individual differences, experimental psychological testing and physiological monitoring procedures can be used, e.g., heart-rate monitoring, as the child negotiates varied settings (M. G. Wade, 1977).

The effects of social–cultural factors such as family life-style, parental attitudes, peer relations, and school settings can be elicited to a degree by formal interviewing. Since the unit of study is the appropriate social organization, group, or institution, longer-term ethnographic "living-in" procedures allow many subtle nuances of day-to-day interaction to be recorded. Hart's (1977) "family studies" are a good example of this approach, so far rarely attempted in *urban* anthropology because of practical difficulties and the time they require.

---

[1] Barker and Wright (1966) assembled complete, highly detailed behavioral Day Records of one boy for one day. The overwhelming amount of data produced demonstrates the need for "methodological filters" to reduce information to levels of discrimination appropriate to range behavior analysis. Geographic diaries, graphic interview, and to some extent guided field-trips each have the effect of introducing a necessary psychic distance between actual behavior and its recollection.

COMPARATIVE SIGNIFICANCE OF INDOORS AND OUTDOORS

It seems clear that children and adults lead very different indoor/ outdoor life-styles. For children "indoors" is a private domain, the source of physical shelter, social security, and psychic support—and also the locus of adult dominance and the limiting effects of "family" and "school." "Outdoors" is a necessary counterbalance, an explorable public domain providing engagement with living systems and the prevailing culture—the locus of volitional learning.

Wright's (1956) data indicate the dominance of home life for Midwest's population as a whole. Of 2,030 behavior settings surveyed in 1952, 1,445 occurred in homes and 585 in more public areas (p. 267), with occupancies of 5.1 million hours and 1.0 million hours, respectively. The proportional split for school children alone was quite different, however; Barker and Wright (1955) state that 43% of children's waking hours were spent in community settings—competing on almost equal terms with home life, rising to a peak in adolescence (Wright, 1956, p. 269, Figure 1).

Hole (1966) includes a rare source of temporal data from Himmelweit, Oppenheim, and Vince (1958) of week-long diary records kept by 77 10-to 11-year-olds in London and four other English towns in 1955. Following is an aggregated summary:

Average hours spent outside during survey week (7 days):	% 10–11 year olds[a]
Up to 8 hours, or 1 hour/day approximately	28
6–14 hours, or 1–2 hours/day approximately	58
over 14 hours, or more than 2 hours/day	14
Total	100

[a] All percentages are rounded out to nearest whole integer throughout the chapter.

Temporal averages are misleading because they level out individual behavior; for example, larger blocks of time may be spent outdoors on weekends rather than smaller blocks each day of the week. Also, without knowing the time of year, it is hard to get a sense of how much total discretionary time was available to the subjects. Nonetheless, the figures give a useful sense of the "temporal scale" of behavior and lead us to urge further investigation in this direction.

The Department of Environment (DoE) report provides indoor/outdoor spatial data of similar generality. From behavior-mapping records, it was found that the aggregate proportion of all resident children seen outdoors was 22%; and for 5- to 10-year-olds it was 30%.[2] Values were

[2] Figures of this kind should be treated with caution (as DoE themselves stress). For example, no compensation could be made for the deflationary effect of unrecorded "off-site" activity or the inflationary effect of "double-counting" in behavior mapping.

also higher for children living at or close to ground level with outdoor access. Again there is a problem of individual variances being obscured by aggregated values. Even so, the fact that one-fourth to one-third of the child population could be expected to be outdoors at any moment during the day gives a useful behavioral perspective.

Simulation and interview data present a more dramatic indoor/outdoor contrast. In the CUULS:US graphic simulations, only 16% of the drawings mentioned building interiors and only 2 out of 265 were devoted entirely to indoor settings (both from inner-city subjects). To counter any suspicion of a California climatic bias, the equivalent figures for the CUULS:BR sample were 4% and 1 out of 96.

CUULS interviews were less extreme. Children were asked two different questions about "favorite place to play": first, "after school"; and second, "at weekends." Responses were divided into three classes:

1. *Homesites* (of subject, relatives, babysitters, and friends);
2. *Community/commercial facilities* (library, church, stores, etc.);
3. *Open spaces/outdoor elements* (parks, playgrounds, streets, vacant land, including responses such as "at the creek," "in my tree," "around the block," etc.).

Average scores for combined after-school/weekend mention rates for the two populations are shown in Table 2.

It should be noted that an ambiguity exists in homesite and community–commercial facilities categories concerning the relative weight of their indoor and outdoor characteristics. At home a child may spend a good portion of time in the garden or yard; at a community facility, such as a recreation center, outdoor activities may be the main attraction. If we take the most conservative case and assume (unrealistically) that home-site and community–commercial facilities provide completely indoor experience, we still find that exactly half the Bay Area mentions and close to three-quarters of the British mentions refer exclusively to outdoor settings.

The significance of the outdoors is reinforced further by DoE, (1973) data. In its interview study, 237 children, living both on and off public housing estates, were asked what they liked about where they lived; 75% of estate children and 45% of the nonestate children answered in terms of "places to play outdoors" (p. 76).

Although our evidence is scattered and light, there is an apparent contradiction here between the overwhelming affective presence of the outdoors in children's minds and emotions, compared to its more modest actual use. The sharp contrast between children's sense of affiliation and physical involvement begs further investigation in a wider range of circumstances than we have been able to tap here.

TABLE 2

COMBINED AVERAGE MENTION RATES OF FAVORITE AFTERSCHOOL
AND WEEKEND PLACES TO PLAY, GROUPED BY SPATIAL REALM, FOR
FIVE BAY AREA SITES AND THREE BRITISH SITES[a]

| | Mention rate[b] | | | |
| | Bay Area | | British | |
Spatial realm	$N = 265$ & 173^c	%	$N = 96$	%
Homesite	.50	27	.34	23
Community-commercial facilities	.44	23	.11	7
Open spaces/ outdoor elements	.94	50	1.05	70
Total	1.88	100	1.50	100

[a] From CUULS Project interviews.
[b] Mention rate (m.r.) is the total number of times an element was mentioned, divided by the number in the sample, to give a clear indication of individual significance. It also allows for consistent aggregation of categories.
[c] Responses for "after school" were elicited from total sample; for "weekend" from 65% of sample.

OUTDOOR BEHAVIOR–ENVIRONMENT CONCEPTS

Three broad concepts are proposed (Figure 2), which together accommodate a full description of children's phenomenal landscapes:

- *Territorial range* defines the collective spatial realm of experiential breadth and diversity.
- *Place* defines the locus of experiential depth and involvement and the source of knowledge and affiliation.
- *Pathway* defines the conjoining network component, threading place and territory together, emphasizing mobility and experiential continuity.

In essence, place and pathway are the concrete, generic units of range; collectively they relate directly to Lynch's (1960) terminology and conceptual scheme. Pathways may function at different times for different people purely as channels of movement from A to B; or at other times they may become significant "linear places" in their own right.

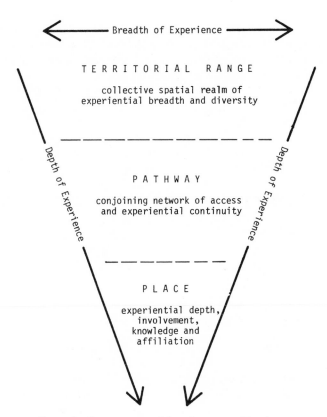

Figure 2. Components of the phenomenal landscape.

MEASURES OF TERRITORIAL RANGE

Territorial range indicates the spatial extent and experiential variety of outdoor places inhabited. It embraces the totality of a child's space–time domain—of familiar places close to home as well as a constantly expanding boundary condition, leading to unfamiliar, challenging encounters in new places.

Territorial range should not be thought of as a gross measure of area within which behavior takes place. Recognizing children's highly selective use of neighborhood space, measurement must take account of the number, variety, occupancy time, and spatial distribution of place-behavior. So far no one has attempted to develop an index or measure combining all these dimensions, though several partial attempts have been made (Moore, 1978).

Barker and Wright (1955) defined territorial range as "the number of community settings inhabited" (p. 99), but failed to take account of their spatial distribution—a crucial need when making physiographic comparisons (between city and suburb for example).

The measure of Mean Home Range (MHR)[3] used by Anderson and Tindall (1972) incorporated the number, variety, and distribution of places. Using data from "geographic diaries," Hart (1977) developed a similar measure, "maximum *daily* (our emphasis) distance traveled"; and a second measure, "maximum distance traveled to a range boundary" (from the homesite during a stated period, indicating the more geographic scale of behavior). Hart's approach, using the "trip" as a basic survey unit, allowed for the more overt, descriptive aspect of range experience to be assessed during a set time interval; e.g., weekday compared to weekend. Graphic simulation techniques have been used to assess territorial range as perceived by the child, with the option of subsequent transfer to a scaled map (CUULS; Ladd, 1970; Maurer & Baxter, 1972).

RANGE EVOLUTION

Territorial range is a dynamic phenomenon, the outcome of complex interactions between organism and environment; it has two distinct aspects: one of "extension," the other of "development."

Range extension is easy to visualize as territorial entrepreneurship from birth onward, with the child constantly striving after new desti-

---

[3] Defined as "total, nonredundant path length" (measured in feet) between "activity nodes," identified by subjects on neighborhood air photos. They suggest this is a less ambiguous and more easily derived measure than "area," because it more closely approximates the structure of behavior. Children do not move indiscriminately over the whole neighborhood domain. Their behavior is subject to a variety of constraints and opportunities. Nonredundant path length is a more satisfactory measure because it allows neighborhood space to be ranked behaviorally, according to how thickly or thinly it is *traversed*. Appleyard & Lintell [1972] provide an example of "street-traversability" as a·function of traffic loadings. Other examples have a potential for study, e.g., block traversability as a function of alleyways, climbable fences, and resident tolerance toward children [as addressed by LeVine & Taylor, 1974]. Path-length measures of range are workable only above a certain spatial scale, where path and place can be behaviorally distinguished. At smaller scales where the density of behavior makes differentiation between "path" and "place" impossible, range concepts are no longer operational and analysis must focus on individual behaviors. All territorial range analyses we have come across relate to home range, where the subjects' home lies at the behavioral center. Several other range types have potential significance, e.g., "park range," extending from a family picnic site; "vacation home range," of rural cabin compared to city hotel; etc.

nations (e.g., front step, friend's house, corner store, park, lake, etc.).
Each extension introduces a new place, which then becomes the temporary landscape marker of the child's "range boundary."

Range extension is a discontinuous process associated with primary social events, such as starting school or learning to ride a bicycle
or using the buses alone. Or consider the new destinations made
possible when permission is finally given to cross a busy street that
had for years been the rigid boundary of the child's world. Extension
is also subject to explicit "range-conditions," i.e., constraints or stimuli
such as parental restrictions, mode of travel, accessibility, private-prop-
erty rights, bureaucratic controls, physical dangers such as traffic, and
the inherent but variable attractiveness of the landscape itself.

Range development is more consistently on-going, related to the
exploration, manipulation, and transformation of newly acquired territory over time. Discovery is not limited to the first visit; each subsequent trip opens up new possibilities for continued involvement.
These may stem directly from new perceptions of familiar places, or
via the collective imagination of peer-groups (Moore, 1974); they may
result from accompanying adult leadership (parents, teachers, older
siblings, etc.); or they may happen because of inherent changes in the
place itself. This last partly explains the significance of natural systems
as a prime source of what might be called "sufficient unpredictability,"
fulfilling children's need for the simultaneous experience of continuity
and change (Mead, 1966).

For each child there exists a repertoire of necessary range behaviors, extending from the strictly routine to exploratory involvements in
a shifting spectrum of places—from familiar to unfamiliar, the known
and the yet-to-be-discovered.

Both ends of this "involvement cycle" are important. The routine
behavior of repeated trips to playground swings, for example, provides
a confirmation of the predictability of social and natural phenomena.
Nonroutine, "experimental" behavior, on the other hand, leads the
child to discover new properties of the world, providing a necessary
testing ground for emergent skills. Children's biological development
must run parallel to range extensions, supplying new material for the
continuing drama of a child's discovery of the world, without which
the acquisition of competence and understanding would be impossible
(Pearce, 1977).

Most studies have taken a rather static view of home range development. It seems important here to clarify the range evolution process
to try to make it more amenable to analysis. The following outline
model is offered, stemming from the CUULS study, with support from

other prime sources. It defines three levels of involvement: "habitual," "frequented," and "occasional."

Habitual range represents close-to-home behavior, incorporating friendship patterns clustered around each child's home, spilling out onto sidewalks, and extending into more accessible neighborhood spaces such as schoolyards, playgrounds, back alleys, lawns, vacant lots, small vegetated grassy areas, etc., where peers can play together. Habitual range analysis is particularly appropriate to the evaluation of residential districts, as we shall discuss later.

Habitual-range development begins during preschool years, initially incorporating the private spaces immediately around the home with later extensions into the contiguous public domain. New social alliances, acquired at elementary school, result in fairly dramatic range extensions to friends' houses and perhaps a corner store, together with sidewalk/street play, which maintains high significance over many years, especially in "dead-end," low-traffic conditions (Zerner, 1974).

The rate of extension depends on local traffic conditions as well as many other controlling factors, including the negotiation of parental restrictions, sex of child, site layout, space availability, microclimate, etc. As children grow in age, an increasing number of range destinations become habituated. Beyond a certain limit, however, temporal constraints require some destinations to be dropped. The picture that emerges (though evidence is skimpy) is of progressive contiguous development up to preadolescence, for most children. In late childhood and adolescence, habitual "turf" remains significant but become fragmented as destinations more distant from home (e.g., friends' houses, soda bar, sports facilities, high school) are substituted for nearby early–middle childhood places.[4]

For all ages, behavior continues to be controlled by temporal constraints, especially during the school year, meaning that periods of play must be wedged between formal school schedules, family mealtimes, extracurricular activites such as music lessons, and (for nearly all urban children) nightfall. There is simply not enough time to wander far from home.

Frequented-range behavior reflects the temporal flexibility of weekend and vacation periods, opening up the possibility of weekly travel to more distant destinations, by children over about 8 years of age—

---

[4] We must stress that this is a highly generalized model and that individual behavior varies tremendously under the influence of social and physical factors [see Barker & Wright (1955); Chapters VIII and IX, for example]; and then there are effects such as residential mobility that have yet to be researched.

especially those on bikes. Typical destinations include preplanned trips to the local ball game, sports field, or swimming pool; excursions downtown; extended visits to parks or libraries; and journeys to special places such as "clubhouses" if not too far away.

In adult terms, most of these destinations are not far from home; but for the child, they lie at a necessary psychological distance, just beyond the habitual boundary, accommodating important qualitatively different, nonroutine experience.

Occasional-range behavior relates to exotic places beyond the frequented range that are the experiential privilege of few children. Trips may be made perhaps once or twice a month or even less frequently. Opportunities arise from a combination of phenomenal factors: the child's own qualities (e.g., independence); fortuitous circumstances presented by the social environment (e.g., tolerant parents); the landscape itself (e.g., a rare feature such as an old quarry or available public transit); and temporal conditions (long summer days, etc.). The variety of potential destinations is dependent upon, and expressive of, local regional characteristics. Mode of travel is obviously a contingent factor; foot, bike, horse, and public transit all embody inherent limitations and potentials. Horse-riding in rural terrain is a particularly potent source of occasional experience.

"Occasional trips" are usually undertaken by peer or sibling groups, as companionship is a necessary condition for journeys into the unknown. When children are chaperoned by an older, more knowledgeable child or adult, experiential quality depends a great deal on the maintenance of a shared understanding as to the role of leadership. In such cases, occasional ranges may include family trips by car to destinations such as vacation homes and large parks, in themselves the potential subject of further range analyses.

CONTROLLING FACTORS ON RANGE DEVELOPMENT

We turn now to empirical sources to illuminate the foregoing conceptual scheme. Coates and Bussard (1974) used three semiequivalent concepts of home-range evolution: "home base," "territorial range," and "chaperoned travel." They looked at range behavior of 4- to 5-, 6- to 9-, and 10- to 12-year-olds in a moderate-density, suburban, planned unit development.[5] According to their results, the range of the youngest group was "bounded in a compact home-base bubble extending about

---

[5] Methods included open-ended and aerial photo-map interviews with children, activity checklists, Activity Day Narratives, and parental interviews ($N = 30$).

50' from the front doors . . . and between 90' and 140' laterally" (Coates & Bussard, 1974, Table 1, p. 138). For half the youngest age group "territorial range" extensions occurred along short paths to playgrounds.

Age and Sex

At elementary-school age, the authors note a dramatic change in range behavior, paralleling Payne and Jones' (1976) observation of less sidewalk and close-to-home play. Coates and Bussard discovered a tenfold increase in "home base area," and a five- to eightfold increase in "path length" (i.e., maximum distance traveled). In the 6–9 age range, all the boys and half the girls traveled to territorial range destinations beyond the home base. Ten- to twelve-year-olds' home base remained about the same, whereas territorial range and number of destinations increased, particularly for girls. Chaperoned travel in both age groups was related primarily to trips to the store.

The Anderson and Tindall study (1972) provides a good example of the simultaneous investigation of several factors controlling range development. Values for MHR of second- and fourth-grade, bike- and non-bike-owning girls and boys were compared for urban and suburban samples.[6] Highest distance scores related to fourth-grade bike-owning boys. Interestingly, urban and suburban MHR values were almost identical: 6,828 feet and 6,820 feet, respectively. A minimum value of 2,699 feet was related to second-grade non-bike-owning urban girls. In all cases MHR was lower for girls than boys and, with the exception of second-grade suburban girls, it was greater for bike owners than non-bike owners. Changes in MHR with age did not follow such an orderly upward progression.

In each age–sex category, MHR was greater for the suburban sample. On the other hand, the number of activity nodes (i.e., range destinations) elicited was greater for the urban sample. A further urban–suburban difference was that the number of "recreation nodes" increased regularly with age and sex in the urban sample, but remained at a constant level in the suburban sample. In other words, the suburban children traveled greater distances for less experience.

The authors suggest three possible explanations: First, suburban back yards (or space immediately around the home) is a more sufficient

---

[6] The study involved "turf-maps" derived from interviews with children using aerial photographs, with samples of black children in inner Baltimore and suburban New England (N = 100 in each case).

play space than the equivalent space around urban homes; second, suburban neighborhoods may provide sparser play "opportunity surfaces." Or, third, range behavior controls are exercised more severely by suburban parents. Our suspicion is that all three factors apply.

Rural, Suburban, and Urban Contexts

Hart's study provides further evidence regarding the effects of age, sex, parental control, and environmental context on range experience. The range distance measure used by Hart[7] was different from Anderson and Tindall's more comprehensive assessment. The mean distance for younger girls was 942 feet, and for boys 1248 feet. In the older group, values were 2,877 and 7,356 feet for girls and boys, respectively. Range Distance Sex Ratios (boys' score divided by girls' score) derived from these figures are 1.32 and 2.56, respectively. The implication is that younger children's range is a great deal more sex-equitable than older children's.

Table 3 includes these values together with equivalent ones from Anderson and Tindall.[8] Ratios for the younger age groups are remarkably close; indeed, the suburban and rural values are almost identical. The indication is of a constancy of sex-difference in the range distance of younger children, irrespective of site context. Ratios for older groups, however, present a different picture. The suburban ratio (1.58) indicates the highest level of equality, with the urban ratio (1.65) following close behind. The rural ratio of 2.56, by comparison, suggests conditions of severe inequality.

Comparison of the differences between sex-ratios indicates increasing sex-disparity between age groups as we move from urban (.19) to suburban (.27) to rural (1.24) situations. The massive difference in rural footage scores between the younger and older boys emphasizes the trend. One possible explanation is that undeveloped rural landscapes offer many more attractive opportunities for range extension, to greater distances, than the more compact homogeneous landscapes of suburbia, or the traffic-constrained, high-density landscapes of the city.

Differences in parental control are certainly also instrumental. Rural girls' range may be restricted more by parental fear and by

---

[7] From children's "geographic diary" records he was able to measure (with a planimeter) maximum daily distances traveled during the week-long survey period, for K–3rd grade and 4–6th grade girls and boys.

[8] Even though identical measures were not used, the comparison of *ratios* appears legitimate as we are interested in differences of scale, rather than kind.

TABLE 3
RANGE DISTANCE SEX RATIOS BY AGE GROUP AND SITE CONTEXT[a]

| | Range distance (ft) | | Ratio difference |
	Younger[b]	Older[c]	
Urban			
Boys	4131	5816	
Girls	2833	3518	
Ratio	1.46	1.65	.19
Suburban			
Boys	5209	6165	
Girls	3962	3905	
Ratio	1.31	1.58	.27
Rural			
Boys	1248	7356	
Girls	942	2877	
Ratio	1.32	2.56	1.24

[a] From Anderson & Tindall (1972) (urban and suburban); Hart (1977) (rural).
[b] *Younger:* urban and suburban, 2nd grade; rural, K–3rd grade.
[c] *Older:* urban and suburban, 4th grade; rural, 4–6th grade.

requirements to do more chores around the home. Suburban girls are probably most free, because chores are more likely to be shared with brothers in middle-class families, and parents consider suburbs more "safe." Even though information on such matters is sparse, we should look at it more closely.

Parental Controls

By relating to parents as well as children, over a considerable period of time, Hart was able to identify subtle negotiations that took place beween them as range became extended step by step. The same was found in CUULS. In some households discussion of children's territorial rights was conducted in an open atmosphere of give-and-take, with very little apprehension overtly expressed by the parents. Both studies found that mothers were more flexible in their judgments, whereas fathers were more authoritarian and arbitrary, more so perhaps in their dealings with daughters than with sons.

Hart and the CUULS study both verify that territorial range rules laid down by parents were more frequently broken by boys, often with the knowledge of parents—and even with the child knowing that the transgression was known. This led Hart to suggest the existence of a double standard of restriction, whereby boys's spatial privileges were accorded a more flexible margin of negotiation with more ambiguous rules, according to the maxim that "boys will be boys." Range rules for girls by comparison were more clear-cut, allowing for less maneuver as circumstances changed, although mothers generally did not seem aware of their preferential treatment toward their sons.

By undertaking long-term ethnographic studies, Hart was able to illuminate further influences of the social environment. He observed the constraining effect of "mothering" duties imposed on older girls and, conversely, the benefits on younger children, who were able to accomplish range extensions in the company of older sisters or occasionally with neighbors acting as surrogate parents.[9] Hart found that range restrictions were more relaxed when both parents were working; and he detected that restrictions of "first born" children are avoided further down the birth order, once older siblings could chaperone younger ones. He also noted that parents generally relax their hold on later children as their parenting skills and confidence mature.

In some cases Hart observed that mothers were unwilling to relinquish their children to the world (cf. Holt, 1975). This was especially true of single parents and last-born children. Most parents, however, transcend this problem and accept the fact that control must inevitably give way to disengagement.

In examining parent–child relations at close quarters, Hart identified three varieties of restrictive *range conditions,* modified by parents and children within a "negotiative" process, to suit prevailing circumstances. The conditions were defined as:

- *Free range*—places allowed to go alone, without asking permission.
- *Range with permission*—places allowed to go alone, but saying where and asking permission first.
- *Range with permission, with other children*—as above, but with other children.

In the CUULS study, a fourth condition was identified, namely:

- *Range with related adults*—accounting for range extensions made in the company of a family member or other adults (recreation leader, teacher, etc.).

From Hart's interviews with children, measures were made of

---

[9] Although the relationship is one of "following" rather than "leading" the trip.

range-boundary extensions under different permission conditions. Findings indicated that the farthest "free-range" distance traveled at first and second grade was about 300 feet, jumping to 786 feet at third grade, rising slightly to about 1,000 feet at fourth grade, jumping again to a maximum of 1,900 feet at fifth grade, and dropping to just over 1,500 feet at sixth grade.[10]

"Farthest distances with permission" followed considerably higher values but in the same relative sequence from just over 1,000 feet at first–second-grade levels to nearly 3,300 feet at fifth grade. Distances "with permission, with other children" still followed a regular progression by age, but again increased from a first–second-grade value of over 1,600 feet to more than 6,000 feet at fifth grade. Range extensions for girls in higher grades arose from domestic-role obligations. Older girls went on errands to stores almost twice as often as boys; but this type of range extension took place within quickly routinized channels, without resulting in an equivalent increase of experiential breadth that such a scale of extension would provide for boys, who were free to come and go as they pleased. Boys were found to mention many more "land-use places" in their diaries than girls, especially in trips alone. Girls became socially isolated in the summer and initiated relatively unimportant trips to the store in order to get away from the house and find contact with other children.

In all cases, under all range conditions, boys' "furthest distances" were greater than girls'. The extreme cases seemed to occur under free-range conditions, at third (Figure 3) and fifth grade, where boys' distances were 2.6 and 2.9 times greater than girls' distances, respectively. At second grade the ratio was still greater than 2.0, as was also the case with fifth graders under "with other children" conditions. At this age, boys experience a dramatic increase of freedom. By fifth or sixth grade, Hart reports, many boys were allowed to go anywhere they chose; and their resultant range-boundary was about as big as it was going to be until they reached driving age. He also discovered that the more advanced extensiveness of the boys' range was stimulated by their earlier bike use. Remaining always one year ahead, they were allowed to ride on sidewalks at third grade, whereas girls were not.

In summary, the Hart findings indicate that older boys especially move around more, further afield, to a greater variety of places. During the same period, girls begin to participate more in the routines of domestic life, with consequential constraints upon both the space and time of their range experience.

---

[10] Values converted from yards and interpolated from bar graphs (Hart, 1977, p. 42.)

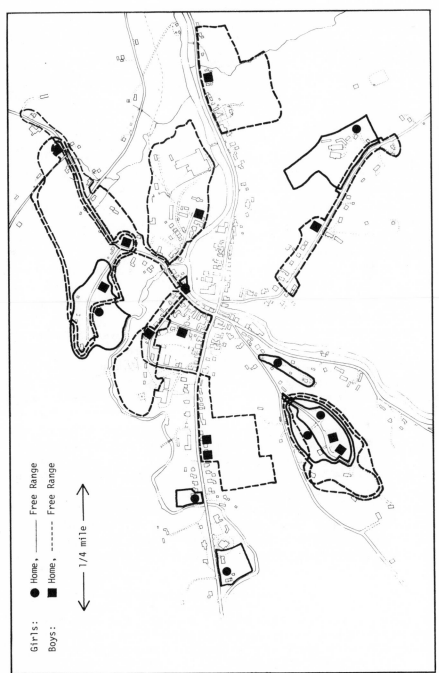

Girls: ● Home, —— Free Range
Boys: ■ Home, ------ Free Range

← 1/4 mile →

Figure 3. Free-range summer boundaries for 8-year-old girls and boys in Inavale, Vermont; showing dramatic sex differences in range development at this age. From Hart (1977, p. 40).

Environmental Fear

Both the Hart and CUULS studies identified several fear-based factors in parental control (which again seemed to affect girls more than boys). CUULS:US subjects were asked *why* use was not allowed of specific named places. Reasons given (as a percentage of total mentions) were: traffic danger, 27%; social apprehension/fear of attack (including not mixing with certain classes of kids, avoiding "winos," and fears of sexual molestation), 25%; "too far/get lost/not old enough" (i.e., a lack of spatial competency), 17%; physical dangers (excluding traffic; but including dogs, snakes, bodies of water, and high places), 17%.

In general the environmental fear of many parents seems out of proportion to statistical reality and gives rise to considerable sex-differentiation toward children, depending on the presupposition of parents. Fathers may think it is "manly" for sons to go out and "conquer" the world, and equally proper for daughters to stay home. Mothers may be far more fearful of sexual interference in respect to daughters, than to sons—and so on, always depending on secondary factors such as urban-rural context.[11]

Similar effects of sex-related spatial behavior were recorded by Payne and Jones (1977) in their study of a Calgary suburb, as well as by Coates and Bussard (1974). The latter again found an emphasis on stricter control, retarding the extension of girls' territorial range. The authors note how specific landscape elements (roads, fences, etc.) were used to mark the range boundaries for girls more precisely than for boys. Hole (1966, p. 24) includes data based on parents' response to a question that asked about maximum free range. For parents of 7- to 8-year olds, 52% said their child was not allowed off the estate; for 9- to 10-year olds the value was down, but was still 23%. In the CUULS:BR study, specific cases were documented regarding where interfaces between new high-rise buildings and old surrounding terraces were used by mothers as rigid, "nonextendable" boundaries, producing a situation of "low negotiative potential" between parent and child. According to Saegart and Hart (1978), such regressive inhibiting of self-deter-

---

[11] A subtle example is taken from the CUULS:US rural sample: the whistling call of fathers was used as a signal for children to come home, who irrespective of sex were allowed to play within "whistling distance." The rural context allowed father and children to have more intimate contact during the day, resulting in more equitable treatment. The expanded point concerns the whistle itself, a common male skill, and the quiet rural surroundings that allowed it to be used by the father in undertaking an important domestic duty (getting children to the table on time).

mination is bound in the long run to result in reduced competence and a multitude of resulting handicaps in dealing with the world.

Covert Equality

The foregoing conclusions are not mirrored in the more covert landscape relationships represented by CUULS graphic-simulation data. Average aggregate mention rates for outdoor place elements were 10.58 elements/drawing for girls and 10.08 elements/drawing for boys. Although there were many sex-differences related to individual classes of element, an aggregate picture of perceptual equality is clearly presented. Whatever differences may exist between girls and boys in their spatial behavior, they are not reflected in the breadth of their schemata. [12] The aggregated CUULS data strongly suggest a covert dimension of landscape affiliation, which seems to provide a countervailing influence upon girls' and boys' relationship with the outdoors. Although particular handicaps may result, as suggested by Saegart and Hart, it is also possible that compensating behavioral shifts occur whereby, for instance, girls gain greater depth of experience via extended involvement in fewer places, versus boys' more extensive but superficial range experience.

Temporal Factors

Temporal constraints on spatial behavior are rarely discussed and have been seldom investigated, yet they have an instrumental effect on children's range experience. CUULS provided mention rates of "after-school" compared to "weekend," "favorite places to play" (Table 4), giving an indication of weekend shifts, presumably from habitual to frequented realms.

A weekend shift away from home is immediately visible, numerically equivalent to the mention rate for weekend family trips, to which it is clearly related in the ecology of behavior. It is interesting to note that the aggregate rates for all nonhomesite destinations are almost identical for both after-school and weekend classes. Numerical equality makes interpretation a simple matter of examining the magnitude of behavioral shifts by destination.

Most scores show a drop in significance from weekday to weekend,

---

[12] This conclusion is further reinforced by Barker and Wright's (1955) finding that very little difference existed between the number and variety of behavior settings occupied by girls compared to boys; 90% of settings inhabited by children and adolescents were inhabited by both sexes (p. 100).

TABLE 4

COMPARISON OF AFTER-SCHOOL AND WEEKEND MENTION RATES
OF FAVORITE PLACES TO PLAY, AGGREGATED BY DESTINATION
TYPE[a]

	Mention rate			
	After school		Weekend	
Favorite places to play	N = 265	%	N = 173	%
Homesite	.63	29	.30	16
Open space	.40	18	.32	17
Community recreation facilities	.35	16	.24	13
Macroelements[b]	.18	8	.23	12
Microelements[c]	.17	8	.12	7
Commercial facilities	.11	5	.06	3
Sports facilities	.11	5	.10	5
Sidewalks/streets	.08	4	.03	2
Nonspecific[d]	.08	4	.12	6
Child-built places[e]	.07	3	.03	2
Weekend family trips	—		.32	17
Aggregate	2.18	100	1.87	100
Minus homesite	1.55	71	1.57	84

[a] From CUULS:US interviews.
[b] E.g., "hills, creeks, fields, railroad tracks."
[c] E.g., "rocks, frogs, crabs, trees, grass."
[d] E.g., "around the block, everywhere."
[e] Included "made" places such as "forts," as well as "found" places such as "hiding places."

indicating that most destination types (open space, community–recreation facilities, microelements, commercial facilities and sidewalks/streets) lie within the habitual range of most 8- to 12-year-olds, and that weekend use is overshadowed by family activity. The lower weekend score for child-built places is surprising and seems to contradict a hypothesis that such places are important destinations in the frequented–occasional realm.[13] On the other hand, the increase of macroelements and nonspecific destinations provides supporting evidence of open-ended weekend range extensions, focused on special landscape features. Collectively, these include a wide range of wild

[13] The "child-built" category included hiding and secret places, etc., that may well have been (by definition, almost) close to home and well within the habitual realm, hence accounting for the low weekend mention rate.

places, rough ground, natural resources, and abandoned artifacts of many kinds. In CUULS:US, weekend macroplaces included "the woods," "the hills," "the fishing pier," "train tracks," "the walnut orchard," "fields," "the creek," "the tunnel," and many others.

The "Pull" of the Landscape

Coates and Bussard's (1974) subjects mentioned "off-site range extensions" with name like "Snake Hill," the "Mountain," and "Closed Road"; in the 6–9 age group, mentions were exclusively by boys. In the 10–12 group, half the girls mentioned wild areas, but the boys still used them more and traveled to more distant ones.

Hart stated that rivers and lakes were the places children valued most and yet the river was forbidden to them until they were at least 8 years old, and the lakes lay well beyond the range of all but the oldest boys. At somewhat more modest scale, brooks and small "frog ponds" were highly valued and used for dabbling in as well as for watching and catching wildlife (micro-elements). Woods, sand piles, quarries, and a variety of "hiding places" and "look-out places" were also highly prized.

In their suburban study, Payne and Jones (1977) note the occasional forays of 8- to 11-year-old boys up "Porcupine Valley"—an adjacent gully of trees and undergrowth, offering places for fort building and hideouts. Another "fringe area" in their study consisted of a large excavated dumping ground, used predominantly by boys to explore and build forts from discarded material.

The foregoing examples of wild and distant places provide a clear illustration of the effect of "place-quality" on range extension, whereby specific features in the landscape exert a "pull" over children, leading them ever further afield.

Investigation of these qualitative attributes of exotic place-elements was of particular concern in the CUULS study. The child-led field trips were especially informative in this respect, enabling the documentation of many subtle characteristics and secondary relationships. In the verbal questionnaire children were asked, "What's the furthest place you've been to on your own or with other kids, without adults going too?" The largest class of response (equal to mentions of commercial destinations) was of macroelements, e.g., "big trees place," "Indian Rock," "down San Carlos to big street," "other side of the mountain," "followed creek three miles to freeway," "followed railroad tracks to recyling plant," "Ellis Lake," with a scattering of "macrotime" responses, such as "all-day hike" (US data).

PLACE

Place is the smallest unit of range, representing the affective hot-spots of a person's schema. The Perls, Hefferline, and Goodman (1951) thesis suggests that place accommodates transactive activity, facilitating learning toward an evolving sense of affiliation and meaning. Organism and environment adapt to each other over relatively long periods of time, coerced and supported by identifiable, measurable elements—space, time, fixed features, loose-parts, natural phenomena, and populations—together with the physical attributes or sensory characteristics of elements and their interactions.

Although "place" is a common term of everyday usage, few attempts, apart from Spivak (1973) and Moore (1977, 1978), have been made to sharpen its theoretical/empirical clarity. Place was used by Hart (1977) as a rubric for the social and geographic (range) factors affecting children's "place experience"; but the influence of the elements and attributes of places were not discussed in detail.

Significant Place Elements

The main source at our disposal is the CUULS graphic simulation data. Multiethnic, 8- to 12-year-old children were asked to make a map or drawing of "all your favorite places, where you go after school or at weekends—around your home and neighborhood, including the summer." From the drawings (Figure 4) 72 categories of place elements[14] were coded. Table 5 gives the complete list in rank order of mention rates.

An overview of the figures indicates that only three elements ("child's own house," "through streets," and "child's mention of self") had a mention rate greater than 0.50, and that a little over half had scores greater than 0.10. Because the sample was drawn from a wide range of settlement conditions, the list can to a degree be taken as a collectively ranked schema of San Francisco Bay region neighborhoods. Note the primary emphasis on the subject's own person and closest friends, together with their homes, the surrounding streets and immediately accessible places such as school, parks, playgrounds, stores, and community facilities. Interspersed within this functional realm are a set of elements of a different type: trees, fences, lawns, stoops, etc.,

[14] In coding, data were disaggregated to a maximum feasible degree, e.g., a park drawn with trees was coded both as "park" and as "single trees." The objective was to be able to code as many as possible of the elements at a scale appropriate to design science and planning policy. From another point of view, the coding procedure adopted was merely a way of showing methodological respect to the integrity of the data.

offering special place-affiliations. Four categories of pathway appear in the upper part of the list: (#2, "through streets," m.r. = 0.79; #20, "trails/shortcuts/paths/alleys," m.r. = 0.20; #21, "sidewalks," m.r. = 0.19; #26, "dead-ends/driveways," m.r. = 0.17). These categories attest to the importance of pathways. The street specifically, as a principal childhood place, is further reinforced by Barker and Wright (1955), who state that traffic ways had the highest occupancy index[15] (7.4) of all community settings for all children, apart from school classes (30.9). On the same scale, open spaces had an occupancy index of 4.3.

In theory, users' mention rates could be compared to actual "occurrence rates" in the environment, indicating the extent to which image and reality coincide. Although the necessary occurrence values are not numerically available, some differences are informally evident. Nonpathway asphalt, for example, has a very low mention rate (0.02) despite its dominant presence in the urban scene. It is apparently a phenomenol nonentity.

Taking an example from the opposite extreme, surely the moderate mention rate for creeks/streams (0.21) indicates a high degree of affiliation compared to their infrequent occurrence in the landscape (many have been culverted). For other elements, mention rates seem equivalent to their frequency of occurrence—trees, for example. Such judgments are based on the presumed *positive* affiliation between person and place. An example of negative "disaffiliation" is indicated by the low 0.26 m.r. given to "traffic" (compared to its ubiquitous presence), reinforced by negative reactions expressed in interviews.

Table 6 shows the 72 place-element categories aggregated into 16 broader place-element classes. The collective prominence of homesite elements comes across clearly with a mention rate of almost 2.00, followed by people (1.49) and vegetation (1.05), each with a value greater than 1.00. Pathways follow closely behind with a mention rate of 0.92. The sizable number of weighty categories mitigates against any kind of stereotypical impression of the child's world being confined to home, school, and playground. There is a diversity here that begs recognition (and further research). Perhaps the most impressive finding is the collective rank of natural systems, accounting for just over a quarter of the aggregate mention rate. Nature evidently has a powerful presence in the world of childhood.

---

[15] *Occupancy index* was defined as the percent of the total occupancy time which a subgroup spent in a setting or group of settings (or the percent of time a class of settings was inhabited). *Territorial index* is also a useful measure of place-significance, defined as the percentage of all community settings inhabited by a subgroup (or the percent of a subgroup inhabiting a class of settings); see Barker and Wright (1955, pp. 99–109).

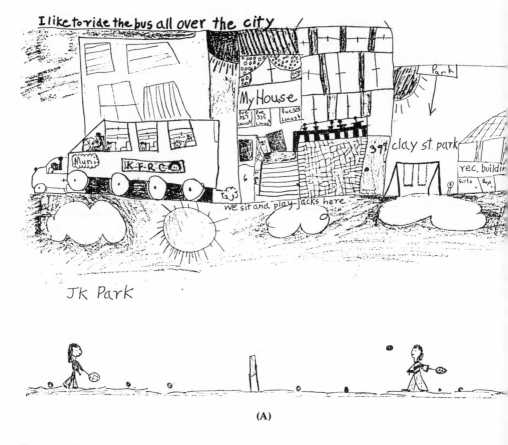

I like to ride the bus all over the city

My House

Park

clay st. park

rec. buildi

Girls Boys

Mun:

K-F-R-C

we sit and play jacks here

JK Park

(A)

Figure 4. Graphic simulations of 12-year-old girls in San Francisco (A) and a nearby suburb (B),
answer to the request, "make a map or drawing of all your favorite places, where you go after scho
or at weekends—around your home and neighborhood, including the summer." As well as providir
useful aggregate data, as discussed in the text, a wealth of possibilities is opened up for the inte
pretation of individual differences. The city child's drawing is subdivided into four distinct enviror
ments: a detailed description of the older apartment building where she lives, including the stoo
where she often plays with her friends; two neighborhood parks within walking distance of h
home; and the "muni" used "to ride all over the city." There is an overall impression of richness i
breadth and depth of experience. The suburban child's drawing clearly reflects a greater sense
environmental continuity, especially in the typical suburban "court" street pattern, which intercor
nects the homes of several friends and supports much bike-riding. Parks are indicated, but with muc
less prominence. The lack of detail gives a feeling of blandness (compared to the city image). Th
"hills" on the right of the drawing were visually prominent in the neighborhood, the "desired
destination of some of the children, but rarely visited because they were "private property." Fro
CUULS Project (1976).

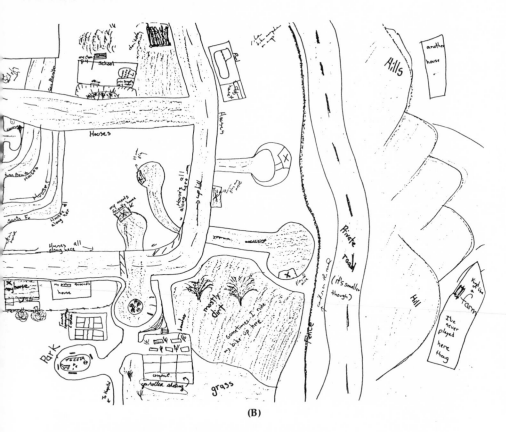

(B)

The only graphic interview data comparable to CUULS are in Maurer and Baxter (1972). They asked a multiethnic 7- to 14-year-old sample to "Draw me a map of how you see your neighborhood, of the place that you live." Their results clearly emphasize vegetative elements, viz.: grass (42%), trees (52%), and flowers (22%) were highly ranked, as were houses (90%) and homes (70%); "other built-structures," e.g., streets (69%), train tracks (25%), and fences (10%) were also significant. An obvious difference to CUULS was the low ranking of playgrounds (7%)—not commented on in the text.

The Berkeley Park Use Study (Mason *et al.*, 1975) presents clear evidence to show that children and adolescents are the predominant users of small neighborhood parks. In five out of six of the parks studied, the under-19s represented more than 75% of the user population. In half the parks 6- to 12-year-old use was particularly dominant.

The study by Lukashok and Lynch (1956) of adults' urban child-

TABLE 5
MENTION RATES OF PLACE ELEMENTS IN RANK ORDER[a]

Place elements	Number of mentions	Mention rate
1 Child's own house	210	.79
2 Through streets	209	.79
3 Child's mention of self	174	.66
4 Friends/relatives home	127	.48
5 Child's school	105	.40
6 Child's friend(s)	94	.35
7 Store(s)	93	.35
8 Community park	90	.34
9 Single trees	82	.31
10 Lawns	82	.31
11 Fences	70	.26
12 Playground/schoolyard/equipment	70	.26
13 Traffic	69	.26
14 Community buildings	69	.26
15 Dwellings/apartments	61	.23
16 Neighbors/sitter's house	57	.22
17 Yard for play/stoop	57	.22
18 Dirt/sand/gravel/tanbark	56	.21
19 Creek/stream	55	.21
20 Trails/shortcuts/paths/alley	53	.20
21 Sidewalks	51	.19
22 Child's parents	51	.19
23 Swimming pool	47	.18
24 Sports field	47	.18
25 Hill/mountains	46	.17
26 Dead-ends/driveways	45	.17
27 Child's siblings	44	.17
28 Building interiors	43	.16
29 Sports playing court	41	.15
30 Topography	38	.14
31 Shrubs	38	.14
32 Buses/BART/stops	37	.14
33 Tall grass/weeds/leaves	37	.14
34 Climbing trees	36	.14
35 Tree clusters	32	.12
36 Child's relatives/other adults	31	.12
37 Cats/dogs	30	.11
38 Climatic conditions	29	.11
39 Agricultural land	27	.10
40 Forts/clubhouses	25	.09
41 Water Play	25	.09
42 Fruiting trees/vines	25	.09
43 Rocks	25	.09
44 Regional park/fairground/campground	24	.09

TABLE 5 *continued*

Place elements	Number of mentions	Mention rate
45 Vacant lot/land under development	24	.09
46 Railroad	23	.09
47 Parking lot	23	.09
48 Misc. buildings/structures for playing	23	.09
49 Shopping/commercial strip	22	.08
50 Pond/lake/reservoir/ocean	22	.08
51 Gas station	19	.07
52 Fish/aquatic life	19	.07
53 Bridges/tunnels	18	.07
54 Dirt roads	18	.07
55 Flowers	18	.07
56 Treehouse	18	.07
57 Garden	16	.06
58 Skating rink/bowling alley	16	.06
59 Church	16	.06
60 Wild animals	16	.06
61 Shopping center/plaza	15	.06
62 Horses	14	.05
63 Abandoned buildings/structures	14	.05
64 Farm animals	13	.05
65 Wild birds/insects	13	.05
66 Movie theater/drive-in	10	.04
67 Tree-swing	10	.04
68 Other domestic animals	8	.03
69 Secret/hiding places	7	.03
70 Asphalt/concrete	6	.02
71 Woodland	5	.02
72 Culvert or stream	2	.01

^a From CUULS:US graphic simulations. N = 265

a From CUULS:US graphic simulations. $N = 265$

hood memories underscores several of the preceding findings, particularly in relation to living elements. From 40 adults interviewed, the following elements were remembered frequently: lawns (27%), ground surface (25%), trees (21%), water (15%). It seems reasonable to conclude that experience of the natural environment is one of the crucial continuities in human life, giving adults a recollected "grounding" in their childhood years.

PLACE ELEMENTS IN THE HABITUAL RANGE

We shift attention now from the aggregate assessment of the place content of the inclusive home range to a closer look at the content of

TABLE 6
AGGREGATED MENTION RATES FOR 16 CLASSES OF PLACE
ELEMENT[a]

Place-element class	Mention rate	%
Homesite	1.99	17
People	1.49	12
N—Vegetation[b]	1.05	9
Pathways[c]	.92	8
Community facilities	.91	8
Open space (official and ad hoc)	.87	7
Through streets	.78	7
N—Natural ground surfaces	.62	5
Sports facilities	.57	4
N—Macro-landscape elements[d]	.55	5
Commercial buildings	.49	4
N—Animals	.43	4
N—Aquatic features	.39	3
Fences	.26	2
Traffic	.26	2
Child-built places[e]	.24	2
Interiors	.16	1
Total	11.98	100

[a] From CUULS:US graphic simulations. $N = 265$
[b] N, natural system elements = 3.04, or 25.4% of total.
[c] Includes all pathway elements except "through streets," because they have a more ambiguous function.
[d] Includes large-scale or ubiquitous elements, such as hills/mountains, climatic conditions, and topography.
[e] Includes forts/clubhouses, miscellaneous structures used for play secret/ hiding places.

places in the habitual realm only (remembering that we have now partitioned off one segment of the ecosystem). At this scale most studies introduce or rely heavily on systematic behavior mapping. An immediate problem with the several good sources available is their categorical mismatch. In an effort to reap the maximum comparative value, findings have been assembled together in two tables. Table 7 contains the results of one German and five American studies. Table 8 contains the more closely coordinated results of two British studies.

The six parts of Table 7 show some clear differences and similarities between the suburban, mixed, and urban contexts. The Aiello *et al.* low-density suburban figures (A), with the smallest number of location categories, indicate a massive 74% of activity actually occurring on the house-site, with 18% occurring on the street (presumably including sidewalks).

The Sanoff and Dickerson figures (B), from a development of similar density, show a much stronger orientation toward the street, possibly reflecting a cultural attribute of the wholly black residents, compared to Aiello *et al.*'s white suburban population. In both cases, public space within or adjacent to the development was hardly used. The most viable explanation seems to indicate the social sufficiency of the house lot and street space.

The Coates and Sanoff figures (C) are from a higher-density, though still suburban, site. Now we see a dramatic shift of activity toward public and community open space (with interest in the street maintained), perhaps indicating the insufficiency of the much smaller attached house lots.

The Auslander *et al.* figures (D), taken from a mix of two urban and a rural site, present a confusing contradiction to the foregoing, with the majority (55%) of activity occurring on the private homesite, and a smaller amount (14%) occurring in public open space and playgrounds. Use of sidewalks (27%), however, remains impressively large.

The other two sets of figures (E and F) were recorded in similar-looking low-rise, "super-block" developments, although in Vogelstang (D) the buildings were more dispersed than at St. Francis Square (E and Figure 5). In these two sites behavior has shifted dramatically from private yards and streets to a variety of designated community spaces, although detailed examination shows considerable disparity between the distributions of activity.

In Vogelstang nearly three times as many children were drawn to play areas as in St. Francis Square, whereas the latters' grassed areas were much more popular. St. Francis Square figures also indicate that over half the outdoor activity occurred on paved areas and sidewalks, whereas the Vogelstang figures show only about a quarter of total activity in these categories.

The reasons for these differences could be many. Our hunch is that they lie more in the physiographic realm than in the social. The major significance of the data is simply to show that there are differences—from which all manner of implications can be drawn (which space does not allow here).

The Cooper Marcus study is unique in also supplying space provision figures, thus enabling Use Space Ratio (USR)[16] values to be

---

[16] Derived from Hole (1966), who used the term Ratio Space Usage (p. 6).

TABLE 7
LOCATION OF CHILDREN'S OUTDOOR ACTIVITIES IN

(A) Aiello *et al.* (1974)		(B) Sanoff and Dickerson (1971)		(C) Coates and Sanoff (1972)	
Frontyard	39%	Front step	6%	Front step and	
Backyard	33%	Driveway	5%	private	
Street	18%	Frontyard	15%	sidewalk	4%
Carport	5%	Backyard	18%	Backyard	4%
Natural areas	5%	Street	23%	Public sidewalk	10%
		Public sidewalk	15%	Street	4%
	100%	Cul-de-sac	8%	Parking lots	9%
		Community		Woods	11%
		center	5%	Public open	
		Open field	3%	space	25%
		Central		Community	
		playground	2%	open space	33%
			100%		100%

a (A) Aiello *et al.* (1974, p. 192). Systematic observation was used to record activities with a total of 30 two-hour observations periods, in a New England suburban development, housing 305 4- to 14-year-olds. (B) Sanoff and Dickerson (1971, derived from Table 1, p. 99). A total of 1941 people were systematically observed in term-time, between 3:30 and 5:00 P.M. with 3- to 13-year-olds accounting for 88% of the total. The site was a 46-acre Turnkey housing project of 216 detached dwellings, housing 1129 total population. (C) Coates and Sanoff (1972, derived from Table 1, p. 13-2-5). A total of 519 people under 18 were systematically observed between 4:30 and 5:30 P.M., on six nonrainy days in March and April 1971, with 3- to 13-year-olds accounting for 71% of the total. The site was an 8-acre Turnkey housing project of attached single-family units, with a total population of 236.

calculated, to indicate the "social effectiveness" of each category of behavior/environment.

Table 8 compares the percentage distributions of activity by location for the two British (public housing) studies. A tendency for play to occur on hard surfaces immediately surrounding residential units is clearly indicated. In low-rise situations considerable use (38%) was made of roads and pavements. In medium-rise situations a shift toward paved courtyard and intermediate areas occurred. In mixed-rise, denser layouts, a further shift occurred toward the buildings themselves, where a full 40% behavior was located in access areas (e.g., stairways and balconies), spaces that are immediately available and offer some degree of enclosure and a feeling of security. In nearly all classes, play on grassed areas was low. Provision of such areas is often low in high-

Six Residential Behavior- Mapping Studies[a]

(D) Auslander et al. (1977)		(E) Dresel (1972)		(F) Cooper Marcus (1974)	% use	% pro-vision	USR
Sidewalks	27%	Play areas	42%	Paved areas	44	20	2.2
Backyards	14%	Paths	21%	Grassed areas ...	19	44	.4
Frontyards	11.5%	Social center	17%	Play equip-			
Front porches ..	10%	Green spaces	6%	ment areas	15	5	3.0
Public open		Entrances to		Perimeter			
space	7%	buildings	5%	sidewalks	12	9	1.3
Playgrounds ...	7%	Spaces not yet		Parking lots	4	21	.2
Side yards	6%	built on or		Other (trees,			
Aprons	5%	landscaped	5%	fences,			
Private		Streets	3%	garbage			
Sidewalk	4%	Garages	1%	sheds, meter			
Street	4%		——	boxes)	6	1	6.0
Back porch	2.5%		100%		——	——	
Alley	2%				100	100	
	——						
	100%						

(D) Auslander *et al.* (1977, p. 6) recorded preestablished data categories directly into a tape recorder, for later transcription. The study covered a predominantly Chicano sample of 3- to 12-year-olds located in three sites: a barrio and a public housing project in Denver and a rural village in the mountains. A total of 4838 observations were made. (E) Dresel (1972, p. 81). Observations were made in a moderate-density development in Vogelstang, a suburb of Mannheim, Germany. (F) Cooper Marcus (1974, p. 202). Behavior-mapping techniques were used to record behavior of people under 18 years old, with 0- to 11-year-olds accounting for 87% of the total. The site was a 300-unit, low-rise moderate-density housing development (St. Francis Square), in San Francisco. Each of 25 subareas was observed 12 times in a period of 5 days, from 8:00 A.M. to 8:00 P.M., in June 1969.

density situations, and that which is provided is invariably "off limits" for children's use. Play in designated playgrounds was also low. The only exception was the 23% playground use in high-density estates, a score practically twice that of the nearest rival. The reason for this, as noted by Cooper Marcus (1974), is that in high-density situations there is frequently nowhere else for children to go, as the rest of the site is given over to buildings and heavily trafficked streets.

Environmentally Dependent and Independent Activity

So far we have looked at the significance of different elements in terms of gross amounts of activity supported. We need also to look at

TABLE 8

Comparison of Locations of Children's Activity in Two British Studies of Public Housing Open-Space Use (%)

Locations	Four low-rise estates[a,b]	Six medium-rise estates[a,b]	Five mixed-rise estates[a,b]	Old housing area[c]	Nine high-density estates[d]	Six low-density estates[d]
	18,102 observations			362 children	5251 children	4659 children
Access areas (i.e., balconies, stairways)	—	23	40	7	15	7
Paved areas (i.e., garage courts)	24	41	23	7	36	35
Roads and pavements (i.e., sidewalks)	39	11	9	54	7	34
Gardens (i.e., private yards)	18	2	1	9	2	—
Play areas	4	11	13	3	23	9
Grassed areas	10	7	8	—	12	13
Wild areas and waste land[e]	5	1	12	14	—	—
Unorthodox areas (garage roofs, etc.)	4	4	2	3	—	—
Planted and other areas	1	5	6	3	—	—

[a] Department of Environment Report (1973), p. 18; 0- to 15-year olds.
[b] Percentages adjusted to exclude the numbers of children observed on the estates which did not have locations in a particular category. Therefore, totals exceed 100%." (DoE 1973, p. 18).
[c] Department of Environment Report (1973), p. 61; 0- to 15-year-olds.
[d] Hole & Miller (1969), p. 1531; ages not given.
[e] "Waste land" applicable to "old housing area" only.

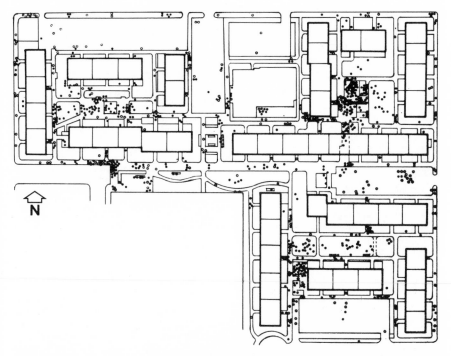

Figure 5. Behavior map of St. Francis Square (a low-rise, moderate-density housing development in San Francisco) representing a "composite day" (8 A.M.–8 P.M.) of behavior, recorded in June 1969. The overall proportion of children (solid dots) to adults (open dots) is almost exactly 7:3, rising to between 5:1 and 7:1 in the interior courtyards. From Cooper Marcus (unpublished source).

variations by types of activity, to give a clearer idea of instrumental significances.

Table 9 includes observational data, from those studies that can be reasonably compared, of activity types occurring mostly within (one may assume) the habitual realm, subdivided according to whether the activity was considered to occur dependently or independently of environmental support.

The figures are remarkably consistent, even though a fairly wide range of density, urban/suburban, and cultural contexts are covered. It is immediately apparent that between one-fourth and one-fifth of activity consists of the more or less immobile social pursuits of children: "hanging out," talking with each other, or playing sedentary games. On the other hand, between one-fourth and one-third of activity is mobile, i.e., children moving around from one place to another, en-

TABLE 9

ACTIVITIES RECORDED BY SYSTEMATIC OBSERVATION IN FOUR STUDIES OF
OUTDOOR SPACE IN RESIDENTIAL AREAS (%)

| Activity type | Department of Environment (1973) | | | | Hole (1966) p. 8 | Cooper Marcus (1974) p. 204 | Aiello et al. (1974) p. 193 |
	Low-rise	Medium-rise	Mixed-rise	Mean			
Environmentally independent							
Sit/stand/lie	19	28	30	27	23	20	15
Walking/running	40	31	30	33	24	37	15
Subtotal	59	59	60	60	47	57	30
Environmentally dependent							
Using playground equipment	3	6	8	7	12	6	8
Wheeled vehicles, roller skates	15	11	9	11	10	4	21
Ball games	6	8	8	8	2	9	7
Subtotal	24	25	25	26	24	19	36
Other	17	16	15	14	29	24	34
Total	100	100	100	100	100	100	100

gaged in chase games, or just wandering around looking for whatever
might come their way. The use of wheeled vehicles is generally in the
range of 10–15%, although with some larger fluctuations. Cooper Marcus found a low of 4% in a low-rise, moderate-density site, Aiello et al. found a high of 21%, in a suburban location. The latter can be
explained in terms of generous suburban space provisions and higher
levels of affluence, resulting in the possession of more wheeled vehicles
(perhaps also reinforced by the example of an auto-dependent life-style).

Playground use and ball games occur at similar levels of frequency:
between 3% and 12%. These activities, as well as larger-scale vehicle
play, are more environmentally dependent than stationary and other
mobile activity, which to a large degree can happen anywhere; whereas
ball play depends on the provision of ball hoops, surrogate goal posts,
sizable flat open areas, walls for bouncing games, and nonprohibitive
management. Wheeled vehicle play is dependent on varied topography, circuitous pathway routes, smooth ground surface, etc. The environmental dependency of playground activity is self-evident.

Totals for the "dependent" and "independent" categories show a high consistency with each other. For the urban sites (first five cases), correlations are very high. The DoE figures indicate almost identical proportions of dependent to independent activity in each case. The proportions of independent activity vary only between 47% and 60%. Agreement between the two low-rise examples (DoE and Cooper Marcus) are particularly notable. Just a few percentage points separate the values taken from two different sites, thousands of miles apart, in two very different cultures and very disparate climatic conditions. A general predictability according to building type, independent of culture, is tentatively suggested by these figures. It is hoped that they may contribute toward further investigation of the degree to which children's play is culture specific or unspecific at different ages.

We turn now to the bottom half of Table 9, showing environmentally dependent activity. The figures indicate that 19–36% of the activity is related to playground equipment (fixed artifact) or wheeled toy and ball play (objects brought to the site, but dependent on specific site characteristics).

The category of "other" activity, which covers 14–34% of all activity, should not be overlooked. On the contrary, this is the area within which the finest grain and diversity of user–site relationships occur, where urban culture has its strongest expression, where personalized differentiations can give users a sense of possession—as exemplified by the use of specialized features in the Cooper Marcus study.

THE CO-ACTION OF RANGE, PLACE, AND PATHWAY

In essence, range development seems to involve children in a combined process of both finding and making places, connected by a network of pathways. Quality-enhancing elements and attributes are very unevenly distributed in the landscape and children are obliged to discover, assemble, and mold combinations to suit their purposes.

Place-making may result from small modifications to fixed resources, a "fort" for instance may exist as an almost inperceptible depression in long grass. The prolific fragments of natural systems can provide the loose-parts (Nicholson, 1971) or behavior objects (Barker & Wright, 1955) necessary to support more open styles of play. As children move through the environment, they may scratch the dirt, pick a couple of mottled stones from the edge of the highway, pluck a few flower heads to decorate their person, or discover some latent play-function in the detritus of modern life: plastic cups, pull-tabs, abandoned domestic apparatus, etc.

Loose-parts are frequently too small to be discriminated in drawings or mentioned in interviews; and they are frequently used in combination with larger fixed features (as documented by both Hart, 1977, and in CUULS). Elements such as a discarded refrigerator case, a small space between buildings, a shady spot under a low-hanging tree provide initial cavelike spaces and are further elaborated and personalized by the addition of small objects and possessions, in much the same way that adults make a house into a home. The scale and symbol system are different, however. This gives rise to political difficulties between children and adults, because children's habitations cannot be given meaning in the conventional terminology used by adults to describe the world.

Data from both Hart (1977) and CUULS indicate the frequent occurrence of small modifications to the landscape. In Inavale they were usually situated within 100 feet of home. Hart recorded that Inavale children spent a large amount of time building places for themselves, and observed that many of the "houses" of children under eight were "found" places with scarcely any major physical modification. They nevertheless served the users well, who modified and differentiated their interiors via their imaginations, rather than by hand. He concluded that the primary factor required to allow building operations was the availability of areas close to home, not dominated verbally by adults or subject to the manicured announcement of adult ownership. A second requirement of building activity was a "flexible landscape" to ensure a ready supply of "loose parts" for construction, provided in Inavale by lush vegetation or snow, depending on the season. Marked girl/boy differences were observed in building places. Whereas boys concentrated on the building structure, girls devoted their attention to details of the interior, often with great imagination. More substantial physical changes such as building clubhouses and tree-forts occurred more rarely. Even in a rural area where opportunities are greatest, the limitations of time, space, availability of materials, and "technical know-how" make construction a haphazard, unpredictable affair. Although this latter scale of activity more readily fits adult stereotypes of a "free childhood," it seems clear that the place transformations most commonly bringing children feelings of proprietorship are quite modest. Hence the viability of the "adventure playground" concept (Cooper, 1970; Bengtsson, 1972; Moore, 1975), with the purpose of providing children with more substantial place-making opportunities close to home.

Only Hart (1977), Gray and Brower (1977), and CUULS looked at children's pathway systems. Two types are identifiable: pathways that traverse exclusive child domains and those that are shared with adults. In CUULS it was found that children frequently switched back and forth between one system and the other. Hart identified 10 child-only paths in his study site, and recorded how some were used to bypass traffic hazards or as places for daring exploits such as setting off fire-crackers. They seemed to serve as ways of escape from adult domination.

In many instances pathways existed as literal shortcuts through small openings, inpenetrable to adults; or they ran across private property where outsiders would not dare to follow, but where children's presence was either tolerated or remained undetected. Hart and CUULS both also discovered examples of so-called shortcuts that geographically were in fact round about routes between stated destinations. But they gave access to a stimulating private landscape, where the normal space-time relations of the functional adult world were suspended. Child-only routes seem to be used as ends in themselves, as places to "dilly-dally on the way"—not so much as movement channels as endless sequences of exploration-for-its-own-sake in *ad hoc* "side-trips." In the most benign examples, there seemed to be no "final destination."

On the other hand, to quote Hart, "considerable value is placed by children in knowing how to get to places. Paths are 'discovered' by them and special pride is exhibited in the finding of 'shortcuts.' This knowledge is shown off to friends with that aura of great excitement which surrounds the sharing of any 'secret.'" Routes are "ritual-ized" by groups of friends, he suggests, "to cope with the uncertainty of too much complexity . . . [making] landmark differentiations highly significant . . . especially for younger children's range-extensions."

A game strategy seems to operate here, echoing Mead's (1966) insistence that both familiarity and challenge be accommodated by the neighborhood landscape. For example, a CUULS expedition led to a description of Golden Gate Park's landscape as a place where, "me and my friends try to get lost . . . running all over without looking where we're going . . . then we find where we are, but we know we got there differently." In this way young explorers extend their schemata of the park, by playing risk-taking "range games," in a landscape ideally suited to the purpose (though probably not designed as such).

Inevitably, the most significant places occur at the intersections of many behavior settings, where the inherent potential of elements and attributes coincide with behavioral competencies of the majority of users. In complex landscapes, pathways and places are so thickly spread on the ground that they form a pyramid of overlapping schemata and interdependent behaviors. Such *multipurposeness* (the capacity of a place to accommodate a variety of activities simultaneously or in sequence) is usually the result of deliberate design, although it may sometimes arise from serendipitous combinations of natural and cultural forces, as in an old rural cemetery (the favorite place of a CUULS boy) containing a mixture of fortresslike monuments, patches of lawn and large mature exotic trees. This kind of juxtaposition provides a powerful stimulus for children, drawing them beyond their habitual domain, into a perceptually more boundless "as if" world where mind, body, and landscape can be in more fluid contact.[17]

CONCLUSIONS AND FUTURE DIRECTIONS

A conclusion that stands out is the evident cultural dependency of children's outdoor relationships. This is not given by any single study so much as by a scattering of indications throughout the body of literature. The impression is strong enough to suggest that every subculture has a significant ethos in childhood environmental experience (Young, 1975). If this is so, two implications immediately follow. The first is that the promotion of environmental awareness, as well as the development of more explicit environmental values in society, must be more firmly recognized as an important responsibility of parents and early–middle childhood public school education. The second implication is the need for more cross-cultural and comparative work at all scales, from interneighborhood studies in the same city to international studies following the directions set by the UNESCO report (Lynch, 1977).

Interrelated with cultural dependencies there also exist, theoretically, more universal species-specific developmental functions, facilitated or constrained as a result of children's outdoor experience. Such functions have so far proved difficult to isolate. Certainly to an extent they can be derived inductively from developmental theory—from Piaget in particular. But the applicative leap required is of immense proportions. Our own suspicion is that once the empirical literature

---

[17] A problem of New Town and suburban environments is that the significance of multipurpose qualities has not been appreciated by those who control the landscape. Complex, naturally formed differentiations are often unavoidably bulldozed during construction, but are not deliberately replaced. The child is faced with an oversimplified lookalike landscape that extends the stereotyped, adult-controlled habitual range instead of providing a contrast to it.

has reached a sufficient magnitude, commonly occurring factors and correlations will begin to be identified. Methodologically, this takes the phenomenological approach to its logical conclusion, i.e., under appropriate ecological conditions children themselves will reveal environmental dependencies that lie beyond the conditioning effects of the particular culture they were born into.

It consequently follows that children must be more directly involved in research and decision-making as co-workers. From our own work, and drawing on that of others (especially Coles, 1964), we are convinced that in essence children are the experts most qualified to make judgments about the categories of behavior and meaning to be applied to their own settings.

The universal needs of children must be clearly articulated and integrated into public decision-making. Empirical pursuit is important as deeper needs may often be overshadowed by more visible cultural attributes, which are not necessarily supportive of physical health and psychic well-being. Both Hart (1977) and Payne and Jones (1976), for example, looked at suburban environments[18] and concluded that they have a detrimental effect on the development of postkindergarten children, providing less and less opportunity for the enhancement of competence. In Chapter 5 of her study of Easter Hill Village, Cooper (1975) presents clear evidence showing how social conflicts between children and adults in housing areas can be exacerbated by a lack of adequate provision to meet children's outdoor play needs. These studies are valuable because they identify a set of physical and social characteristics that define unsatisfactory ecological conditions, thus paving the way for further research focused on the more effective management of residential settings to promote child-development more adequately.

Age and range extension are clearly correlated, but because of the variety of secondary factors involved it is difficult and probably futile to try to specify detailed norms of range extent by age. More appropriate is the clarification of general stages of range development within broad age limits that should be expected (e.g., in "early," "middle," and "late" childhood), in relation to specific controlling factors in particular contexts.

Sex differentiation emerges very clearly as a major issue for further research. We have quoted findings that clearly indicate that at most age levels boys' territorial ranges are more extensive than girls' ranges, in some contexts by a large amount. Yet on the other hand, according

---

[18] Hart's study area included a new hilltop suburban subdivision, providing an ideal opportunity for comparison with the old town.

to two sources (CUULS and Barker and Wright, 1955) covert environmental relationships appear to be more or less equitable. Thus, overt
use is not a sufficient indicator of landscape significance. Indeed, evaluations based solely on direct observation of behavior (especially in
ecologically partitioned, "official" settings), will more likely result in
only minor improvements to the status quo, rather than broaden the
spectrum of needed solutions.

The problem for individual investigators is to recognize their own
personal values, as developed from field experience, combined with
sources of introspection and apply them explicitly to interpretation and
future research design. In this way the values of "others" will be more
clearly identifiable. It cannot be directly proved, for example, that
children's involvement with natural systems is absolutely essential to
their well-being, yet one can be led toward this conclusion by working
closely with children in ecologically viable settings. This in turn will
affect future research design, resulting inevitably in the reinforcement
of previously tentative conclusions. The outcomes of such an evolving
epistemology will be very different from those predetermined by theoretical suppositions.

Cross-cultural, comparative study, identification of universal dependencies, closer scrutiny of environmental sex differentiation and
the pursuit of in-depth, co-working relationships with children in
education, and research seem to be, in summary, general directions to
be followed. We conclude with a list of specific research questions and
tasks within this perspective, appearing to us as priorities under the
broad areas of range, place, and pathway analyses.

RANGE ANALYSIS

1. In the assessment of a greater variety of contexts, special attention should be paid to (a) *urban–suburban landscape variables:* density,
land-use pattern, pathway networks, traffic distributions, age of landscape and buildings, presence of natural systems; (b) *climatic differences:* (studies so far are biased toward warm, summer months); (c)
temporal factors of seasonal daylight hours, weekday/weekend, school
time/vacation, etc., and how they effect indoor/outdoor investment of
discretionary time; (d) *influence of television,* role of parents as monitoring agents.[19]

---

[19] Although many children watch a lot of television, it is not so far all children. A wide
range of TV-watching behavior was recorded in CUULS, reflecting differing parental
values.

2. Investigations of range conditions that tend to foster outdoor experiential equality between girls and boys.

3. Extended exploration of the roots of parental fears compared to factual reality. More adequate data are required concerning actual (as opposed to imagined) physical and social dangers faced by children, to help reduce parental apprehension in some cases and to focus political awareness in other cases.[20]

4. Methodologically, the development of diary methods and graphic-simulation techniques show considerable promise as efficient data-gathering tools.

Place Analysis

1. Much more work is required in order to understand the relationships between *involvement* and *affiliation*, i.e., how does physical engagement contribute toward a lasting image of place or, indeed, does involvement necessarily need to come first? This is a particularly pertinent question vis-á-vis girl/boy differences.

2. Following from the above, extended studies of outdoor activity are required, leading eventually, we hope, to a set of agreed-on topologies. At the moment this is lacking in the literature and greatly limits opportunities for interstudy comparison. Sharper attention must also be paid to the different biases inherent in activity classification, according to the sex of the investigator, her/his disciplinary background, the overall scale of study, and interpretations of predominant molar categories versus weighty categories of miscellaneous "other" activity. An attempt to standardize activity topologies will require formal meeting and negotiation between experienced field workers. There is a similar need to standardize age groupings and temporal units of analysis.

3. Deeper analyses need to be made of place experience, conducted over a relatively long period of time, so that the two measures of involvement, "frequency of visit" and "duration of stay," can be recorded in sufficient volume to guarantee statistical relevance when correlated with physical and social variables. With sufficient records, places and their constituent place elements should be able to be ranked

---

[20] There is an overwhelming issue of liability insurance and its detrimental effect on the quality of children's environments, which in turn is related to insurance companies' profit motives on the one hand and the public's propensity to sue on the other. Empirical data would contribute a great deal toward public education in this area.

according to an index of involvement. This will make possible the projection of range "opportunity surfaces" in new residential development, at a greater level of specificity.

4. At a deeper level still, assessment of specific dependencies between particular activities and particular place elements and attributes will be of great benefit to decision-makers. Involvement and affiliation do not develop without some degree of dependency on elements and attributes. However, some activities are supported by a wide range of circumstances, others are place and time specific. This distinction needs greater clarification in terms of specific elements and activities to help define the most potent components of multipurpose environments.

5. Related to paragraph 4, above, is the need for further comparative studies of nontraditional, unofficial, or esoteric play environments. These include adventure playgrounds[21] children's use of wild areas in parks and elsewhere; miscellaneous uncontrolled areas such as waterfronts, renewal sites, waste-land, construction areas, etc. A specific subarea includes the places children find and make for themselves, including forts, hideaways, secret places, and tree houses.[22]

6. Homesite architecture, i.e., spaces inside and immediately around, above, and below the child's residence, beg further research (although the same ethical caveat applies). A considerable contribution has been made by the cited work. Pollowy (1977) has published a useful introductory text. So far, the majority of studies have focused on a fairly narrow band of moderate- to high-density housing types. This may be a priority place to start, but extensions need to be made into a much broader range of housing while also paying greater attention to the effects of family and peer relationships. Barbey (1974) has presented a highly suggestive direction, based on children's graphic conceptions of house design. Ladd (1972) also demonstrated the possibilities of co-working relationships by asking black adolescents to contrast present housing conditions with imagined future hopes.

7. Generally speaking, we favor a deliberate bias toward the comparative case study of "success" environments (chosen on the basis of user-consensus), rather than "problem" environments; seemingly the latter attract a disproportionate amount of attention.

---

[21] Considering how long adventure playgrounds have been in existence, especially in Europe, there is a mystifying paucity of empirical literature.

[22] Such studies, conducted in the field, raise serious ethical questions concerning children's rights of privacy and proprietorship, however.

Pathway Analysis

1. Elements and attributes that provide good pedestrian pathway networks need documentation, especially in high-density/high-traffic conditions. Appleyard and Lintell (1972) have already documented the dramatic negative effect of traffic on the general quality of street life. Further studies are needed to show the especially severe effects of traffic on children's use of sidewalks and streets.

2. Much more information is required concerning how children move around their block, neighborhood and city. Durlack, Duncan, and Emby (1976) have made a beginning contribution, vis-à-vis 10- to 16-year-olds in suburban Toronto. But key controlling factors need more precise identification and analysis, in a broader range of contexts.

3. Research and development work is required in relation to bikeway and horse-trail networks. Successful examples need study, to isolate transferrable principles and attributes. Cycle-range studies need to be conducted in parallel with pedestrian studies, using the same techniques and measures.

REFERENCES

Abercrombie, M. L. J. *The anatomy of judgement*. Baltimore: Penguin Books, 1969.

Aiello, J. F., Gordon, B. & Farrell, T. J. Description of children's outdoor activities in a suburban residential area: Preliminary findings. *In* R. C. Moore (Ed.), *Childhood city man-environment interactions*. Vol. 12. D. Carson (general ed.). Milwaukee: EDRA, 1974. Pp. 187-195.

Anderson, J. & Tindall, M. The concept of home range: New data for the study of territorial behavior. *In* W. J. Mitchell (Ed.), *Environmental design: Research and practice*. Proceedings of the EDRA3/AR8 Conference. Los Angeles: University of California, 1972. Pp. 1-1-1-1-1-7.

Andrews, H. F. Home range and urban knowledge of school-age children. *Environment and Behavior*, 1973, *5*(1), 73-86.

Auslander, N., Juhasz, J. & Carrusco, F. F. Chicano children and their outdoor environments (summary report), unpublished manuscript. Department of Psychology, University of Colorado, Boulder, 1977.

Appleyard, D. & Lintell, M. Environmental quality of the city street. *American Institute of Planners Journal*, 1972, *38*(2), 84-101.

Baltimore Departments of Planning, and Housing and Urban Development. *Community renewal program interim report*. Baltimore, May 1972. P. 149.

Bangs, H. P. J., & Mahler, S. Uses of local parks. *American Institute of Planners Journal*, 1970, *36*(3), 330-334.

Barbey, G. F. Anthropological analysis of the home concept: Some considerations based on the interpretation of children's drawings. *In* R. C. Moore (Ed.), *Childhood city, man-environment interactions*. Vol. 12. D. Carson (general ed.). Milwaukee: EDRA, 1974. Pp. 143-149.

Barker, R. G., & Wright, H. F. *Midwest and its children*. White Plains, New York: Row, Peterson and Company, 1955.

Barker, R. G. & Wright, H. F. *One boy's day*. New York: Archon Books, Harper and Row, 1966.

Bartlett, F. *Remembering*. Cambridge: Cambridge University Press, 1932.

Bengtsson, A. *Adventure playgrounds*. New York: Praeger, 1972.

Boulding, K. *The image: Knowledge in life and society*. Ann Arbor: University of Michigan Press. 1956.

Brower, S., Gray, L. Stough, R. *Doll-play as a tool for urban designers*. Department of Planning, Baltimore, Md., April 1977.

Brower, S. N., & Williamson, P. Outdoor recreation as a function of the urban housing environment. *Environment and Behavior*, 1974, *6*(3), 295–345.

Byrom, J. B. *Shared open space in Scottish private enterprise housing*. The Architectural Research Unit, Dept. of Architecture, University of Edinburgh, 55 George Square, Edinburgh 8. Report A43:R2. July 1972.

Coates, G. & Bussard, E. Patterns of children's spatial behavior in a moderate-density housing development. *In* R. C. Moore (Ed.), *Childhood city, man-environment interactions*. Vol. 12. D. Carson (general ed.). Milwaukee: EDRA, 1974. Pp. 131–141.

Coates, G. & Sanoff, H. Behavior mapping: The ecology of child behavior in a planned residential setting. *In* W. J. Mitchell (Ed.), *Environmental design: Research and practice*. Proceedings of the EDRA3/AR8 Conference. Los Angeles: University of California, 1972. Pp. 13-2-1–13-2-11.

Cobb, E. The ecology of imagination in childhood. *In* P. Shepard & D. McKinley (Eds.), *The subversive science*. Boston: Houghton Mifflin, 1969 Pp. 122–132.

Coles, R. *Children of crisis*. New York: Dell, 1964.

Cooper, C. C. Adventure playgrounds. *Landscape Architecture*, 1970, *62*(1), 18–91.

Cooper, C. C. *Easter Hill Village: Some social implications of design*. New York: The Free Press, 1975.

Cooper Marcus, C. Children's play behavior in a low-rise, inner-city housing development. *In* R. C. Moore (Ed.), *Childhood city, man-environment interactions*. Vol. 12. D. Carson (general ed.). Milwaukee: EDRA, 1974. Pp. 197–211.

Cooper Marcus, C. & Moore, R. C. Children and their environments: A review of research 1955–1975. *Journal of Architectural Education*, 1976, *29*(4), 22–25. (Also published as Reprint #132, Institute for Urban and Regional Development, University of California, Berkeley.)

Department of Environment (DoE). *Children at play*. London: Her Majesty's Stationary Office, Design Bulletin 27, 1973.

Downs, R. & Stea, D. *Image and environment: Cognitive mapping and spatial behavior*, Chicago: Aldine, 1973.

Dresel, P. Open space in new urban areas. *Open space in housing areas*. National Swedish Institute for Building Research, 1972 (Box 1403, S-111 84, Stockholm).

Durlak, J. Duncan, B. Emby, G. *Suburban children and public transportation in metropolitan Toronto*. Urban Studies Program, York University, Downsview, Ontario. Report prepared for Ministry of State for Urban Affairs, January 1976.

Gould, P. & White, R. *Mental Maps*, Baltimore: Penguin Books, 1974.

Gray, L., & Brower, S. Activities of children in an urban neighborhood. Department of Planning, Baltimore, Md., April 1977, (unpublished manuscript).

Hart, R. *Children's experience of place: A developmental study*. New York: Irvington Press, 1978.

Hayward, D. G., Rothenberg, M., & Beasley, R. R. Children's play and urban playground environments: A comparison of traditional, contemporary and adventure playground types. *Environment and Behavior,* 1974, 6 (2), 131–168.

Himmelweit, H. T., Oppenheim, A. N., & Vince, P. *Television and the child.* London: Nuffield Foundation, 1958.

Hole, V. *Children's play on housing estates.* National Building Studies Research Paper 39. London: Her Majesty's Stationary Office, 1966.

Hole, V., & Miller, A. Children's play on housing estates. *Architect's Journal,* 1966, 143 (25), 1529–1536.

Holt, J. *Escape from childhood: The needs and rights of children.* Baltimore: Penguin Books, 1975.

Ladd, F. Black youths view their environment: Neighborhood maps. *Environment and Behavior,* 1970, 2(2), 74–99.

Ladd, F. Black youths view their environments: Some views of housing. *American Institute of Planners Journal,* 1972, 38 (2), 108–116.

Lee, T. Urban neighborhood as a socio-spatial scheme. *Human Relations,* 1968, no. 21, 241–268.

LeVine, J., & Taylor, J. W. *Manipulability and meaning in public space.* Cambridge, Mass. Harvard Graduate School of Design, May 1974 (unpublished Master's thesis).

Lukashok, A., & Lynch, K. Some childhood memories of the city. *American Institute of Planners Journal,* 1956, 22(3), 142–152.

Lynch, K. *The image of the city.* Cambridge, Mass.: MIT Press, 1960.

Lynch, K. (Ed.). *Growing up in cities: Studies of the spatial environment of adolescence in Cracow, Melbourne, Mexico City, Salta, Toluca and Warsawa.* Cambridge, Mass.: MIT Press, 1977.

Mark, L. S. Modeling through toy play: A methodology for eliciting topographical representations in children. *In* W. J. Mitchell (Ed.), *Environmental design: Research and practice.* Proceedings of the EDRA3/AR8 Conference. Los Angeles: University of California, 1972. Pp. 1-3-1–1-3-9.

Martensson, B. Observations of outdoor activities in some housing areas. *Open space in housing areas,* National Swedish Institute for Building Research, 1972 (Box 1403, S-111 84, Stockholm).

Mason, G., Forrester, A., & Hermann, R. *Berkeley park use study: A working report to guide the acquisition and development of New Parklands.* Berkeley: Department of Parks and Recreation, 1975. (Available from Design Section, Civic Center Building, 2180 Milvia Street, Berkeley, Calif. 94704, price $1.00.)

Maurer, R., & Baxter, J. C. Images of the neighborhood and city among Black-, Anglo- and Mexican-American children. *Environment and Behavior,* 1972, 4 (4), 351–388.

Mead, M. Neighborhoods and human needs. *Ekistics,* 1966, 21 (123), 124–126.

Moore, G. T., & Golledge, R. G. *Environmental knowing.* Stroudsburg, Pa.: Dowden, Hutchinson and Ross, 1976.

Moore, R. C. Patterns of activity in time and space: The ecology of a neighborhood playground. *In* D. Canter and T. Lee (Eds.), *Psychology and the built environment,* London: Architectural Press, 1974.

Moore, R. C. The place of adventure play in urban planning for leisure. *Adventure playgrounds and children's creativity.* Report of the Sixth International Conference of the International Playground Association, Milan, Italy, Sept. 1975. (Available from I.P.A., 12 Cherry Tree Drive, Sheffield, England, S11 9AE.)

Moore, R. C. The environmental design of children—nature relations: Some strands of applicative theory. In *Children, Nature and the Urban Environment: Proceedings of a Symposium-Fair.* Northeast Forest Experiment Station, Upper Darby, Pa. Report #NE-30, 1977.

Moore, R. C. Meanings and measures of children/environment quality: Some findings from Washington Environmental Yard. *In* W. E. Rogers & W. H. Ittelson (Eds.), *New directions in environmental design research EDRA 9.* Washington, D.C.: Environmental Design Research Association, 1978 (L'Enfant Plaza Station, P.O. Box 23129, Washington, D.C. 20024).

Moore, R. C., & Wochiler, A. An assessment of a redeveloped school yard based on drawings made by child-users. *In* R. C. Moore (Ed.), *Childhood city, man-environment interactions.* Vol. 12. D. Carson (general ed.). Milwaukee: EDRA, 1974. Pp. 107–119.

Nicholson, S. The theory of loose parts. *Landscape Architecture,* 1971. *62* (1), 30–34.

Payne, R. J., & Jones, D. R. W. Children's urban landscapes in Huntington Hills, Calgary. *In* P. Suedfeld & J. A. Russel (Eds.), *EDRA 7: The behavioral basis of design, Book 2.* Stroudsberg, Pa.: Dowden, Hutchinson and Ross, 1977.

Pearce, J. C. *Magical child; Rediscovering nature's plan for our children.* New York: E. P. Dutton, 1977.

Perls, F., Hefferline, R. F., & Goodman, P. *Gestalt therapy.* New York: Dell, 1965 (first published, 1951).

Pollowy, A. M. *The urban nest.* Stroudsburg, Pa.: Dowden, Hutchinson and Ross, 1977.

Rivlin, L., Rothenberg, M., Justa, F., Wallis, A., & Wheeler, F. G., Jr. Children's conceptions of open classrooms through use of scaled models. *In* R. C. Moore (Ed.), *Childhood city, man-environment interactions.* Vol. 12 D. Carson (general ed.). Milwaukee: EDRA, 1974. Pp. 151–160.

Saegert, S. & Hart, R. The development of sex differences in the environmental competence in girls and boys. *In* P. Stevens Jr. (Ed.), *Studies in the anthropology of play: Papers in memory of B. Allan Tindall,* Cornwall, N.Y.: Leisure Press, 1978.

Sanoff, H. & Dickerson, J. Mapping children's behavior in a residential setting. *Journal of Architectural Education,* 1971, *25* (4), 98–103.

Southworth, M. *An urban service for children based on analysis of Cambridge boys' conception and use of the city.* Cambridge, Mass.: MIT, 1970 (unpublished Ph.D. dissertation).

Spivak, M. Archtypal place. *In* W. Preiser (Ed.), *EDRA 4.* Vol. 1. Stroudsburg, Pa.: Dowden, Hutchinson and Ross, 1973. Pp. 33–46.

Tuan, Y.-F. *Topophilia: A study of environmental perception, attitudes, and values.* Englewood Cliffs, N.J.: Prentice Hall, 1974.

Wade, G. R. *A study of free-play patterns of elementary school age children in playground equipment areas.* Department of Physical Education, Pennsylvania State University, Dec. 1968 (unpublished Master's thesis).

Wade, M. G. Method and analysis in the study of children's play behavior, *Quest,* 1977, Vol. XXVI.

Wright, H. F. Psychological development in Midwest. *Child Development,* 1956, *27* (2), 266–286.

Young, D. G. *A particular kind of world: A search for relationships of quality between children and their environments.* Berkeley: University of California, Dec. 1975 (unpublished Master's thesis).

Zerner, C. *Tin pods, asphalt streams, Gotham's rodeo arena: The street hearth of play.* Portland, Ore.: The University of Oregon, Dec. 1974 (unpublished Master's thesis).

4

School Environments

PAUL V. GUMP

INTRODUCTION

From kindergarten through the twelfth grade, the average young person will spend about 14,000 hours in schools; if preschool and college are added, this can rise to 20,000. This is an awesome amount of time and it is important to recognize that it is not devoted exclusively, some would say not even primarily, to learning of a curriculum. This large portion of young lives goes into *living* in schools—and we would assume that the quality of this living is an important matter. In the discussion to follow, it is assumed that the quality of child life is very much affected by the quality of the environments they inhabit. We are interested in studies that can tell us something about environmental characteristics and their behavioral and experiential effects.

As matters ecological have become prominent, the words *environmental* and *ecological* have been employed to refer to many kinds and levels of phenomena. The resulting confusion requires some clarification of meanings. The question now posed is: "When you speak of a school or classroom *environment*, what are you talking about?"

A variety of phenomena can be crowded under the word *environment*: physical context, action context, social climate, life space, etc. This can be illustrated if, instead of turning to definitions, we turn to

PAUL V. GUMP · Department of Psychology, University of Kansas, Lawrence, Kansas.

a sample of the reality in question—to a classroom in operation. If an observer spent an hour-and-a-half, first thing on a Monday morning, in a third-grade classroom, what would he see? What might he report?

On entry, the observer notes that the room is a rectangle 30 × 40 feet; moveable desk-seats are placed in five-by-five columns and rows. In a back corner, chairs circle a table. At the front but to one side, a teacher's desk faces obliquely toward the student desk-seats. An American flag hangs from a wall holder near this desk. Our observer notes the many behavior objects that children and teachers use: books, posters, science material (including gerbil cages and fish bowls), and so on. The room stimulates a blend of observer reactions: a sense of openness punctuated by clusters of interesting objects.

So far the observer has noted physical milieu, and "milieu" can be one meaning for the word *environment*. The observer could describe this milieu objectively (e.g., so much room, so many seats arranged in certain ways), or he can speak subjectively of the meanings or feelings elicited by the milieu ("interesting objects," "a sense of openness").

The observer shifts attention from milieu to events; he records that when the teacher announces, "All right, class, it's time to get started," the children, who have been cruising about or visiting, come to stand by their seats facing the flag. A group salute is followed by teacher and class singing *America*. As the students sit, the teacher calls for the "Weekend News." Several students share their families' excursions and experiences. The teacher listens carefully but after the fourth weekend report, many children are stirring restlessly and looking about; a few converse in whispers. The teacher shifts the program to consideration of what will be done today; pointing to the board, she shows assignments for the Red Birds, the Gophers, and the Pacers. She illustrates how certain social studies questions can be approached.

The teacher then signals, "All right, Red Birds," and nine children go to the back, assembling around the table; the remainder are arranging papers, pencils, and books at their desks.

Determining to focus upon the Red Birds, the observer watches the teacher manage discussion–review of story material. She offers bits of content and students volunteer more content to complete the story sequences. After this "warm-up," the teacher asks individual children to read a paragraph aloud. Between readings she comments about content, asks about phonics for particular words. The routine continues for 20 minutes.

In the meantime, most of the students at their seats in the main part of the room keep oriented to the books and the writing, but some do not. Joe, with a new group of baseball cards, is trying to get Sam's attention. Sam reaches for the cards; Joe furtively checks on the teacher and discovers that although she still sits in the reading circle, she is frowning straight at him. Quickly he puts the cards away and takes up his spelling book.

The teacher returns attention to the Red Birds, who apparently did not notice her silent reprimand. She explains what they will be reading next time and dismisses the group. As the Red Birds return to their regular seats, another group appears at the circle. This second group (the Gophers) apparently uses the return of the first group as the signal to move; the teacher has not addressed them. A second session of reading, following the format of the previous one, is now carried out.

After 20 minutes, the teacher sends the Gophers back to join the rest of the class. She goes to the front and takes out some large flash cards with a multiplier and a multiplicand on one side and a product on the other. She announces, "Well now, before recess, let's see how sharp you are." The children attend immediately; they know what this means. The teacher holds up a card and children shout an answer; then she turns the card over so children can see if they were correct. This sequence takes less than 3 seconds and the teacher moves right on to the next problem. Now, the teacher calls out a row number and then flashes a card for just the children in that row. The game moves rapidly as rows are called in random order. The observer notes that many children are leaning forward in their seats and shouting with vigor; they seem deeply involved. A few give little yelps of triumph as they see they have answered correctly. One child, however, never responds quickly; he warily listens to the others and then chimes in. For him, the game seems more of a threat than an opportunity.

After about 10 minutes, the teacher stops, saying, "Good! Most of you are becoming sure of these combinations. Now, let's put our materials away, and get ready for recess." The children immediately comply. The observer infers that this is because the teacher begins to dismiss them by rows, "most quiet row first." In a minute, the room is empty.

Primarily, this description deals with matters for the class as a whole, or for major sections of it, but the observer also referred to some matters that applied only to particular children. Further, most of the account deals with directly observable phenomena; it is objective. However, there are portions in which meanings and feelings of persons were inferred, that is, there was also subjective description. With the general versus the individual dimension and the objective versus the subjective dimension in mind, it is possible to describe several kinds of environments appearing in the observer's notes.

The Objective or Milieu-with-Program Environment

The observer's account shows that an action structure operated in this classroom. This structure combined with the milieu to create four different environments during the first part of the morning: the opening or getting started period, the seat work sessions operating parallel to the reading circles, and then the total group involved in a multiplication drill or game. Much of what the teacher did was to signal and maintain the appropriate action structure for the various environments. Much of what students did—singing, listening, reading aloud, shouting answers—was their part of the program. Although the teacher did much to maintain the program, it would be incorrect to say that her ongoing behavior *was* the program. Some movements were made without her signal (the Gophers arrive at the reading circle). Even when she gave signals, their content was sparse compared to the actual behaviors students carried out ("Let's get started" yielded return to seats, standing at attention, and readiness to salute).

The physical space and objects of the classroom and the program were very much joined. The flag was placed where it was easily faced by saluting students, the chairs in the reading circle faced inward to facilitate sending and receiving intragroup messages. Even the sitting behavior of students involved a shape that suits the shape of their desk-chairs. This congruence between milieu shape and behavior shape is "synomorphy" and is described by Barker and Wright (1955). Environmental units made up of temporally and spatially bounded sections of milieu-program phenomena are called *synomorphs* (Barker, 1968). Synomorphs are real (not subjective) sections of the external environment; while they have relevance to individual inhabitants, they are not described from the point of view of any one inhabitant (they are extraindividual). Synomorphs are contexts for behavior with dependable, enduring inputs to inhabitants. The four environments in the classroom were each synomorphs. When synomorphs change, much of the behavioral opportunities and limitations for inhabitants also change: for example, one could do things in the multiplication game quite different from the things done in seat work.

The Objective Individual Environment

Although he did not choose to do so, the observer could have decided to follow behavior of one child throughout the morning. He would have noted all of the events and objects that impinged upon the behavior of this child. The operation of the milieu-program environment would have appeared frequently in this behavior, but the overlap would not have been complete. Parts of the child's behavior bring up elements of the environment not related to program (Sam was intrigued by Joe's baseball cards, which were not part of the milieu for this program). Parts of the child's behavior may elicit special treatment by the program (Joe's behavior brought him a teacher reprimand, a counter-deviancy action to protect the program). For conceptual clarity it is important to note that the individual environment can be just as objective as the milieu-program environment. Different things do happen to people in the same subsetting and these things can be described without appeal to inferences regarding the meanings that the individual develops, the feelings he experiences. Also, it is important to recognize that these individual environments are, to varying degrees, determined by the individual. Joe brought the frowning-teacher input upon himself. When we try to determine how the environment affects an individual who nevertheless is creating an idiosyncratic environment, there are problems of circularity.

THE SUBJECTIVE ENVIRONMENT

Logically, both a general, nonindividual, subjective environment and an individual one can be proposed. The observer referred to "interesting objects" and to "feelings of spaciousness." If one assumes that most individuals entering the room would experience these meanings, then a general subjective environment is described. But one cannot be sure about this generality; all we know so far is that aspects of the milieu appealed to the observer's psyche in the manner described. It will be prudent to speak of subjective or phenomenological environments without distinction as to their generality or individuality. The subjective environment is the one which refers to the meanings people develop for the events they experience; it may be heavily affected by motivations of inhabitants. Inferences from the objective reality to the subjective environment can be of a low or high level. For example, the observer's interpretation that the children seemed deeply involved in the multiplication game was a low-level inference well supported by evidences such as "children leaning forward in their seats" and "shouting with vigor." To assume that the boy who always first waited to see what others would say saw the game as "a threat" is a more tenuous high-level inference referring to a highly individual subjective environment.

One can develop a subjective description of the environment by direct observation with no dependence upon self-report. For example, Wright, Barker, Null, and Schoggen (1955) have an account of the environment of one boy that is highly subjective or—in Lewin's terms—concerned with the individual's life space. Although the primary data are fairly objective (specimen records), inference made about the experienced situation points to the subjective world. For example, various episodes are rated regarding the "geniality of the situation." Other research on subjective environments asks for individuals' perceptions and interpretations of reality (e.g., Wahlberg, 1969).

Use of a subjective environment has been strongly supported. Wahlberg (1978) believes that the environment-as-perceived is a potent source of variables with which to explain behavior. However, the circularity problem, noted above in relation to the objective individual environment, is compounded with the subjective environment. Not only is the individual developing an environment unique to himself because his particular behavior elicits unique inputs, but the individual's previous experience, his predispostions, his intelligence, and other "personal variables" enter into the picture given of the environment. The issue, of course, is not whether this is a "true environment"; the issue is whether one can develop an environmental description which is independent of a particular individual and which points to a reality that can be directly manipulated, one not a product of circularity. In the sequence of areas used to explain behavior by relating it to environment, the subjective environment takes a position as a late intervening variable, not a primary source of environmental effect; for the problem we are considering in this chapter, qualities describing subjective environments are closer to *dependent* than to *independent* variables.

In the material to follow, most emphasis will be upon studies that emphasize aspects or parts of the "milieu-with-program" or synomorph environment. Least attention will be paid to studies manifestly using subjective variables as a base from which to describe environments.

The organization to follow appeals more to common sense than to conceptual analysis. Studies that deal with preschool, elementary school, high school, and university will be considered in that order. Where similarities of concepts, methodologies or findings persist across these divisions, those similarities will be developed. The reader must be prepared, however, for the fact that conceptual integration in this field of study is underdeveloped.

ENVIRONMENTS IN EARLY CHILDHOOD

The first research with preschool environments emphasized their relation to development of intelligence. The question was: "Would nursery school experience make the child smarter?" Early results seemed to say, "Yes." At least sizable gains in scores on intelligence test scores were reported by investigators (Swift, 1964). Later studies examined the success of nursery schools by noting how well graduates from such environments performed in public school. As more data have been assembled, it has become clear that matters are not as straightforward as early investigators had thought. Test gains were not always significant, nor was it always the case that nursery school better prepared children for kindergarten or first grade. Reviews and evaluations of the intellectual and adjustment effects of nursery school and enriched day-care experience are available but will not be discussed in any detail here (Swift, 1964; Horowitz & Paden, 1973). Two aspects of these studies need to be underlined as a basis for our discussion.

First, the dependent variables were those related to behavior in future environments (e.g., intelligence). Not much attention was paid to what was happening to the child while *in* nursery school. Second, very little systematic and quantitative resource was devoted to measurement of the nursery school environment. The environmental side of the relation between environment and children's lives tended to be expressed as the labels "with nursery school" and "without nursery school," rather than as a set of measured dimensions.

As research developed, changes in the field became apparent. There has been an interest in how the child behaves and what the child experiences in the nursery school process; there have been beginnings in measurement of the nursery school environment. The attention to what happens to children in nursery school (as opposed to what happens to them as a consequence of having gone through nursery school) is important for two reasons. First, if we are to understand the long-term effects of nursery school training, we must measure nursery school inputs and the child's reaction to these inputs. Another reason for becoming systematically informed about nursery school operations is that children are living in these operations and the qualities of this living should be optimum. Day-by-day experience in the preschool should be good because living should be good.

In the studies to follow, both nursery school and day-care environments will be considered. Studies are limited to those dealing with children around three to six years of age. Some of the preschool researches have dealt with general labels or variables for preschool environments while others have paid attention to various settings within those environments. Such a division is maintained below.

GENERAL ENVIRONMENTS FOR PRESCHOOLERS

The "environment" of a preschool study is often described in label form. For example, an investigation by Berk (1971) compared a Montessori and a traditional university-sponsored nursery school. Although differences in program were not systematically measured, they were used to explain differences in the behavioral situations of children. These situations were recorded and analyzed according to methods devised by Schoggen (1963). Briefly, this analysis focuses upon the relation between what the environment "wants" from the subject and what the subject is trying to do. Schoggen referred to these interactions as Environmental Force Units (EFUs) and Berk isolated those EFUs in which conflict existed between the desire of the nursery school children and persons or happenings appearing in their behavior streams. Berk also went beyond the analysis of what happened to children in the two environments to the adaptations children made to the various conflict EFUs. In Berk's overall conceptualization of the problem, variations in program requirements produced variations in the conflict EFU and these, in turn, were reflected in variations in children's responses or adaptations.

The Berk data are rather complex but their major thrust can be illustrated. The Montessori system involved a prearranged and highly structured program which, it was hypothesized, would result in relatively more EFU conflicts between desires of the child and those of the teacher. Results amply confirmed this hypothesis: Three times as many "child desire–teacher expectation" conflicts appeared in the Montessori environment as in the university nursery school. Since children usually responded to teacher–child EFU conflicts with compliance (72%), the percentage of dependent–compliant behavior at the Montessori nursery school was almost twice as great as that at the traditional nursery school.

A less expected finding of the study related to occasions presenting a conflict between the desire of the observed child and his capacity to manage certain challenges in the environment. These EFUs were much more prominent in the traditional than in the Montessori school. Since adaptation to such EFUs was often one of "persisting," persistent behavior was more frequent in the traditional nursery school.

Although the latter finding was not predicted, it fits with the difference in program emphasis: Montessori presents carefully graded environmental challenges; the traditional nursery school left children free to engage the environment as they wished—whether or not they were ready for its difficulties.

The Berk study illustrates various levels of research in preschool environments: the program emphasizes (unfortunately not formally measured in this research) the environmental events involving inhabitants (which are heavily influenced by program dimensions), and the adaptations taken to these environmental events.

Investigations comparing environments in day-care centers, in families, and in home and nursery school combinations have been reported by Prescott (1973). She characterized seven day-care centers as closed and seven as open; child versus teacher choice of activity was the major dimension defining closed versus open. Family care referred to care in homes *outside* the child's own; the home and nursery care referred to the child's own home and half-day attendance at a nursery school. One level of environment in these investigations was the contexts as just described, but another was the individual environments of children as these occurred from moment to moment within the contexts.

Prescott noted the kinds of activities that engaged the children and found more "closed activity" in the closed centers. (Closed activities are those inherently discouraging exploration and self-developed elaborations such as copying tasks or puzzles; doll or block play are open activities.) Activities could also be described in terms of the amount of associated physical mobility. Highly mobile segments constituted only one-tenth of the closed-center activity but was double this amount in the other three contexts.

The proportion of time taken for transitions (official and unofficial) in the closed centers was 26%, in the open centers 14%, and only 7% in the family and 8% in the home and nursery arrangements. The fact that over one-fourth of a child's time in the closed center was taken up in changing activities indicates a kind of regimented environment. Data on *how* activities got started and stopped reinforced this impression: Adults pressured the initiation of 58% of the activity segments in the closed centers but only 20% in open centers and 13% and 9% in family care and home and nursery care, respectively. At the closed center the kinds of activities provided and the preponderance of adult pressure meant that child behaviors rated as creative or exploratory was relatively infrequent; these behaviors increased as one moved to the open center, the family, and the home-and-nursery contexts.

Prescott did not present quantification on most aspects of physical milieu, but she did propose a "softness rating" to reflect presence or absence of such items as "cozy furniture" (rockers, couches, lawn swings), rugs, grass (which children could play on), dirt (which children could dig in), water and other "messy" material for play, fondable pets, adult laps, and so on. Prescott reported that such "soft" items were substantially absent from the closed centers but more available in the open ones and in the homes and nursery school. Prescott pointed to further differences between the contexts: contacts with the world outside (vistors, tradesmen, trips to stores, etc.) were much less frequent in centers than in homes; mixture of various age levels of children were absent in closed centers, somewhat more likely in the open ones, and quite frequent in the family, and home and nursery settings.

As in the Berk study, the Prescott material showed that the kind of context (open, closed, etc.) with its associated staff practices and physical environment impinges upon the directly experienced individual environment in a fashion that is intuitively understandable. One can go a step further on the environmental side of the problem and ask what seems to influence whether a center will be closed or open. Center size seemed to be important. Prescott sought a variety of sizes for the day-care centers but all closed centers that she was able to locate were large ($N > 60$); further, no small centers ($N < 30$) showed a closed structure. These observations suggest that the size of children's environments may influence the program that comes to operate as a part of those environments.

ISSUES OF SIZE AND DENSITY

So far attention has been given to preschool environments characterized as to type: Montessori or traditional, closed or open. Other studies have focused upon a major variable label. One of the most popular of such labels has been size. The size issue may refer to number of children served (as in Prescott's "size of center" above) or number of children in relation to some aspect of environmental capacity; the latter are density studies.

Some studies have reported that increases in child density lead to increased difficulties in social interaction (Hutt & Vaizey, 1966; Jersild & Markey, 1935; Loo, 1972; Swift, 1964). However, the tendency for density or crowding to be associated with increased aggressivity has not been consistent; children often adapt well to high density; further, different kinds of density yield different effects (Swift, 1964).

McGrew (1972) has proposed two kinds of density: social density, referring to a high number of persons in an area or institution, and spatial density, meaning restricted space for a given number of persons. A large room with many inhabitants—even if space per person is quite adequate—has high social density. If the same number of persons are required to use one-half of the room, spatial density is also high. McGrew found that changes in space changed the frequency of running behavior—for many or few children; with space held constant and number of children changed, running behavior was not affected.

Spatial density could be considered a particular example of a more basic kind of density: the number of persons in relation to their behavioral resources. Smith (1974) showed that changes in available toys and apparatus were accompanied by changes in social behavior. The decrease of physical behavioral resources produced several effects: increased social interaction, more large groups and fewer "loners," more aggression and more stress behaviors. An earlier study by Johnson (1935) yielded analogous findings; when playground equipment was reduced, children responded with more social interaction and more conflict.

Rohe and Nuffer (1977) showed that increased spatial density (produced by dividing a room in half) significantly reduced preschoolers' cooperative behavior but only tended to increase aggression. Sheltering and bounding various activity areas by inserting partitions 4 × 4 feet increase cooperative behavior and, in high-density conditions, markedly increased constructive behavior. Finally, choice of program alternatives by children was affected by partitioning and by density; for example, high density discouraged selection of activities requiring high concentration.

Relative deprivation of behavior objects in the nursery situation can increase behaviors interpreted as creative—putting chairs in a line and "playing train," arranging tables end-to-end to create a sidewalk and walking prams along this path (Smith, 1974). In general, when toys were reduced but "apparatus" remained available (furniture, climber, etc.), children often responded with increased sociality and inventiveness. The removal of apparatus and the maintenance of toys did *not* lead to a similar result. Clearly, the number of persons present is only a starting datum for studies on size or density; the availability and the kinds of behavioral resources are necessary considerations.

One behavioral resource in a preschool environment is the number of adults available who can respond to children. A study by O'Conner (1975) compared situations in which 3.5 versus 7.1 children per teacher were present. More adult presence led to more social exchange with adults and less with children, to more reassurance obtained from adults, and to less positive attention paid to other children. An interesting additional result was that children who were measured as more dependent sought out the adult more frequently *only* in the school where fewer adults were present; apparently adult-seeking is less likely to indicate a dependency trait when adults are easily available.

The complexity of the size and density issue is illustrated by Fagot's investigation of Dutch and American nursery schools (1977). Dealing only with four-year-olds, Fagot compared very-high-density schools in the Netherlands (1.2 m² per child) with schools in the United States of moderate (2.3 m²) and very low density (10.5 m²). The general findings did not support the idea that increased density leads to increased negative effects; to the contrary, the few significant results obtained showed that the "crowded" Dutch children spent more time in positive interactions than the American children. Fagot does not report differences between the moderate and the low American densities.

Perhaps the most important aspect of the Fagot study relates to observations (not quantified) regarding the programs of the high-density (Dutch) schools. The management of child behavior in the Dutch schools involved much more directiveness in program arrangements (not in individual contact with students). For example, in the Dutch system, children were assigned to room areas; free choice of play spaces and materials was not possible. Large motor activity indoors was quite limited, although outdoor activity was always provided.

Enough has been learned about size and density issues to convince one that no simple relationships between density and child behavior exist. Spatial density yields different effects than social density; effects of density vary depending upon whether partitions are employed and whether behavioral opportunities are maintained or reduced. Further, density influences children's choice of setting or activity, which, in turn, influences the qualities of child behavior. Finally, in real situations (not experiments) size and density shape the very establishment of the program before children have an opportunity to react to size *per se*. (The reader will recall that Prescott found large centers associated with "closed" programs; Fagot noted that very high density was found with directed, highly regulated programs.) Research on how size and density shape program formation might be more strategic than research on direct child effects. The effects of various nursery school programs is our next concern.

INTRASCHOOL SETTINGS AS ENVIRONMENTS FOR PRESCHOOLERS

Global descriptions of preschool environments usually ignore their clear internal milieu and program structure. A sample of school structure for the third grade was offered at the beginning of this discussion. Daycare centers and nursery schools exhibit their own structure of settings; there are times, places, objects, and action structures for nutrition, for rest, for directed activity, for free play, and so on. Any careful description of the preschool environment will take account of this internal ecological differentiation.

An early book by Hartley, Frank, and Goldenson (1952) described how various nursery school activities (some of which become nursery school settings) encouraged various child behaviors and experiences. Block corners tend to be associated with both cooperative group play and yet also more conflict. Painting, work with clay, and other common nursery school activities were discussed in terms of their capacity to support expression of various child interests or needs.

The Hartley work, although based on much nursery school experience, offered no hard data for its assertions. Shure (1963) did classify and count behaviors associated with five nursery school subsettings: art, books, dolls, games, and blocks Block areas were more likely to attract boys than girls, yielded moderately high social interaction, and more destructive behavior than the other settings. Active social exchange was frequent in the doll area but relatively low in art.

Sometimes investigators study problems not manifestly related to the ecological structure of the nursery school but then discover that this structure is influencing their results. For example, Harper and Sanders (1975), studying sex differences, found that these differences operated first in choice of activity, place, and objects Boys tended to choose outdoor play, to use more space, to employ sand, tractors, climbing structures in their play; girls were more frequently indoors enjoying craft tables and kitchen activities. These same researchers (Sanders & Harper, 1976) found that the amount of fantasy exhibited related to place and sex interacting: boys outdoors increased their fantasy over girls; indoors, girls manifested more fantasy than boys.

Quite thorough investigations of nursery school settings have been carried out by Kounin and his colleagues at Wayne State University (Kounin, 1977). The basic data sources have been videotape recordings of two aspects of nursery school operation: one set of tapes recorded a half-day session for each of 37 children. For the most part, these tapes recorded extensive free play situations during which children chose their places, objects, and activities; the environment was relatively passive. Another set of tapes depicted 598 different lessons—periods in which small groups of children were taken to a small room and a particular program was established (the teacher read a story, the group explored with magnets, the children created paper pie plate faces, etc.); in these lessons, the environment was not passive; it did not permit a wide variety of child choices but presented a single set of imposed milieu and program operations. Working with both the free play and the lessons, the Kounin group demonstrated the effects of variation of nursery school settings upon various dimensions of child behavior; once these relations were established, the next search was for the dimensions of setting (as opposed to setting labels) associated with the behavioral contrasts. The availability of taped material, which could be searched (and "re-searched") for conditions antecedent and consequent to selected behavioral events, greatly enhanced the possibility of inferring relationships.

A broad view of nursery school settings and their child inhabitants has been provided by Rosenthal's work (1973) with tapes of the half-day sessions. The long periods within the session that could be termed "free play" were investigated (preparation–cleanup or snacks–lunch, for which teachers structured a regime, were omitted.) One question for these time periods might be: "How 'free' is free play?" Prescott (1973), it may be recalled, found that, in closed day-care centers, activities were more often entered because of adult pressure than by child free choice. Rosenthal could identify children's attendance at an activity center, reverse the tape, and study the conditions operative at the time the child started the activity. She found that most activity entries were made by child choice: teachers were made responsible for only 9% of the activity-setting entries.

Rosenthal also delineated two aspects of child involvement in the various settings: attraction power (how many children appeared), and holding power (how long children remained in the setting); Rosenthal found that blocks and art were both popular as measured by attraction power but that art had significantly greater holding power.

Using the same tapes, Houseman (1972) focused upon varous forms of child conflict. Total conflicts of all kinds were quite frequent, occurring at a rate of about 14 per hour per child; however, most persisted less than 15 seconds and exhibited minimal effect upon subsequent child action and emotion. Houseman found, as did Shure (1973) that frequency of conflicts was related to activity settings or synomorphs. The climber, the kitchen, and the large block area were associated with more conflicts than art, clothing, and snacks–lunch. By searching the tapes Houseman identified events antecedent to conflict. She found that a number of children used the block area and "needed" the blocks being used by others; this presence of interchangeable materials offered one source for conflict. (Such interchangeability was absent in puzzles, and conflict was lower at the puzzle table.) Conflicts also arose because floor space in blocks was common rather than individual; further, large houses and forts produced "insiders" (those who built) and "outsiders" (those who did not); conflict arose between the groups. A parallel examination of the art area, where conflict was quite low, showed few such sources of conflict.

The incidence of positive social interaction as this related to settings and behavior objects was investigated by Doyle (1975), who employed the full range of settings in the taped half-day sessions. Doyle found that relatively high usage of an area was not sufficient for high social interaction in the area, the latter being more determined by the prevailing action structure. High sociality was associated with preparation–cleanup, role play, and those large-muscle objects that could accommodate more than one child user at a time (e.g., climber); in contrast, social exchange was low in puzzles, small model props, and single-person large-muscle objects (tricycles, rocking horse). Much *positive* sociality was highly likely in role play and in multiple-person large-muscle activity; positive sociality was infrequent or absent when children played with the science objects or engaged in art. Antisocial interactions (teasing, ridiculing, and quarreling) were relatively frequent in small toy activities (doll house, standing figures, small vehicles); antisocial actions were few in snack–lunch, art, and large-muscle, single-person activities.

As can be seen from these various researches, the sociality variable can be approached at various levels: number present at an activity setting, amount of social exchange, and amount or proportion of positive and negative social interaction. The first levels may be preconditions for following ones but they are not sufficient conditions. Art is well attended but shows few social exchanges (although those exchanges are rarely negative); small toys provide low population, low exchange, but the proportion of negative interaction is quite high.

The repeated association of activity setting or synomorph with measures of child involvement and social behavior suggests that one look at those basic dimensions of the synomorphs that might account for the relations. Kounin has suggested that activity involvement is related, for example, to variety and complexity of different constituent behaviors required by an activity. Many different behavior possibilities are called upon in art projects that involve cutting, pasting, and coloring. Interchangeability of materials and single versus multiple person for large-muscle equipment are dimensions related to child interaction. One of the major ideas from the Kounin group which yields dimensions for activities, rather than labels, has to do with research in the lessons and the concept of *signal systems*.

For any activity setting one may ask: "If a child were placed in this ongoing operation, what would be the signals which would tell him when to do what?" And more basically, "What are the qualities of this signal set?" Signals to children for a lesson involving teacher reading a story tend to be continuous and from one single, competent source; signals for a lesson in which children are to recall and discuss what jobs mother and father have are less steady and continuous and come from a number of different, less competent, child sources. Discussion contributions from nursery school children are occasionally halting or off-topic, creating gaps in the signal delivery. The amount of involvement children show in activities is related to two issues: the steady, clear delivery of task-furthering signals to the participants, and the prevention of other, task-competing, inputs.

Kounin and Gump (1974) found that involvement or on-task behavior of children in settings where there was a relatively steady single source of signals (e.g., the teacher-reads format) was higher than when the signals came from multiple child emitters (small-group discussion and talks). The prevention of competing inputs in certain activity formats is well illustrated in the individual construction or arts and crafts lessons. For example, a teacher may suggest that the "lesson" will be making pictures or collages of desserts. Each child is given necessary objects: scissors, paste, sheet of paper, and magazine pages showing various foods. The signal system now relates to the results of the child's own activity upon the external world. Cutting a picture suggests applying paste and putting it on the sheet; the presence of one food on the sheet suggests returning to the food pictures for more cutting, followed by pasting. A continuous signal system operates as one action by the child and its immediate consequence provide thrust and direction for the next. This signal system is relatively continuous but it has another quality. The child, because his own physical actions produce immediate consequences which push to further action, is more *insulated* from competing stimuli than even the child listening (with others) to teacher reading a story. Data showed that individual construction lessons yielded significantly more on-task behavior than any other format—including the teacher-reads format, which was itself relatively high in involvement. The hypothesis that the individual construction project provided protections against possible competing inputs received further support when more child involvement was found in *individual* construction than in *group* construction (projects for which children must track and relate to signals from each other as well as to direct consequences of their own actions).

The continuity and the insulation dimensions are qualities that can be applied to formats as wholes. The model for the teacher-reads format involves a single continuous emitter. In actual practice, teachers diluted this monopoly of signal output by periodically requesting children to show their own reactions to the story. Thus, it is possible to categorize activity format according to their dominant and enduring signal system, but one may also investigate the moment-by-moment condition for the group activity.

Kounin and Doyle (1975) reasoned that within the teacher-as-emitter formats (teacher reading, teacher demonstrating) high child involvement would occur when the teacher maintained her signal continuity but low involvement would result if too much signaling came from child contributors. A study of the actual situations developing within formats of high and low involvement showed this prediction to be correct—with certain modifications: the total amount of child contribution was not predictive; rather the number of *extended* child contributions was the crucial factor. If the teacher kept such contributions short, thus limiting the gaps in signal continuity, high involvement was maintained.

Most nursery school studies of activities have selected on-task behavior or social interaction as their dependent variables. An investigation by Sherman (1975), using the Kounin lesson tapes, was refreshing in that the dependent variable was child glee. This investigator noted that lesson playback often produced sharp outbursts of laughter and shouting; he identified each incident of group glee and studied the tapes to discover their contextual and eliciting conditions. A major part of Sherman's analysis employed the signal system description of lessons developed by Kounin and Gump 1974; he demonstrated that group glee was quite infrequent in the individual construction lessons, in which continuity and insulation were predominant and signals were quiet and matter of fact. Glee outbursts were only moderately frequent in the teacher-led story demonstration and discussion format, but they were very frequent in the music and movement formats (10 times as frequent as in individual construction). It was proposed that the intense signals that come from musical beats and from large-muscle movement, in a context of similarly stimulated peers, were factors contributing to glee outbursts. Sherman found that glee was also associated with relatively large lesson groups (5–9 children) rather than small (3–4) and mixed-sex rather than single-sex groups.

The replay capacity of the videotapes was especially highlighted when Sherman determined whether glee resulted from a simultaneous reaction of several children to an eliciting event or from behavioral contagion (i.e., one child's outburst became the stimulus for the next child). By examining momentary events immediately preceding the glee incident, Sherman showed that 70% of the incidents were not spontaneous but a consequence of contagion. Davenport (1976) later showed that deviancy contagion was also greatest in the music and movement formats and least in the individual construction lessons.

The Kounin researches make amply clear that aspects of settings are consistently associated with child behavior variables. Further, some analyses of events within settings (e.g., Kounin & Doyle, Sherman, Davenport) reveal ongoing processes that intervene between qualities of the overall format and of child behavior outcomes. For example, the glee and the deviancy in the music and movement format was based on a contagion process that operated quite readily in that ecology but not in individual construction settings.

EXPERIMENTAL AND APPLIED FOCI IN PRESCHOOL ENVIRONMENTS

The behavior analysis group in psychology has become increasingly concerned with ecological matters. The incidence of peer reinforcement in nursery school was shown by Charlesworth and Hartup (1967) to be greater in dramatic play and lesser in "table activites." The sequence of influence seemed to be that activities determined extent of sociality, which in turn influenced frequency of peer reinforcement.

A later essay by Ann Rogers-Warren (1977) described how to analyze the environment in which behavior modification is planned. Pertinent issues include the cues and reinforcements for target behavior that already exist in the environment and the ease with which milieu, program, and staff can manage a proposed intervention. Illustrations are offered for environmental analyses showing that environmental issues pertinent to behavior modification are becoming explicitly recognized.

Some researchers from the behavior-modification tradition have gone further; they have manipulated ecological variables to achieve behavioral effects that might otherwise be achieved by contingent reinforcement. A paper by Risley (1977) reviews these efforts and a few examples can be described here.

LeLaurin and Risley (1972) dealt with the excessive amount of time children devote to transitions in some day-care centers, a problem noted above in Prescott's studies (1973). These investigators developed a procedure that made teachers responsible for activities and areas; children moved to these areas as they became ready (this program arrangement was given the basketball label, *zone defense*). In the contrasting (and usual) arrangement, teachers were responsible for a group of children and, as all in the group became ready, all moved with the

teacher to the new activity (labeled *man-to-man defense*). Careful alternation of zone and man-to-man defenses demonstrated that the zone
approach yielded more child time in appropriate activity engagement,
much less time in transition.

Two researches reported by Krantz and Risley (1977) are instructive
since they compare effects produced by ecological versus reinforcement
manipulations. The attentiveness of kindergarten children to teacher's
story was measured when all children crowded in front of the teacher
and again when each child sat on a marked separate space on the floor.
Attentiveness was clearly superior under the second condition. While
the authors attribute results to the crowding (children close together),
the clarity of each child's area should also be considered. Work by the
Kounin group suggested that clarity of one's activity boundary (e.g.,
Houseman, 1972) appears associated with minimum conflict, which, in
turn, relates to better activity engagement. Using contingencies, Krantz
and Risley also increased attentiveness in the crowded condition but
not to any greater degree than by the provision of marked spaces. It
would appear that the ecological arrangements were more simple and
less intrusive than the reinforcement efforts.

Not only is the quality of the ongoing setting important in determining a child's behavior, but the temporal relation between various
settings can be crucial. Which activity setting follows which? Krantz
and Risley demonstrated that if story presentation followed settings
emphasizing physical action (outdoor play, dance, musical chairs), only
63% of the sampled behaviors in the first 15 minutes of the story time
were attentive; if the story followed a rest period, attentiveness rose to
86%.

The foregoing studies along with others not described (Doke &
Risley, 1972; Hall, Delquardi, & Harris, 1977; Montes & Risley, 1975;
Quilitch, Christophersen, & Risley, 1977) are perhaps indications of a
developing speciality—that of "applied micro-ecological psychology."
The more conceptual and extensive field works of researchers such as
Kounin or Prescott provide data identifying those aspects of preschool-
ers' environments which are associated with various child behaviors.
The direct manipulations by Risley and others add experimental evi-
dence and illustrations of practical application.

A major problem running through most of the previous research
is the weakness of program measurement. The environmental side of
the investigations has been described by names for concrete places and
objects (e.g., block corner), or general labels (e.g., Montessori or traditional), and some high or low points on dimensions usually derived
after data collection (e.g., continuity of signals). Missing have been

quantifications along preestablished program dimensions. Some advance in measurement of such dimensions has appeared in studies of preschool regimens established to improve the functioning of the disadvantaged. An extensive study by Miller and Dyer (1975) dealt with the operations and the effects of four preschool programs (Montessori, Bereiter-Engleman, Darcee, and Head Start enrichment). Much of the research concerns the pedagogic aspects and effects of the various operations and is beyond our focus here on preschool environments. However, pertinent are ideas regarding program measurement and illustration of their use in collecting data on certain ecological dimensions.

Miller and Dyer first worked to clarify the *model* of each preschool regime. (These authors actually used the word *program* for what is a model; since we have used *program* in a somewhat different sense, we will avoid confusion by referring to "model" rather than "program".) The model is the statement of "how things should go" if the educational orientation was to be represented accurately and refers to matters of philosophy, methods and curriculum, role of the teacher, and goals for children. Models can be measured by determining how well given definition statements represent a particular orientation; experts in the particular schooling philosophy can make such judgments.

In contrast to models are *treatments*. Model statements are translated into dimensions to which observed events in the classroom may be coordinated. Treatment, then, is a quantification of what actually happens in carrying out the model.

The Montessori model suggests much individualization of activity, few small working groups, and much manipulation activity. Repeated observation in the classroom would record the extent to which these aspects of model were realized in treatment: How often did the observer note that small groups of children had formed? How many children in each observational sample were engaged in manipulation of materials? Other treatment dimensions relating to ecological conditions were considered: How often do children engage in the same or different tasks? How frequently is verbal recitation the major activity? What is the frequency of role playing?

Although logically each treatment dimension is independent of every other, empirically the dimensions were found to cluster. For example, the presence of all-on-the-same-task activity was associated with infrequent formation of small groups. The Montessori school exhibited less same-tasks activity (as prescribed by its model) but considerable small-group activity (not as prescribed). High manipulations and conversation clustered together and was most heavily operative in the Montessori treatment.

The use of treatment dimensions enable measurement of the extent to which program models are realized in actual operation. Further, the treatment dimensions can be used to describe the operating environmental contexts and processes with which certain behavioral outcomes are associated. The treatment measurement in the Miller and Dyer study can be related to a gain in children's competence. For example, the more didactic treatments (Darcee and Bereiter-Engelman) yielded the most immediate gain in cognitive areas; however, certain cognitive competence measures taken after several years did not favor the didactic programs.

The Miller and Dyer material can be related to the discussion that opened this chapter. The use of models and treatments is a way of describing official and operating programs of nursery schools; settings or synomorphs provide naturally occurring environmental units which constitute those programs.Some of the findings reviewed here relate to global programs and some to dimensions operating in specific units. It would appear that one set of environmental variables important to child behavior is that dealing with size and density. Another set relates to "openness" or degree of child choice in selection of activity. Further, size and openness interact—a fact with implications for those who would reform children's environments.

Within the synomorphs of nursery school environments, the nature of the signal systems that guide child behavior appear important if one wishes to affect on-task behavior, social interaction, or even child glee.

As a group the preschool environments have been described using direct observation rather than interviews or questionnaires; this has encouraged more objective description than will be the case with high school and university environments to be described later.

We turn now to a review of elementary school environments.

ENVIRONMENTS IN ELEMENTARY SCHOOLS

Qualitative Pictures

Some investigators immerse themselves in classroom action and, from the experience, portray how life goes for pupils and teachers. Although the pictures presented are not quantitative, they often include analyses and generalizations which bear upon important issues. An impression of the reformist flavor of some of the accounts can be gained from scanning a sample of titles: *The Way It Spozed to Be* (Herndon, 1968); *Death at an Early Age* (Kozol, 1967); *The Urban School: A Factory for Failure* (Rist, 1973).

Qualitative analyses from the ethnographic tradition have become increasingly frequent (Wolcott, 1975); some of the works have focused upon important agents in the educational environment such as the principal (Wolcott, 1973) and the teacher (Doyle, 1977; McPherson, 1972); other efforts have attended to behavior and situations of students (Erickson, 1977; Goetz, 1976). The need to present statements of "what really happens in classrooms" has been strong enough to induce psychologists trained in experimental and quantitative methods to offer trenchant yet qualitative reports about life in the classroom (Jackson, 1968; Smith & Geoffrey, 1968). An advantage to such reports is that they suggest new variables for quantitative efforts. Jackson notes that for children in the "daily grind" of school, the environment tends to present repeated experiences involving denial, delay, interruption, and distraction. These four aversive qualities may be responsible for the decrease in children's proschool motivation as they advance through the school grades. The nonquantitative accounts challenge some long-held assumptions about the nature of the classroom enterprise. Jackson even questions the belief that teachers are mostly devoted to issues of learning. He finds the immediate attentions of teachers center on activity management, not on "teaching" in the strictly pedagogic sense. Is Jackson correct? A study of almost 50 elementary classrooms showed only 30% of a teacher's time invested in academic instruction and learning; various efforts to maintain activities were more frequent (Conant, 1973). Clearly it would be important for educational researchers to examine the nature of the classroom activities managed and the management practices teachers employ.

Children in Global School Environments

Early quantitative studies often approached school environments by a focus upon individual inhabitants. The data from a sample of individual environments became data on the environment. Since the major source of significant input to the child has been assumed to be the teacher, the nature of teacher–child encounters was investigated. A large research literature on teacher behavior has been thoroughly reviewed by Dunkin and Biddle (1974) and will not be repeated here. A sociological theory of what schools are supposed to do and the nature of the operations by which they do it has been proposed by Parsons (1955), who makes central the role of the classroom teacher. The teacher is not seen as mother-surrogate but as one who presses pupils away from exclusive familial ties. The teacher deals with children in a universalistic, not individualistic fashion, responding less to their emotional needs and more to the necessity for them to become task and achievement oriented.

Two studies from ecological psychology yield data relevant to Parsons' view. Dyck (1963) examined encounters between parents and children and between teachers and children in a small Midwestern town. Parents, much more frequently than teachers, responded *to* their children's activity, their overt expressions, their state, or condition; teachers were much more likely to seek activity *from* the child. Schoggen (1975) found interactions between children and parents to be more frequent, more individualized, and more tinged with negative affect than interactions between children and their teachers; on the other hand, teachers were more likely to make extensive demands on children and to be successful in influencing the children's behavior. Taken together, Dyck and Schoggen empirically ground Parsons' concept of the teacher as a relatively impersonal, task-centered agent of socialization.

Not all schools have been organized around traditional values. Berk and Lewis (1977) studied social input and social response in four schools whose environments were described as: Traditional, Transitional (between Traditional and more "open" arrangements), Progressive (following a Dewey or open philosophy), and Romantic (reflecting a Rousseau or laissez-faire approach). Direction of daily activities was most exclusively under teacher control in the Traditional school, and was less so in the Transitional; a balance of teacher–child control existed in the Progressive school, and children were in control of most activities in the Romantic school.

In the Transitional and Progressive schools, children quite frequently initiated social interchange with adults; such adult-seeking was somewhat lower in the Romantic school and very low in the Traditional environment. In relationship with peers, the most teacher-controlled school (Traditional) produced very few extended peer interactions but also few negative exchanges; the school controlled by children (Romantic) yielded the most extended peer interactions and the most negative ones. Of additional interest was the issue of opposite-sex interaction, which occurred much more frequently in the Progressive School than in any of the others.

Although Berk and Lewis did not systematically measure the program aspect of these four environments, they refer to program and milieu informally and have presented evidence to show that the children's social experiences can be much affected by the school they inhabit.

A very ambitious attempt to measure classroom types and their effects occurred as a part of the national Follow-Through program sponsored by the U.S. Office of Education. A longitudinal quasi-experimental project was established to measure the operations and the effects of seven different kinds of intervention in grades one through three. Rather complex measurements of classroom procedures and associated child outcomes have been described by Stallings (1975). A total of 166 classrooms were observed for three days each; described were physical facilities, major activities, groupings, and specific child and adult behaviors. From concrete events in these areas, it was shown that the ideologies of the various types of intervention were, for the most part, being actualized; for example, positive reinforcements were offered in the reinforcement classrooms, small groups of children working without continual teacher supervision were established in the more "progressive" or open classes. The events of the classroom were related to child-test and child-behavior variables. A fundamental finding was that academic gain was related to amount of class time devoted to the particular academic area. Further, the more structured, reinforcement-oriented programs, in general, produced higher gains in reading and mathematics.

In contrast to the structured, didactic programs were others which might be labeled "flexible." In the flexible environments, children were more likely to choose their own seat location (at least part of the time) and to engage in a wider variety of activities. An immediate concomitant of procedures in the flexible classrooms was more child initiative in verbal exhanges. Children in flexible, as opposed to structured, classrooms gained more on the Ravens Test (1962)—presumably a measure of spatial and nonverbal intelligence—and they indicated more proschool motivation by their superior daily attendance. (Support for the idea that attendance does reflect proschool motivation comes from the finding that more smiling and laughter was recorded in the better attended classrooms.)

Certain child behaviors in classrooms were also related to the kind of program sponsored. Cooperation was less frequent in the structured programs and task persistence was more frequent. However, one cannot assume that cooperation or persistence were being developed as child *qualities*; these behaviors may have simply reflected program requirements and not tendencies developed in the child.

The Follow-Through data are a valuable addition to our understanding of children's school environments. Although the investigators did not always separate classroom program variables from those of individual pupil behavior, they have demonstrated that what actually happens in classrooms can be reliably measured and the results of such measurement can be sensibly related to important child development outcomes.

CHILDREN AND INTRASCHOOL SETTINGS

Field Studies

In the preceding studies the basic units of analysis have been classrooms and individual pupils. In the introduction to this chapter, a picture was drawn of classroom objects and events organized into subenvironments or synomorphs (opening session, reading circles, and so on). Classrooms, especially in elementary school, represent not one but a cluster of settings and what happens to children is highly dependent upon which setting in the cluster is occupied.

Some investigators have identified subsections of the classroom by subject matter. Adams and Biddle (1970) studied videotapes of arithmetic and social studies lessons. Using these samples of classroom operations, the investigators established a number of interesting results. For example, in both kinds of lessons, the extent to which children interact with the teacher is very closely related to where they sit. Several seats across the front of the room and several more down the center account for the large majority of teacher–pupil interactions.

Such an association has been known for some time (Dawe, 1934; Sommer, 1967), but it has sometimes been attributed to seat preference (Farnsworth, 1933). However, a recent study by Koneya (1976) indicates that seating location in a group setting influences social interaction even when preference is controlled. A child's effective environment depends on where the child is physically located within the classroom.

Adams and Biddle showed that certain child and teacher behaviors related to subject matter. For example, corrective behavior from the teacher was more prominent in mathematics than in social studies. However, a chain of effects seemed operative: teachers in social studies usually interacted continually with the entire class. In mathematics, teachers often dealt with individuals or were otherwise "disengaged" from most of the class. Without direct supervision pupils showed more off-task behavior, which aroused more teacher correction.

The relationship between subject matter and classroom organization points to an important issue in the description of intraclass units. Two approaches may be used but they should not be confused: a lesson or other section of the environment can be described according to its subject matter or it can be described in terms of what might be labeled its program or *format*. The same subject matter can be handled in quite different formats. In the introduction to this chapter, the subject matter, mathematics, was handled by a flash card drill. The environment represented by the drill format is quite different from a mathematics format requiring children to compute worksheet problems at their desks. Format directly specifies many more aspects of the child's school environment than does subject matter; those correlations between child behavior and subject matter that do appear probably do so because certain formats tend to be associated with certain subject matters.

Other investigators have dealt with the sample subsettings in classrooms. Hughes and associates (1959) obtained specimen records for 35 elementary teachers and found that teacher behavior varies between lessons; for example, more negative affect by teachers to pupils occurred in arts and crafts than in academic lessons. Kounin (1970) examined videotapes of half days in elementary classrooms using a subsetting approach to locate those portions of the classroom events upon which he wished to focus. Pupil off-task behavior was higher in teacher-absent seatwork than in teacher-present reading circles or recitations. Furthermore, the delineations of subsettings highlighted the concept of transition between subsettings. Focus upon certain dimensions of teacher behavior at transition led to sensible correlations between teacher scores on these dimensions and pupil on-task behavior.

The success in establishing relationships between sample settings and inhabitants' behavior encouraged Gump (1967, 1969) to attempt a more comprehensive approach in which full days of classroom activities would be analyzed according to their ecological or setting structure. Teacher behavior as well as child behavior would be viewed as fitting this structure; teachers were assumed to be at least as influenced by the environments they selected and maintained as were children. Gump used specimen records to preserve teacher activity and time-lapse photography to record pupil behavior. The material was unitized first, not into behavioral bits, but into the twenty or so subsettings that occurred throughout the school day. (The chapter introduction illustrates several of these subsettings). A "map" could be drawn showing the operation of these settings over time; on some occasions the total class would occupy one setting, at other periods, the pupils would be divided between several simultaneously operating settings.

Once identified, the subsettings could be categorized along a number of facets: the business or concern of the subsetting, the teacher's action role, the grouping arrangement, the extent to which active events external to pupils paced their activity, and so on. The general questions asked were: What is the nature of this third grade environment? What is the relation between aspects of this environment and the behavior of teachers and children?

With a map of subsettings available, both teacher and pupil behaviors could be coordinated to the settings and transitions in the map, and the relationship between inhabitant acts and ecological structure could be obtained. For example, teacher acts handling deviating behavior rose at transitions and fell off in the main body of the segments. Teachers were very busy, averaging almost 1300 recorded units of verbal action per day. And the amount of such action varied systematically with the subsetting the teacher occupied. Class-wide recitation formats yielded 50% more teacher acts than did reading circles. Such data made it quite clear that teachers were heavily influenced by the subsettings they established.

Pupil behavior was also related to setting qualities. When the setting was coded as providing continuous active external input (as in a recitation), pupils were more on-task than when the external input was passive (as in seatwork). Among the active input settings, there were variations in group size (small teacher-led groups, e.g., reading circles, as opposed to full class recitations); on-task behavior was significantly higher during the small-group sessions. Finally, subsettings dominated by pupil presentations showed relatively low on-task scores for pupils—an outcome consistent with the later Kounin and Doyle (1975) finding that extended pupil contributions led to less pupil involvement in nursery school.

Evidence from the Gump material supported several assertions: the classroom is an ecologically differentiated phenomenon whose segments may be reliably identified and described. These segments influence pupil behavior and experience directly, and the segments also coerce teacher behavior which then influences the pupil.

The research also shows that a sample of lessons is not an adequate sample of children's school environments. Some 12% of pupil time is spent in procedural synomorphs, not in lessons (Gump, 1967). (This is time required for housekeeping, for orderly exits and entrances, etc.) Further, the time *between* lessons yields different action than time *during* lessons. (The increase in teacher counter-deviancy rates at transition, cited above, is a major example.)

Overall, the Gump research encourages a perspective that sees improvement in the quality of classroom life resting upon upgrading the settings that teachers and pupils inhabit.

Experiments

The association of certain setting qualities with particulars of student behavior and experience suggests that settings might be manipulated to produce favorable results. Hundreds of experiments dealing with teaching methods might be seen as relevant. A set of reviews in this area has been presented by Gage (1976). Attention here will be limited to those variations in school environments aimed at variables other than academic learning (e.g., enjoyment, pupil–pupil interaction).

The appreciation of what might be accomplished with novel formats in classrooms is probably enhanced when one realizes how completely two formats dominate most classroom environments. The first format is pencil–paper seatwork which requires much pupil time—in the Gump study it was 36%. The other most ubiquitous arrangement is the recitation (37% of pupil time). Recitation usually involves several cycles per minute of teacher questioning, pupil answering, and teacher reacting. Frequent use of this format accounts for the very high number of teacher verbal acts during the school day. The weaknesses of the recitation were pointed out by Stevens in 1912: Teachers, not pupils, become the busy persons in the classroom, bits of knowledge rather than ideas or reflections are made central, individual needs are ignored, and students are often pressed into a tense or competitive situation. Yet the recitation format has been exceedingly durable; studies made 60 years after Stevens' criticisms show that teachers are talking and questioning for about two-thirds of the classroom time; students are rarely seen questioning or elaborating on material (Hoetker & Ahlbrand, 1969). If the domination of seatwork and recitation formats could be challenged by successful introduction of novel formats, a significant accomplishment would have been achieved.

Usual classroom formats have been criticized because they place students in competitive relationships with one another. Certainly the recitation often involves questions of who will answer correctly and who will be wrong. Ways by which cooperative formats could operate and a review of research showing good effects of cooperation have been offered by Johnson and Johnson (1975). A cooperative (as opposed to competitive) format for social studies programs was shown to increase liking for social studies and for elements involved in cooperative classroom work (e.g., sharing information, receiving group grades as opposed to individual ones; Wheeler & Ryan, 1973). Racially or sexually heterogenous teams were established for instructional games by De Vries and Edwards (1974); the amount of cross-sex and cross-race helping increased over participations in less cooperative formats. The same investigators were also able to show that task satisfaction and peer tutoring in the general student population would increase when games and teams were established (De Vries & Edwards, 1973).

The use of simulation games, not only to assist academic learning, but to enrich classroom experience, has been increasing. A review of approaches and findings has been contributed by Seidner (1976), who claims that the games change the age-old pattern of teacher–pupil interaction, increase legitimate peer interaction, give students a sense of control over their immediate environment, and improve their motivation. Interestingly, Seidner maintains that cognitive learning is not necessarily greater when game simulations are employed. Certainly a major factor in the games is that most students (about 80%) say they enjoy them. The amount of enjoyment is very closely related to group size. Since a part of pleassure in the games is the opportunity to "do something," it is important to note that the larger the game population, the fewer moves made by any one child—and the less the child's enjoyment (Inbar, 1968).

Before leaving the issue of games it should be noted that they represent one of the most comprehensive and coercive program forms available. Games specify the ends of behavior, the kinds of behavior, and the action relationships among participants. Game play involves a basic cooperation for all participants in the sense that even competitors agree to mesh specified behaviors toward the working out of a challenge. Cooperation appears again in two forms: the interlocking of team members' behaviors and the sharing of action goals or rewards. Introduction of games into classroom environments might be expected to create important changes in pupil–pupil and pupil–teacher interaction.

For more and more children, one out-of-class but school setting is the bus. About 44% of American children are said to begin and end their school day by riding a bus. Although many problems have arisen on bus rides, very little research is available. A study by Berk and Berson (1975) offers a beginning in the area. Using specimen records of children, these investigators sought to determine what happened to children riding a bus to a university laboratory school. Data obtained before experimental manipulation showed that behavior going to school in the morning is much more outgoing, positive, and socially interactive than behavior returning home in the afternoon. In an attempt to increase pleasure and sociality on the bus ride, toys, sedentary games, and art supplies were made available through adults riding the bus. This setting manipulation created emphatic behavioral changes, but many were in opposite directions for boys and girls. The boys became quite involved in puzzles and games using them socially and competitively with peers; as a result there occurred more social episodes, more squabbles, and more intervention by adults. Girls selected dolls, knitting, and art supplies and engaged in less social interaction and less conflict and experienced less intervention by adults. Although conditions on the bus were reasonably favorable for both boys and girls under both regular and treatment conditions, the manipulations showed that the quality of the bus ride can be changed if educators wish to do so. Since almost half of America's children spend several hours each week on the bus, the plea of Berk and Berson for a designed, not laissez-faire, bus environment seems quite justified.

OPEN SCHOOL ENVIRONMENTS

Widespread construction of open-space schools has been encouraged by two quite different considerations. Ideological support, for example, has come from descriptions of an open philosophy operating in some of the British Infant Schools. Practical pressures have begun with the economy of school building construction—an economy more pertinent to initial cost of the building than to the long-term expense of the total facility.

In the United States the movement toward open schools began in the late 1950s, peaked in the late 1960s, and is probably now on the decline (Myers, 1974). Compilations of open-school studies are available (e.g., Metropolitan Toronto School Board, 1974); a short general review has been prepared by Gump (1975). Several studies have cast doubt on the efficiency of the open program (as generally implemented) to yield academic gains beyond those obtained in traditional regimes (Bennett, 1976); in fact, for inner-city children, the open arrangement may prove inferior to the more traditional one (Traub, Weiss, Fisher, & Musella, 1974).

Open programs, when they do operate, present children with more opportunities related to facilities, activities, and persons; more necessity to develop their own directions and means for learning; more intimate but much less frequent guidance from the teacher. In schools where open program seemed generally successful, students do report experiencing more initiative, more responsibility to self, and more autonomy (Traub *et al.*, 1972). Observation of children may show less positive results: children may spend more time in movement and transition and may be seen more frequently "disengaged" from educational activity (Fisher, 1974; Gump, 1974).

Since open programs in schools may be becoming less frequent and many open-space schools never had open programs, the question of what open space does to classroom functioning becomes important. (The open-space schools will be with us for some time; the school systems that built them are "married" to these buildings, and the marriage will be maintained—if not for the sake of the children, then for the sake of the taxpayer.) A major principle in ecological psychology is that of *synomorphy*; the proposition is that, in settings, standing patterns of behavior (programs) and the physical milieu (space and facilities) become *synomorphic* or "similar in shape." Brunswik (1957) expressed a similar idea when he wrote of environment and organism "coming-to-terms." With traditional school programs being pressed to use open physical designs, the usual synomorphy between behavior and milieu is violated. However, the need for a coming-to-terms continues. What, then, happens to the programs and the spaces in these classroom environments?

In a traditional arrangement, many teachers isolate their particular children from surrounding distraction. Placed in open schools these teachers attempt to establish substitute walls by using book-cases, file cases, chart and map easels, portable dividers, and the like. These arrangements do not effectively block out sounds, but they screen off what might be seen of the sound source (Gump & Ross, 1977a). Noise may also be reduced by assignment of loud activities (and loud people) to the most remote areas. Changes in program are also made: large group recitation become less frequent because the amount of sound required might distract nearby groups; for the same reason, audiovisual devices become rarely employed in individual classes. The physical mobility made possible by open space often results in those students visiting more different places (and people) in their school day than did students in schools of traditional architure (Gump, 1974). The coming-to-terms of milieu and program, then, means that certain features of both may drop out and that new features may be added until some steady state is achieved.

Of 21 Midwestern schools, all manifesting varying degrees of *physical* openness, two-thirds were shown to have little or no *program* openness (Gump & Ross, 1977b). It might be thought that the more open the physical design, the more open the program, but many teachers modified the openness by inserting wall substitutes. Analysis showed no correlation between *original* physical openness and program openness; as would be predicted by the synomorphy hypothesis, a strong positive relationship did obtain between *modified* physical openness and program openness.

A final fact relates to teachers. A minority were involved in open programs and expressed solid satisfaction with their open buildings; however, those teachers who led traditional programs in unmodified open buildings were quite dissatisfied—a dissatisfaction that might have implications for the students in their charge.

Before leaving elementary school environments, it might be noted that children entering first grade are exposed to invitations and pressures which, although operative in nursery school, now are more persistent and intense. Formal learning becomes a requirement, not merely an opportunity. Children are asked for a more fundamental reorientation. They are to reduce their relatively exclusive dependence on family and accept somewhat transitory and impersonal teachers; they are to give and get support from peers; they are to reduce their pleasure seeking and find satisfaction in tasks and their completion; they are to become industrious. Research on elementary school environments reflects this change. On-task measures become, after learning, the major dependent variable. But attention is also given to peer relationships and program variations that influence them. Although there may be some agreement on what the child is to become, there is conflict over the extent to which direction from outside or direction from within the child is to be depended upon for his maturing. Thus, research develops around the dimension of amount of child choice in school activities. Studies of flexible or open programs show that while these may enhance satisfaction and peer relations, they often do not increase learning.

HIGH SCHOOL AND UNIVERSITY ENVIRONMENTS

Research at the high school and university levels takes a considerably different shape from that available on earlier school environments. Since extracurricular affairs become much more important after elementary school, research dealing with this area appears. Except for questionnaire research, not much classroom investigation appears. At the university level a new environment—student housing—becomes important. In all, however, the environmental research at this level is not extensive and is not easily comparable to that of the lower-level school situations.

A major set of studies regarding high school environments has centered on the variable of size (e.g., Barker and Gump, *Big School, Small School,* 1964). At the outset, student population may be taken as a simple index of school size. However, size also refers to environmental extent. The number of behavior settings in the school is one measure of environmental size. The relation between the two sizes provided the theoretical direction for the research. As school population size increases, the number of settings also increases but at a slower rate; the consequence is that large high schools have more students per setting than do small high schools. This undermanning of settings in the small school is especially influential in extracurricular settings where pressures upon youth to enter, to participate, and to accept responsible roles are greater than they are in large schools. As a result of these pressures, young people in small high schools are relatively more likely to occupy central setting positions (program chairman, secretary, jounalist, actor, varsity athlete, cheerleader, etc.).

As a result of their more central activity in extracurricular settings, students in small high schools report satisfactions different from those of large-school students. For example, the small-school students emphasize the gratification of gaining competence, of meeting challenges, of success in small-group activity, of realization of cultural or religious values; large-school students report vicarious satisfactions, satisfactions in affiliation with a powerful institution, with being given "points" for supporting certain extracurricular affairs.

The differences in felt invitations and pressures to participate in large and small schools were directly measured by Willems (1967), who found that a sense of responsibility to school affairs was stronger in small schools. Of special interest in Willems' findings was the fact that academically marginal students in large high schools felt almost no responsibility for their school's extracurricular settings; many such students in the small school reported feelings of responsibility—more than large school nonmarginal or "regular" students and as many as the small school regular youth.

The general findings for the large and small school have been replicated (Baird, 1969; Wicker, 1968). It should be recognized how powerful, relative to "in-the-person" variables, undermanning can be. For example, an attempt to relate degree of responsible participation to a plausible personality variable (audience sensitivity) was not successful (Willems, 1965). Further, although the variable of intelligence is clearly related to degree of responsible participation *within* large or small schools, it is also true that students of slightly less than average

IQ in small schools participated responsibly in more settings than did students of high IQ in large schools (Barker & Gump, 1964, p. 88).

The ecological variable of population exchange has been applied to high school environments. Kelly (1969) found that students in a school with high population turnover showed more behavioral variation, more multiple-group membership, and more "exploratory activity" than students in less transient schools. Insights from this study prompted Kelly to attempt a much more ambitious investigation of the course of high school life for boys from contrasting high schools. Certain research vicissitudes diminished the contrasts between schools and the centrality of the idea of exploratory activity, but the research report (Kelly, 1978) provides important ideas. The extent to which the boys in two large typical suburban schools expressed either dislike or very minimal acceptance of their school life was sobering. For most boys, the high school environment was a bland experience, one in which it was difficult to engage and to exercise one's capacities.

Students at one suburban school (Wayne) did accept school and school staff better than at the other (Thurston). A map of how staff used settings at the schools showed that staff at Wayne were frequently present at many settings also used by students. For example, staff at Wayne more often entered students' "free time places" and athletic settings. It was likely that mutuality of setting use not only reflected a better staff–student relationship at Wayne, but sustained and perhaps even generated some of this better student-staff relationship as well. The work of Kelly and his associates has other valuable facets that the reader may wish to pursue.

THE "QUESTIONNAIRE ENVIRONMENTS"

Although some previous research employed specially devised questionnaires as a part of the measurement methodology, other investigations have established a standardized questionnaire as the main measurement device. The research pattern has involved selection of a setting or setting cluster representing a particular type of environment and administration of a standardized questionnaire to inhabitants.

The exclusive use of questionnaires raises more methodological problems than can be analyzed here; one issue demands attention, however. Most of these instruments, as developed, combine data from quite different realms, an amalgam that limits interpretation of results. For example, certain items will deal with basic qualities of program operation ("To what extent does all the class work on the same material?"), other items probe for judgments about peer relationships ("Are there cliques in this class?"), and still other questions invite projections of the respondent's motivations ("Do most pupils find the work interesting?"). When scores are reported, it is difficult to know (without study of item content) whether the variables represent material about program, for which the student respondent can be used as an *informant*, or material about personal, emotional reactions to the environment, for which the student is made a *subject*. From the perspective of this chapter, the questionnaire environments mix scores for setting operations with scores for highly subjective reactions to such operations. In analyzing findings, the safest interpretation is to treat the questionnaires as measures of the perceived environment, i.e., as inhabitant response to the ecological habitat. In spite of the neglect of the objective program environment, the standarized questionnaires have become salient in the environmental literature and several illustrative examples of the research will be considered.

The Learning Environment Inventory was developed by Wahlberg (1969) to measure the classroom "environment" of secondary students. Variables quantified include peer relationships, felt challenge of tasks, availability of materials, and student motivation toward class activity. That the inventory represents differences in persons (as well as in environments) was established when it was shown that respondents' personality and biographical measurements were well correlated to their questionnaire report of their environments (Wahlberg & Ahlgren, 1970). Such a result would dismay investigators who hoped to use students as objective informants but is quite appropriate for Wahlberg, who maintains that the *perceived* environment makes the important difference in behavior (Wahlberg, 1978). Evidence from several studies did show that a more positive picture on the Learning Environment Inventory was related to better academic achievement (Wahlberg, 1969; Anderson, 1970). As might be expected, different subject matters tended to produce different "environmental" profiles; e.g., biology classes were perceived as least difficult and quite diverse; physics classes as most cohesive and satisfying (Lawrenz, 1976).

A Classroom Environmental Scale for use at the secondary level has been published and early research findings reported (Trickett & Moos, 1973; Moos & Trickett, 1974). The scale deals with nine facets of classroom events. Students were found to be more satisfied with classes where there was high involvement, innovative teaching methods, and clarity of rules; teacher support emerged as a particularly important aspect of high school classrooms. Classrooms in which students felt that much was learned were described in somewhat similar terms except that competition (for grades and recognition) and good class-room order also typified the high-learning environments.

One more high school "environmental" scale, the Classroom Activities Questionnaire (Steele, Hause, & Kerins, 1971) has yielded interesting results. Scale items attempt to measure the extent to which teachers employ "thought questions" as well as the amount of class time devoted to various classroom activities (discussion, lecture, etc.). The possibility that students' responses might be used as reliable reports of what really happens in class (and not limited to the perceived environment) received some support on the issue of "teacher talk." A direct observation of amount of teacher talk was taken and compared to students' and to teachers' reports of how much teachers talked. A correct estimate (within 10%) was made by only 16% of the teachers but by 58% of the students!

Investigations of college environments by use of a standardized student questionnaire appear in the works of Astin (1968), Pace and Stern (1958) and Pace and Baird (1966). The size of the institution proved to be an important ecological factor; for example, the smaller the size, the more cohesive the social ties among peers (Astin, 1968; Clark, 1962). Standarized questionnaires have also been employed to measure the "environments" of living groups on campus. For example, Moos, Van Dort, Smail, and De Young (1975) administered their University Resident Scale to 100 different living groups and were able to show that certain measurement clusters typified various living groups. As examples, the all-male groups were high in *competition,* the all-female groups emphasized *traditional social values.* Marked social-climate differences obtained between fraternities and men's dormitories (Gerst & Moos, 1972). Data are accumulating to show that *where* young persons live at a university may have more to do with what they experience than *which* university they select.

Student reactions to aspects of dormitory life appeared in an early work by Van der Ryn and Silverstein (1967) and have been reviewed by Heilweil (1973). A major dormitory variable in many studies is size. The high-rise or "megadorm" is reported by Wilcox and Holahan (1976) to yield relatively less-positive scores in the University Residence Environmental Scale. Compared to students in smaller domitories, those in the megadorms reported less involvement in their residence, less emotional support, less control of events, and less order and neatness; they report more "independence"—a variable which could just as well be labeled "indifference to social conventions and constraints."

Questionnaire and behavioral data were used to compare reactions to dormitories of three density or size levels (Bickman, Teger, Gabrick,

McLaughlin, Berger, & Sunaday, 1973). Helpful behavior, as measured by the lost-letter technique, increased as dormitory populations decreased. Questionnaire data demonstrated that as size decreased, fellow residents were perceived as more friendly, more considerate, and more independent; with size decrease, even the buildings were perceived as more friendly, cheerful, and unrestrictive. The Bickman investigation involved several kinds of measurements and replications. The negative evidence against the megadorm would appear to deserve sober consideration prior to the construction of more such living quarters.

The preceding dormitory methods are clearly useful in measuring the human effects of certain environmental arrangements. However, just what happens in the various living arrangements to yield the results is not well advanced by such studies. The standardized questionnaires are roughly analogous to thermometers used to assess human health; both tell us about a resulting state rather than about generating conditions.

DIRECTIONS FOR RESEARCH

The phenomena involved in environment–child relationships may be divided into three realms: the environmental side presenting a succession of milieu-program units or settings; an interface between inputs arising in the settings and a child's action and reaction to these inputs; and a set of changes or developments in the child, related to the encounters along the interface. The first area represents the objective setting environment referred to in the introduction; the interface can be expressed as the objective individual environment. The subjective environment can involve the child's emotional reaction to interface events, although enduring changes in thought and attitude regarding the external world (the third realm) can also be referred to as the subjective environment.

A full understanding of the relation of children to their school environment will require coordination of data from all three realms. The preceding review of studies shows that this sort of coordination has sometimes been attempted; the Follow-Through studies presented by Stallings (1975) are examples. Most often investigators have chosen to deal with only part of the trio of events. For example, Kounin (1977) investigated qualities of settings in relation to the interface and to the children's immediate reaction; no attempt was made to discover lasting changes in the children. Other investigators skip aspects of the three realms and simply label the environmental side (large or small, structured or flexible) and then measure subjective reactions by question-naire; the operating nature of the environment is ignored, as are events along the interface. Since what actually happened (in terms of environmental operation and subject behavior) is unknown, findings for these studies are of uncertain value.

Selection of variables to employ in the three realms is a matter for some debate. In terms of a variable that seems to have marked and diverse effects, it would appear that *size* makes a reasonable choice. Size effects were noted for students in nursery schools and in university dormitories. Size changes result in changes in the milieu-program unit as well as in its inhabitants. Unfortunately for environmental research, no other variable has been identified as having the power of the size dimension.

Variables in the child-change realm would seem very important, and some of these have not been well measured. Present-day tests can reveal changes in certain curricular competencies but have not been reliably employed to learn about changes in the child's cooperativeness, self-confidence, or desire and capacity to care for others. We would presume that such change in the child would be desirable.

Variables most neglected are probably those on the environmental side, those prior to the interface variables. Our capacity to measure a program or to recommend research-based improvements is quite limited. When psychologists measure a child's behavior or his qualities, they are on familiar ground; when asked to measure environmental contexts, they have difficulty. It might be important for more investigators to turn from a child-centered approach to one in which the context for the child furnishes *dependent* variables and forces impinging on that context contribute the *independent* variables. If a science of school environments is to be developed, we need to know more than "what's best for the child." Many times we already know that. What is not known is why, for example, a subsetting like recitation, which is presumed to be a poor format, persists over generations of critics. Why do the innovations and improvements for the school (such as those involved in open education) fail to survive?

For those interested in child development, the schools' environments offer an especially important source of understanding. In schools there exist natural experiments (contrasts of conditions) that provide a necessary change from too much of child development research, which Bronfenbrenner has criticized as being based in strange situations with strange adults covering very short time periods (1977). Schools have been and will be offering contrasting programs which span relatively long time periods and in which significant changes in

children will often occur. If we can learn how to measure the changes—
and, just as important, how to measure the programs—we may comprehend the school environment and its effects much better than we
do now.

REFERENCES

Adams, R., & Biddle, B. J. *Realities of teaching: Explorations with video tape.* New York:
    Holt, Rinehart and Winston, 1970.
Anderson, G. J. Effects of social climate on individual learning. *American Educational
    Research Journal,* 1970, *1,* 135–151.
Astin, A. *The college environment.* Washington, D.C.: American Council on Education,
    1968.
Baird, L. L. Big school, small school: A critical examination of the hypothesis. *Journal of
    Educational Psychology,* 1969, *60,* 253–360.
Barker, R. G. *Ecological psychology: Concepts and methods for studying the environment of
    human behavior.* Stanford, Calif.: Stanford University Press, 1968.
Barker, R. G., & Gump, P. V. *Big school, small school.* Stanford, Calif.: Stanford University
    Press, 1964.
Barker, R. G., & Wright, H. F. *Midwest and its children.* New York: Harper & Row, 1955.
    (Reprinted by Hampden, Conn.: Archon Books, 1971).
Bennett, N. *Teaching styles and pupil progress: Do open classrooms really work?* Cambridge,
    Mass.: Harvard University Press, 1976.
Berk, L. E. Effects of variations in the nursery school setting on environmental constraints
    and children's modes of adaption. *Child Development,* 1971, *42,* 839–869.
Berk, L. E., & Berson, M. P. The school bus as a developmental experience for young
    children. *Illinois School Research,* 1975, *11* (3), 1–14.
Berk, L. E., & Lewis, N. G. Sex role and social behavior in four school environments.
    Elementary School Journal, 1977, *77* (3), 205–217.
Bickman, L., Teger, A., Gabrick, T., McLaughlin, C., Berger, M., & Sunaday, E. Dor-
    mitory density and helping behavior. *Environment and Behavior,* 1973, *5,* 465–490.
Bronfenbrenner, U. Toward an experimental ecology of human development. *American
    Psychologist,* 1977, *32,* 513–531.
Brunswik, E. Scope and aspects of the cognition problem. *In* J. Gruber, R. Jessor, & K.
    Hammond (Eds.), *Cognition: The Colorado symposium.* Cambridge: Harvard Univer-
    sity Press, 1957.
Charlesworth, R., & Hartup, W. W. Positive social reinforcement in the nursery school
    peer group. *Child Development,* 1967, *38,* 993–1002.
Clark, B. R. *Educating the expert society.* San Francisco, Calif.: Chandler, 1962.
Conant, E. *Teacher and paraprofessional work productivity.* Lefington, Mass.: D C Heath,
    1973.
Davenport, G. G. The effects of lessons' signal systems upon the duration and spread of
    children's deviance. Unpublished doctoral dissertation. Wayne State University,
    1976.
Dawe, H. C. The influence of size of kindergarten group upon performance. *Child
    Development,* 1934, *5,* 295–303.
De Vries, D. L., & Edwards, K. J. Learning games and student teams: The effects on
    classroom process. *American Educational Research Journal,* 1973, *10,* 307–318.

De Vries, D. L., & Edwards, K. J. Student teams and learning games: Their effects on cross-race and cross-sex interaction. *Journal of Educational Psychology*, 1974, *66*, 741–749.

Doke, L., & Risley, T. The organization of day-care environments: Required vs. optional activities. *Journal of Applied Behavior Analysis*, 1972, *5*, 405–420.

Doyle, P. H. The efficacy of the ecological model: A study of the impact of activity settings on the social behavior of preschool children. Doctoral dissertation, Wayne State University, 1975.

Doyle, W. P. Learning the classroom environment: An ecological analysis of induction into teaching. American Educational Research Association Meeting, New York, 1977. *Journal of Teacher Education*, in press.

Dunkin, M. J., & Biddle, B. J. *The study of teaching*. New York: Holt, Rinehart & Winston, 1974.

Dyck, A. J. The social contacts of some Midwest children with their parents and teachers. In R. Barker (Ed.), *The stream of behavior*, New York: Appleton-Century-Crofts, 1963.

Erickson, F. Some approaches to inquiry in school-community enthography. *Anthropology & Education*, 1977, *8*, 5869.

Fagot, B. I. Variations in density: Effect on task and social behaviors of pre-school children. *Developmental Psychology*, 1977, *13*, 166–167.

Farnsworth, P. R. Seat preference in the classroom. *Journal of Social Psychology*, 1933, *4*, 373–376.

Fisher, C. Educational environments in elementary schools differing in architecture and program openness. American Educational Research Association Annual Meeting, Chicago, Ill., 1974. Available from author: Far West Laboratory for Educational Research and Development, 1855 Folsom Street, San Francisco, Calif. 94103.

Gage, N. The psychology of teaching methods. *Seventy-Fifth Yearbook of the National Society for the Study of Education*. Chicago: University of Chicago Press, 1976.

Gerst, M. S., & Moos, R. H. The social ecology of university student residences. *Journal of Educational Psychology*, 1972, *63*, 513–525.

Goetz, J. P. Behavioral configurations in the classroom: A case study. *Journal of Research and Development in Education*, 1976, *9*, 36–49.

Gump, P. V. Intra-setting analysis: The third grade as a special but instructive case. In E. Willems & H. Raush (Eds.), *Naturalistic viewpoints in psychological research*. New York: Holt, Rinehart & Winston, 1969.

Gump, P. V. Operating environments in open and traditional schools. *School Review*, 1974, *84* (4), 575–593.

Gump, P. V. The classroom behavior setting: Its nature and relation to student behavior. U.S. Office of Education Cooperative Research Branch, Project NO. 5-0334. Final report; 1967. Mimeo.

Gump, P. V. Ecological psychology and children. In E. Hetherington (Ed.), *Review of child development research*. Chicago: University of Chicago Press, 1975.

Gump, P. V., & Ross, R. The fit of milieu and programme in school environments. In H. McGurk (Ed.), *Ecological factors in human development*. New York: North-Holland Pub. Co., 1977a.

Gump, P. V., & Ross, R. What's happened in schools of open design? Mimeo. Department of Psychology, University of Kansas, 1977b.

Hall, R. V., Delquardi, J., & Harris, J. Opportunity to respond: A new focus in the field of applied behavior analysis. Mimeo. Human Development and Family Life, University of Kansas, 1977.

Harper, L. V., & Sanders, K. M. Pre-school children's use of space: Sex differences in outdoor play. *Developmental Psychology*, 1975, *11* (1), 119.

Hartley, R. F., Frank, L., & Goldenson, R. M. *Understanding children's play*. New York: Columbia University Press, 1952.

Heilweil, M. The influence of dormitory architecture on resident behavior. *Environment and Behavior*, 1973, *5*, 377–412.

Herndon, J. *The way it spozed to be*. New York: Bontain, 1968.

Hoetker, J., & Ahlbrand, W. P. The persistence of the recitation. *American Educational Research Journal*, 1969, *6*, 145–167.

Horowitz, F. D., & Paden, L. Y. The effectiveness of environmental intervention programs. *In* B. M. Caldwell & H. N. Ricciute (Eds.), *Review of child development research*. Vol. 3. Chicago: University of Chicago Press, 1973.

Houseman, J. An ecological study of interpersonal conflict among preschool children. Unpublished dissertation, Wayne State University, 1972.

Hughes, M. M., & Associates. Assessment of the quality of teaching in elementary schools. Unpublished report, Cooperative Research Project No. 353, Office of Education, U.S. Department of Health, Education and Welfare, 1959.

Hutt, C., & Vaizey, M. Differential effects of group density on social behavior. *Nature*, 1966, *209*, 1371–1372.

Inbar, M. Individual and group effects of enjoyment and learning in a game simulating a community disaster. *In* S. Boocock & E. Schild (Eds.), *Simulation games in learning*. Beverly Hills, Calif.: Sage Publication, 1968.

Jackson, P. *Life in classrooms*. New York: Holt, Rinehart & Winston, 1968.

Jersild, A. T., & Markey, F. V. Conflicts between pre-school children. *Child Development Monographs*, 1935, No. 21.

Johnson, D. W., & Johnson, R. T. *Learning together and alone*. Englewood Clifs, N.J.: Prentice-Hall, 1975.

Johnson, M. W. The effect on behavior of variations in amount of play equipment. *Child Development*, 1935, *6*, 56–68.

Kelly, J. G. Naturalistic observations in contrasting social environments. *In* E. Willems & H. Raush (Eds.), *Naturalistic viewpoints in psychological research*. New York: Holt, Rinehart & Winston, 1969.

Kelly, J. G. *The high school: An exploration of students and social contexts in two Midwestern communities*. Hillsdale, N.J.: Lawrence Erlbaum Associates, 1978.

Koneya, M. Location and interaction in row-and-column seating arrangements. *Environment and Behavior*, 1976, *8* (2), 265–282.

Kounin, J. S. *Discipline and group management in the classrooms*. New York: Holt, Rinehart & Winston, 1970.

Kounin, J. S. Some ecological dimensions of school settings. American Educational Research Association Meeting, New York, 1977.

Kounin, J. S., & Doyle, P. Degree of continuity of a lessons signal system and the task involvement of children. *Journal of Educational Psychology*, 1975, *67*, 159–164.

Kounin, J. S., & Gump, P. V. Signal systems in lesson settings and the task related behavior of preschool children. *Journal of Educational Psychology*, 1974, *66*, 554–562.

Kozol, J. *Death at an early age*. Boston: Houghton Mifflin, 1967.

Krantz, P. J., & Risley, T. R. Behavioral ecology in the classroom. *In* K. D. O'Leary & S. G. O'Leary (Eds.), *Classroom management: The successful use of behavior modification*, 2nd Edition. New York: Pergamon Press, 1977.

Lawrenz, F. Student perception of the classroom learning environment in biology, chemistry, and physics courses. *Journal of Research in Science Teaching*, 1976, *13*, 315–323.

LeLaurin, K., & Risley, T. R. The organization of day-care environments: "Zone" versus "man-to-man" staff assignments. *Journal of Applied Behavior Analysis*, 1972, *5*, 225–232.

Loo, C. M. The effects of spatial density on the social behavior of children. *Journal of Applied Social Psychology*, 1972, *2*, 372–381.

McGrew, W. C. Interpersonal spacing of preschool children. *In* J. S. Bruner & K. J. Connolly (Eds.), *The development of competence in early childhood*. London: Academic Press, 1972.

McPherson, G. *Small town teacher*. Cambridge: Harvard University Press, 1972.

Metropolitan Toronto School Board. *Study of educational facilities*. (Annotated bibliography of research on open schools). Toronto: Metropolitan Toronto School Board, 1974.

Miller, L. B., & Dyer, J. L. Four preschool programs: Their dimensions and effects. *Monographs of the Society for Research in Child Development*, 1975, No. 162.

Montes, F., & Risley, T. R. Evaluating traditional day care practices: An empirical approach. *Child Care Quarterly*, 1975, *4*, 208–215.

Moos, R. H., & Trickett, E. J. *Classroom environmental scale manual*. Palo Alto, Calif.: Consulting Psychologists Press, 1974.

Moos, R. H., Van Dort, B., Smail, P., & De Young, A. J. A typology of university student living groups. *Journal of Educational Psychology*, 1975, *67*, 359–367.

Myers, D. Why open education died. *Journal of Research and Development in Education*, 1974, *8* (1), 60–71.

O'Conner, M. The nursery school environment. *Developmental Psychology*, 1975, *11*, 556–561.

Pace, C. R., & Baird, L. Attainment patterns in the environmental press of college subcultures. *In* T. Newcomb & E. Wilson (Eds.), *College peer groups*. Chicago: Aldine, 1966.

Pace, C. R., & Stern, G. G. An approach to the measurement of psychological characteristics of college environments. *Journal of Educational Psychology*, 1958, *49*, 269–277.

Parsons, T. The school class as a social system: Some of its functions in society. *Harvard Educational Review*, 1955, *29*, 297–318.

Prescott, E. *Who thrives in group daycare?* Pacific Oaks College, 714 W. California Blvd., Pasadena, Calif. 91105. 1973. Mimeo.

Quilitch, H. R., Christophersen, E. R., & Risley, T. R. The evaluation of children's play materials. *Journal of Applied Behavior Analysis*, 1977, *10*, 501–502.

Raven, J. C. *Raven's coloured progressive matrices*. New York: Psychological Corporation, 1962.

Risley, T. R. The ecology of applied behavior analysis. *In* A. Rogers-Warren & S. Warren (Eds.), *Ecological perspectives in behavioral analyses*. Baltimore: University Park Press, 1977.

Rist, R. C. *The urban school: A factory for failure*. Cambridge, Mass.: MIT Press, 1973.

Rogers-Warren, A. Planned change: Ecobehaviorally based interventions. *In* A. Rogers-Warren & S. Warren (Eds.), *Ecological perspectives in behavioral analyses*. Baltimore: University Park Press, 1977.

Rohe, W. M., & Nuffer, E. L. The effects of density and partitioning on children's behavior. Presented at the 85th meeting of A.P.A. San Francisco, Calif., 1977. Mimeo.

Rosenthal, B. An ecological study of free play in a nursery school. Unpublished doctoral dissertation, Wayne State Unversity, 1973.

Sanders, K. M., & Harper, L. V. Free play fantasy behavior in pre-school children:

Relations among gender, age, season, and location. *Child Development*, 1976, *47*, 1182-1185.

Schoggen, P. Environmental forces in the everyday lives of children. *In* R. Barker (Ed.), *The stream of behavior.* New York: Appleton-Century-Crofts, 1963.

Schoggen, P. An ecological study of children with physical disabilities in school and at home. *In* R. Weinberg & F. Wood (Eds.), *Observation of pupils and teachers in mainstream and special education settings: Alternative strategies.* Minneapolis: Leadership Training Institute, University of Minnesota, 1975.

Seidner, C. J. Teaching with simulations and games. *In* N. Gage (Ed.), *The psychology of teaching methods. Seventy-Fifth Yearbook of the National Society for the Study of Education.* Chicago: University of Chicago Press, 1976.

Sherman, L. An ecological study of glee in small groups of preschool children. *Child Development*, 1975, *46*, 53-61.

Shure, M. B. Psychological ecology of a nursery school. *Child Development*, 1963, *34*, 979-992.

Smith, L. M., & Goeffrey, W. *The complexities of an urban classroom.* New York: Holt, Rinehart & Winston, 1968.

Smith, P. Aspects of the playgroup environment. *In* D. Canter & T. Lee (Eds.), *Proceedings of the conference: Psychology and the built environment.* London: Architectural Press, 1974.

Sommer, R. Classroom ecology. *Journal of Applied Behavioral Science*, 1967, *3*, 489-503.

Stallings, J. Implementation and child effects of teaching practices in Follow-Through classrooms. *Monographs of the Society for Research in Child Development*, 1975, *40* (7-8).

Steele, J. M., House, E. R., & Kerins, T. An instrument for assessing instructional climate through low inference student judgments. *American Educational Research Journal*, 1971, *8*, 447-466.

Stevens, R. *The question as a measure of efficiency in instruction: A critical study of classroom practice.* New York: Teachers College, Columbia University, Contributions to Education, 1912, No. 48.

Swift, J. W. Effects of early group experience: The nursery school and day nursery. *In* M. Hoffman & I. Hoffman (Eds.), *Child development research.* Vol. 1. New York: Russell Sage Foundation, 1964.

Traub, R. E., Weiss, J., Fisher, C. W., & Musella, D. Closure on openness: Describing and quantifying open education. *Interchange*, 1974, *3*, 69-84.

Trickett, E. J., & Moos, R. H. Social environment of junior high and high school classrooms. *Journal of Educational Psychology*, 1973, *65*, 93-102.

Van der Ryn, S., & Silverstein, M. *Dorms at Berkeley*, Berkeley, Calif.: Center for Planning and Development Research, 1967.

Wahlberg, H. J. Social environment as a mediator of classroom learning. *Journal of Educational Psychology*, 1969, *6*, 529-542.

Wahlberg, H. J. Psychology of learning environments: Behavioral, structural, or perceptual? *In* L. S. Shulman (Ed.), *Review of research in education.* Vol. 4. Itasca, Ill.: F. E. Peacock, in press.

Wahlberg, H. J., & Ahlgren, A. Predictors of the social environment of learning. *American Educational Research Jounral*, 1970, *7*, 153-167.

Wheeler, R. C., & Ryan, F. L. Effects of cooperative and competitive classroom environments on the attitudes and achievement of elementary school students engaged in social studies inquiry activities. *Journal of Educational Psychology*, 1973, *65*, 402-407.

Wicker, A. W. Undermanning, performances, and students' subjective experiences in behavior settings of large and small high schools. *Journal of Personality and Social Psychology*, 1968, *10*, 255–261.

Wilcox, B. L., & Holahan, C. Social ecology of the megadorm in university student housing. *Journal of Educational Psychology*, 1976, *68* (4), 453–458.

Willems, E. P. Participation in behavior setting in relation to three variables: Size of behavior settings, marginality of persons, and sensitivity to audiences. Unpublished doctoral dissertation, University of Kansas, 1965.

Willems, E. P. Sense of obligation to high school activities as related to school size and marginality of student. *Child Development*, 1967, *38*, 1247–1260.

Wolcott, H. *The man in the principal's office: An ethnography*. New York: Holt, Rinehart & Winston, 1973.

Wolcott, H. (Ed.) Ethnography of schooling. *Human Organization*, 1975, *34* (2), 111–127.

Wright, H. F., Barker, R. G., Null, J., & Schoggen, P. Toward a psychological ecology of the classroom. *In* A. Coladarci (Ed.), *Readings in educational psychology*. New York: Holt, Rinehart & Winston, 1955.

5

Childhood and Privacy

MAXINE WOLFE

INTRODUCTION

In 1930, Plant cited lack of privacy as a factor contributing to children's emotional disorders. Since then, the topic of privacy and its relation to child development and experience has all but disappeared from available literature. Child psychology books contain few if any references to "privacy" but are replete with references to social development, social interactions, and children's behaviors in groups. Yet it is untrue that the child development literature had nothing to tell us about "privacy." Rather, it is the word "privacy" that rarely if ever appears. The present chapter attempts to answer the questions: "What role might privacy experiences play in child development?" "What is the nature of privacy experiences during childhood?" "How do childhood experiences contribute to or affect children's patterns and concepts of privacy?" To answer these questions, I focus, first, on the general issue of conceptualizing the nature of human privacy. This conceptualization will provide a perspective for understanding age and age-related experiences as well as the role of cultural and sociophysical environmental factors. Research about privacy for children will be described and its contribution to our understanding of the role of privacy in child development will be explored. Finally, I attempt to suggest new and unexplored areas of research which might fruitfully extend our present knowledge.

MAXINE WOLFE · Environmental Psychology Program, City University of New York Graduate School, New York, New York.

A PERSPECTIVE FOR UNDERSTANDING PRIVACY

Background of this Approach to the Problem of Human Privacy

The present work grew out of interests in two seemingly separate aspects of the problem of human privacy: My interest was in understanding human behavior and the physical environment. Privacy was a longstanding issue in environmental design and evaluation (Chermayeff & Alexander, 1963; Kira, 1966). Empirical work had produced a body of data relating to "privacy" (Bracy, 1964; Kuper, 1970; Lawton & Bader, 1970; Marshall, 1972; Proshansky, Ittelson, & Rivlin, 1972), but these data had limited applicability because of the lack of a conceptual framework for understanding privacy as an environmental concept. The word *privacy* appeared consistently, but with many meanings (see Altman, 1975). At the same time, it was treated as a unidimensional, all-encompassing construct on the assumption that it had a clear, singular meaning; environmental researchers uniformly asked questions about "privacy" (Do you have enough "privacy" here?), but neither asked nor told even the respondents what privacy meant. *Answers to questions concerning the sources of the desire for privacy, alternative means of achieving privacy—physically, psychologically, behaviorally—remained speculative and unexamined.*

The direct involvement of my colleague, Robert Laufer, in a political–legal question turned my full attention back to the question of human privacy. To be more specific, the interest of the Constitutional Litigation Clinic of Rutgers University in the issue of invasion of privacy and its consequences for political behavior led to a systematic review of literature on the effects of surveillance or invasion of privacy on human behavior (Levin *et al.*, 1971). What was found was fragmentary and very often only tangentially relevant. In fact, those engaged in the project discovered that *it was impossible to discuss the consequences of invasion of privacy in the absence of any systematic knowledge of the nature of privacy.*

Our seemingly separate interests were brought together in 1971 at the Privacy Committee meetings of the Society for the Psychological Study of Social Issues. Sharing our analysis of the state-of-the-art in our respective fields, Bob Laufer, Harold Proshansky, and I formed an interdisciplinary seminar focused on conceptualizing the problem of human privacy. The interdisciplinary focus was intentional and members included sociologists, anthropologists, psychologists, architects, and planners. We saw *the problem of privacy as cutting across traditional disciplinary boundaries*. This seminar led to a paper (Laufer, Proshansky,

& Wolfe, 1973) in which we proposed that rather than attempting to seek a global definition of privacy, the problem of privacy could be viewed along a series of dimensions that might aid the development of theory, research, and application. The seminar generated our first research project, which focused on the development of concepts and patterns of privacy in childhood and adolescence and on the role of sociophysical factors in affecting these concepts and patterns.[1]

The developmental-environmental perspective did not emerge simply out of a desire to understand more about children and their development nor from a belief that the sociophysical environment was the *sole* determinant of concepts and patterns of privacy. Rather, it evolved out of an attempt to clarify the basis for the distinctions between the wide range of meanings that seemed to be associated with the word *privacy*; to provide a coherent framework for diverse empirical data in a variety of fields by specifying how the sources of privacy in human relationships were given form and feeling in everyday life; and to attempt to understand privacy as a future as well as contemporary social issue. Over the last four years, the seminar has continued, a range of research has evolved out of it (Wolfe & Laufer, 1975; Wolfe, Schearer & Laufer, 1976; Wolfe & Golan, 1976; Golan & Justa, 1976; Laufer & Wolfe, 1976), and we have used these data as well as data from others' research to rework our initial conceptualization into a multidimensional developmental theory of privacy (Laufer & Wolfe, 1977).

PRIVACY AS A CONCEPT AND A SOCIAL ISSUE: A MULTIDIMENSIONAL DEVELOPMENTAL THEORY

Our theory describes the elements that must be taken into account to understand a given individual's perception and experience of privacy and invasions of privacy. We have combined these elements into *environmental, interpersonal,* and *self-ego* dimensions of privacy (Laufer & Wolfe, 1977): The individual concretely experiences privacy on a daily basis in the interpersonal dimensions of a given situation. Privacy, in whatever form, presupposes the existence of others (including the self-as-other, objects, and physical stimuli) and the possibility of a relationship with them. The acting out of this relationship has two

[1] This research was supported by a research award from the Faculty Research Award Program of the City University, by the Society for the Psychological Study of Social Issues, and by the Center for Human Environments of the City University of New York.

elements:

- *Interaction management:* privacy as interaction management is actually a form of noninteraction or a choice of the parameters of interaction with specified others including the nonhuman environment.
- *Information management:* privacy as information management relates to the individual's desire to manage past and present information about him/herself and attempts to gauge his/her behavior in terms of future and present consequences (calculus of behavior).

Yet in order to understand when, why, and how a person desires to manage information or interaction *and* the meaning of the actual experience for the individual, we must be able to understand the self-ego and environmental dimensions of privacy.

In our society development is conceived of as a process focusing on individuation—autonomy and, by implication, personal dignity. This is what we call the *self-ego dimension* of privacy. Thus, the relationship between autonomy, privacy, and privacy behavior

> can be described in terms of individuals' freedom to choose their own movement across the boundary which distinguishes them as being and functioning alone versus being a separate individual interacting and functioning with others.

Yet privacy is related to the self in two other ways. Privacy, in its various forms can be seen

> as a way of both enhancing the self and protecting the self . . . and . . . because of the high value our culture places on privacy as an expression of personal dignity, options for privacy are connected with self-esteem. (Laufer & Wolfe, 1977, p. 27)

However, privacy options and one's perception of privacy options are clearly related to the environmental dimension of privacy. The environmental dimension is composed of a series of elements that act as boundaries of meaning and experience:

- *Cultural element*: the mores of a community limit the perceived options available to any person or group . . . and play a decisive role in the way an individual defines privacy situations,
- *Sociophysical element*: privacy can be understood in terms of the ecological and physical properties of the environmental settings that circumscribe human behavior, including available technology, numbers of people and their relation to one another, types of tasks required, and specific ritualistic activities.

- *Life-cycle element*: the cultural and sociophysical limits on possible privacy experiences will apply differentially to individuals at various stages of the life cycle. The individual's concepts and patterns of privacy are not static throughout life.

Applying this dimensional analysis to understanding a given individual's perceptions and experience of privacy and invasion of privacy in a particular situation we begin by asking: What does "privacy" mean, to whom, in what situation? But, we are not asking *only* a phenomenological question. As Westin (1967), we are concerned with the role of social, historical, political, and economic factors in privacy and privacy invasion. "From our perspective, *the individual and normative aspects of privacy are interdependent.* Time provides the dynamic basis for the interdependence. The individual experiences time as growing or aging while the sociocultural system experiences time as historical and technological development" (Laufer & Wolfe, 1977).

The interdependence of the phenomenological and normative aspects of privacy means that *concepts and patterns of privacy and privacy invasion are strongly tied to or defined by the experiences of given situations* because understanding of and behavior related to privacy evolve out of concrete transactions with the world we live in, act in, and have to comprehend. The types and limits of lived experience will be a function of the historical tradition of the society, the available technology, the ecological setting, the stage of the individual's life cycle, the individual's sense of self, and the nature of interpersonal relationships. Thus, our emphasis on the developmental aspects of privacy grew out of a perspective which assumes that desire for a given form or quantity of privacy (Altman, 1975) is not context-free and that the *individual's understanding and experience of privacy and invasion of privacy will be related to his/her growth and life, over time, within a particular social-historical-political-economic-physical environment.*

Using the dimensions we attempt to understand how the types of lived experience and the limits of lived experience embodied in concrete situations and events affect individuals' understanding of what privacy is, their conscious labeling of specific situations as privacy-related, their ability to predict whether or not given situations or events will be experienced as invasionary, their subsequent behavior based on that understanding, and new understanding based on the behavior. By comparing individuals with different experiences, we attempt to understand why certain individuals may perceive specific situations as private or invasionary when others do not; why certain individuals may not be consciously aware of and, therefore, do not demand or seek certain rights or experiences, yet may still be affected by the absence of certain privacy-related experiences.

In our theory *control/choice* (Westin, 1967; Proshansky, Ittleson, & Rivlin, 1970; Altman, 1975) *is treated as a mediating variable in the privacy system. "Control/choice" is not synonymous with "privacy."* Control/ choice has been part of every conceptualization of privacy (Westin, 1967; Proshansky *et al.*, 1970; Altman, 1975). It is also central to many issues in Western society and is emphasized in a highly individualistic society such as ours. We distinguish between control/choice as a generic concept and control/choice in relation to privacy. Thus, a situation is not necessarily privacy-related simply because an individual perceives, experiences, or exercises control/choice. Conversely, the individual may not experience, perceive, or exercise control/choice, yet other elements may create a privacy situation. Specific situational dimensions and their elements define control/choice as a privacy-related concept.

Finally, we assume that *the quantity and form of possible privacy experiences within a given society and for given individuals within a society (especially during childhood, but continuing throughout the life cycle) have implications for the quality of life.* The lack of specific forms and/or amounts of privacy experience may result in impaired physical or mental well-being (D'Atri, 1975; Plant, 1930) or in limited political or social involvement (McCarthy & Saegert, 1978). We believe that in order to understand these possible outcomes, we must first understand what privacy means to different people and the ways in which concrete daily life experiences can affect these meanings. We have approached this issue through the environmental dimension of the privacy system.

THE ENVIRONMENTAL DIMENSION OF PRIVACY

The elements of the environmental dimension—cultural, life cycle, and sociophysical—act as boundaries of meaning and experience by delimiting (1) the quantity and form of privacy granted and (2) the quantity and form of privacy that might consciously be desired and/or exercised. These environmental elements neither exist nor have their impact in isolation from one another. However, to underscore their contribution to the individual's understanding and experience of privacy, I will discuss each as separately as possible while at the same time emphasizing their interrelationships. I begin by looking at the life-cycle element of privacy indicating how and why age-related experiences in general, and childhood experiences in particular, are relevant to the individual's understanding and experience of privacy.

PRIVACY AND THE LIFE CYCLE

The concept of the life cycle is critical to an understanding of privacy. As an individual progresses through the life cycle, from birth to death, (1) the society imposes different demands and requirements; (2) the individual assumes different roles; (3) the individual's activities and environments change; (4) the society is changing; and (5) the individual's experiences, needs, activities, desires, and feelings change. Over the life cycle individuals will experience a range of concrete situations that have different privacy-related possibilities and actualities. Thus, their concepts and patterns of privacy should also change.

The phrase "life-cycle stage" does not simply refer to "age" as a singular and static variable that somehow *naturally* defines the individual's range of abilities of experiences. Rather, it is a holistic concept referring to the relationship of each stage to the totality of the life cycle, the types and qualities of experiences possible within it, and the values attached to it. The totality of the life cycle, as well as its individual stages, are neither static nor invariant. For example, while a human female cannot bear children until she is physiologically capable, the age at which child-bearing begins, the length of this stage of the life cycle, the quality of the experience, and its value vary across societies, within a particular society at different points in history, and even within a particular society for different individuals or groups of individuals. From birth, a female child within a particular society at a particular time will be exposed to certain experiences and treated in certain ways related to that eventual stage and all of its implications.

In applying the life-cycle concept to an individual's understanding and experience of privacy, we have to analyze: (1) how that particular stage is viewed at a particular time within a particular society and how the range of privacy experiences individuals can *potentially* have reflect as well as support that view; (2) the *actual* privacy experiences of individuals compared to *potential* privacy experiences; (3) the potential as well as actual privacy experiences in prior life-cycle stages to determine their influence on present behavior and concepts; and (4) the actual and potential privacy experiences this individual may confront in the future.

Privacy and Childhood

The early years of life, within any society, form a crucial life-cycle stage. Individuals can and do change and grow over the life cycle, yet it is during the early years that our most basic understandings of the world are formed. In this sense, all of child development is socialization (Ingelby, 1974). Regardless of genetic differences, structured development of intellectual functioning, and so on, the kinds of lived experiences children have and the evaluation of these experiences by the adult world tell children what they are capable of doing and being in the present as well as the future.

In the next section I want to show how childhood experiences within our society act to socialize children to understand privacy in specific ways. To do this, I will provide a description of what is considered to be "appropriate or normal" childhood experience and the ways in which privacy seems relevant to this course of events. However, the reader must keep in mind that these ideas largely reflect the predominant mores and myths of our culture at this time. The role of the child, the definition of childhood and its relation to the rest of the life cycle, and therefore the nature of childhood experience has changed from medieval to modern times and is continuing to change. In medieval times, from about *age 7*,

> children were mixed with adults . . . they immediately went straight into
> the community of men, sharing in the work and play of their companions,
> old and young alike . . . the movement of collective life [left] nobody any
> time for solitude and privacy . . . in these crowded, collective existences
> there was no room for a private sector. (Ariès, 1962)

By the eighteenth century the modern nuclear family, living in its own home, was a predominant way of life. Privacy became a way for the middle-class family to withdraw and protect itself and its children from viewing and being influenced by lower-class existence. Family and school removed the child from adult society, providing a life experience that supposedly reflected the desire for individualism. Yet Ariès believes that the modern nuclear family and education outside of the home actually *limit* individualism and support conformity by limiting the experiences of children to given groups of people. Thus, we should be cautious about accepting modern notions of childhood as absolutes, and we should be aware of the possible contradictions that may exist between the values our experiences are supposed to reflect and the reality of these experiences and their outcomes. On the latter point, Philip Slater (1970) argues that in contemporary middle-class homes we communicate conflicting values regarding privacy. We stress cooperation, community, and the sharing of experiences. Indeed, according to Slater, in the middle-class home the child has little psychological privacy. Sensitivity to the psychological needs and states of children motivates middle-class parents to know what children are thinking and feeling in addition to what they are doing. On the other hand, we stress competition and privacy and support the view by providing children with their own rooms and a status model consisting of the private office and the private home.

Slater's analysis also emphasizes another caveat for the reader. This prevailing description of normal childhood experience reflects an underlying assumption of a given life experience—middle-class, white society. In reality the lived experiences for children of the same ages but within different groups in our society are quite varying (Slater, 1970; Lewis, 1970; Coles, 1970; Silverstein & Krate, 1975). Therefore, the general description I provide is not intended to be construed either as "what is" or as what I believe "should be" for all children. It does, however, reflect what is perceived to be the "normal" life experience of children in our society. Children whose life experiences are different should form a different understanding of privacy. In later sections, we will use this description as a basis against which to compare the varying conditions that do exist, exploring the role of cultural and sociophysical elements and their relationships at different ages to concepts and patterns of privacy, and attempting to show how varying experiences impact on the lives of specific children, both positively and negatively.

Privacy and Childhood in the United States

The essence of most views of child development in our society is that the child who is to develop into a healthy adult must have experiences that allow for the growth of autonomy, the developent of a sense of competence and mastery, and supportive relationships with others. All children are in a subordinate power position in relation to adults and do not have much control over their own lives. The general view is that children gain control through the provision of appropriate incremental experiences of physical and psychological separateness (Bowlby, 1969). The goal, within the limits of conformity required by the society, is to create an independent being (a self), but a being who is nevertheless "social."

Developmental theorists view the development of the self as a process of the separation of the person from the social and physical environment (Piaget & Inhelder, 1969; Werner, 1948; Freud, 1962;

Searles, 1960). Indeed, in order for the child to have a general understanding of the world and meaningful social relationships, it has been
postulated that the child must first develop a sense of him/herself that
is separate from others. This process of psychological separation, i.e.,
the formation of the self, begins with birth and at different stages of
development will be characterized by certain conflicts, accomplishments, and types of behaviors and supported or inhibited by the
provision or absence of certain types of life experiences.

Thus, while the word *privacy* does not appear in this literature,
these views suggest that the separation and individuation of the self
necessarily require that the child experience aloneness in one form or
another (i.e., psychological or physical). Schwartz (1968) suggests that
privacy is expressed differently at each developmental stage and that
the manner of its expression varies in terms of the ego's relation to
those from whom privacy is sought and the manner in which withdrawal *can* be accomplished. Simmel (1971) views the development of
the self through the life cycle as an alteration of conflict and consensus
with society; the individual raises and lowers boundaries—perhaps
both physically and socially—between him/herself and others, i.e.,
alternately seeking privacy and interaction. In the formulation presented earlier, this is part of what I have called the self-ego dimension
of privacy experience.

Yet at early ages either physical or psychological separation can be
a negative experience. It is generally imposed by others and the child
may have fears or may be ambivalent about his/her ability to function
alone (Bowlby, 1969). In this sense the developmental task of learning
to function independently adds a critical aspect to the relationship
between the self and privacy experience—volition: the *desire* to choose
aloneness (physically or psychologically) when capable of functioning
in aloneness.

Yet given the child's role as a nonperson within the society, desire
and capability are not enough to ensure the exercise of choice vis-à-vis
privacy. We must, therefore, look at those aspects of the child's daily
experiences which create an awareness of situations as actually or
potentially involving privacy and which place limits on the child's
options for managing aspects of privacy relevant to a situation. To do
this, I will take the reader on a brief trip through childhood and
adolescence, attempting to point out the privacy-related aspects of
children's lives. This excursion will necessarily be limited and is not
intended to touch upon all aspects of children's lived experiences.
Rather, by using major developmental tasks, I hope to give the reader
some sense of the possible relationship between privacy and the life-

cycle stages of childhood and adolescence. It is hoped that the reader can expand this view into other aspects of the developmental process.

The ability to exercise choice is experienced in any privacy situation as the ability to choose how, under what circumstances, and to what degree the individual is to relate to others (animate or inanimate) or separate him/herself from others (physically or psychologically). The ability to perceive options and to exercise choice among options develops out of a complex relationship between the evolving sense of self in interaction with the environment (in its broadest sense) through experience in specified situations.

At early ages children have little or no choice of privacy situations. Interaction management is severely limited because children's time and space are controlled by adults. The extent of this control varies with caretaker's perceptions of children's ability to handle freedom from surveillance in a particular setting, i.e., with the perception of the extent to which the child will have internalized behavioral norms and will act appropriately without surveillance, given the nature of the sociophysical environment.

As children become capable of being intruders, by being able to walk and talk, adults begin to set limits, which are the beginnings of the child's understanding of transgression (Erikson, 1963; Simmel, 1971). At the same time, children have little control over other's or their own access to anything except, in limited ways, their own object possessions. Adults and older children freely enter children's rooms, inspect their belongings, and interrupt their activities. The child's earliest experiences with the management of interaction is as it is exercised by others in authority: The child is either an intruder (intentional or unintentional) or one intruded upon.

In order to choose *consciously* to manage interaction or information between self and other, the individual must have an awareness of a situation as actually or potentially involving privacy. This is not always possible because over the life cycle, and especially at young ages, we are constantly exposed to unanticipated situations. Furthermore, over the life cycle our roles and goals are changing and there is a problem of limited understanding of a situation until it is experienced personally. Often it is only in hindsight that a situation is experienced or perceived in terms of its privacy potential or invasionary qualities (Fischer, 1971).

Information management first becomes possible when children can give up the notion that authority is omnipresent (Piaget, 1966). Initially, children have a belief that even when behaviors are not seen, they are known about and will eventually bring reward and/or punishment. To a large extent this belief reflects the reality of the children's experience. Until about age 7 or 8, children's limited range of movement and adult control over their lives means that adults generally have access to and/or knowledge about children's activities. Yet caretakers cannot and generally do not want to be with children all of the time. As the adult's perception of the need for surveillance decreases, children are allowed greater range of movement and will be alone more often and for longer periods of time, increasing the possibility that adults will not know about all of their children's behaviors. We give children clues to the limits of our information when we ask questions about their activities during periods of our absence.

The nonchosen aloneness created by decreased surveillance is a significant experience. The act of aloneness (physical or psychological) and adult reactions can become experiential determiners of future experience sought, expected, or defined as private. Children can experience concretely their own ability to survive and the possibilities of choosing what to do under these circumstances; adult reactions make it clear that information about this experience is not automatically known. Since children are rewarded and/or punished for behaviors or thoughts at variance with adult desires, experience revealing adults' limited access expands children's understanding of the use of information and interaction management. A successful first lie (Tausk, 1933) or hidden behavior brings awareness that many things are not known until volitionally revealed—awareness of the ability to control access to information about one's own thoughts and behaviors. Freud (Ekstein and Caruth, 1972) believed that, in our society, the child's first lie was a sign of the beginning of the separation and individualization of the self. While the management of information vis-à-vis *behavior* in these early childhood years is limited by the difficulties of interaction management, information management is more possible and is probably an early form of consciously sought privacy experience and an early expression of autonomy.

The ability to exercise choice in relation to privacy also varies depending on the nature of the interpersonal context. Privacy involving the individual alone provides as total choice as is possible in the human situation. As the size of the group increases, collective norms begin to govern choice over the degree, form, and extent of information and interaction management. Also, when we move from the interpersonal to the institutional level (i.e., school), each individual's ability to choose decreases or increases relative to his/her position in the social structure.

As children grow older they are gradually allowed to be alone without supervision and spend more time away from home, some alone and some with peers. Being able to go outdoors alone and entering school are two of the first extrafamilial situations the child experiences. Being more often in public situations, children are exposed to community norms. Spending larger portions of time away from home, whether outside or in school, gives children greater options for managing information about their behavior vis-à-vis the family. At the same time, the school environment, both physically and socially, is more structured. There is generally less opportunity for children to manage interaction or to choose the circumstances of interaction. The child spends time in shared spaces with other children whom he/she has no voice in choosing and little chance of physically avoiding. Schoolwork, which requires concentration, along with institutional norms against the sharing of intellectual information, gives children their first solid experience of using interaction and information management in relation to task demands. In our society school is an important socializing influence relative to the uses of interaction and information management for competition and achievement.

Between entrance into school and adolescence, children focus more on peer relationships. The sharing and withholding of information and the extent and nature of interaction with peers is one way of defining the nature of friendship. The range of peer groups expands; children affiliate differentially with other children depending on activities. Based on abilities, needs, and the social composition of these groups, the child takes on different roles. Interaction and information management can support the exercise of behavior in one role context which may conflict with other role definitions. For example, preadolescents may be rebellious to authority when with their peers and respectful to authority when with their parents; they may be leaders in certain groups and followers in other groups. Being able to manage information and interaction between these groups maintains the validity of these behaviors in each separate context (Wolfe & Laufer, 1975) and limits the potential negative consequences. Therefore, spending larger portions of time away from home exposes the child to a broader range of situations in which interaction and information management must and can be used.

The extended range of interactions and patterns of associations means that children usually engage in more social interactions *per se* as they grow older. At the same time task demands increase. School becomes a more serious enterprise: more homework is required; the child is told that performance will affect future life possibilities. Within the family the child may be required to take on certain responsibilities. Interests change: reading, listening to music, individual hobbies may become more valued activities. The increase in demanded as well as actual interactions, along with the broadened range of interest and responsibilities, all have implications for the uses of interaction management. Children may want or need (1) consciously to withdraw from social interactions or from the demands of others, both family and peers, (2) to control stimulation, from both social and physical sources, (3) to rehearse aspects of behavior that will be included in social interactions, using role-playing and fantasy as ways of reality-testing the nature of interactions (Erikson, 1963). These are all situations in which the child, on a daily basis, can learn the uses and limits of interaction management.

As children approach adolescence, sexual maturation is an increasingly important aspect of daily life—physically as well as psychologically. Children begin to have an awareness of their own sexual development and their own questions and ideas about intimate interpersonal relationships. At the same time specific societal and family norms relating to these behaviors will begin to reflect the adult world's perception of these children as "near-adults." Implicitly or explicitly, information will be transmitted about which topics may be discussed, which activities are allowed and not allowed, and under which conditions these activities may occur.

As children enter adolescence, they are given more independence from their families. They have more freedom from surveillance; their range of movement from the home increases; they are more often in public, nonfamily, situations. This is the time for trying out new activities that appear to be at variance with the norms of the older generation. Adolescents will attempt to use interaction and information management as a way of engaging in these behaviors while limiting conflict and avoiding present or future consequences. But this requires control over access to some *relevant* aspects of a situation. Depending on the specific situation, this relevant aspect may be distraction, interruption, observation of activities, knowledge of thoughts, or information of specified types. It might require a locked door, a private diary, a secret, or directing and choosing the type and intensity of stimulation (from people, noise, or visual stimuli) desired and consistent with or relevant to other needs. Yet adolescents may not always be able to anticipate what is relevant and, furthermore, what is perceived as relevant is already a function of previous experience. In addition, even when adolescents know what aspects are relevant, they are rarely in a position to make meaningful choices. Thus, the form and amount of privacy possible will clearly be related to the degree of personal autonomy in a specific situation and to the ecological environment in which privacy can be sought, achieved, or experienced.

Since adolescents are still dependents living with their families, the form, quantity, and quality of interaction management within the confines of the home remains difficult if not impossible. It is not until people have a place of their own that they can experience, within their living space, control over access to their person or belongings or the active choice of the conditions of privacy situations. As a result, adolescents may frequently spend greater portions of time outside the home as a way of attempting (1) to manage interaction with family members, (2) to limit the family's access to information about their behavior, and (3) to set the conditions of interaction with their peers. Yet there are few options outside the home for choosing the types of situations the adolescent might perceive as being necessary and relevant for the experience of privacy (Ladd, 1974). The beginning of search for intimacy and the desire for sexual experimentation will make the management of interaction and information more salient but still difficult to achieve. The privacy-related elements of available situations under which these activities can occur (for example, cars, movie theaters) may have a significant impact on the way in which, as adults, we eventually come to understand these behaviors. Thus, while adolescence is considered to be a critical phase in the formation of self-identity (Erikson, 1963), the experiences of adolescence socialize the person to the limits of independence and self-identity within a particular society; privacy experiences are an important aspect of this socialization process.

In summary, through their daily experiences children and adolescents develop an understanding of the uses and limits of interaction and information management in everyday life. They develop a sense of themselves as separate from and connected to others, an understanding of the conditions under which to seek physical and psychological aloneness or interaction, an understanding of the possible range of such experience, and the uses of each of these for self-enhancement or regrouping. At the same time, these experiences give children and adolescents a view of societal norms with respect to certain behaviors and activities and provide a way of interpreting these as valued or not valued, good or bad. In this way children's experiences with privacy feed back into their sense of self-esteem and help define the range, limits, and consequences of individual autonomy within our society.

These ideas, derived from the application of my theoretical perspective to what are viewed as ordinary childhood and adolescent experiences, are given support from research focusing on the general quality and limits of children's and adolescents' experiences and understanding of privacy and the extent and nature of changes with age.

I will describe this research and then leave the realm of the "generalized childhood experience" by indicating how specific cultural and socio-physical environmental experience can create significant differences in the experiences particular children have and subsequently affect their concepts and patterns of privacy.

The Meaning of Privacy in Childhood and Adolescence

Much of the data to be presented in this paper are drawn from a study conducted by Robert Laufer and myself (Wolfe & Laufer, 1975; Wolfe, *et al.*, 1976; Laufer & Wolfe, 1976; Wolfe, 1977). It was an interview study[2] with 900 children and adolescents, ages 5–17, and was designed to gain understanding of concepts of privacy and to assess whether the meaning of privacy is related to age, sex, socioeconomic status, racial/ethnic group membership, or place of residence and, in addition, to children's experiences with and opportunities for physical privacy within the family dwelling.

Since all of the interview questions were open-ended, the structure emerging from a content analysis of responses is a reflection of the nature of children's and adolescents' concepts of privacy. Table 1 lists the 39 coding categories that emerged from responses to the definitional question: "Would you please tell me all the things the word privacy means to you?"

The responses reflected many of the dimensions and elements of privacy discussed in the literature (Westin, 1967; Laufer *et al.*, 1973; Altman, 1975) and in the perspective presented earlier. The self-ego dimension is reflected in responses such as "doing what you want to do" (113, an autonomy component) and "being alone when emotionally aroused" (108, a self-protective component). The sociophysical element of the environmental dimension is reflected in responses such as "being alone in a room or place" (109), "quiet" (132), "having a room of my own" (127), "doing and thinking alone" (106), "being in the bathroom" (135), and "sex" (131). The interaction management element of the interpersonal dimension is represented by responses such as

[2] See Wolfe and Laufer (1975) for a complete description of methods and procedures. My thanks to the children, teachers, and administrators of all the schools for their cooperation and support; to Sue Fox, Rich Olsen, Jan Zyniewski, Carlos Hernandez, Cynthia Cook, Josh Holahan, and John Krogman for their help in interviewing; to Nathan Auslander for his patience in transcribing; to Mary Schearer, who has shared many hours of coding, data analysis, and discussion; and to John Best for computer programming.

TABLE 1

CODING CATEGORIES[a] FOR "TELL ME ALL THE THINGS PRIVACY MEANS TO YOU"

101	Alone, being alone, alone with self
102	Being able to be alone
103	Feeling of being alone
104	Seclusion
105	Alone and unbothered, undisturbed
106	Doing and thinking alone (being alone to read, to think, to play)
107	Being alone when you want to
108	Being alone when emotionally aroused (mad, hurt)
109	Being alone in a room, in a place
110	Alone with somebody
111	Being away from people (don't want anyone around)
112	To be with others without interruption or without being bothered
113	Doing what you want to
114	Doing what you want to without being disturbed or bothered
115	Doing what you want to and no one knows
116	Being able to do what you want (must have words: being able to)
117	Being able to do what you want to without being interrupted
118	Being able to do what you want to and no one knows
119	Doing what you want to alone
120	Being able to do what you want to alone
121	No one bothering me, unbothered
122	Wanting to be alone
123	Controlling access to information (knowing something you don't want anyone to know about; or keeping something to yourself; secrets or sharing secrets; you don't want anyone to see what you are doing)
124	Controlling access to spaces (no one being able to go into my room; no one can come in unless I want them to)
125	Controlling access to things (like having something no one can bother—diary, toys)
126	Private things—without elaboration (the words: my diary, toys, without elaboration)
127	Having a place or room of my own
128	Private place—statement like private house, room, without any elaboration
129	Abstract concept of "having your own"
130	Private activities (mention of a behavior with no explanation, sleeping, reading, etc.)
131	Sex, your own sexual ability, kissing boyfriend, being alone and having a girl with you, divorce, abortion, intimacy
132	Quiet
133	Quiet as a condition for doing something
134	Peace or peaceful
135	Being in the bathroom in and of itself as a private thing
136	Using the bathroom for nonbathroom aloneness (reading, thinking)

[a] Code numbers were used for computer programming. In the text, references are made to both the code number and the descriptive phrase.

"alone" (101), "being alone when I want to" (107), "alone with some-body" (110), "being away from people" (111), and "no one bothering me" (121), while responses such as "knowing something you don't want someone else to know or having secrets" (123) reflect the infor-mation management element.

Each of the questions we asked elicited responses that reflected at least two, if not all three, dimensions. When asked to describe "a time when you felt very private," respondents *spontaneously* gave informa-tion about the presence or absence of others, who the people were, the type of place they were in and its physical characteristics, whether the situation was sought or imposed, and whether they were involved in a specific type of activity. Descriptions of invasion experiences in-cluded spontaneous mention of places and their physical characteris-tics, perceived intentionality of the invader, and the normative sanc-tions attached to respondents' reactions, as well as the probable consequences of their action. Descriptions of private thoughts and feelings focused on the nonnormative or nonacceptable nature of these feelings and thoughts and the meaning for self-esteem and self-evalu-ation. Limits of space preclude a complete description of coding cate-gories for each question.[3] However, in Table 2, I have abstracted what seem to be the key elements of responses given to the definitional question and for descriptions of "a time you felt very private," "a time someone or something disturbed your feeling of being private," "a private place," and "a private talk."

Aloneness and managing information were the most frequently given elements in the abstract definitions of privacy (Column A). Yet 30% of the respondents did not use either of these elements in their definitions. For this latter group, "no one bothering me," "controlling access to places," "autonomy/choice," and "quiet" were the most fre-quent elements used. This finding cautions against assuming that pri-vacy has a singular abstract meaning for all children and adolescents. Furthermore, the findings below indicate that the understanding and evaluation of specific situations involves a complex of elements inter-acting with one another.

We analyzed the extent to which these key elements were paired in responses to definitional questions. This analysis indicated that aloneness was a major connector: aloneness/no one bothering me ac-counted for 13.9% of the 908 pairs of responses; aloneness/managing information, 13.5% of the pairs; aloneness/choice-autonomy, 10.4%; aloneness/doing and thinking, 6.2%; aloneness/controlling access to

[3] Copies of the interview and coding categories may be obtained from the author.

TABLE 2

NUMBER AND PERCENTAGE OF RESPONDENTS USING A KEY ELEMENT IN DEFINITIONS OF PRIVACY, DESCRIPTIONS OF PRIVACY EXPERIENCES, INVASIONS, PRIVATE PLACES, PRIVATE TALKS

Key element	(A) Definition of[a] privacy		(B) Description of privacy experience		(C) Description of invasion		(D) Reason why "place private"		(E) Reason why "talk private"	
	(f)	(%)[b]	(f)	(%)	(f)	(%)	(f)	(%)	(f)	(%)
Aloneness	(441)	56.1	(170)	23.8	(88)	12.1	(221)	35.5	(45)	8.8
Management of information	(307)	39.1	(134)	18.8	(107)	14.8	(26)	4.2	(319)	62.5
Being unbothered, undisturbed	(182)	23.1	(66)	9.3	—	—[d]	(124)	19.9	—	—
Controlling access to places	(150)	19.1	(71)	10.0[c]	(76)	10.5	(85)	13.7	(15)	2.9
Autonomy/choice	(128)	16.3	(81)	11.4	(86)	11.9[e]	(81)	13.0[f]	(38)	7.4
Doing and thinking	(71)	9.0	(64)	9.0[c]	(263)	36.4	(64)	10.2	—	—
Quiet	(62)	7.9	(64)	9.0	—	—	(41)	6.7	—	—
Self-evaluation/protection	(13)	1.6	(61)	8.5	—	—	—	—	—	—
	N = 786		N = 713		N = 722		N = 622		N = 510	

[a] For all questions, except this one, respondents appear in only one category. For the definitional question, respondents can appear in more than one category, but are counted in each category only once. For example, a respondent would be counted once in "alone" category if they gave one or more responses which included the word "alone" (101–111, 119, 120, or 122), with 30.5% being a simple statement of "alone." "Information" category includes: 115, 118, 123, with 36.6% in category 123. "Unbothered" includes 105, 112, 114, 117, 121, with 11.5% being a simple statement of "not being bothered." "Places" includes 109, 124, 127, 128, with 8.2% being in category 124. "Autonomy/choice" includes 107, 113–120. "Doing and thinking" includes 106 and 130. "Quiet" includes 132, 133, 134.

[b] Percents based on total number of respondents answering each question, excluding "don't know" responses.

[c] In descriptions of privacy experiences, 67.6% of respondents mentioned being in a specific place but only 10.0% described this as the "reason it was private"; similarly, 55.3% described an activity, but only 9.0% described this as the "reason it was private."

[d] Would not be included as description since it was part of the question: "Describe a time when someone or something disturbed your feeling of being private."

[e] This reflects the attempts of others to lessen autonomy/choice, mainly by questioning a child about behavior.

[f] Includes "no one knowing where I am, where it is."

space, 4.1%; and aloneness/quiet, 4.4%. Managing information was not paired to any significant extent with other elements; its next highest pairing was with choice/autonomy—3.3%. Choice/autonomy and no one bothering me were most often combined with aloneness, followed by their combination with one another (4.8%).

An analysis of paired elements in reasons given for "why a place was private" revealed essentially the same pattern, except that ownership became an additional key descriptor (Wolfe, et al., 1976). Four constellations of meanings were found. One was related to a private place as a place to think and reflect—similar to Westin's (1967) self-evaluation function and to the self-identity functions described by Altman (1975) and in my own perspective. This experience included aloneness, quiet, and lack of disturbance and interruption. Two constellations were related to autonomy. One reflected the exercise of autonomy vis-à-vis controlling access to place: a place that's mine—no one knows where it is or where I am—I control access—I'm alone—no one bothers me. The unknown location and control over access seem to represent the exercise of autonomy, while the aloneness and lack of disturbance seem to be secondary outcomes. The second autonomy constellation connects privacy with choice of activity as expressed through aloneness and concretized in the ownership of a space that guarantees nonintrusion; it's my place—I can be alone—no one bothers me—I can do what I want to do. Finally, there was an information-control grouping that fits the most usual definitions of what privacy means: a desire to be alone—doing a specific activity—no one bothers me and *no one knows what I am doing*. In the latter instance the place seems to be a privacy mechanism in Altman's (1975) sense of the term, while for the autonomy constellations, having a place seems to be central to the understanding of what privacy means.

If we compare children's abstract conceptualization of privacy (that is, their response to the definitional question) with their descriptions of private times, places, talks, and invasions we get some sense of the source of these abstract elements in their everyday experience. In descriptions of "a time you were very private," although 55% of the respondents described themselves as engaging in some activity and 79% mentioned being in a specific place, the key elements in the situation which led to its being perceived as "private" were aloneness and information management (Table 2, Column B). Thus, the successful privacy experience may include an activity component and a place component, but for most children this is secondary to the experience of aloneness and/or information management.

Invasion experiences, on the other hand, are unsuccessful privacy experiences. Most children (except at the youngest ages) described invasions as situations in which they wanted to be alone rather than being forced to be alone through punishment or exclusion or they wanted to manage information rather than being excluded by someone else's management of information; the most frequently described invasion experience was the interruption of activities (such as reading, homework, playing, and thinking; Table 2, Column C). The autonomy/choice element refers here to the attempts of others to lessen autonomy largely by questioning the child/adolescent about his/her behavior.

Understanding of privacy as the management of information comes primarily from children's experiences of private talks (Table 2, Column E); talks were private because "no one heard what was said or should know what was talked about." These talks most often took place at the request of parents and authorities. Their content was described primarily as dealing with problems or being arguments about the child's behavior. Information management was also described as a central element of descriptions of private thoughts and feelings and both of these included a strong use of self-protective, self-evaluation elements.

Some children understood each of the experiences in terms of their exercise of autonomy, but it was not *the* major definer for most of the children and adolescents we interviewed. This finding reflects the reality of most children's and adolescents' experiences. They are still dependent children, all of them living at home and spending large portions of their time in the home or in other environments (school) where others control much of their activity and movement. There is limited opportunity for privacy as the exercise of autonomy in interaction management, i.e., in terms of choosing the conditions, extent, and types of these experiences. Given the problematic nature of managing interaction, information management may be the more possible alternative but not necessarily the privacy situation that would be actively chosen if choice were possible. Furthermore, problems of interaction management may make information management difficult to achieve. Finally, an understanding of privacy as information management comes most often from experiences of attempts by others to lessen children's autonomy, i.e., talks initiated by authority figures and focused on the problematic aspects of children's behavior.

The ritual aspects of privacy, its relation to sex and to bathroom activities, were mentioned only rarely. One possible explanation, especially in relation to sexual activity, may be that most of the sample were preadolescents. Alternatively, the privacy-related aspects of these activities are so normative that they may be nonconscious: acted upon but not verbalized or even consciously thought about (Bem, 1970) unless they are absent. Data to be presented later, which relate the use of these elements to age and to environmental experiences, lend support to both explanations.

To sum up, children know what privacy is, it is meaningful in their lives, and the elements of their abstract conceptualizations seem to come from concrete experience of various types of situations. The most frequently described elements of these situations are aloneness, information management, the lack of disturbance and interruption of activities, the control over access to spaces, autonomy, and quiet. The association of privacy with the exercise of choice/autonomy was infrequent, reflecting both the limited opportunities for actively managing interaction and the experience of information management primarily in situations where autonomy was lessened. Children's and adolescents' concepts of privacy and descriptions of privacy-related experiences show that privacy is complex, involves a range of elements in combination with one another, and militates against a single definition or the use of a single element as the definer of the experience. However, it is also clear that for each child one of the key elements becomes central to the understanding of privacy as an abstract concept. The next sections will present an interpretation of how particular aspects of children's lives may make one element more salient than another.

Age-Related Experiences

In my general perspective I stated that it was the interaction of normative and individual factors, concretized in children's daily life experiences that would interact to create children's and adolescents' concepts of privacy. In applying the life-cycle element of the environmental dimension to ordinary childhood and adolescent experience, I tried to suggest ways in which changes in children's experience might relate to changes in patterns and concepts of privacy. There is some clear research support for these hypotheses.

Studies on "home range" and on children's use of outdoor play space indicate that the distance children travel away from the home increases with age, with dramatic differences between children younger than eight and those older than eight. The evidence also suggests that limitations are set by the children themselves as well as by their parents (Anderson & Tindall, 1972; Hart, 1978; Saegert & Hart, 1975). Once children can move outside the home, it is also clear that their age will influence privacy-related experience. For example, in a public situation, children who invaded the personal space of adults were reacted to differently depending on their age: 5-year-old invaders received a positive reaction, 8-year-olds were ignored, and 10-year-olds received a negative reaction similar to that received by an adult in a similar situation (Fry & Willis, 1971).

In our own study we asked respondents to tell us the ways in which "other family members let you know when they (family member) want to be private." Answers were coded according to person(s) described, whether the cue(s) described was verbal, nonverbal, or both, and the type of verbal or nonverbal cue(s) given. Most children, at all ages, described one or both of their parents, while siblings were more likely to be described by older children. Verbal cues predominate; nonverbal cues are given less often and children rarely describe others as giving both types of cues. Respondents in all age groups more often describe their mothers as giving verbal cues; fathers are described as using nonverbal cues by twice as many respondents as describe mothers in that way. However, children below age 13 describe parents' responses as more verbal than nonverbal, while above age 13 the nonverbal cues predominate.

A content analysis of descriptions of verbal cues yielded three types: (1) statements of *personal need* for privacy or for some specific type of privacy, sometimes including an explanation: "I want to be alone," "I want privacy," "I don't want to be disturbed," "I have work to do," "I don't want you to see or hear this"; (2) *direct commands* telling the child what to do with no explanation of what the adult was doing or its relation to that person's privacy needs; "get out of here," "leave me alone," "don't bother me," "don't come in"; (3) *hints* given to the child: "why don't you go someplace else," "don't you have something else to do." At all ages direct commands were the rule, accounting, on the average, for about 50% of all verbal cues given. But these are highest in the 8–12 age group, accounting for 63% of all the verbal statements parents are described as making. The youngest children describe more personal statements, while more of the oldest group describe their parents as giving hints.

The nature of the statements within categories also changes with age. Personal statements made to children below the age of 13 are more often explanatory ("I have a headache," "I need to work"), while those made to children 13 years and older assume the child's understanding ("I want privacy"). The direct but nonexplanatory command of "go away, stay out" increases with age, while more specific commands like "be quiet" drop as age increases. Parents seem to be assuming that the youngest children need a personal explanation and the oldest already have an understanding. Parental reactions to the 8- to 12-year-old group seems especially problematic and least stabilized. Eight- to

12-year-olds are given verbal cues to the same extent as younger children but those are more likely to be direct commands, with no explanation.

Nonverbal cues also change according to the age of the child. There were three types of nonverbal cues: (1) *the person is described as going to another place,* inside or outside of the house: "leaves the room," "goes to the sewing room," "goes somewhere for a ride in the car"; (2) the person is described as *using markers or consistent patterns of behavior* related to physical objects: "closing doors," "locking doors," "putting up a sign," "sitting in a certain chair"; (3) statements suggesting *use of more subtle cues,* including facial expressions and ignoring, and children's inability to pinpoint exactly what the cue was ("you can just tell"). Below age 13, the most frequently described nonverbal cue was that the parent "went someplace else." For the 13- to 17-year-olds, the more subtle indicators and the inability to specifically describe these ("you can just tell") were given as often as the first type.

Examining the specific nature of the nonverbal cues within types we again find differences with age. When the youngest children describe their parents as going to another place, that place is within the house and no specific room dominates. The oldest group describe parents as leaving the house. Children 8 to 12 year old overwhelmingly describe their parents as "going into the bedroom." While respondents at all ages describe parents as closing doors, 8- to 12-year-olds describe this marker exclusively. In the oldest group, equal percentages of respondents describe door closing *and* habitual patterns of behavior such as parents' sitting in a certain chair.

In sum, the socialization pattern emerging from the descriptions of verbal and nonverbal cues gives us a picture of parental styles of privacy being transmitted to children at different ages. First, children are mainly given cues about interaction management. The youngest children experience their parents as remaining in the home, going to one room or another although not using a particular room consistently; the children link this behavior to specific personal need. Parents of 13- to 17-year-olds assume that their children already have an understanding of privacy, need little explanation, and can either be left alone in the house and/or will respond to hints to leave the room or the home. For the 8- to 12-year-old group the situation is more ambivalent and problematic for both parents and children. Children at this age are too capable to be kept out of most spaces, and yet parents probably do not view them as capable enough to be left alone or to go out by themselves as often as older children. The parents' choice, limited by these factors, seems to be to retreat into the bedroom, to define this clearly as the parents' territory, and simply to command the child to stay out without explanation.

A study by Parke and Sawin (1975) provides further data that privacy patterns change with age and reflect the interaction of both children's and parents' behavior and understanding. Defining privacy as the extent to which access to space in the home environment was limited by the principal occupant of the space (similar to what I have called control over access to places), they had parents fill out a questionnaire for themselves and for each of their children describing the use of physical markers (closed doors) and social rules (knocking requirements and access restrictions) to control access to bedrooms and bathrooms. They had responses for 112 children, ranging in age from 2 to 17, who were from 48 middle-class families participating in the Fels longitudinal study.

Parke and Sawin found that as children develop they make greater use of privacy markers, such as closing a door in a room they are occupying. The greatest increase in closing bathroom doors was between ages 2–5 and 6–9. The closing of bedroom doors increased steadily with age, but showed the greatest increase between ages 6–9 and 10–13. In addition, parents knock more often both on bedroom and bathroom doors with older children. Child occupants actively restricted parents' access to bathrooms more as they got older, the largest increase occurring between the 6- to 9-year-old group and the 10- to 13-year-old group. One variable that seemed to contribute to children's active restriction was their physical maturity. The more physically mature children (defined as the early appearance of secondary sex characteristics) were more likely to restrict access. Thus, the kinds of experiences we have associated with privacy change as children move through childhood into adolescence.

Our respondents' descriptions of invasion experiences also change with age, with the interruption of activities being cited less often and the inability to manage information cited more often as the child enters adolescence. More of the adolescents, as compared to children 12 and younger, describe being questioned about their behavior and/or having someone find out something they did not want known. And compared to younger children, when adolescents describe these invasion experiences, the information they have not been able to manage is more likely to be related to sex, smoking, and drugs—all "deviant" activties.

Our data show that these changing experiences are paralleled by changes in children's concepts of privacy (Wolfe & Laufer, 1975; Wolfe et al., 1976). The complexity of children's concepts of privacy increase with age (Wolfe & Laufer, 1975). Most responses reflecting autonomy/

choice ("doing what I want to, being alone when I want to") are not given by children under age 8. Responses dealing with sex and seclusion do not appear until age 13. Table 3 shows the key elements used in definitions of privacy by children in different age groups.

While aloneness and managing information ("no one knows") are clearly the most frequent elements mentioned at all ages, the younger group, compared to the older group (8 and above), mentions aloneness significantly less often. It should also be noted that this category increases for older children largely through the addition of meanings which involve aloneness but are more complex (e.g., being alone when I want to). The management-of-information element is used significantly more often by 13- to 17-year-olds than for the two younger groups. Controlling access to spaces is given most often by the 8- to 12-year-old group, whom, as we have seen above, are most usually given cues of this sort by their parents. Quiet as a key element drops with age, paralleling the finding above that parents stop giving this as a specific command with age. Autonomy/choice elements increase gradually but significantly for each group, reflecting the increased home range, parents' use of space outside the home for their own privacy needs, and parents' hints to their older children to leave the house.

Data from children's descriptions of private places are entirely consistent (Wolfe et al., 1976). Older children are more likely to describe an outdoor place as their private place, while younger children describe various rooms in the house, giving none predominance. Although all children primarily describe private places as "alone" places, more of the youngest group describe the presence of at least one, if not more, people, the 8–12 age group has the highest percent of "alone" responses, and the 13–17 age group begins to mention the choice of being alone or with others. At all ages the lack of noise was the predominant physical descriptor used. However, equally prominent in the 8- to 12-year-old group (significantly more so than for the other groups) was the presence of doors or doors with locks. The inclusion of specific furniture and the use of "keep out" signs drops with age, while using the separation of the space (apart/secluded) as a physical descriptor increases with age.

Thus, the data on *changes in children's concepts of privacy provide a striking parallel to data on their changing daily experiences with interaction and information management, especially in relation to their family and family environment.*

Yet, families and family environments differ, and childhood experiences with privacy might be dramatically different in different

TABLE 3

KEY ELEMENTS USED IN DEFINITIONS OF PRIVACY[a] AS A FUNCTION OF AGE

Key element	4-7 years		8-12 years		13-17 years		Comparisons		
	(f)	%[b]	(f)	%	(f)	%	4-7 vs 8-12	8-12 vs 13-17	4-7 vs 13-17
Aloneness	(57)	40.1	(169)	57.5	(215)	61.4	<.01	N.S.	<.01
Managing information	(39)	27.4	(98)	33.3	(170)	48.6	N.S.	<.01	.01
Controlling access to place	(26)	18.3	(71)	24.1	(53)	15.1	N.S.	<.01	N.S.
Unbothered, undisturbed	(24)	16.9	(72)	24.5	(86)	24.6	N.S.	N.S.	N.S.
Quiet	(18)	12.7	(26)	8.1	(18)	5.1	N.S.	.05	<.05
Autonomy/choice	(9)	6.3	(38)	12.9	(81)	23.1	.05	<.01	<.01
	N = 142		N = 294		N = 350				

[a] For the definitional question, respondents can appear in more than one category but are counted in each category only once. For example, a respondent would be counted once in "alone" category if he gave one or more responses which included the word "alone" (101–111, 119, 120, or 122). "Information" category includes 115, 118, 123. "Unbothered" includes 105, 112, 114, 117, 121. "Places" includes 109, 124, 127, 128. "Autonomy/choice" includes 107, 113–120. "Quiet" includes 132, 133, 134.
[b] Percent based on number of respondents in each age group who gave a definition.

cultures (Bettelheim, 1969; Talmon, 1972), for children living in specific communities within a culture (Slater, 1970; Coles, 1970; Lewis, 1970), and for specific families in those communities (Simmel, 1971). In the next section, I will focus on the cultural element and its contribution to our understanding of privacy in childhood. I will describe some recent findings of a study conducted in Israel and then focus on sex differences and family socialization practices within our own culture which seem to influence the form and extent of privacy experience children have.

THE CULTURAL ELEMENT

Altman (1975) and others (Roberts & Gregor, 1971) have shown that different cultures have different patterns and forms of privacy. Cultural norms limit the perceived options available to any specific person or group within the culture, and within a culture the individual or group's position will also be a factor creating different ranges of options. Even in complex societies, however, the dominant perspective of the culture will have a significant impact on the way an individual defines privacy situations, because the concrete experiences people can and do have are, in many ways, limited by these perspectives.

Children in Different Cultures

We have some evidence of the cultural differences between children from an unpublished study by Churchman (1977). Using our interview questions with Israeli-born children, grades 2, 4, and 6, living in suburbs of Haifa, Churchman compared her data to the responses from our suburban sample. In contrast to the U.S. suburban respondents, who rarely cited ownership as a definition of privacy, approximately 33% of the Israeli children defined privacy in these terms. Of the Israeli children, 51% said ownership was the "reason why a place was private," compared to only 8.0% of the U.S. sample. Israeli children also spoke of the permanence of private places ("it's where I live and I'm not going to leave it") a response that did not arise in the U.S. sample. In accord with our findings, changes with age indicated association of privacy with autonomy. We might speculate that the ownership and permanence aspects of privacy gain their salience from Israel's historical importance for the Jewish people as their "own state" and the ever-present instability of that situation. Furthermore, in urban and suburban areas ownership of one's house or apartment has become both the norm and the ideal. Even the traditional agricultural communes (i.e., the Kibbutzim) have been moving toward relegating communality to the joint ownership and working of the land, while providing more privacy in the form of separate living arrangements and ownership of personal property. There is little other available literature on differences between children in different cultures, but it is an area that is ripe for research.

Within our own culture, however, we can examine the influence of the cultural element by looking at sex differences and family socialization patterns.

Privacy and Sex Differences

In recent years a great deal has been written about the influence of sex-role stereotyping on the behavior of boys and girls (Maccoby & Jacklin, 1974). Sterotyped descriptions of girls include their greater modesty, their greater sociability and desire to be with people, their lesser independence or greater dependence—many characteristics that appear relevant to the types of experiences with interaction and information management discussed earlier. Individual families will differ in the treatment of their male and female children, but the predominant perspectives within our culture exert their influence.

Research points to differences between male and female children in what we have described as possible privacy experiences during childhood. The available data on personal space led Altman (1975) to conclude that (1) girls form more stable social distance patterns at earlier ages, reflecting the earlier cultural training of girls in regard to rules for social interaction; (2) males have larger personal-space zones than females; and (3) people generally maintain greater distance from males than from females. Several studies have found that females become more prosocial under crowded conditions while males become more aggressive (Saegert. Mackintosh, & West, 1975). Data show sex differences in self-disclosure—part of information management. Cozby (1973), in a review of that literature, concluded that studies show either no sex differences or females disclosing more than males; no study has reported greater male disclosure. Little of this research focuses on children, however, and when gender has been included as a variable in this research it has rarely been the main focus (Altman, 1975).

One area that seems particularly relevant for understanding the differences between the privacy-related experiences of male and female children is research on "restrictedness" versus "autonomy-granting" socialization practices. Maccoby and Jacklin (1974) initially suggest that the literature in this area shows no sex differences in independence granting. However, Saegert and Hart (1975) question this conclusion on two grounds: (1) the focus, in available child development research, on the 4- to 5-year-old age group and (2) the omission from Maccoby and Jacklin's review of five studies of spatial range, which show consistent and significant sex differences. On the former point, Saegert and Hart point out that Maccoby and Jacklin cite recent evidence of emerging sex differences in autonomy-granting experiences beginning at about 7 years of age. Newson and Newson, who in an early study of child-rearing in Nottingham, England (1968), had found no differences in 4-year-old boys' and girls' range of movement inside or outside of the home, report that at age 7 the girls as opposed to the boys (1) are being met after school more often than boys; (2) must make their whereabouts known more; an (3) are more often in the company of an adult.

In recent studies of home range, consistent sex differences have been found to emerge between 8 and 10 years of age. Beginning at about 9 years of age, boys are allowed to go further from the home without asking permission (Hart, 1978); differences are proportionately greater at age 10 than at age 8 (Anderson & Tindall, 1972); mothers are more likely to check up on their girl children than on their boy children (Landy, 1957); older boys have more free or undirected time than older girls (Munroe & Munroe, 1971); and, while boys and girls are equally likely to be sent on errands, domestic chores, especially staying around the house and looking after young children, are commonly the duties of daughters, not sons (Hart, 1978).

Saegert and Hart (1975) and Hart (1978) suggest that these restricted ranges for girls and greater freedom for boys are not simply a matter of protection of female children. They are partly based on the notion that "boys will be boys" and must have this experience in order to develop into appropriate men. Furthermore,

> after 6 to 7 years of age, when utilitarian roles are found for children, while girls become less "clingy" and become more of a "companion" to the mother, they are not given greater freedom of physical mobility as are the boys. The mother, usually responsible for caretaking of the children, brings girls more quickly into line with the woman's role in the home than the father or mother does for boys. (Saegert & Hart, 1975, p. 6)

The net result of these attitudes is that girls are likely to be home more often, with fewer possibilities for achieving privacy as physical aloneness and less choice in type and extent of privacy situations.

The findings of Wolfe et al. (1976) on children's concepts of private places parallel Saegert and Hart's findings. Beginning at 8 years of age, boys were more likely than girls to describe outdoor places and indoor places other than their own home. With increasing age, girls were more likely to describe a private place as either "an alone place or a with other place" while for boys this change did not occur as dramatically. More girls than boys focused on doors as a primary physical descriptor of a private place, reflecting their greater restriction to the home. Boys were more likely than girls to describe their ability to control access as the reason a place was private. In our study, as well as in Saegert and Hart's, these sex differences were affected by place of residence—urban versus suburban/rural. I will describe these data later. First, I will focus on other differences in the general socialization patterns of boys and girls with respect to specific types of privacy experiences.

Parke and Sawin (1975), in their study of the use of closed doors, knocking requirements, and access restriction, provide additional evidence of differing privacy socialization practices for boys and girls. For bedroom use, opposite-sex parents and siblings knock more often, are restricted more in their access, and have doors closed more frequently in their presence. Yet, both parents and siblings observe bedroom knocking rules *far more often for girls*.

Access to the bathroom showed similar cross-sex interaction and was strongly related to developmental trends as well as to the nature of bathroom activities. Girls showed the greatest increase in restricting bathroom access from ages 10 to 13, especially for fathers. It was not until 14–17 that boys became as restricting as girls. Both boys and girls restrict access for dressing, toileting, and bathing. However, mothers have more access during these activities than fathers regardless of who is the occupant.

These data reflect the earlier socialization of girls for bodily privacy, especially in relation to men, probably due in part to the earlier appearance of secondary sex characteristics. In addition, the role-models girls and boys are seeing are different: mothers are not restricted as much as fathers and girls' privacy behavior is more closely related to the parent of the opposite sex than is that of boys.

Children's and adolescents' descriptions of their mothers' and fathers' privacy-seeking patterns is consistent with the home range, access, and private-place data. Both boys and girls describe fathers as using nonverbal cues more than mothers. But while mothers and fathers behave differently toward their daughters, they behave similarly toward their sons: girls describe their fathers as using nonverbal patterns twice as often as their mothers, while for boys there is not as great a difference reported. More boys as compared to girls describe receiving direct commands from *both parents*. In describing parents' use of nonverbal privacy cues, more boys and girls describe their mothers as "closing doors." However, twice as many girls as boys describe their fathers as doing this, while equal percentages of boys and girls describe their mothers as using this pattern. Boys and girls equally mention their parents' main nonverbal mode as "going some-place," yet fathers are twice as often described as "leaving the house." Finally, both boys and girls are more likely to be unable to articulate their fathers' pattern ("you can just tell").

Our respondents' description of parents' door-closing patterns complement the children's patterns described by Parke and Sawin, while fathers' greater use of the outdoors would be consistent with the differing socialization patterns revealed by the data on spatial range and use of private places. The childhood differences seem to reflect the modeling of parents' patterns as well as the overlay of cultural sex-role stereotyping, which begins to appear most strongly during preadolescence.

These differences in behavioral patterns are clearly reflected in our data on boys' and girls' definitions of privacy. The element of aloneness is given by somewhat more males than females but is most strongly affected by age rather than sex differences. More of the youngest boys define privacy as controlling access to places than their female age cohorts. Yet the percentage of boys using this element remains constant through preadolescence while the percentage of girls using it increases up to the boys' level at ages 8–12, and by 13–17 both use it less often. This increase in use of controlling access to places as a definer of privacy is consistent with Parke and Sawin's findings on increased use of restricted access in the home for girls during the preadolescent period.

By 13–17 the two elements that distinguish between boys' and girls' definitions are the use of autonomy/choice vis-à-vis interaction management (e.g., "being alone when I want to") and controlling access to information (e.g., "knowing something I don't want anyone else to know"). Use of choice/autonomy element increases with age for both boys and girls, but between 8–12 and 13–17 the percentage of boys using this element increases dramatically, and by ages 13–17 significantly more boys than girls use it to define privacy. For girls, on the other hand, it is the information-management element that shows increased use from preadolescence to adolescence and is used by significantly more girls in the adolescent age group.

It is clear from this research that privacy patterns and concepts are a significant part of sex-role socialization. In terms of the potential costs of the absence of certain types or amounts of privacy-related experiences, many of the issues raised by the women's movement of recent years would seem to be related to privacy sex-role socialization experiences. Sex-role socialization for privacy may be related to the lessened sense of autonomy many women have; the higher incidence of agrophobia among women (Chesler, 1972); their phenomenological favoring of crowdedness, along with lack of awareness of its negative effect on their performance (Saegert *et al.*, 1975); their overextensive bodily modesty, especially in relation to the opposite sex; their use of disclosure/nondisclosure as a way of relating to others; and their use of more personal statements of need in relating to other individuals. Women seem to be socialized to use information management as their primary privacy pattern, except in relation to ritual privacy, where interaction management via controlling access to spaces is a legitimate mode. Males, on the other hand, are being socialized to view privacy in terms of autonomy and freedom of movement, to be less verbal, and, when verbal, to be less expressive of their personal needs.

Privacy and Family Socialization Patterns

Other issues raised by the cultural dimension are the relationship between patterns and concepts of privacy and the specific family socialization patterns, including social class and ethnic patterns. At this time, few data are available. Since Parke and Sawin's respondents were part of the Fels Longitudinal sample, they had for their 2- to 7-year-old middle-class respondents concurrent child-rearing practice ratings using the Fels Parent Behavior Rating Scales. For this limited age and class sample they found that (1) mothers rated as restrictive and coercive exercised more control over children's uses of privacy as control over access to places and (2) affectionate and approving mothers had children who controlled access to places less during personal activities. Cozby (1973) cites data mainly with middle-class college students, suggesting that disclosure to parents correlated with respondents' ratings of parents as warm and friendly, but concludes that the limited literature indicates that family relationships may be more important in determining to *whom* a person discloses (family or friends) than in the absolute *level* of disclosure. He also reports differences between first and later borns in self-disclosure, the latter disclosing more. Schachter's original data (1965) could be interpreted as showing that later borns prefer physical aloneness (privacy) when they are anxious.

Few studies are available which focus on class and ethnic differences. Ethnic differences in self-disclosure seem to disappear when social class is held constant, and Cozby suggests that class differences in parent-child verbalization interactions may lead to variations in self-disclosure in adulthood. Earlier we described Slater's analysis of the conflicting privacy experiences of middle-class children (see Childhood and Privacy, above).

These aspects of the cultural element—i.e., family child-rearing practices, social class, ethnicity—have rarely been the main focus of privacy research; existing evidence is fragmentary and unconnected by a unified theoretical approach. One way of understanding these family socialization patterns and their implications for privacy within our culture is to look at them in terms of the actual daily life situations of children and their parents. In order to do this, I will turn my attention to the sociophysical element of the environmental dimension of the privacy system.

The Sociophysical Element of Privacy

As I have stated elsewhere:

> The concrete experiences with privacy are transmitted through the institutional fabric of a society experienced through the socio-physical environment. Privacy can be understood in terms of the ecological and physical properties of the environmental settings that circumscribe human behavior. (Laufer & Wolfe, 1977)

Simmel (1971), for instance, differentiated between open and closed family systems and their relevance to privacy. In the closed family, which he equated with the *city* family, no one is allowed in the house without special invitation and children are not free to roam into other houses; the family controls its own children and does not allow others to do so, developing norms of its own; seeks to maintain its difference from others; and is likely to give less psychological and personal privacy to the child within the family structure. Simmel interpreted this pattern as a way of dealing with the heterogeneity of urban life. The open family, generally found in *small towns* and *rural areas*, utilizes social control by others as opposed to internalized mechanisms for self-control. The homogeneity of the setting means that parents are not concerned about their children being subject to varying influences and allow others in the community to supervise the children. Thus, Simmel is suggesting that living one's daily life in a city or in a rural area will have implications for the patterns and concepts of privacy the person develops.

There is need, however, for a more fine-grained analysis of the differences between these two styles of life and some analysis of suburban life, especially in terms of the daily life experiences of children.

The amount of available land in these areas and other economic conditions may determine the type of housing available (high density versus low density; high rise versus low rise; single versus multiple family dwellings). Socioeconomic factors can also determine the type of neighborhood in which a family can live and therefore children's freedom of movement outside the family dwelling. Thus, Anderson and Tindall (1972) found that urban children have a much more limited home range than suburban children, especially at younger ages, making interaction management more problematic. The amount and type of indoor and outdoor space in combination can severely alter the experience of privacy *within* the house because the number of people present at any one time, and over time, will partly be a function of the available outdoor alternatives. A finite amount of indoor space in one residential area may provide for more privacy than it would in another residential area. In each of these areas the means of transportation and the level of stimulation can also alter the essential means and conditions of privacy. These factors impinge on the daily lives of parents and their children; there is evidence to suggest that privacy-related experiences of children, as well as their understanding of privacy, are different depending on these sociophysical variables.

In our own study, we compared patterns and concepts of privacy for children living in a suburban/rural area and children living in an urban area (Wolfe, 1977). We determined socio-economic status by using the North-Hatt scale and creating four groups using quartiles. In analyzing definitional data we found that socioeconomic status influenced both the urban and suburban samples, aloneness being used more by the highest socioeconomic-status respondent, with information management being used more by the lowest group. Socioeconomic comparisons produced neither as many nor as strong differences as did the home-environment variables. The explanation seems to lie in the extent to which home-environment variables correlate with socioeconomic status within each residential setting. In the suburban/rural area the income distribution was bimodal, with lower-middle-class and middle-class groups predominating. Our sample reflected this distribution, with few children falling into the extreme groupings. In addition, 73% of housing units were built between 1950 and 1964, 84% are owner occupied, and only 20% have more than nine living units. The urban area, on the other hand, had a wider income distribution, many more renters, much larger houses, and housing units that varied considerably in age.

Thus, in our suburban/rural sample, the correlations between home-environment variables and socioeconomic status were extremely low, with the highest (r = 0.31) between socioeconomic status and sharing or having one's own room. In the urban sample, the correlations were generally higher, with the highest correlation between socioeconomic status and household density (r = 0.51). These differences reflect the reality of urban and suburban living environments. And since children's daily experiences center around their home environments, the range and effect of possible privacy experiences will vary according to the nature of the relationship between these environments and socioeconomic status, within a particular community and between communities.

Thus, data on children's and adolescents' concepts of private places (Wolfe *et al.*, 1976) indicate that for children the urban versus suburban/ rural distinction has its major impact in terms of the availability of the outdoors as an alternative place for privacy. Suburban/rural children, especially those who shared a room, were more likely to describe outdoor places (treeforts, beaches, the woods)—these becoming more relevant during adolescence, when freedom of movement is greater. Urban children and adolescents overwhelmingly cited house-related areas as private places regardless of age. If they had their own bedroom, it was more likely to be the private place mentioned, especially as they approached adolescence. Urban adolescents who shared a room either made the wishful statement that "my own apartment *would* be a private place" or, under the highest levels of density (more than 1.0 person per room), cited their bedroom as a private place, probably because the alternative (more people in other house areas) was even more problematic.

The outdoor alternative in the suburban/rural area colored all other findings. For example, compared to suburban/rural females, fewer urban females describe a private place as an "alone" place, with the differences being especially strong at the adolescent age and for girls who share a bedroom. There were no such differences between urban and suburban males on this basis. In terms of the home range data presented earlier, our data support the idea that part of limiting a girl's movement, especially in urban areas, may be a function of parents' perceptions of the outdoors as a dangerous place along with their belief that their girl children must be protected more than boy children. The limit this places on girls' experience of aloneness in the urban environment is compounded when the home environment provides only limited opportunities for aloneness—when a girl shares a bedroom.

Yet female children are not the only ones affected by the limited availability of the outdoors in the urban environment. Even under the lowest-density home-environment conditions (.00–.79 occupants per room) more suburban/rural respondents characterize a private place as an "alone" place than do their urban counterparts. The availability of the outdoors also created the major difference in reasons respondents gave for why a place was private. Compared to the urban group, the suburban/rural group was more likely to say "no one knows where it is or where I am." This difference between residential groups was most pronounced for males 8–12 years of age, suggesting that suburban/rural males are experiencing privacy-as-autonomy at an earlier age than urban males. The limited use of the outdoors in urban areas also meant that invasions were more likely. Suburban/rural children were better able to match their need for privacy with a place that would not be invaded, i.e., an outdoor place.

While sharing or having one's own room influenced respondents' concepts of private places in both urban and suburban/rural areas, given the lack of the outdoors as an alternative, other internal home environment characteristics (number of people per room, number of rooms, and number of people) either alone or in combination with room status (having or sharing a bedroom) influenced urban respondents more. In the urban area, even under low-density conditions, respondents who had their own room were more likely than those who shared to describe a private place as an "alone" place. As the number of rooms in the house increased, more children who had their own rooms described "separation" as a physical characteristic, while there was no difference between children who shared a room under varying amounts of space. At the highest number of occupants (> 7) more urban respondents with their own rooms than sharing a room said that a private place was private because they could control access to it. As the number of occupants in the household increased, regardless of room status, there was a decrease in the number of respondents citing "aloneness" as a reason why a place was private, and as density increased respondents were *less* likely to say that being "unbothered" defined a private place.

It is common statement that under crowded conditions "at least the bathroom can be used as a private place." Our own data give exactly the opposite picture. The urban respondents were more likely to mention the use of the bathroom, yet those who did had their own rooms and lived in households with the fewest number of occupants and the lowest number of occupants per room. Ladd (1972) found the same thing for a low-income black sample as did Parke and Sawin (1975) for a middle-income sample: less privacy (defined as being able to control access to bedroom and bathroom spaces) was afforded to children in smaller homes.

The impact of internal home-environment characteristics on children and adolescents' understanding of privacy is substantiated and elaborated by our data definitions of privacy. In the suburban/rural sample, interaction of sharing or having one's own bedroom and age of the child created the strongest differences in abstract understanding of privacy. There were hardly any differences between own and shared room suburban/rural children at the youngest age. Yet more own-room than shared-room preadolescents (8–12 years of age) defined privacy using the elements of aloneness and autonomy/choice, while more shared-room respondents defined it in terms of controlling access to information. Equal percentages of own-room and shared-room adolescents in the suburban/rural areas use the element of "aloneness," probably because of the availability of the outdoors; but more own-room adolescents, as compared to shared-room adolescents, use autonomy/choice and controlling access to places, while most of those who share focus on being unbothered. The only other effect of internal home-environment variables within the suburban/rural group was that increases in the number of occupants in the household as well as household density (the number of occupants per room) meant that fewer children defined privacy as aloneness. The number of rooms *per se* had no effect on the use of aloneness, and other elements (autonomy/choice, etc.) were uninfluenced by any other home-environment variables.

In the urban samples internal home-environment characteristics had a stronger effect than sharing or having one's own room. The use of aloneness as a definer of privacy decreased as a function of decreased rooms, increased occupants, and increased density. Decreases in the percentage of respondents defining privacy as controlling access to places were related to increased numbers of occupants and increased density, while the number of rooms in the dwelling did not seem related to respondent's use of this definer. The definition of privacy as being "unbothered" was related to the number of rooms: as the number of rooms in the house decreased, the use of "unbothered" as a definer decreased. Use of this definition was also less likely as density increased, but number of household occupants had no effect. The only difference between urban shared-room and own-room preadolescents was that more own-room respondents used aloneness as a definer. Having a bedroom became important for the urban adolescent group, and more of this group, as compared to those who share a room, mentioned their own room as a private place and also defined privacy as aloneness, autonomy/choice, and being unbothered. The use of controlling access to information and access to spaces as definers of privacy did not differentiate between shared room and own room in the urban sample.

Quiet as a definer of privacy was used more often by the suburban/ rural sample, varying little except in terms of whether children shared a bedroom. Shared-room suburban/rural children use it more often than the own-room group, especially at preadolescent ages. In the urban sample, quiet as a definer of privacy was used by more children as the number of occupants increased and as density increased. In both areas its use seems to represent more of what children desire than of what they have. Our data on private places support this idea since "no noise" was a more likely definer of a private place for urban children who shared a room or lived under higher-density conditions (Wolfe *et al.*, 1976).

We looked at the group of home-environment characteristics that might produce the most difficult living conditions for children to see what impact place of residence might have. Under the highest-density conditions (more than 1.0 person per room), suburban/rural children are more likely than their urban counterparts to define privacy in terms of choice/autonomy and being unbothered. In households with the fewest number of rooms and in households with the highest number of occupants suburban/rural respondents use autonomy/choice and un-bothered as definers of privacy more than their urban counterparts, who use controlling information more. Thus, regardless of where children live, extreme limits on physical privacy within the home means that privacy is less likely to be connected with aloneness and controlling access to spaces. But under these same conditions in suburban/rural areas, the association of privacy with autonomy/choice and being un-bothered is stronger than in urban areas, while in the urban areas the focus is placed on controlling access to information.

CONCLUSIONS AND IMPLICATIONS

I began this chapter with a perspective for understanding privacy in childhood and adolescence, suggesting that:

1. An individual's understanding of privacy is the outcome of the interdependence of phenomenological and normative factors, as they are embodied in the experience of concrete stiuations and events.
2. Through an understanding of these experiences from a multi-dimensional developmental perspective, we could describe their privacy-related elements.
3. Using this approach we could begin to understand how and

why an individual develops a desire for a given form or quantity of privacy.

4. This knowledge might serve as a basis for understanding the implications of presence or absence of certain kinds or amounts of privacy-related experiences for child development and for the quality of our lives as both children and adults.

The available research suggests that children's and adolescents' concepts of privacy do parallel their daily life experiences. The most frequent conceptions of privacy include interaction management and information management. Yet a substantial number of our respondents *do not* define privacy in this way but focus on environmental management (controlling access to places, the absence of noise), while a smaller number focus on autonomy/choice. Thus, there is no singular understanding of privacy.

PRIVACY AS AN EXPERIENCE OF SEPARATION

While we can speak abstractly about privacy as interaction management, meaning the *choice of* aloneness or interaction, children and adolescents define privacy in terms of "aloneness" and describe privacy experiences mainly as "alone" experiences. Few of our respondents focused on being with others. Information management was mainly described as *nondisclosure* of information rather than sharing information, and environmental management was described as *"not* letting people in" and "no noise." Thus, while we may speak of privacy as a dialectic (Altman, 1975), it is mainly experienced and understood by children and adolescents as a unidirectional or one-sided experience. This reflects the reality of their lives, the nature of their roles as nonpersons in society, and the connection of "growing up" with increased possibilities for experiences of psychological and physical *separateness.* As children grow older, the experiences they are "granted" are experiences of aloneness, freedom of movement, the possibility of restricting access to spaces, etc. This socialization pattern reflects our society's heavy emphasis on individualism and self-reliance, which focuses on the *separation* of the individual from others.

PRIVACY PATTERNS AND AUTONOMY

These childhood and adolescent socialization experiences also reflect the general historical understandings of privacy within U.S. culture (Westin, 1967), including the contradictory messages Slater (1970) described. The protection of property was the original basis for privacy rights within our legal system. This is still a strong value expressed by the ideal of the private home, private office, and private car and the ways in which these are viewed as giving one the freedom to behave as one wishes.[4] Given the age of our sample (4–17) and their possible privacy-related experience, autonomy/choice was not frequently associated with privacy. However, those respondents who did associate it with privacy largely connected it to interaction management: being alone when desired and being able to sustain aloneness or some alone-activity without interruption or disturbance. These interaction-management experiences were strongly associated with environmental management: the possession of a place that seemed to legitimate the act of restricting others' access. The possibility of possessing a place was related to living in environments with more rooms, fewer people, and few people per room and/or to residential environments in which children had access to the outdoors. Aloneness via the possession of a place, as well as the experience of possessing a place and hence the experience of controlling access became associated with privacy-as-autonomy and with the possibilities it afforded for self-reflection and thinking. These findings echo statements made by Plant in 1937:

> Our work in suburban and rural districts has convinced us that periods of being alone, of playing alone, of having the privacy of one's own room, are important fostering agents in feelings of individuality, of self-sufficiency. (p. 214)

> Among these individuals of crowded areas and crowded families there is what one describes as the phenomenon of being so much in the world that there is no chance to look at it. (p. 228)

The association of autonomy with information management was very infrequent. A child's first lie may be an early indication of the separation of the self from others, but we must ask about the quality of the form of separation, especially since it is more prevelant among children who do not have opportunities for privacy as interaction or environmental management. Children's and adolescents' descriptions of information management experiences involve the attempts of others' to lessen their autonomy, i.e., experiences with the loss of control over information which have negative consequences for the child or adolescent. With age, unsuccessful information management experiences (invasions) become increasingly associated with "deviant" behavior.

---

[4] Some years ago, there was an attempt to pass a law requiring drivers to use seat belts. This event aroused cries of "invasion of privacy" on the basis that one's car was private transportation and gave one the right to do as one wished.

Thus, while the withholding of information is self-protective and, hence, a statement of the separation of self, this form of separation is connected with negatively valued experiences—the fear of future consequences and lessened autonomy. This is what we have called the "calculus of behavior" aspect of privacy as information management (Laufer & Wolfe, 1977).

Furthermore, the research suggests that the development of a style of privacy seeking is connected to a range of elements that circumscribe the kinds of privacy-related experiences a child or adolescent can have. These elements can also make information, interaction, and environmental management more or less independent of one another. Specifically, age-related, sex-related, and sociophysically related experiences made the possession of a place, the freedom of movement, and the experience of certain types of invasions more or less likely to occur. A child who, because of his/her age, sex, or the nature of external and internal home environment, is confined to the home or other adult-controlled environments will have limited possibilities for privacy as interaction management (aloneness, the lack of interruption) and limited choice of privacy-seeking patterns. Such children could attempt to refrain from engaging in behavior that they think is at variance with adult desires (in legal terms, this is called the "chilling" effect; see Levin & Askins, 1977), yet it is often hard to gauge what will be considered "appropriate" rather than "deviant," especially at younger ages. Children may attempt to achieve privacy as information management, that is, engage in certain behavior and hope they will be able to keep it hidden. In this case, the same elements that push the child toward this mode increase the likelihood that information management will be unsuccessful. And each of these alternatives means that the privacy experience will be one of lessened autonomy.

The foregoing discussion is not meant to suggest that privacy as interaction management has to be a more positive experience than privacy as information management. In fact, evidence would suggest that the significant issue is the ability to exercise choice of the types and conditions of privacy situations relevant to other needs. But the person must be able to perceive choice, and the choices available must in fact be meaningful and without negative consequences. Thus, Wolfe and Golan (1976) found that in a children's psychiatric hospital the only place for privacy—uninterrupted and chosen aloneness—was a seclusion room. Given the lack of alternatives, the children said they often feigned emotional upset or "acted out" in order to be sent there. However, the unintended consequences were that they defined privacy as "being alone when emotionally upset" and that the staff attributed this behavior to the children's pathology and used it as a basis for continued hospitalization. Clearly, then, we must begin to understand how certain experiences limit the perception of choice or the ability to exercise choice vis-à-vis privacy as well as the consequences of these limitations.

Privacy and Positive Social Behavior

If, in fact, we as a society actually value cooperation, sharing, and a style in which people choose to relate to others, it seems essential to understand those experiences that actually support the choice of social interaction or the sharing of information. Research has indicated that being in the continual presence of others (nonchosen) does not support positive social interaction but in fact may encourage severe psychological withdrawal or aggressive behavior, while experiences with chosen aloneness can lessen this behavior. Golan (1978) found that in a children's psychiatric hospital children who more often experienced privacy as chosen aloneness engaged in fewer aggressive behaviors when in the presence of others and were significantly more likely to define privacy in terms of interaction rather than information management. Murray (1974) found that high levels of within-household density (as measured by number of people per room and/or high numbers of people) meant that children were more aggressive in school settings. These and other studies (Loring, 1956; Hutt & Vaizey, 1966; Wolfe & Golan, 1976; Wolfe, 1975) provide empirical support for a statement made by Plant (1937) when he spoke of "mental strain" as being an effect of crowded living conditions that limited the child's ability to be alone:

> The results, when these periods of freedom are lacking, are those of somewhat forbidding negativism or of irritable outbursts of temper which belong definitely to the phenomena of fatigue. (p. 227)

And while it seems that these conditions are related only to urban environments, our data indicate that in both urban and suburban/rural areas within-household density had similar effects, limiting children's understanding of privacy as aloneness. The advantage of the suburban/rural environment was largely in terms of the availability of the outdoors. Yet considering the rapid urbanization of suburban areas and the increases of crime even in rural areas (New York Times, 1978), the continued availability of the outdoors for children is questionable.

PRIVACY AND SELF-ESTEEM

Other consequences of limited amounts or types of privacy experiences may be in terms of the child's sense of self-esteem. Self-esteem can be generally defined as the evaluation individuals customarily maintain with regard to themselves. As Golan (1978) has pointed out, high levels of self-esteem have been shown to be positively correlated to positive social participation, creativity, independence, leadership, a healthy nonconformity, self-reliance, and self-respect. Within our individualistic culture, all of these are viewed as positive qualities. What role might certain privacy experiences play in the development of self-esteem? Golan (1978) found that within two psychiatric hospitals, those children in single-occupancy bedrooms had significantly more experiences of privacy as chosen aloneness and had higher levels of self-esteem than children in multiple-occupancy bedrooms, even though the staff rated them as equally ill, equally likely to socially participate, etc. It may be that in our culture the high value or status accorded to the sole possession of a place means that it becomes a symbol for self-worthiness, especially in a setting where other signs of self-worth are absent. Perhaps, as Plant (1937) described, it provided opportunities for chosen aloneness which gave children more of a sense of objectivity and an ability to see themselves and the institutional environment more clearly. Or since they could control access at least in relation to the other children, perhaps having their own room gave them a sense of autonomy. Aloia (1973) found that for the elderly, perceptions of limited privacy options were connected with perceptions of low self-esteem and that the relationship between these differed depending on the type of place in which elderly respondents lived (an apartment in a community, a senior citizens home, or a convalescent home).

SOME UNANSWERED QUESTIONS

Research specifically focusing on privacy is in its infancy. Needed at this point are studies that focus on the effects of the lack of specific forms or quantities of privacy-related experiences. Can we more directly show that the lack of amounts or types of privacy lead to the use of other privacy-seeking behaviors which may be physically, psychologically, or socially deleterious? What is the relationship between the lack of certain privacy experiences and anxiety or stress? Are private rooms the answer to providing experience with privacy as autonomy or merely patchwork for other societal problems and simply another step in the pursuit of loneliness (Slater, 1970)? Do the privacy-related aspects of certain childhood environments have implications for children's development of skills and competence? For instance, research on social facilitation indicates that children learn new skills better when they are alone but perform learned skills better when they are in groups. To what extent is this the result of the privacy-related aspects of present school environments, which emphasize learning as an individual, competitive experience, not sharing intellectual information, being in the presence of others during performance?

Is there continuity between childhood experiences and concepts of privacy and adult experiences and concepts? Since privacy becomes defined within a given context, do these definitions and experiences become the basis of future desire? What are the long-range effects of specific privacy experiences available within a given life-space context? Children in highly urbanized areas are likely to live in home environments (high-rise, little space) that provide for little aloneness and allow for little freedom from noise and disturbance of activities. The findings of Cohen, Glass, and Singer (1973) and of Wilner, Walkley, Pinkerton, and Tayback (1962) indicate that these conditions can lead to poor school performance. Children in low-income families are likely to live in neighborhoods that are high in density and allow limited freedom of movement. They may go to schools that are large and crowded and recreate in environments that allow for little aloneness or quiet. Although limitations on privacy-related experience for these children may be seen as just one aspect of their lives, privacy-related questions persist: Are these experiences consistent enough to have enduring effects by creating "a desire" for privacy which reflects past experience rather than future possibilities? Do they create a sense of self and self-esteem which limits the capacity for effecting change? These are the types of questions relative to privacy experiences in childhood and adolescence that need to be addressed.

ACKNOWLEDGMENTS

The theoretical perspective presented in this paper is the combined effort of myself and Robert Laufer and grew out of an earlier paper written by us and Harold Proshansky (Laufer, Proshansky, & Wolfe, 1973). My special thanks to Harold Proshansky for first getting me interested in the topic of privacy and to our colleagues who participated in the seminar and conducted research that contributed to our thinking, especially Marian Golan and Fran Justa.

REFERENCES

Ariès, P. *Centuries of childhood: A social history of family life.* New York: Vintage Books, 1962.

Aloia, A. Relationships between perceived privacy options, self-esteem and internal control among aged people (Unpublished Doctoral dissertation, California School of Professional Psychology, 1973). *Dissertation Abstracts International, 1973, 34,* 5180B. (University Microfilm N. 74-7922)

Altman, I. *Environment and social behavior: Privacy, territoriality, personal space and crowding.* Monterey, Calif.: Brooks Cole, 1975.

Anderson, J., & Tindall, M. The concept of home range: New data for the study of territorial behavior. *In* W. Mitchell (Ed.). *Environmental design: Research and practice.* Los Angeles: University of California, 1972.

Bem, D. *Beliefs, attitudes and human affairs.* Monterey, Calif.: Brooks Cole, 1970.

Bettelheim, B. *The children of the dream.* London: Macmillan, 1969.

Bowlby, J. *Attachment and loss.* New York: Basic Books, 1969.

Bracy, H. *Neighbors: Subdivision life in England and the United States.* Baton Rouge, La.: Louisiana State University Press, 1964.

Chermayeff, S., & Alexander, N. Y. *Community and privacy: Toward a new architecture of humanism.* New York: Doubleday, 1963.

Cohen, S., Glass, D. C., & Singer, J. E. Apartment noise, auditory discrimination, and reading ability in children. *Journal of Experimental Social Psychology, 1973, 9,* 407–422.

Coles, R. *Uprooted children: The early life of migrant farm workers.* New York: Harper & Row, 1970.

Chesler, P. *Women and madness.* New York: Doubleday, 1972.

Churchman, A. Concepts of privacy of Israeli children. Unpublished paper. Haifa, Israel: Technion, 1977.

Cozby, P. C. Self-disclosure: A literature review. *Psychological Bulletin, 1973, 79,* 73–91.

D'Atri, D. A. Psychophysiological responses to crowding. *Environment and Behavior, 1975, 7,* 111–126.

Ekstein, R., & Caruth, E. Keeping secrets. *In* M. Giovacchinni (Ed.), *Tactics and techniques in psychoanalytic psychotherapy.* New York: Science House, 1972.

Erikson, E. *Childhood and society.* 2nd Edition. New York: Norton, 1963.

Fischer, C. T. Toward the structure of privacy: Implications for psychological assessment. *In* A. Giorgi, W. G. Gischer, & R. Von Eckartsberg (Eds.), *Duquesne studies in phenomenological psychology.* Pittsburgh: Duquesne University Press, 1971.

Freud, S. *The ego and the id* (J. Strachey, Ed., and J. Riviere, trans.). New York: Norton, 1962 (originally published, 1923).

Fry, A., & Willis, F. N. Invasion of personal space as a function of the age of the invader. *Psychological Record, 1971, 21,* 385–389.

Golan, M. B. Privacy, interaction and self-esteem. Unpublished Doctoral dissertation, City University of New York, Environmental Psychology Program, 1978.

Golan, M. B., & Justa, F. The meaning of privacy for supervisors in an office setting. Paper presented at the meeting of the Environmental Design Research Association, Vancouver, British Columbia, May 1976. City University of New York Graduate School: Center for Human Environments, No. 76-6.

Hart, R. *Children's sense of place.* New York: Halstead Press, 1978.

Hutt, C., & Vaizey, M. J. Differential effects of group density on social behavior. *Nature, 1966, 206,* 1371–1372.

Ingelby, D. The psychology of child psychology. In M. P. M. Richards (Ed.), The integration of a child into a social world. London: Cambridge University Press, 1974.

Ittelson, W. H., Proshansky, H. M., & Rivlin, L. G. Bedroom size and social interaction of the psychiatric ward. Environment and Behavior, 1970, 2, 255–270.

Kira, A. The bathroom. Ithaca, N.Y.: Cornell University Center for Housing and Environmental Studies, 1966.

Kuper, L. Neighbor on the hearth. In H. M. Proshansky, W. H. Ittelson, & L. G. Rivlin (Eds.), Environmental psychology: Man and his physical setting. New York: Holt, Rinehart & Winston, 1970.

Ladd, F. Black youths view their environments: some views on housing. Journal of the American Institute of Planners, March 1972, 28, No. 2.

Ladd, F. The lack of amenities for adolescents in urban environments. Paper presented at City University of New York, Environmental Psychology Program, 1974.

Landy, D. Tropical childhood. New York: Harper & Row, 1965.

Laufer, R. S., Proshansky, H. M., & Wolfe, M. Some analytic dimensions of privacy. In Kuller, R. (Ed.), Architectural psychology. Stroudsberg, Pa.: Dowden, Hutchinson and Ross, 1973.

Laufer, R. S., & Wolfe, M. The interpersonal and environmental context of privacy invasion and response. Paper presented at the Fourth International Architectural Psychology Conference, Strasbourg, France, June 1976.

Laufer, R. S., & Wolfe, M. Privacy as a concept and a social issue. Journal of Social Issues, 1977, 33, 22–42.

Lawton, P., & Bader, J. Wish for privacy in young and old. Journal of Gerontology, 1970, 25, 48–54.

Levin, H. et al. "A social science appendix" to Tatum vs. Laird. Appeal from U.S. District Court of Columbia. Directed April 21, 1971.

Levin, H., & Askin, F. Privacy in the courts: Law and social reality. Journal of Social Issues, 1977, 33, 138–153.

Lewis, O. Privacy and crowding in poverty. In H. M. Proshansky, W. H. Ittelson, & L. G. Rivlin (Eds.), Environmental psychology: Man and his physical setting. New York: Holt, Rinehart & Winston, 1970.

Loring, W. C. Housing and social problems. Social Problems, 1956, 3, 160–168.

Maccoby, E. E., & Jacklin, C. N. The psychology of sex differences. Stanford, Calif. Stanford University Press, 1974.

Marshall, N. Privacy and environment. Human Ecology, 1972, 2, 93–110.

McCarthy, D., & Saegert, S. Residential density, social overload and social withdrawal. In J. Aiello & Y. Epstein (Eds.), Crowding and residential environment. New York: Plenum Press, in press.

Munroe, R. L., & Munroe, R. H. Effects of environmental experience on spatial ability in an East African society. Journal of Social Psychology, 1971, 83, 15–22.

Murray, R. The influence of crowding on children's behavior. In D. Canter & T. Lee (Eds.), Psychology and the built environment. England: Architectural Press, 1974.

Newson, J., & Newson, E. Four years old in an urban community. England: Pelican Books, 1968.

The New York Times: Character of Rural Life Changing with Dramatic Increase in Crime, Dec. 27, 1977.

Parke, R. D., & Sawin, D. B. Children's privacy in the home: Developmental ecological and child-rearing determinants. Paper presented at the IIIrd Biennial Conference of the International Society for the Study of Behavioral Development, Guilford, England, July 1975.

Piaget, J. *The moral judgement of the child*. New York: Basic Books, 1966.

Piaget, J., & Inhelder, B. *The psychology of the child*. New York: Basic Books, 1969.

Plant, J. Some psychiatric aspects of crowded living conditions. *American Journal of Psychiatry*, 1930, *9*, 849–860.

Plant, J. *Personality and the cultural pattern*. New York: The Commonwealth Fund, 1937.

Proshansky, H. M., Ittelson, W. H., & Rivlin, L. G. Freedom of choice and behavior in a physical setting. *In* H. M. Proshansky, W. H. Ittelson, & L. G. Rivlin (Eds.), *Environmental psychology: Man and his physical setting*. New York: Holt, Rinehart & Winston, 1970.

Roberts, J. M., & Gregor, T. Privacy: A cultural view. *In* J. R. Pennoch & J. W. Chapman (Eds.), *Privacy*. New York: Atherton Press, 1971.

Saegert, S., & Hart, R. The development of sex differences in environmental competence of children. *In* P. Barnet (Ed.), *Women in society*. Chicago, Ill.: Maroufa Press, 1975.

Saegert, S., Mackintosh, E., & West, S. Two studies of crowding in urban public spaces. *Environment and Behavior*, 1975, *7*, 159–184.

Schachter, S. *The psychology of affiliation: Experimental studies of the sources of gregariousness*. Stanford, Calif.: Stanford University Press, 1965.

Schwartz, B. The social psychology of privacy. *American Journal of Sociology*, 1968, *73*, 741–752.

Searles, H. *The non-human environment in normal development and in schizophrenia*. New York: International Universities Press, 1960.

Simmel, A. Privacy is not an isolated freedom. *In* J. Pennock & J. Chapman (Eds.), *Privacy*. New York: Atherton Press, 1971.

Silverstein, B., & Krate, R. *Children of the dark ghetto: A developmental psychology*. New York: Praeger, 1975.

Slater, P. *The pursuit of loneliness*. Boston: Beacon Press, 1970.

Talmon, Y. *Family and community in the kibbutz*. Cambridge, Mass.: Harvard University Press, 1972.

Tausk, V. On the origin of the "influencing machine" in schizophrenia, *Psychoanalytic Quarterly*, 1933, *2*, 519–556.

Werner, F. *Comparative psychology of mental development*. New York: International Universities Press, 1948.

Westin, A. F. *Privacy and freedom*. New York: Atheneum, 1967.

Wilner, P., Walkley, R. P., Pinkerton, T. C., & Tayback, M. *The housing environment and family life*. Baltimore, Md.: Johns Hopkins Press, 1962.

Wolfe, M. Room size, group size and density: Behavioral effects in a children's psychiatric facility. *Environment and Behavior*, 1975, *7*, 199–224.

Wolfe, M. *Growing up in cities: the concept of privacy in childhood and adolescence*. Paper presented at the IVth Biennial Conference of the International Society for the Study of Behavioral Development, Pavia, Italy, 1977.

Wolfe, M., & Golan, M. B. *Privacy and institutionalization*. Paper presented at the meeting of the Environmental Design Research Association, Vancouver, British Columbia, May 1976. City University of New York Graduate School: Center for Human Environments, No. 76-5.

Wolfe, M., & Laufer, R. S. The concept of privacy in childhood and adolescence. *In* D. H. Carson (Ed.), *Man–Environment interactions: Evaluations and applications*. Part II. Stroudsberg, Pa.: Dowden, Hutchinson & Ross, 1975.

Wolfe, M., Schearer, M., & Laufer, R. S. *Private places: The concept of privacy in childhood and adolescence*. Paper presented at the meeting of the Environmental Design Research Association, Vancouver, British Columbia, May 1976. City University of New York Graduate School: Center for Human Environments, No. 76-8.

6

Stalking the Elusive Cognitive Map

THE DEVELOPMENT OF CHILDREN'S REPRESENTATIONS OF GEOGRAPHIC SPACE

ALEXANDER W. SIEGEL
KATHLEEN C. KIRASIC
AND
ROBERT V. KAIL, JR.

INTRODUCTION

Most mornings you manage to find your way from home to office. This "way-finding" typically is accomplished around diversions, occlusions, and traffic, without a compass or road map, and, most important, without getting lost. Similarly, most mornings our children get from home to school without getting lost, even though the routes that children take on their journeys often are not direct (see Figure 1). Both adults and school-age children, then, seem to be able to get from a starting point to a not-simultaneously-perceivable endpoint in large environments, without navigational aids and without getting lost. In contrast, in Western society we rarely permit 3- and 4-year-olds to make such a journey, in spite of various protections (e.g., street-cross-

ALEXANDER W. SIEGEL, KATHLEEN C. KIRASIC, AND ROBERT V. KAIL, JR. · Psychology Department, University of Pittsburgh, Pittsburgh, Pennsylvania. Preparation of this paper was made possible, in part by NICHHD Grant No. 09694 to the first author.

223

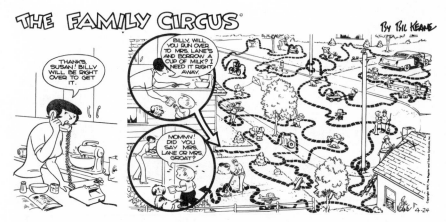

Figure 1. "The Family Circus" by Bil Keane, copyright 1977, reprinted courtesy of The Register and Tribune Syndicate, Inc.

ing guards). Societal wisdom tells us that the very young child, unlike his slightly older sibling, has limited way-finding skills—that he cannot travel between two points unless the end can be seen from the outset.

These developmental changes in way-finding seem to be attributable, in large part, to developmental changes in cognitive-mapping skills (Siegel & White, 1975): We assume that accurate way-finding in the large environment is guided by some reasonably accurate internal representation of that environment—a cognitive map (Downs & Stea, 1973a)—and that the characteristics of these internal representations change developmentally (Stea & Blaut, 1973).

Our primary purpose in this chapter is to provide an integrative review of the literature of children's cognitive-mapping skills. Before turning to this literature, we wish to consider three more general issues. First, the notions of representation in general and cognitive maps in particular need to be examined so it will be clear how we plan to use these terms. Second, critical methodological problems are encountered in attempting to determine children's knowledge of large-scale space (i.e., the nature of their cognitive maps), and these need to be considered in some depth. Third, we will argue that the developmental stages of spatial knowledge parallel different levels of the nervous system.

COGNITIVE MAPS

The nature of representation has been of tremendous concern to both cognitive and developmental psychologists. Representation has been conceptualized as variously perceptual or abstract in nature. That is, investigators vary in the extent to which they conceptualize "representation" as a more or less iconic copy of an event (e.g., Kosslyn, 1975; Shepard, 1975) or an abstract schematization in concrete (Hochberg, 1972), propositional (Bobrow & Norman, 1975), or analog (Holyoak, 1977) terms. In addition, "constructive" theories of development have proposed that the representation becomes progressively more differentiated and integrated over development (Piaget, 1960; Werner, 1948).

Space limitations preclude a detailed examination of the general problem of representation. (For relevant discussions, see Anderson, 1976, and Pylyshyn, 1973.) We do, however, wish to make one point clear concerning the representation of knowledge of large-scale environments. The term *cognitive map* is actually misleading. Tolman (1948) suggested that, rather than merely remembering specific spatial relations to which it has been exposed, an organism constructs an "overview" of the implicit spatial relations in a space. [Maier (1936) drew similar conclusions when children were given experience in a maze and were then able to find a reward from different starting points.] Tolman (1948) thus conceptualized the representation of real-life space, even in rats, as being similar to a map. However, the theoretical arguments and empirical data of Appleyard (1970), Hochberg (1972), Kosslyn (1975), and others have shown that the internal representations of our surroundings that guide our spatial behaviors cannot contain the innumerable details and dimensions of our environment as portrayed in a "road map." Rather, the representation [much like Bartlett's (1932) "schema"] is more probably a stripped down and encoded map of our world in which appropriately chosen features are central (Menzell, 1973; Tolman, 1948; Trowbridge, 1913). Additionally, we find from Appleyard (1969), Ladd (1970), Lee (1970), and Lynch (1960) that these representations are often distorted, fragmented, and inaccurate (both in a projective and Euclidean sense). Even so, for purposes of linguistic economy, we will use the term *cognitive map*, knowing that it is a convenient fiction.

The Development of Cognitive Maps

Since we assume that children's way-finding in large-scale environments is guided by cognitive maps, it is important to understand how these cognitive maps develop. Siegel and White (1975) have recently proposed a conceptual framework for understanding and studying the development of spatial representations of large-scale environments that we will use later to organize our discussion of the literature. On the basis of empirical and theoretical literature in neurology, urban design, and psychology, the following analyses were postulated: Descriptions of space reflect models of the environment. These models can be called cognitive maps (or spatial representations) and are constructed by the integration of successive percepts over time. It seems likely that humans are neurologically disposed to create and organize such models (Fishbein, 1976a; Herrick, 1956; Jackson, 1874). The capacity to build such models develops (Bergson, 1911; Gladwin, 1970; Werner, 1948). The models are initially figurative constructions which arise and jell out of a foundation of perceptions and practical activity. Eventually, they become coordinated to social terminology and become schematized and metricized. Landmarks and routes are the predominant elements of these representations; higher-order configurational elements are also used, but they develop late (Downs & Stea, 1973b; Shemyakin, 1962).

Siegel and White (1975) further postulated that the development of spatial representations in children conforms to the sequence identified in the construction of spatial representations in adults: First, landmarks are noticed and remembered. The child acts in the context of these landmarks, and given landmarks and action-sequences, route formation is accomplished. Landmarks and routes are formed into clusters, but until an objective frame of reference is developed, these clusters remain uncoordinated with each other. Although the spatial representations of adults and those of children differ in detail, the underlying developmental process is the same: The sequence of going from landmarks, to route-representations to configurational-coordinated representations is a process of going from association to structure (Mandler, 1962) and of deriving simultaneity from successivity.

Why Cognitive Maps?

The basic purposes of cognitive maps are to permit way-finding in the large-scale environment without getting lost and to serve as organizers for the organism's experience (Lynch, 1960). Both Kaplan (1973) and Fishbein (1976b) have argued that man's ability to construct cognitive maps of the environment is a canalized social competency; that is, over the course of human evolution, the ability to construct cognitive maps gave humans a selective evolutionary advantage and became incorporated into the epigenetic system of the hunter-gatherer ancestors of man. The ability to cognitively map "geographic space" aided cooperative hunting of big game and facilitated the seasonal-selective search for fruits and vegetables. One hardly need elaborate the positive adaptive value of remembering the locations in the environment where particular kinds of game and food can be found and the negative adaptive value of not remembering one's bearings relative to a home base.

The many functions of cognitive maps for contemporary man have been documented in numerous domains of research. For example, it is again clear from the literature of urban planning that one important function of cognitive maps is to organize cognitive and social experience. Appleyard (1970), Lee (1968), and Lynch (1960) have shown how one's conception of the spatial environment influences and organizes one's social and cognitive experiences (Berger & Luckmann, 1967; Maurer & Baxter, 1972). A cognitive map can serve, for example, as a device from which one can generate decisions about action and planning of sequences of action. It is certainly easier for a New York taxi driver to plan a route from the Brooklyn Battery Tunnel to the Empire State Building if he has an overall "mental map" of New York City as opposed to an almost unlimited number of serial point-to-point associations. In other words, a cognitive map permits greater *cognitive efficiency* (Lynch, 1960; Neisser, 1976). Finally, cognitive maps can be used to understand fundamentally nonspatial domains of experience. For example, if one has a coherent representation of the city of Boston, this can be used to decide the location of the best place to park during rush hour, to derive a list of Chinese restaurants within a five-minute walk of Harvard Square, or to reject the proposition that someone walked from the airport to downtown in five minutes (Siegel, 1977a).

In summary, the term cognitive map is, in a sense, a misnomer, for these internal representations do not correspond literally to maps. Instead, they are configurations of landmarks and routes, configurations that are often distorted or even inaccurate. The fundamental purpose of a cognitive map is to organize knowledge of geographic space, thus resulting in greater efficiency and accuracy of movement within that space.

METHODOLOGICAL ISSUES

It seems to be characteristic of researchers and clinicians that judgments of children tend to center on cognitive competence rather than performance; that is, observed changes in cognitive performance typically are assimilated rapidly into hypotheses and statements about cognitive competence. Equating performance with competence ignores powerful situational effects on performance. A child's performance can be moved "upward" or "downward" by the load or difficulty placed on the child by the situation (White & Siegel, 1976). Consider, for example, the Piagetian finding that preoperational children typically encounter difficulty in recalling the events of a story in the appropriate order (Piaget, 1968). Based on this performance phenomenon, Piaget has speculated about underlying capacities for reversible thought (Piaget & Inhelder, 1969) and egocentrism (Piaget, 1926). Brown (1976) pointed out that the method used by Piaget to assess the child's competence—verbal recall—is one that is particularly difficult for young children. When Brown (1976) used a nonverbal measure of story recall, she found that even 5-year-olds were quite capable of recalling the events of a story in their appropriate order. Thus, since children fluctuate in their *apparent* ability depending upon a variety of factors, it becomes critical to measure a child's performance in several conditions or contexts before reaching conclusions regarding that child's competence.

These considerations are particularly relevant to the phenomenon of cognitive mapping, in which the key methodological issue involves "externalizing" the map (Milgram, 1973). Most of our knowledge about cognitive maps in adults is based on research in which adults are asked to report verbally their impressions, experiences, and knowledge of a particular environment or to draw a free-hand sketch map of the layout of the features they consider to be significant (Appleyard, 1970; Carr & Schissler, 1969; Lynch, 1960). These techniques are quite restricted in their applicability to young children. Young children's verbal reports of things and events experienced typically are neither terribly accurate nor reliable. In addition, young children's drawings are not to be trusted (Kosslyn, Heldmeyer, & Locklear, 1977); having the child draw a sketch map confounds cognitive (i.e., internal) mapping ability and "externalizing" ability (i.e., understanding and producing conventions and symbolizations). It is surely the case that young children's cognitive maps of environments are more accurate than the products they draw to "represent" those environments.

Problems also exist with nonverbal or "constructive" measures of mapping. One of the experimental factors that has contributed significantly to an underestimation of the young child's cognitive mapping abilities is that children's knowledge of large environments has only rarely been tested in a layout of the same scale. Thus, developmental change in the ability to translate from the large-scale environment to a small-scale model (or vice versa) is confounded with the child's actual knowledge of the layout. Such problems of translation almost certainly are not trivial for young children, as has been shown in research on children's "egocentrism" in tasks requiring a change of perspective (e.g., Huttenlocher & Presson, 1973).

Most of the studies in the developmental literature utilize environments in which most of the layout is visible at any one time. In getting from point A to point B in the real world, however, the route taken is typically indirect and accomplished around obstacles and occlusions. In constructing cognitive maps of the real world, elements and relations not directly perceivable during a single environmental encounter are included (Kosslyn, Pick, & Fariello, 1974). Thus, conclusions reached from research regarding the nature of cognitive maps are limited in generality by the extent to which the real world is simulated in detail (i.e., obstacles, occlusions) as well as in size.

A final issue or problem in the externalization of young children's cognitive maps is that whereas, in the real world, children develop their knowledge of macrospace over varied and repeated encounters with the environment, most of the research done to date has not tested that knowledge in a similar fashion. Typically, a child is asked to construct or recall either the environment or a model only once or after only one exposure. If, indeed, cognitive maps of macrospace develop and become elaborated via a mechanism of integration of percepts over time and repeated encounters, research has, at the very least, the obligation to test the child in an analagous fashion (Siegel, 1977a).

In summary, the process of revealing a child's cognitive map is a complicated affair. The method of assessment should provide a view of a child's cognitive competence that is relatively unbiased by irrelevant performance factors. Drawings and verbal reports are poorly suited for this purpose, as are methods that require the child to translate between environments of different sizes or scales. Unfortunately, these are the sorts of methods that most researchers have relied upon in their studies of children's knowledge of large-scale space. Consequently, most of the studies to be discussed later deserve careful scrutiny on methodological grounds before conclusions are reached regarding the level of competence imputed to the children in these studies.

NEUROLOGICAL BASES OF SPATIAL KNOWLEDGE

We argued in the previous section that spatial development has important neurological and epigenetic underpinnings. In the present section we provide evidence to support this argument. Our discussion has two parts. First, we will argue that the developmental progressions found in cognitive mapping rest on a neurological substrate—the construction of the central nervous system and the principle that secondary cortical adaptations must be established on the base of subcortical adaptations.[1] Second, we will review evidence documenting the importance of specific cortical areas (i.e., the parietal lobes) for the development of cognitive mapping.

Parallels between Spatial Development and Levels of the Nervous System

In the latter part of the nineteenth century, under the influence of evolutionary thinking, contemporary philosophical psychology was merged with theory and data regarding the organization and function of the nervous system. Perhaps the foremost figure in this enterprise was John Hughlings Jackson, "the father of modern neurology." Borrowing heavily from the Development Hypothesis of Herbert Spencer (Spencer, 1862/1892), Jackson (1884) argued that the growth of knowledge and the evolutionary organization of the nervous system rested on a hierarchical system of experiential analyses. This argument, taken by Cassirer (1955) and Piaget (1960), suggested that spatial knowledge arises out of a hierarchical nervous structure in which space is presented, then represented, then re-represented to the organism. Cassirer (1955) postulated three levels of spatial knowledge: active, perceptual, and symbolic space. At the first level, active space, is the "hardwiring" which permits sufficient spatial calculations to arrange the organism's movement in space. Built upon this lower level, with further evolution of the brain, a second-order analysis is possible—perceptual space (i.e., knowledge of arrangements of things in space). Finally, with the possession of frontal, temporal, and parietal cortex, one gets in man re-representation and the possibility of symbolic space (i.e., formal representations of space; Werner & Kaplan, 1963).

The mechanism that allows for the ontogenetic and phylogenetic progression between these levels is that of temporal integration—a process by which successive events or percepts are converted into a simultaneity. Cassirer's three levels of space can be construed as spatial knowledge existing at three levels of temporal integration. At the first level, rapid temporal co-occurrences permit object manipulation, co-

---

[1] For example, destruction of the hippocampus in rats produces poor performance in such spatial tasks as mazes and those requiring alternation of responses or successive trials. One of the major hypotheses regarding these deficits is that the primary function of the hippocampus is to construct a cognitive or spatial map of its environment. O'Keefe and Dostrovsky (1971) suggest that ". . . it is the loss of this spatial reference map which results in all or most of the behavioral deficits reported for hippocampectomized rats" (p. 175). The hippocampus is thus a subcortical structure on which the higher-order organization of the cortex is superimposed in man.

ordination of hand and eye, etc. (Blumenthal, 1977).[2] At level two, sensory encounters over longer temporal spans permit the assembly of the landmarks and routes of spatial representation. At the third level, symbolic space, a higher-order integration allows construction of more distal arrangements of space mapped out in nonvisible units such as angstroms or light-years. That is, at this highest level, perceptual space is "remodeled" such that coordination and extrapolation of and from perceptual space is permitted.

The Right Parietal Lobe: Seat of Spatial Knowledge?

It should be noted that what has seemed "higher" in neurological and philosophical discussions has been incorporated as a directional principle in current conceptualizations of cognitive development. The development of the child is seen as the working out of such an evolutionary tendency. Using similar reasoning, there has been a pervasive tendency to conceptualize pathology as dis-evolutionary (Teitelbaum, 1977).

The importance of the right posterior hemisphere [and especially the secondary associational cortex (Luria, 1966)] for spatial knowledge has been demonstrated repeatedly in the literature of neurology (Harris, 1976). Critchley (1971) documented extensively that damage of the parieto-occipital region of the right hemisphere produced various disturbances in visuospatial functioning, loss of map-reading ability, visual agnosia (inability to recognize objects), loss of topographical memory (memory for familiar places), prosopagnosia (loss of the ability to recognize faces), and constructional apraxia (e.g., loss of drawing or constructional ability).

The relationship between the dissolution of spatial knowledge in brain damage and its ontogeny in children has been made explicit in a paper by DeAjuriaguerra and Tissot (1969) in which the apraxias are viewed as disturbances in mastery of space:

> It does seem possible at the present time to classify apraxias according to the type of space in which they are realized . . . . Each of the classical forms

---

[2] Hart and Moore (1973) propose a distinction similar to that of Cassirer by separating basic spatial concepts (orientation and locomotion in proximate space in which the goal can be directly perceived) and macro-spatial cognition. The coordination of the visual, vestibular, and verticulomotor systems by the brain determines an individual's knowledge of the basic dimensions about which all information is organized: up–down, front–back, and left–right (Harris, 1976). The problem of basic spatial concepts and macro-spatial cognition are not independent—but our primary concern here is macro-spatial cognition.

of apraxia corresponds to the disorganization of a type of space which is "genetically distinct": constructional apraxia corresponds to Euclidean space, ideomotor apraxia to the space centered on the body, ideational apraxia to the concrete space of manipulation. It may be thought that in the place of a descriptive system of classification meant to be physiopathological we are substituting a purely phenomenological but equally descriptive system of classification. In a sense that is true, but it is an objective type of phenomenology, namely, that of the development of the child. This reformalization has an advantage in that it enables us to understand why the different types of apraxia appear to be of an almost predetermined nature. They are but the reappearance, in a form more or less distorted by pathological conditions, of levels of adaptive organization of the central nervous system laid down in the course of development. (p. 63)

Thus, much of the research from neurology indicates that damage to the parietal area in the minor hemisphere (in most adults) seems to selectively impair configurational spatial knowledge.

It was argued earlier (and will be documented later) that the development of configurational or survey maps is ontogenetically late, relative to the development of landmark or route knowledge. Recent evidence suggests that this late development of configurational knowledge may represent the relatively late maturation of parietal lobe (or parietal-occipital-temporal cortex). Specifically, recall that one of the most common sequelae of right parietal lobe damage is prosopagnosia—the loss of ability to recognize familiar faces. In a series of provocative papers, Carey and Diamond (1977; Diamond & Carey, 1977) have demonstrated that the young child's recognition of faces is not unlike that found in patients with right posterior lesions. Specifically, these patients, as well as 6- to 8-year-olds, recognize inverted faces as capably as do older children and normal adults. In contrast, when upright faces are shown, patients with right posterior lesions and children younger than age 10 are not as accurate in their recognition of faces as are adults.

Why should developmental differences be found for upright but not inverted faces? Carey and Diamond (1977) argued that faces can be differentiated on two bases: features and gestalts (relational, higher-order, or configurational properties). The development of the ability to encode faces configurationally might account for the marked improvement in recognition accuracy of upright faces between ages 6 and 10. It is likely that configurational encoding is responsible for the improvement since isolated distinguishing features could be encoded from inverted faces almost as well as from upright faces, while configurational encoding is much more difficult with inverted faces. Thus, it may be that the immaturity of the cortical areas mediating face perception in the adult—or the lack of commitment of these areas to the functions they will subserve in adulthood—places a limit on the young child's capacity to represent new faces. Although similar performances need not imply the operation of identical neural structures, it would appear that age 10 marks an inflection point in the development of right hemisphere specialization, and thus, possibly, in the development of configurational spatial representation.

Summary

Research on the development of spatial knowledge in children, as well as data from the literature of clinical neurology, seems to indicate that levels of spatial knowledge parallel levels of the nervous system. In the following section we will use these three stages of spatial knowledge—landmarks, routes, and configurations—to organize our discussion of the literature of children's cognitive mapping.

THE DEVELOPMENT OF COGNITIVE MAPS

In this section we will try to specify and document what seems to be a general sequence in the development of cognitive mapping. The documentation will be selective rather than exhaustive. The specification of the sequence will be considered in three major sections conforming to the model of the elements of cognitive maps specified by Siegel and White (1975): landmarks, routes (sequences), and configurations.

THE DEVELOPMENT OF LANDMARK KNOWLEDGE

We argued earlier that the basic elements of the cognitive map were landmarks—those salient objects or points of decision in the environment that are noticed and remembered and around which the child's action and decisions are coordinated. Landmarks are unique patterns of perceptual events that identify a specific geographical location. The Place de l'Etoile is as much a landmark as the Washington Monument, or a billboard advertising Noxzema shaving cream. For children, landmarks might be the candy store, the playground, and the school crossing. These landmarks are the strategic foci to and from which a person moves or travels, are predominantly visual, and are used as proximate or intermediate devices to maintain one's course. Children's and adults' descriptions of environments typically begin with the mention of landmarks (Appleyard, 1970; Downs & Stea, 1973a;

Gladwin, 1970). Thus, it seems logical to begin this discussion with a consideration of the development of landmark knowledge.

We can identify at least two developmental levels of landmark knowledge. The first is recognition or identification—knowledge that a landmark is familiar, that it has been seen before. The second, which presupposes the first, is knowledge that landmarks can be *used* to facilitate the placement of other landmarks and events; that is, at this level, landmarks can be used to organize past and future experience. This kind of knowledge, almost a "meta-knowledge" of landmarks (à la Flavell & Wellman, 1977) probably shows the greatest developmental differences in the childhood years, as will be shown.[3] Two specific questions concerning landmark knowledge guide our discussion: (1) To what extent does the ability to recognize and identify landmarks change with development? (2) What is the developmental progression in how location information is remembered and used?

Recognition of Landmarks

The first question can be dispensed with rather easily. The capacity for recognition of single, relatively discriminable objects remains essentially invariant from at least 4 years of age to adulthood (e.g., Brown, 1973). Sheer landmark recognition appears, in essence, to be developmentally insensitive or invariant, and thus can be assumed to be, at least in large part, "hardwired" or "canalized" (Hochberg & Brooks, 1962). Furthermore, spatial locational knowledge seems to be encoded with minimal conscious effort on the part of the child (e.g., Mandler, Seegmiller, & Day, 1977; von Wright, Gebhardt, & Karttunen, 1975).

Use of Landmarks

The situation is far more complex with regard to how spatial locations are used to organize spatial experience. Here a bifurcation appears in the literature. The majority of studies concerned with the development of children's spatial knowledge have typically used a

---

[3] A third level of knowledge is knowing that not only can landmarks serve as organizers of spatial experience, they can also serve the purpose of organizing more symbolic, semantic kinds of "nonspatial" knowledge. For example, Huttenlocher (1968) has shown that subjects solve reasoning problems of the type: "Fred is taller than Harry; Jim is taller than Fred. Who is the tallest?" spatially. They first imagine arranging the two items from the first premise, and then imagine placing the third item with respect to these fixed items (i.e., landmarks or anchors) according to the description in the second premise. Thus, subjects spatialize certain "nonspatial" dimensions, and this spatialization determines how they set up such problems.

small-scale environment as the environment to be "mapped." In other words, research has typically focused on children's spatial knowledge in arrays of objects that are small, novel, simple, and thus artificial. Little attention has been paid to children's knowledge of the actual and familiar large-scale spaces in which real children develop real knowledge about the spatial layouts of their world. Recently, however, attempts have been made to study children's cognitive maps of large environments (or at least in "simulations" of large environments) (Herman & Siegel, 1978; Kosslyn et al., 1974).

Micro- and Macro-Spatial Landmark Knowledge. It is important to distinguish between these two literatures. Micro-spatial cognition may well involve processes different from those of macro-spatial cognition. Additionally, as was argued in the Introduction, in asking a child to pretend that a small space stands for a large environment, the interpretation of a child's poor performance is ambiguous. It might be due to a lack of macro-spatial knowledge, a problem in translating macro-spatial knowledge to a micro-spatial domain, or some combination of both. Recent evidence highlights the danger in equating the results of micro- and macrospatial studies. For example, Acredolo (1976) found that preschoolers' coding of spatial location and their ability to coordinate perspectives in a small-scale space was markedly inferior to their ability to do so in large-scale space. Similarly, in a study by Siegel and Schadler (1977) kindergartners who constructed relatively inaccurate models of the spatial layout of their classroom had little difficulty remembering the locations of these objects in the actual classroom. Thus, generalizations regarding developmental differences from one scale of space to another would seem ill-advised. This is not to say that the particular results obtained in one or the other domain are inaccurate or invalid. Rather, statements regarding a child's competence in cognitive mapping (or landmark knowledge) in the large environment cannot be inferred merely from performance in small-scale space.

Frames of Reference. A key issue in the use of landmark knowledge for the placement of other landmarks is that, in so doing, the child must create and operate within some objective frame of reference. Outside features or landmarks become organized into systems in space. Piaget and Inhelder (1967), Moore (1976), and others have suggested that part of what is involved in this process is a progressive differentiation of self-orientation from outside-orientation, and the development of an objective sense of bearing (Minnigerode & Carey, 1974; Siegel & White, 1975; Werner, 1948). Similarly, Wapner, Cirillo, and Baker (1971) and Pick (1970) have argued that a frame of reference is necessary in order to remember and reconstruct the location, orientation, and interobject relationships accurately. Thus, it would appear that second-order landmark knowledge (i.e., knowledge of the use of landmarks) is intimately tied to the development of frames of reference.

The child's construction of frames of reference seems to progress through a series of stages from egocentrism to flexible objectivism. Moore (1975) describes this progression as going (a) from undifferentiated egocentric, (b) to differentiated and partially coordinated into fixed sub-groups, and (c) to abstractly coordinated and hierarchically integrated. This description bears more than a surface similarity to Piaget's descriptions of progression from topological to coordinated-Euclidean concepts of space. Inherent in such a transition is an increase in the child's awareness and utilization of the viewpoints of others and the rules for ascertaining those viewpoints. Pufall and Shaw (1973), for example, asked 4-, 6-, and 10-year-old children to copy an object's location and orientation within a two-dimensional spatial layout under two conditions: when the experimenter's standard board and that of the subject were in the same orientation and when they were rotated 180° from each other. Their analyses of children's performances seem to indicate that a frame of reference develops in at least two sequential phases. Once the frame is developed, it organizes relations among objects if there are no distinctive features to serve as unique reference points. They found that for 4-year-olds, "near-far" and "left-right" appear to function independently and do not form a single system. In the second phase, 6-year-olds are capable of using relations among reference features within the space (if nonrotated) in addition to using a purely egocentric frame of reference. That is, in the second phase, the child knows not only that a landmark is "near" some distinctive feature but also that the landmark is in a specific orientation (e.g., left-right) relative to that distinctive feature (Coie, Costanzo, & Farnill, 1973; Harris & Strommen, 1972). As the child develops, he shifts from an egocentric to a more fixed frame of reference, and then finally becomes able to use this framework in a flexible and adaptive manner. He begins to use landmarks to anchor, organize, and coordinate his cognitive map.

Piaget's Description of the Development of Landmark Knowledge. The most complete account of the development of landmark knowledge and frames of reference is derived from Piagetian theory (Laurendeau & Pinard, 1970; Piaget & Inhelder, 1967). According to Piaget, the young child encodes spatial location in relation to himself (an egocentric system) rather than in terms of its relation to other objects in the spatial array (an objective frame of reference). The child progresses from a coding system based on the relationship of landmarks to his own body

and own perspective (Wapner *et al.*, 1971) to a system in which landmarks become central features for partial coordination of space (a fixed
frame, topological in nature), and finally to a coding system based on
abstract axes, thereby facilitating full coordination in space (i.e., to a
coordinate frame of reference that is Euclidean in nature). (See also
Moore, 1976.)

The most convincing evidence favoring the developmental sequences described by Piaget comes from the work of Acredolo (1976,
1977) and her colleagues (Acredolo, Pick, & Olsen, 1975). In several
studies, Acredolo has provided children with contrasting frames of
reference which they must use to determine the location of an object.
In one study (Acredolo, 1977, Expt. 1), the task was to learn in which
of two locations on opposite sides of the room an object had been
hidden. The child stood at the point labeled A in Figure 2 and closed
his eyes while the experimenter hid a trinket under one of two identical
cups. The trinket was consistently placed under one of the two cups.
After the child had correctly located the trinket on five consecutive
trials, he was moved to the opposite side of the room (point B in Figure
2) and was asked to locate the trinket again which remained under the
same cup. If the child relied upon egocentric cues—making the same
bodily response (e.g., left turn)—then he would select the wrong cup.
Only by using the landmarks in the room and ignoring bodily cues
could the child respond correctly. Between ages 3 and 5 years, the
percentage of children relying upon such landmarks increased from 50
to 100. Stated another way, half the 3-year-olds relied upon egocentric
cues while no 5-year-olds did. When the two cups were differentiated
by placing distinctive tablecloths under each, the percentage of 3-year-

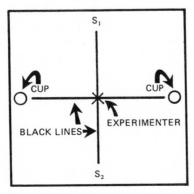

Figure 2. The experimental space used by Acredolo (1977).

olds using these landmarks rather than relying on an egocentric frame of reference increased from 50 to 75.

The results of this study are important for two reasons. First, the results support the sequence of spatial development described by Piaget and Inhelder (1967) in that young children responded on the basis of an egocentric frame of reference while only older children were likely to respond on the basis of an objective frame. Second, Acredolo's results attest to the importance of the differentiation of the environment for successful use of landmarks. Even in the most undifferentiated environments, a person familiar with the area and its linguistic conventions can detect and discriminate landmarks that would be undetectable to an outsider. In other environments, landmarks are so salient and differentiated that even a stranger would have difficulty getting lost. Thus, the development of accurate cognitive maps of large-scale space would seem to be highly dependent on the differentiatedness of landmarks.

The importance of differentiated environmental cues on children's ability to remember the location of events in a large-scale environment was clearly demonstrated by Acredolo et al. (1975). Children were taken on a walk down a relatively long corridor. For some children, the corridor was empty; for others, two chairs were added as landmarks. During the walk, the experimenter "accidentally" dropped her keys at a particular location. A few minutes later the child was asked to return to the spot where the experimenter had dropped her keys. When no landmarks were available, 3- and 4-year-olds were much less accurate than 8-year-olds, but age differences disappeared when landmarks were present. Acredolo et al. (1975) argued that the younger children used only topological cues provided by the landmarks, but the 8-year-olds were, in addition, using Euclidean spatial relationships. "An understanding of Euclidean spatial concepts, particularly metric distance appears to have enabled the older children to code location in space relatively accurately in the absence of distinctive landmarks so that the addition of such landmarks made no significant difference to their performance" (Acredolo et al., 1975, p. 500). Thus, so far it appears that, just as Piaget would have us believe, young children are not capable of using Euclidean spatial relationshps.[4]

The Role of Experience. Consider the nature of the preceding ex-

---

[4] However, as Williams and Jambor (1964) point out: "The manner in which topographical orientation is developed in children and the stages through which it passes are not altogether clear from past work; Piaget's studies have been concerned with elucidating the development of 'concepts' of space rather than the manner in which children find their way about in it" (p. 56).

periments. The child was given but one exposure to the environment prior to being tested. As we indicated earlier, children typically have repeated encounters with environments during which they develop their spatial knowledge (Munroe & Munroe, 1971; Nerlove, Munroe, & Munroe, 1971). Repeated experience in the environment is thought to be necessary for the integration of successive percepts with the movements associated with those percepts in order for the child to develop an accurate cognitive map (Siegel & White, 1975). The importance of such repeated exposure to the environment can be seen in a study by Herman and Siegel (1978). Children from kindergarten, second, and fifth grade were taken on a walk through a spatial layout of buildings in a 4.9 × 6.1 m room. Half the children at each grade were given three walks through the environment prior to their first reconstruction; the other half were allowed to reconstruct the layout after each walk. For all children, accuracy of construction improved as a function of experience (i.e., the number of walks): children who constructed the town the first time after three walks produced more accurate models than those who constructed it after only one walk. On the first construction, fifth graders were more accurate than either group of younger children (see Figure 3). The age differences on the first construction look surprisingly like those data reported by Piaget and Inhelder (1967) and by Laurendeau and Pinard (1970).

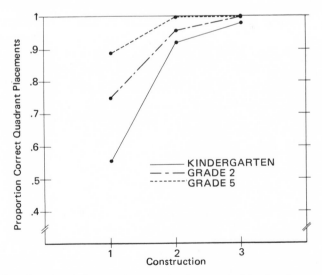

Figure 3. Developmental changes in accurate placement of landmarks as a function of repeated experiences. Adapted from Herman and Siegel (1978).

If the experiment had stopped here and the child not been given additional opportunities to reconstruct the layout, the data would have supported the simple argument that not until the child can utilize an abstract frame of reference will he be able to accurately localize and remember landmarks in the environment. However, as is clear from Figure 3, the performance of even the kindergarteners eventually became as accurate as that of fifth graders. By the third construction, the performance of the kindergarten children was asymptotic. Whereas performance on the initial construction is consistent with the data of Acredolo and Piaget, the data from the final construction are clearly in conflict. It is not difficult to reconcile this disagreement: children in the previous studies were not given the repeated opportunity to interact with the environment, and such repeated interaction is not only paradigmatic for young children's interactions with real-world space, but also facilitates the process of integration of percepts with movements.

Of course, all experiences are not equal in their effects on the development of spatial knowledge. Locomotion on the part of the traveler seems to be critical for the development of memory for environmental landmarks. Appleyard (1970) found that the extent of direct contact in the environment, such as length of residence in an area, or driving as opposed to taking a bus, was related directly to the quality of residents' cognitive maps of a city (as inferred from their sketch maps). Ladd (1970) had black urban adolescents draw sketch maps of their neighborhoods and found that the configurational quality and accuracy of the map, as well as the richness of detail (landmarks), increased with experience in the environment and with an increased sphere of functional activity of the youths. Ladd argued that "walking is intimate to the environment and therefore articulates the schema" (p. 97). These and other studies with adults (Carr & Schissler, 1969; Lee, 1968, Lynch, 1960) seem to indicate that actual locomotion may be an almost essential condition for the construction of accurate cognitive maps.

Summary

Sheer recognition and identification of landmarks is a relatively early-developing ability that improves little over ontogenetic development. In constrast, the meta-knowledge of landmarks—knowing that something you recognize can be used to organize interrelationships among other objects within an objective frame of reference—increases significantly with development. In other words, knowing not only that you have seen something before but where and when you have seen it seems to develop in concert with more general cognitive abilities. The development of landmark knowledge seems to be another example of the development of "applied cognition": Development comes in knowing that knowing something about landmarks is spatially useful.

THE DEVELOPMENT OF ROUTE LEARNING

Although landmarks are essential to way-finding in the large environment, they are insufficient for constructing a cognitive map unless they are embedded in a context of effective action, i.e., a method for getting from landmark to landmark: A primary function of a landmark is to help maintain one's passage on a particular route. Routes can be considered as nonstereotypic sensorimotor routines permitting the traveler to go from Landmark A to Landmark B. One has a route if one has (expects, imagines) a particular landmark at the beginning and knows that a succession of landmarks in a particular order will follow if a particular direction/heading is taken; the last landmark in the succession is the destination. In other words, route knowledge is fundamentally a form of sequence knowledge (Siegel & White, 1975). If the sequence of landmarks experienced while traveling does not conform to expectations, one quite quickly has the feeling of being "lost." Routes can then be seen as a kind of spatial glue—strands of spider thread connecting the nodes (landmarks). Routes give shape to the spatial representation.

Thus, we reencounter a set of mechanisms first met in the development of landmarks knowledge: locomotion and the concomitant temporal integration permitted by it. Beck and Wood (1976) suggest that one must move through the environment for an evnironmental experience to take place. In so doing, one must necessarily organize these temporally successive "motion-events" into a single linear stream—a simultaneity from a successivity, a structure from a set of associations (Mandler, 1962)—a coherent event with quality and texture (Jenkins, Wald, & Pittenger, 1976).

Thus, we can conceptualize the environment (and one's cognitive map of that environment) as consisting of landmarks connected by routes, which are guided in some way by sequence learning. What is the mechanism of the "sequence learning" or process of route formation? Although we are not in a position to provide a formal analysis, the following would seem to be four essential characteristics of a route-learning system.

1. A route must involve a sequence of decisions—what we would typically call changes in bearing (e.g., Kuipers, 1976; Siegel & White, 1975). The organism must typically compute its decision in terms of an

orientation or the direction of the organism with reference to some feature(s) of the environment. Route formation is dependent logically upon landmark knowledge.

2. The knowledge of a route might be constructed by means of a kind of serial learning—a memorized series of decisions. However, it is more likely that a memorized route would be similar to paired-associate learning, with changes in bearing associated with the arrival at "stimulus" landmarks.

3. To some extent, learning between landmarks is incidental and irrelevant—except to the extent that intermediate landmarks serve as course-maintaining devices (i.e., as landmarks associated with no change in bearing). Thus, a conservative route-learning system would be, in effect, "empty" between landmarks. All of the learning would be organized around the nodes of the decision system, the landmarks.

4. In the adult's construction of a cognitive map, routes become scaled by landmarks in an ordinal and roughly interval sense—but this issue need not concern us now. That is, to some extent, the "empty" space between landmarks gets "scaled" during extended experience with the routes. This scaling may be of significance in the ultimate elaboration of what Shemyakin (1962) has called "survey" maps.

In the remainder of this section, we will examine research concerning the development of route knowledge. Two types of evidence are particularly relevant. As has been mentioned previously, route knowledge is a type of sequence knowledge. Consequently, studies of children's recognition and reconstruction of sequences may provide insights into the development of route knowledge. Of course, as has been argued throughout this chapter, it is risky to make inferences about children's cognitive-mapping skills based on their performance in microspatial tasks. We will, therefore, also examine studies of the development of route knowledge in large-scale or in simulations of large-scale space.

Recognition and Reconstruction of Sequence

According to Piaget (1968) recognition memory is the most primitive form of memory, depending only on sensorimotor schema. In reconstructive memory, the child must have a schema that can be activated with much less stimulus support than is the case with the recognition memory. In fact, a consistent theme in the developmental literature is that a child is often able to recognize a sequence prior to being able to reconstruct that sequence. Blackstock and King (1973), for example, demonstrated that preschoolers were able to recognize a seriated configuration (i.e., find an M & M that is under a seriated set and not under a nonseriated set) well before they were able to reconstruct a seriated array (i.e., make yours like mine).

The manner of stimulus presentation has also been shown to play a significant role in memory for sequences. Pufall and Furth (1966), for example, found that preschoolers could more accurately reconstruct sequences presented simultaneously than sequences presented successively. They suggested that a successive sequence must be internally structured and maintained and that the resulting cognitive load is too great for the preschool child. In a rather interesting way, the simultaneous presentation of a series of events provides a kind of stimulus support not present when the events are presented successively. This is reminiscent of a well-established finding in the literature of learning in children—simultaneous discriminations are far easier than successive discriminations (Gollin, 1965).

When we consider sequences that are ordered *logically* rather than physically (Huttenlocher, 1968), a similar pattern of developmental change emerges. Brown and her colleagues (Brown & Murphy, 1975; French & Brown, 1975) presented several toys to preschoolers, about which they were told a story. The stories were constructed either such that each item played an integral part in the plot (i.e., the items were presented in a logical order), or such that no apparent relationship existed among the items (i.e., the items were presented in random order). When the children were asked to reconstruct the stories, even the preschoolers were able to retell the story that had been presented to them in a logical sequence. As might be expected, the younger children had considerable difficulty in reconstructing the series that had been presented to them randomly.

Route Learning in Large-Scale Spaces

Given this discussion of sequence knowledge of microspace, it is of interest to ask what developmental research has been done to investigate the development of route knowledge in the large environment. Brown and Lawton (1975) required preschoolers to reconstruct the route taken by a baby elephant through several locations in a 1.2 × 2.2 m model jungle. Along the way, the elephant stopped at 5 of 12 possible locations. Three experimental variables were manipulated. Children in a *passive* condition sat and watched the experimenter take the elephant through the model; children in an *active* condition walked around the model with the experimenter and moved the elephant from location to location. A second variable was the "connectedness" of the locations. In one condition, a story tied together or logically ordered the sequence of locations visited by the elephant in his walk through the jungle; in the other condition, descriptions of locations were independent and the stories nonconnected—the experimenter's descriptions merely pinpointed the elephant's location, and the descriptions were linguistically connected only by "and then he went to the lake and then he went to the village," etc. The final variable manipulated was the mode of reconstruction. Half the children reconstructed the sequence from the beginning; other children reconstructed the sequence in reverse, starting from the last location visited. Generally, active subjects performed better than passive subjects, and connecting stories produced better reconstruction of the sequence than nonconnected stories. Finally, preschoolers could readily reconstruct the route if they started at the beginning, but regardless of the other variables, reconstruction of the sequence in reverse proved far too difficult for them. Brown and Murphy (1975) concluded that prior to the period of concrete operations, young children can readily trace and construct a series of events in a forward order, but are unable to do so in a reverse order. That preschoolers would have difficulty in reconstructing a route in reverse is consonant with Piaget's arguments and data; the fact that these children can construct a forward sequence is dissonant with Piaget, who argues that most sequence construction is not readily performed until the period of concrete operations.

A recent study by Herman and Siegel (1978) is relevant here. Although previously described earlier in this chapter let us recapitulate the central details. Kindergarten, second, and fifth graders were asked to reconstruct from memory the spatial layout of buildings in a large (4.9 × 6.1 m) model town. They were told to put each of eight buildings exactly where they had been in the model they had just encountered. Those buildings with definite topological cues (buildings at the end of a road or railroad track) were not only the most accurately placed by all children (even for the youngest children on the first construction), they were also typically the first and last buildings that the child put down while building his model. This finding seems directly related to Trabasso's (1975) and Siegel, Allik, and Herman's (1976) concept of end-anchors. The recall of the first and last items in a serial array is facilitated because they are spatially unique—they are the only stimuli which have other stimulus items only on one side. Endpoints alone are unambiguous with respect to comparative relationships with the other items.

Summary

The development of route construction seems to parallel our description of the development of landmark knowledge presented in the previous section. Landmark knowledge develops from knowing that something has been seen to knowing *where* that something has been seen (and that such knowledge can be useful). It appears that route construction similarly goes from knowing that a particular landmark is associated with a particular bearing or heading to knowing that a sequence of landmarks is associated in time with a sequence of headings or bearings. In both instances, the lower-level processes of landmark recognition or landmark-bearing associations seem hardwired and present at an early age. What seems to evolve with development is a kind of higher-order knowledge. Specifically, increased capability of temporal integration permits, not only a meta-knowledge of landmarks, but also conversion of landmarks associated with bearings into simultaneous temporal and spatial sequences, which may conveniently be called routes.

The extent to which successions of elements can be transformed to a simultaneity (or structure derived from associations) seems to be related directly to the information-processing capacity of the organism, which clearly increases with development. Perhaps the most sophisticated statement of this argument is Pascual-Leone's (1970) construct of M-space: "A central computing space—M is the maximum number of schemes, items, or discrete chunks of information that can be attended to or integrated in a single act" (p. 307). An increase in the capacity of M-space with development would allow for the simultaneous entry of sufficient discrete chunks of the environment (e.g., landmarks) to be encoded, transformed, and coordinated.

The Development of Configurational Knowledge

Landmarks and routes seem, then, to constitute a first-order, "enactive" and possibly second-order "integrative" representation of the terrain. One can conceive, in effect, of an environment as consisting of potential landmarks connected by potential routes. Similarly, one can picture a cognitive map as landmarks (visual "pegs") connected by routes (sensorimotor "lines"). However, storing 10 to 100 or 1000 different separate routes through a city is cognitively unwieldy, in terms of both storage and retrieval. Somehow, a means must be found or created to store all the way-finding information about an environment (e.g., where routes cross, landmarks common to two routes, which routes are adjacent, parallel, etc.) in a single cognitive structure. Such "gestalt" or configurational knowledge is a sophisticated "twist" that gives its possessor an edge in way-finding and organizing environmental experience. These configurations enhance way-finding, and they may be a necessary condition for invention of new routes.

There are in all likelihood a number of levels of sophistication of survey maps, probably corresponding to levels of temporal integration that permit increasingly flexible ways in which the representation can be used. The level of sophistication is probably related to the degree to which the map is "association" or "structure" (Mandler, 1962), is successive or simultaneous. "Simultaneity of survey, that is the simultaneous embracing of a multitude of details, is characteristic of these representations" (Shemyakin, 1962, p. 226).

A number of authors have discussed two levels of maps and have argued that "route" maps (i.e., landmarks connected by routes but without a sense of the interrelationships) are developmentally prior to "survey" maps (i.e., in which routes are integrated). Survey maps become possible only after two accomplishments—the establishment of routes and an objective frame of reference. They appear as coordinations of routes within such an objective frame of reference. This distinction appears frequently in literature other than that of developmental psychology. We turn to this literature first, prior to consideration of the developmental data.

A common thread that runs throughout the literature of neurology and urban design is that "route" maps are microgenetically prior to "survey" maps. Critchley (1971), Luria (1966, 1973), and others have found that parieto-occipital damage in the right hemisphere destroys the ability to produce a "survey" representation. In the literature of cognition of urban environments, a similar argument is made regarding the microgenesis of people's perceptions of and attitudes toward urban locales. Appleyard (1969, 1970) had adults draw sketch maps of both their whole city and their local areas. On the basis of these maps, he distinguished two main categories of production: sequentially dominant and spatially dominant. Appleyard noted that many persons built their drawings along paths of movement. As familiarity (e.g., length of residence) with the area increased, persons were less likely to build their drawings along paths of movement and were more likely to present configurations that integrated the various landmarks and routes.

Turning to the literature of developmental psychology, one finds a similar sequence. Piaget, Inhelder, and Szeminska (1960) asked children 4–12 years old to draw (and then construct from their drawing a three-dimensional model of) the school buildings and the principal features in the immediate locale, and to reconstruct the route from school to a well-known landmark. Piaget characterized the performance of young children (up to 6 or 7 years) as performances in which landmarks were uncoordinated. In constructing their map, younger children described changes of position (i.e., rotation) in terms of end-anchors only, while older children compared paths of movement (routes). Younger children made no attempt to link endpoint with starting point, nor did they consider both in terms of a larger frame of reference. At a more advanced level, children reconstructed routes and used subsystems of reference. However, the various routes and subsystems were not coordinated as a whole. "Their plan of the district is made up of several portions which are correct in themselves but do not agree with one another" (p. 8). Thus, to this point, Piaget's research, consistent with our previous arguments, provides evidence for the primacy of landmarks, followed by landmarks connected by routes. In contrast, at the next level, children reproduced a coordinated whole in sketching their journeys. "What began as a sketch-plan of a route finishes as a general map of the district" (p. 20). "Ala (8;3) thinks of 24 separate features and arranges them correctly. Now and again, in bringing in a new object, he is driven to build up a sub-group involving fewer relations, but each time he succeeds, almost immediately, in integrating this sub-group with the main plan" (p. 19). Piaget *et al.* (1960) argued that older, concrete-operational children can construct " . . . a topographical schema in line with a two-dimensional coordinate system, though the various intervals are not always strictly proportional to each other . . . a complete coordination is achieved at level IIIB" (p. 20).

Shemyakin's (1962) description of the development of spatial representations agrees in large measure with that of Piaget. Shemyakin asked adults and children to draw sketch-maps of their neighborhoods. Young children (6-7 years) typically drew only those routes over which they traveled frequently. Turns of the street on the route "home from school" were produced accurately. However, children drew only those sections of routes over which they actually traveled, rather than the whole street, and certainly did not include adjacent streets. Older children (9-10 years) produced more complex drawings and "branches" from the main route, although these branches were not interconnected. By 12 years, children presented the locality in the form of a "closed aggregate."

Shemyakin's (1962) account can be reconceptualized in the following way. At first, children represent a locality only by taking some specific point in it (a feature or landmark) as the initial or reference point. Representations produced by these children are referred to by Shemyakin as "route maps," a cognitive map produced by a relatively lower-order "enactive" method: "a topographical representation of a 'route-map' type which reflects a locality in the form of mentally traced routes of locomotion, corresponding to the first of these methods" (p. 220). At some later point, a "survey map," a higher-order representation, becomes possible:

> A topographical representation of the "survey-map" type which reflects a locality in the form of a system of the mutual disposition of local objects, corresponds to the second method . . . . Representations of the "route-map" type develop earlier than do the "survey-map" type of representations. (p. 220)

Thus, the work of both Piaget and Shemyakin seems to indicate the existence of two levels of maps—a lower-level, primarily enactive, sensorimotor, feature-based plan of a locale; and a higher-order, coordinated plan within a frame of reference.

Hardwick, McIntyre, and Pick (1976), while in basic agreement with Piaget and Shemyakin, provide a slightly different account of the developmental progression of configurational maps. Their general view of a cognitive (configurational) map is that it provides one with information as to where objects and places are located relative to one's own position in the environment. The composition of a map consists of various types of information content (e.g., size, distance, direction). They suggest that the cognitive maps of adults are multilevel representations of spatial information. These levels can be conceptualized both as cognitively hierarchical and temporally stacked (White, 1965). Level 1, the "bottom of the stack" so to speak, is a general level containing a single coordinate representation of the *ordinal* relationships between features (e.g., a global conception). Level 2 is a more specific level, containing a series of smaller subrepresentations, each associated with a particular point of view within the total cognitive map. "Initially the individual makes a decision about a direction, then proceeds to 'fine tune' [his] response in order to specify an object's exact location in relation to [himself]" (Hardwick et al., 1976, p. 49).

The "model" of Hardwick et al. (1976) can be described using the metaphor of a microscope with lenses of increasing degrees of magnification. On first examining a specimen, the technician sets the power at, say, 20×, in order to get an overall "feel" for the texture, quality, and "gestalt" of the specimen. Once the specimen has been "defined," the technician switches to, say, a 100× magnification to examine more closely a particular subregion of the specimen from a particular vantage point. This process can be continued iteratively such that each subregion can be examined in detail. The child's "view of the world" is analogous to that provided by the 100× lens: It can examine closely one region at a time, but cannot examine closely two or more regions simultaneously. What appears to be most difficult for the young child is to integrate the different subregions of a larger existing configuration into a unified whole. Analogous to Piaget's class-inclusion problem, the child can attend to the whole in a global sense, or the parts, but not both.

Recent evidence seems to demonstrate the utility of this metaphor. Siegel and Schadler (1977) asked kindergarten children to construct from memory a three-dimensional model of the arrangement of the furniture within their classroom. Clusters of furniture in the classroom were reproduced accurately, but the relationships among clusters (subregions) were not reproduced accurately. Siegel and Schadler's results can be interpreted as indicating that the children's cognitive maps of their classrooms consisted of several "mini-maps"—each constituting a subregion defined by a feature or feature cluster. Like the Hardwick *et al.* (1976) younger children, Siegel and Schadler's kindergarteners were able to construct an accurate representation of several subregions separately, but were unable to build up a coherent and accurate representation of the environment as a whole.

CONCLUDING REMARKS

SUMMARY

Several general threads of themes have emerged in this review of research related to the development of cognitive mapping:

1. There seems to be reasonable evidence for a developmental sequence in the construction of cognitive maps of the large environment. Landmarks are the essential visual pegs—points of decision and salience that are noticed and remembered. Following this, children and adults act in the context of these landmarks and, as they do so, routes are constructed. At a primitive level, then, cognitive maps can be conceptualized as uncoordinated networks of landmarks, connected by routes. The final phase in the sequence seems to be one in which these elements are coordinated into a more comprehensive configuration within some objective frame of reference. This sequence seems to obtain both in the development of children's cognitive maps over years and adults' cognitive maps over shorter periods of time.

2. The sequence we have just outlined—from landmarks to routes to configurations—can be conceptualized as defining a horizontal dimension of spatial development. There is a second "vertical" dimension. Within each domain, two levels of spatial knowledge are found: At the lowest, most primitive level is enactive, sensorimotor knowledge—knowing that one has seen a landmark, knowing that one can get from A to B, and recognition of elements within a spatial configuration. Developmental differences at this level of knowledge are minimal. A second kind of knowledge, call it spatial meta-knowledge or meta-cognition, seems to stem from, become superimposed upon, and integrate that first-order knowledge. It is at this level that one finds developmental differences and relatively less-robust structuration (i.e., less resistance to factors such as load, stress, etc.). Examples of this kind of meta-knowledge are (a) knowing not only that you have seen a landmark before but also where you have seen it and that this knowledge can be useful in organizing a spatial representation of the environment; (b) knowing not only that you can get from A to B, but also that a number of landmarks can be placed ordinally on such a dimension and that you can start at any point on the dimension, and with appropriate bearing can get to either terminal landmark; (c) knowing not only that you can recognize a particular landmark in a large array, but also that particular subregions can be coordinated with each other.

3. Within each "vertical domain" one can see the progression from Level 1 to Level 2, in both children and adults—increased temporal integration, the ability to convert successivity to simultaneity, to convert association to "structure," to consider parts and wholes simultaneously. Each progressive expansion of the temporal integrative capacity not only permits greater scope and comprehensiveness of the map, but permits it to be used more flexibly (i.e., things can be looked at from multiple vantage points), not only in the domain of things spatial, but in the extension of the map for the understanding of nonspatial (perhaps semantic) phenomena. The development of this critical cognitive capability is undoubtedly related to the maturational state of the nervous system and the demands of the social environment, and thus probably develops synchronously with other cognitive capacities.

4. Thus far, our discussion has centered primarily on cognitive and neurological processes and mechanisms. An additional factor influencing the development of cognitive maps is a motivational one—the purposes or agendae of the traveler. As Wapner, Kaplan, and Cohen (1973) point out, the "cognizer" or "map-constructer" does not traverse environments in a motivational vacuum. It would seem, for example,

that a taxi driver in New York—whose livelihood depends on an extensive landmark and route knowledge of the city—would be more "motivated" to construct as accurate and flexible a representation as possible, whereas the casual visitor would not feel compelled to construct such a detailed representation. This problem, one of the interaction of cognitive and "social" or "motivational" variables, has not yet been considered empirically. A more complete understanding of the development of cognitive mapping requires such consideration.

RESEARCH IMPLICATIONS

Several obvious problems for further research surface quickly within the context of our proposed framework. For example, we argued that a second level of landmark knowledge was not only that a landmark was familiar, but also that it has been seen in a particular location and time (i.e., spatiotemporal context). Within a recognition-in-context memory paradigm, subjects could be presented a series of objects and/ or events in controlled spatial and temporal contexts (pictures, slides, or films), and be asked subsequently to identify from an array both the objects (or events), *and* the context in which they had been presented originally. These studies would be designed to specify the features and boundary conditions (e.g., affective, spatial, and temporal) of landmarks that get registered in memory and how these change with development.

A second line of research stemming from our framework would involve studies designed to specify the developmental course of how the landmarks become integrated into configurations (Siegel, 1977b). To assess the process of configuration construction, subjects could be given a series of encounters (varying in setting conditions, frequency, the nature of the environments, etc.) with spatial layouts of landmarks and routes in large-scale space. Following each encounter, either immediately or after some delay, the subjects would be instructed to reconstruct the layout. The subjects' construction performance might well be videotaped so that a "real-time" analysis of their constructions could be conducted.

It is also important to consider the broader "strategic context" within which such studies are carried out. In our derivation of the sequence of the development of cognitive maps in children, a fair amount of stock was placed in a particular kind of argument—the use of parallels. Many of the ideas proposed regarding the sequence of map development in children were derived from the literatures of disciplines concerned primarily with *adult* functioning (i.e., neurology and urban design). Since there is relatively little "direct" evidence on map development in children, we looked for "similarities" in these other disciplines.

Teitelbaum (1977) has referred to this kind of argument as "synthesis by parallel":

> "Synthesis by parallel" . . . in essence says that something new is like something else that is already familiar. A parallel is a similarity, and the more detailed it is the more confidence we have that the similarity is not mere coincidence. One uses this method from the conviction that nature is parsimonious: if a given phenomenon works in a particular fashion, it is likely that the same method is used to produce other phenomena which up to now we have not recognized as being the same. Therefore, look for a parallel. (p. 10-11)

That is to say, a thorough understanding of one behavioral or cognitive system may be potentially useful in gaining an understanding of a second, unfamiliar system that is similar to the first in some meaningful way. In such cases, understanding proceeds in large measure by looking for parallels, "analogies" (Lorenz, 1974), "partial isomorphisms" (Piaget, 1971), or "formal identities" (Miller, 1956). This is particularly the case in underdeveloped domains of knowledge, where, in large measure, the most productive kind of research is hypothesis-generating, rather than hypothesis-testing. Cognitive mapping, now in the fetal rather than in the embryological stage, is still such a knowledge domain. Thus, we feel that progress can best be made in understanding cognitive mapping by studying concomitantly both the development of landmark registration and of layout reconstruction (1) in children over long periods of time (i.e., years), (2) in children over shorter periods of time (i.e., minutes, hours, or days as in experimental sessions), and (3) in adults over short periods of time (i.e., minutes, days, or weeks).

THE BIGGER PICTURE

Our goal in this chapter has been to characterize the developmental sequence of cognitive mapping. While the research and theory described has involved children, it would be a mistake to assume that this literature is important only for developmental psychologists. On the contrary, we believe that the study of the development of cognitive mapping may ultimately provide the core for an integrated theory of environmental cognition.

To understand this contention, consider the diversity of research domains currently included under the general rubric of environmental cognition. A partial list of topics would include environmental assessment, environmental preference, and spatial behavior (Moore & Golledge, 1976). What do these domains have in common? We would argue that the core issue in environmental cognition is the nature and development of internal representations (cognitive maps) of that environment. Adaptive action in an environment, decision-making in an environment, attitudes toward that environment, and feelings about that environment are all fundamentally based on internal representations of that environment that are constructed by the "cognizer." In other words *all* human cognition and action is guided by internal representations of external events. Consequently, to understand an individual's attitude toward, action in, or decisions about the environment, it is necessary to be able to characterize that individual's representation of that environment and specify how that representation is developed and/or constructed. The characterization of cognitive maps and their development are the primary concerns, albeit sometimes implicit, of the research described in this chapter. Achieving such a theoretical and empirical understanding of cognitive maps and their development in children and adults is a fruitful, and perhaps necessary, first step in understanding the more general problem of environmental knowing.

ACKNOWLEDGMENT

The authors wish to thank J. F. Herman for his comments on an earlier version of the manuscript.

REFERENCES

Acredolo, L. P., Frames of reference used by children for orientation in unfamiliar spaces. In G. Moore & R. Golledge (Eds.), *Environmental knowing*. Stroudsburg, Penn.: Dowden, Hutchinson & Ross, 1976.

Acredolo, L. P. Developmental changes in the ability to coordinate perspectives of a large-scale space. *Developmental Psychology*, 1977, *13*, 1-8.

Acredolo, L. P., Pick, H. L., & Olsen, M. G. Environmental differentiation and familiarity as determinants of children's memory for spatial location. *Developmental Psychology*, 1975, *11*, 495-501.

Anderson, J. R. *Language, memory and thought*. Hillsdale, N.J.: Lawrence Erlbaum Associates, 1976.

Appleyard, D. Why buildings are known. *Environment and Behavior*, 1969, *1*, 131-156.

Appleyard, D. Styles and methods of structuring a city. *Environment and Behavior*, 1970, *2*, 100-118.

Bartlett, F. C. *Remembering*. Cambridge: Cambridge University Press, 1932.
Beck, R. J., & Wood, D. Cognitive transformation from urban geographic fields to mental maps. *Environment and Behavior*, 1976, *8*, 199–238.
Berger, P. L., & Luckmann, T. *The social construction of reality*. New York: Anchor, 1967.
Bergson, H. *Creative evolution* (A. Mitchell, trans.). New York: Henry Holt, 1911.
Blackstock, E. G., & King, W. L. Recognition and reconstruction memory for seriation in four- and five-year-olds. *Developmental Psychology*, 1973, *9*, 255–260.
Blumenthal, A. L. *The process of cognition*. Englewood Cliffs, N.J.: Prentice-Hall, 1977.
Bobrow, D. G., & Norman, D. A. Some principles of memory schemata. *In* D. G. Bobrow & A. M. Collins (Eds.), *Representation and understanding: Studies in cognitive science*. New York: Academic Press, 1975.
Brown, A. L. Judgments of recency for long sequences of pictures: The absence of a devlopmental trend. *Journal of Experimental Child Psychology*, 1973, *15*, 473–480.
Brown, A. L. The construction of temporal succession by preoperational children. *In* A. D. Pick (Ed.), *Minnesota symposia on child psychology*. Vol. 10. Minneapolis: University of Minnesota Press, 1976.
Brown, A. L., & Lawton, S. C. Age differences in the ability to retrace a journey in forward or reverse sequentiality. Unpublished manuscript, University of Illinois, 1975.
Brown, A. L., & Murphy, M. D. Reconstruction of arbitrary versus logical sequences by preschool children. *Journal of Experimental Child Psychology*, 1975, *20*, 307–326.
Carey, S., & Diamond, R. From piecemeal to configurational representation of faces. *Science*, 1977, *195*, 312–314.
Carr, S., & Schissler, D. The city as a trip: Perceptual selection and memory in the view from the road. *Environment and Behavior*, 1969, *1*, 7–36.
Cassirer, E. *The philosophy of symbolic forms*. Vol. 2. *Mythical thought*. New Haven: Yale University Press, 1955.
Coie, J. D., Costanzo, P. R., & Farnill, D. Specific transitions in the development of spatial perspective-taking ability. *Developmental Psychology*, 1973, *9*, 167–177.
Critchley, M. *The parietal lobes*. New York: Hofner, 1971.
DeAjuriaguerra, J., & Tissot, R. The apraxias. *In* P. J. Vinken & G. W. Bruyn (Eds.), *Handbook of clinical neurology*. Vol. 4. Amsterdam, North-Holland, 1969.
Diamond, R., & Carey, S. Developmental changes in the representation of faces. *Journal of Experimental Child Psychology*, 1977, *23*, 1–22.
Downs, R. M., & Stea, D. Cognitive maps and spatial behavior: Process and products. *In* R. M. Downs & D. Stea (Eds.), *Image and environment: Cognitive mapping and spatial behavior*. Chicago: Aldine, 1973a.
Downs, R. M., & Stea, D. (Eds.), *Image and environment: Cognitive mapping and spatial behavior*. Chicago: Aldine, 1973b.
Fishbein, H. D. An epigenetic approach to environmental learning theory: A commentary. *In* G. Moore & R. Golledge (Eds.), *Environmental knowing*. Stroudsburg, Penn.: Dowden, Hutchinson & Ross, 1976a.
Fishbein, H. D. *Evolution, development, and children's learning*. Pacific Palisades, Calif.: Goodyear, 1976b.
Flavell, J. H., & Wellman, H. M. Metamemory. *In* R. V. Kail & J. W. Hagen (Eds.), *Perspectives on the development of memory and cognition*. Hillsdale, N.J.: Lawrence Erlbaum Associates, 1977.
French, L. A., & Brown, A. L. Comprehension of before and after in logical and arbitrary sequences. Unpublished manuscript, University of Illinois, 1975.
Gladwin, T. *East is a big bird*. Cambridge: Harvard University Press, 1970.

Gollin, E. S. A developmental approach to learning and cognition. *In* L. P. Lipsitt & C. C. Spiker (Eds.), *Advances in child development and behavior.* Vol. 2. New York: Academic Press, 1965.

Hardwick, D. A., McIntyre, C. W., & Pick, H. L. The content and manipulation of cognitive maps in children and adults. *Monographs of the Society for Research in Child Development*, 1976, 41 (3), Serial No. 166.

Harris, L. J. Sex differences in spatial ability: Possible environmental, genetic, and neurological factors. *In* M. Kinsbourne (Ed.), *Hemispheric asymmetries of function.* Cambridge: Cambridge University Press, 1976.

Harris, L. J., & Strommen, E. The role of front-back features in children's "front," "back," and "beside" placement of objects. *Merrill Palmer Quarterly*, 1972, 18, 259–271.

Hart, R. A., & Moore, G. T. The development of spatial cognition: A review. *In* R. M. Downs & D. Stea (Eds.), *Image and environment: Cognitive mapping and spatial behavior.* Chicago: Aldine, 1973.

Herman, J. F., & Siegel, A. W. The development of cognitive mapping of the large-scale environment. *Journal of Experimental Child Psychology*, 1978, in press.

Herrick, C. J. *The evolution of human nature.* Austin: University of Texas Press, 1956.

Hochberg, J. The representation of things and people. *In* E. H. Gombrich, J. Hochberg, & M. Black (Eds.), *Art, perception, and reality.* Baltimore: Johns Hopkins University Press, 1972.

Hochberg, J., & Brooks, V. Pictorial recognition as an unlearned ability: A study of one child's performance. *American Journal of Psychology*, 1962, 75, 624–628.

Holyoak, K. J. The form of analog size information in memory. *Cognitive Psychology*, 1977, 9, 31–51.

Huttenlocher, J. Constructing spatial images: A strategy in reasoning. *Psychological Review*, 1968, 75, 550–560.

Huttenlocher, J., & Presson, C. C. Mental rotation and the perspective problem. *Cognitive Psychology*, 1973, 4, 277–299.

Jackson, J. H. On the nature of the duality of the brain. Originally published in *Medical Press and Circular*, 1874. Reprinted in J. Taylor (Ed.), *The selected writings of John Hughlings Jackson.* Vol. 1. New York: Basic Books, 1958.

Jackson, J. H. Evolution and dissolution of the nervous system (Croonian Lectures). Published in parts in the *British Medical Journal, Lancet,* and *Medical Times and Gazette*, 1884. Reprinted in J. Taylor (Ed.), *The selected writings of John Hughlings Jackson.* Vol. 2. New York: Basic Books, 1958.

Jenkins, J. J., Wald, J., & Pittenger, J. B. Apprehending pictorial events: An instance of psychological cohesion. *In* C. W. Savage (Ed.), *Minnesota studies in the philosophy of science.* Vol. 9. Minneapolis: University of Minnesota Press, 1976.

Kaplan, S. Cognitive maps in perception and thought. *In* R. M. Downs & D. Stea (Eds.), *Image and environment: Cognitive mapping and spatial behavior.* Chicago: Aldine, 1973.

Kosslyn, S. M. Information representation in visual images. *Cognitive Psychology*, 1975, 7, 341–370.

Kosslyn, S. M., Heldmeyer, K. H., & Locklear, E. P. Children's drawings as data about internal representations. *Journal of Experimental Child Psychology*, 1977, 23, 191–211.

Kosslyn, S. M., Pick, H. L., & Fariello, G. R. Cognitive maps in children and men. *Child Development*, 1974, 45, 707–716.

Kuipers, B. Spatial knowledge. Massachusetts Institute of Technology Artificial Intelligence Laboratory, Memo 359, June 1976.

256 Alexander W. Siegel et al.

Ladd, F. C. Black youths view their environment: Neighborhood maps. *Environment and Behavior*, 1970, *2*, 64–79.

Laurendeau, M., & Pinard, A. *The development of the concept of space in the child.* New York: International Universities Press, 1970.

Lee, T. R. Urban neighborhood as a socio-spatial schema. *Human Relations*, 1968, *21*, 241–268.

Lee, T. R. Perceived distance as a function of direction in the city. *Environment and Behavior*, 1970, *2*, 40–51.

Lorenz, K. Z. Analogy as a source of knowledge. *Science*, 1974, *185*, 229–234.

Luria, A. R. *Higher cortical functions in man* (B. Haigh, trans.). New York: Basic Books, 1966.

Luria, A. R. *The working brain.* London: Penguin Press, 1973.

Lynch, K. *The image of the city.* Cambridge: MIT Press, 1960.

Maier, N. R. F. Reasoning in children. *Journal of Comparative Psychology*, 1936, *21*, 357–366.

Mandler, G. From association to structure. *Psychological Review*, 1962, *69*, 415–427.

Mandler, J. M., Seegmiller, B., & Day, J. On the coding of spatial information. *Memory and Cognition*, 1977, *5*, 10–16.

Maurer, R., & Baxter, J. C. Images of the neighborhood and city among Black, Anglo- and Mexican-American children. *Environment and Behavior*, 1972, *4*, 351–388.

Menzell, E. W. Chimpanzee spatial memory organization. *Science*, 1973, *182*, 943–945.

Milgram, S. Introduction. In W. H. Ittelson (Ed.), *Environment and cognition.* New York: Seminar Press, 1973.

Miller, J. G. Toward a general theory for the behavioral sciences. In L. D. White (Ed.), *The state of the social sciences.* Chicago: University of Chicago Press, 1956.

Minnigerode, F. A., & Carey, R. N. Development of mechanisms underlying spatial perspectives. *Child Development*, 1974, *45*, 496–498.

Moore, G. T. Spatial relations ability and developmental levels of urban cognitive mapping. *Man-Environment Systems*, 1975, *5*, 247–248.

Moore, G. T. Theory and research on the development of environmental knowing. In G. T. Moore & R. G. Golledge (Eds.), *Environmental knowing.* Stroudsburg, Penn.: Dowden, Hutchinson & Ross, 1976.

Moore, G. T., & Golledge, R. G. (Eds.), *Environmental knowing.* Stroudsburg, Penn.: Dowden, Hutchinson & Ross, 1976.

Munroe, R. L., & Munroe, R. H. Effect of environmental experience on spatial ability in an East African society. *Journal of Social Psychology*, 1971, *83*, 15–22.

Neisser, U. *Cognition and reality: Principles and implications of cognitive psychology.* San Francisco: W. H. Freeman & Co., 1976.

Nerlove, S. B., Munroe, R. H., & Munroe, R. L. Effect of environmental experience on spatial ability: A replication. *Journal of Social Psychology*, 1971, *84*, 3–10.

O'Keefe, J., & Dostrovsky, J. The hippocampus as a spatial map: Preliminary evidence from unit activity in the freely-moving rat. *Brain Research*, 1971, *34*, 171–175.

Pascual-Leone, J. A mathematical model of the transition rule in Piaget's developmental stages. *Acta Psychologica*, 1970, *32*, 301–345.

Piaget, J. *The language and thought of the child.* New York: Harcourt & Brace, 1926.

Piaget, J. The general problems of the psychological development of the child. In J. M. Tanner & B. Inhelder (Eds.), *Discussions on child development: Proceedings of the World Health Organization study group on the psychobiological development of the child.* Vol. IV. New York: International Universities Press, 1960.

Piaget, J. *On the development of memory and identity.* Worcester, Mass.: Clark University Press and Barre Publishers, 1968.

Piaget, J. *Biology and knowledge.* Chicago: University of Chicago Press, 1971.

Piaget, J., & Inhelder, B. *The child's conception of space.* New York: Norton, 1967.

Piaget, J., & Inhelder, B. *The psychology of the child.* New York: Basic Books, 1969.

Piaget, J., Inhelder, B., & Szeminska, A. *The child's conception of geometry.* New York: Basic Books, 1960.

Pick, H. L. Systems of perceptual and perceptual-motor development. *In* J. P. Hill (Ed.), *Minnesota symposia on child psychology.* Vol. 4. Minneapolis: University of Minnesota Press, 1970.

Pufall, P. B., & Furth, H. G. Recognition and learning of visual sequences in young children. *Child Development,* 1966, *37*, 827–836.

Pufall, P. B., & Shaw, R. Analysis of the development of children's spatial reference systems. *Cognitive Psychology,* 1973, *5*, 151–175.

Pylyshyn, Z. W. What the mind's eye tells the mind's brain: A critique of mental imagery. *Psychological Bulletin,* 1973, *80*, 1–24.

Shemyakin, F. N. Orientation in space. *In* B. G. Ananyev *et al.* (Eds.), *Psychological Science in the USSR.* Vol. 1. Part 1. U.S. Office of Technical Reports (#11466), 1962.

Shepard, R. N. Form, formation, and transformation of internal representations. *In* R. L. Solso (Ed.), *Information processing and cognition: The Loyola Symposium.* Hillsdale, N.J.: Lawrence Erlbaum Associates, 1975.

Siegel, A. W. "Remembering" is alive and well (and even thriving) in empiricism. *In* N. Datan & H. W. Reese (Eds.), *Life-span developmental psychology: Dialectical perspectives on experimental research.* New York: Academic Press, 1977a.

Siegel, A. W. The development of cognitive maps of large-scale space. Paper presented at the biennial meeting of the Society for Research in Child Development, New Orleans, March 1977b.

Siegel, A. W., Allik, J. P., & Herman, J. F. The primacy effect in young children: Verbal fact or spatial artifact? *Child Development,* 1976, *47*, 242–247.

Siegel, A. W., & Schadler, M. Young children's cognitive maps of their classroom. *Child Development,* 1977, *48*, 388–394.

Siegel, A. W., & White, S. H. The development of spatial representations of large-scale environments. *In* H. W. Reese (Ed.), *Advances in child development and behavior.* Vol. 10. New York: Academic Press, 1975.

Spencer, H. *First principles.* 4th Edition. New York: Appleton, 1892 (1st edition, 1862).

Stea, D., & Blaut, J. M. Toward a developmental theory of spatial learning. *In* R. M. Downs & D. Stea (Eds.), *Image and environment: Cognitive mapping and spatial behavior.* Chicago: Aldine, 1973.

Teitelbaum, P. Levels of integration of the operant. *In* W. K. Honig & J. E. R. Staddon (Eds.), *Handbook of operant behavior.* Englewood Cliffs, N.J.: Prentice-Hall, 1977.

Tolman, E. C. Cognitive maps in rats and men. *Psychological Review,* 1948, *55*, 189–208.

Trabasso, T. Representation, memory, and reasoning: How do we make transitive inferences? *In* A. D. Pick (Ed.), *Minnesota symposia on child psychology.* Vol. 9. Minneapolis: University of Minnesota Press, 1975.

Trowbridge, C. C. Fundamental methods of orientation and imaginary maps. *Science,* 1913, *38*, 888–897.

Wapner, S., Cirillo, L., & Baker, A. H. Some aspects of the development of space perception. *In* J. P. Hill (Ed.), *Minnesota symposia on child psychology.* Vol. 5. Minneapolis: University of Minnesota Press, 1971.

Wapner, S., Kaplan, B., & Cohen, S. B. An organismic-developmental perspective for understanding transactions of men and environments. *Environment and Behavior,* 1973, *5,* 255–289.

Werner, H. *Comparative psychology of mental development.* New York: International Universities Press, 1948.

Werner, H., & Kaplan, B. *Symbol formation: An organismic-developmental approach to language and the expression of thought.* New York: Wiley, 1963.

White, S. H. Evidence for a hierarchical arrangement of learning processes. *In* L. P. Lipsitt & C. C. Spiker (Eds.), *Advances in child development and behavior.* Vol. 2. New York: Academic Press, 1965.

White, S. H., & Siegel, A. W. Cognitive development: The new inquiry. *Young Children,* 1976, *31,* 425–435.

Williams, M., & Jambor, K. Disorders of topographical and right-left orientation in adults compared with its acquisition in children. *Neuropsychologica,* 1964, *2,* 55–69.

Wright, J. M. von, Gebhardt, P., & Karttunen, M. K. A developmental study of the recall of spatial location. *Journal of Experimental Child Psychology,* 1975, *20,* 181–190.

7

Children as Environmental Planners

JILL N. NAGY
AND
JOHN C. BAIRD

INTRODUCTION

The importance of internal representations of a large-scale environment has long been recognized (Trowbridge, 1913), but only recently has the nature and use of such representations been the subject of intensive experimental study (for review, see Hart & Moore, 1973; Siegel & White, 1975). These reviews focus on issues raised within the context of environmental psychology. However, investigations of spatial knowledge also encompass concerns basic to the understanding of human memory and problem solving. The construction of internal, spatial arrays as mediators of semantic organization and logical inferences is under investigation in both children (Trabasso & Riley, 1973; Trabasso, Riley, & Wilson, 1975; Huttenlocher, 1967) and adults (Potts, 1972, 1975). It appears that in some instances a spatial dimension is added to information in order for certain relationships to be more easily perceived, remembered, or utilized. Likewise the current trend in data analysis involving scaling techniques highlights the usefulness

JILL N. NAGY · Department of Psychology, Loyola University, Chicago, Illinois JOHN C. BAIRD · Department of Psychology, Dartmouth College, Hanover, New Hampshire.

of superimposing a spatial dimension onto information involving complex relationships.

Thus, there are several reasons why the study of spatial representations deserves careful attention. Within an environmental framework, information about one's spatial world serves the obvious function of facilitating location and movement within that space and so deserves attention in its own right. But the more general question of how people take in, code, and utilize information containing a spatial dimension (either inherent or imposed) can also be addressed within an environmental framework.

Most investigations in environmental psychology have focused on the content of spatial knowledge by testing the accuracy of a person's awareness of the arrangement of objects in space. Developmental studies generally compare the accuracy of children's awareness to that of adults. In 1970, Stea and Downs suggested a system to classify investigations of the development of large-scale cognitive representations. The three areas noted at that time still encompass most studies of environmental representations. These include (1) the elements comprising the spatial representation, (2) the relationships between and among elements, and (3) the final configuration that results from the elements and their relations.

Developmental differences have been found in each of these areas. Landmarks, the salient elements of the spatial image, are visual tools used as the starting point of a representation and as course-maintaining devices. Both the quality and quantity of landmarks have been found to change with age. Whereas neighborhood maps of young children tend to involve local objects (e.g., houses, trees), older children substitute abstract summarized points for specific elements (Shemyakin, 1962).

Ladd (1970) found that the quality and production of neighborhood maps were positively related to the extent of the child's normal activity range, suggesting the importance of sensorimotor input in the formation of children's spatial representations. The importance of the child's movement within the environment has since been noted by Acredolo (1976), Hardwick, McIntyre, and Pick (1976), and Herman and Siegel (1977). Yet vision also plays a significant role in the internal representation of spatial relations (Smothergill, 1973; Keogh, 1969, 1971).

Once landmarks are established, the child is thought to make a set of decisions using these elements as anchor points (Siegel & White, 1975; Piaget & Inhelder, 1971). Such decisions connect the landmarks through a series of routes. The most significant developmental change has been observed in the associative nature and distance these routes can extend. Kindergarten children in reconstructing their classroom were found to correctly reproduce several subparts of the room but were not able to build up a representation of the environment as a whole (Siegel & Schadler, 1977). Others have also noted that primary school children have accurate, differentiated schema for circumscribed areas (Kosslyn, Pick, & Fariello, 1974; Lee, 1963–64; Lord, 1941).

A key issue in this developmental literature is the child's frame of reference (Acredolo, 1976; Siegel & White, 1975). It is argued (Piaget, Inhelder, & Szeminaka, 1960; Shemyakin, 1962) that the child's associative route map cannot become a gestalt configuration until a projective referent system is achieved. Within the Piagetian framework this is thought to be related to the concrete stage of cognitive development occurring around the age of eight. However, more recent studies (e.g., Borke, 1975; Fishbein, Lewis, & Keiffer, 1972; Herman & Siegel, 1977; Ives, 1977; Shantz & Watson, 1971) suggest that spatial knowledge is determined more by environmental conditions (e.g., opportunities to walk through the environment) than by stage-related cognitive maturity.

Although this research has succeeded in isolating several elements relevant to the development of spatial images, it is directed toward the structural aspects of environmental cognition (Hardwick *et al.*, 1976). The majority of research has been concerned with examining the structure of what a person remembers to be true about a segment of his environment. It does not address the psychological processes underlying the development of spatial representations. Why do these representations vary under different experimental conditions and with different age subjects? Is there an internal representation that changes with age? Does the process of creating this representation change with age? In sum, what is the process of creating a spatial representation of any kind, and what developmental changes are critical to this process?

We will leave complete discussion of the development of environmental awareness to the other authors of this volume. In this chapter we focus on a series of studies undertaken to investigate the placement of objects in space. This issue includes the planning of new arrangements as well as the reproduction of old ones. The methodological basis derives from the insights into the planning process suggested by the direct mapping technique used by Baird, Degerman, Paris, and Noma (1972). Because of the centrality of this approach to our present concerns, some time is spent describing the reliability of the method as well as subjects' preference for this procedure as a reflection of their viewpoints. The major part of the chapter covers a program of research into the development of the planning process underlying the production of spatial configurations. Finally, we offer a model of the planning sequence, noting the underlying psychological process and how they might develop.

METHODOLOGICAL CONSIDERATIONS

Invesigation of cognitive representations of spatial relations has utilized two procedures: (1) numerical judgments of the relative distances between pairs of items (e.g., Ekman & Bratfisch, 1965) and (2) direct mapping of items in a two-dimensional space (Lynch, 1960). It is not clear whether these two methods reveal the same underlying spatial representation or, if not, which method best answers the important issues within a substantive area.

The numerical technique requires that the subject make sequential judgments about the relative distances between each item and every other item within the spatial context. The data are then analyzed utilizing psychophysical procedures and multidimensional scaling (MDS). Studies utilizing such pairwise comparisons have generally been concerned with the accuracy of cognitive maps. The results for large-scale environments have been inconsistent. Most studies find that adults tend to underestimate distance (e.g., Ekman & Bratfisch, 1965; Briggs, 1973; Cadwallader, 1973; Canter & Tagg, 1975). Yet some report that subjects are quite accurate at making relative distance estimates (Golledge & Zannaras, 1973). It appears that distance judgments as measured by this technique are influenced by factors other than the cognitive representation of the spatial environment: the type of response scale, the subject population, the particular city, and geographical terrain (e.g., rivers, mountains).[1] In addition, judgments of large-scale environments are based on cognitive representations of locations, not on actual stimuli, thereby introducing a memory component into the behavioral measurement.

The second approach to the investigation of the awareness of physical distances involves the direct mapping of items in a two-dimensional plane. In the "cognitive mapping" technique introduced by Lynch (1960), subjects sketch maps of specified environments such as a city (for review, see Saarinen, 1976). This technique is a rich source of data, as it more closely taps the presumed multidimensional character of environmental awareness. However, the interpretation and analysis of such data are by no means trivial exercises. Subjects vary

[1] These influences are similar to those encountered when subjects judge stimuli which are available to direct perception (Baird, 1970).

not only in sketching ability but also in level of detail and use of scale. Potentially, however, direct mapping has distinct advantages over methods of pairwise comparisons. Similar statistics can be used (e.g., psychophysical functions), and the need for MDS solutions for individual subjects is eliminated since the dimensionality of the space is a constraint of the task. Moreover, MacKay (1976) has shown that drawn maps of city locations are judged to be more accurate than MDS maps derived from subjects sorting item pairs into similar distance categories.

In order to provide a technique encompassing the qualitative advantages of direct mapping together with the quantitative power of numerical judgments, a modified direct-mapping technique was developed (Baird et al., 1972). A series of studies was undertaken to assess the validity and reliability of this approach. Subjects were given a set of facilities to be placed within a specified space. In this way, sketching ability and level of detail were eliminated as factors influencing the resultant map, and the necessary control for quantitative analysis was provided.

Subjects were given an empty space (either a plain piece of paper or a matrix) and a set of items relevant to the experimental context to be mapped (town or campus buildings). The name of each item was written on an individual square and all items were presented in a random order next to the board. The subject was asked to plan[2] a particular environment (e.g., ideal town, college campus) by placing the items within the space such that their spatial arrangement represented the environment specified. A computer analog of the task (Baird, Merrill, & Tannenbaum, 1978) was used in the college studies reported here. This technique is more expedient, maintains the same task requirements, and produces the same data base as the noncomputerized version used with the children and high school students.

Subjects made their plans within the constraint that once an item was established on the board that item could not be moved. Although this requirement adds to the task difficulty, the constraint was necessary in order to allow for measurement of planning strategies. Early in the research program, data were collected without this constraint. Adults moved a few items minimally, while most children (fourth graders) did not move any. At the completion of their design, if the children were reminded that facilities could be moved, either they

---

[2] The creation of a spatial representation will be distinguished in two ways throughout this chapter: (a) map—refers to the creation of an actual environment as it physically exists in the real world; (b) plan—refers to the creation of a hypothetical environment that does not physically exist in the real world. In this case, it is an ideal environment.

moved none or they completely erased the board and began all over again. It seemed that those children who initiated so drastic a maneuver interpreted the remark as a rebuff to their plan, and so began again. More important, the plans for subjects without the constraint were similar to those with it.

A series of experiments was performed with college students to investigate the feasibility of direct techniques for the study of cognitive mapping. Results from pairwise judgments and direct mapping were compared in two experimental tasks: representation of a familiar college campus and planning of a hypothetical, ideal town (for details of these studies see Baird *et al.*, 1978; Merrill & Baird, 1978; and Baird & Merrill, 1978). Pairwise judgments were obtained with a modified version of magnitude estimation in which subjects indicated the relative distance (real or ideal) between a pair of buildings (campus or town) on a scale from 1 to 100. The direct mapping data were gathered in the manner described above. Subjects mapped their real campus given a set of 11 buildings (e.g., dormitory, library) and their ideal town given a set of 11 facilities (e.g., home, school, fire department).

For the college campus, there were three maps for each subject: the "actual" map of the campus as it physically exists, the "direct" map of the campus, and the "pairs" map derived from multidimensional scaling of the pairwise distance judgments.

For each environmental context, the data were organized for analysis of map congruence and map preference between the direct and pair configurations as well as for reliability and validity. The results for the real campus indicated that the measurement of the cognitive representation of a familiar environment is consistent with the actual spatial relations within that environment. No matter what method of measurement was used, the location of points was similar for all buildings.

Map preference was determined by asking subjects to express an opinion about the relative accuracy of their two individual maps (direct and pairs) and the actual map. A series of pairwise combinations of all maps was presented and subjects chose the more accurate representation. There was no clear preference for the actual over the pairs map, but a strong preference for the direct map over the pairs. Thus, although the accuracy of both the pairs and direct maps is high for the familiar campus, subjects perceived the direct map to be more accurate.

Investigation of the ideal town was carried out in a fashion similar to the campus study. Subjects were asked to create a representation of their ideal town by direct planning and by giving pairwise distance preferences. MDS was used to construct a two-dimensional plan from each subject's pair preferences. This pairs plan was then presented alongside the direct plan of the ideal town and subjects selected their preferred configuration. In addition, the consistency of each method was determined by asking each subject to complete the task again, four months after the initial session.

For each method, pairs and direct planning, a measure of reliability between sessions 1 and 2 was obtained by correlating distances between items in each subject's plans. The levels of correlation were similar for the pair and direct planning procedures and reveal substantial individual differences (ranging from $r = .13$ to .87). Quantitative comparison of the direct and pairs configurations indicated that the two plans of ideal towns were not in close agreement for most subjects, suggesting differential results as a function of measurement technique. When confronted with a choice between their pair and direct configurations (presented side by side), 8 out of 10 subjects in the initial session said they preferred their direct plan over their pairs plan. Four months later, 9 out of 10 subjects expressed a preference for their direct plan.

These methodological studies suggest that a technique using pairwise distance judgments and MDS is as accurate as the direct technique for uncovering distance relations in a familiar environment. However, it should be remembered that although the pairs map is as accurate as the direct map, subjects report that the direct is more like the real than is the pairs map. For investigating spatial representations of hypothetical environments, direct planning is clearly more appropriate than pair judgments. Within an ideal context in which the subject is asked to plan a new spatial arrangement, the two techniques do not yield similar results. And, as with the familiar environment, subjects prefer their direct plans. Furthermore, in the direct method, since the subject has control over the mapping process, it is possible to investigate the strategies utilized in producing or reproducing a spatial environment. This marks an important advantage of direct planning over pair judgments. It provides the opportunity to study the planning process and the way in which spatial representations are developed.

DEVELOPMENTAL STUDIES

The Town Study

In our investigation of children as environmental planners, we have taken various approaches to tease apart the parameters critical to this process. This work derives from the study of children planning their ideal towns utilizing the direct planning technique (Nagy & Baird, 1974). A preference task in which subjects are given a set of familiar, common items and asked to create a new "ideal" spatial arrangement of these items provides a framework within which to investigate the processes underlying the creation of spatial arrangements. Preferences of environmental design are multidimensional in character, in this case involving element interrelations, patterns, and sequences as well as wholes (Lynch, 1960). By systematically varying the age of the subjects, one may look at the possible change in both environmental preferences and the cognitive processes involved in developing these ideal arrangements.

The subjects participating in these studies were all students from a rural New England town (population of 10,000) attending the same school. The youngest children were in the 4th grade while the adults were in the 12th grade of the same school or were undergraduates from nearby Dartmouth College. Since no significant differences were found between 12th graders and college students, both these age groups will be considered "adults" interchangeably in the following discussion.

One possible outcome of the experimental task is represented in Figure 1. Initially, the subjects were given an empty 5 × 5 matrix and

		Hotel		Factory
Offices	Police Department		Hospital	
	Bus St.		Fire Department	Church
Playground	School	Apartment	Shopping Center	
Home		Museum		Movie Theater

Figure 1. A possible response matrix representing a subject's ideal town plan.

15 two-inch squares representing the various town facilities. The 15 town facilities were placed to the left of the matrix board. The fourth graders were asked to read each item as it was placed to the left of the board. For all other subjects the items were already next to the board when they came into the experimental room, and they were asked to look over the items to be certain they understood them. All subjects were told that the empty squares on the board were to be considered as park land. The students were then asked to plan their ideal town, given the constraint that they could not change the placement of an item once it has been established. More specifically, they were told to plan a town in which they would like to live. The children were given careful instructions about the fact that items which were close together on the board would be close together in their town and ones far apart on the board would be far apart in their town. At the completion of the instructions, they were reminded that they were to plan the town the way they would want it to be. All children seemed immediately to grasp the meaning of these instructions.

A composite plan[3] for each age group was created by MDS (McGee, 1966) based upon the average distance matrix of items. The output of this analysis is treated as a composite representing the combined designs of all subjects within an age group. As indicated by the work measure,[4] good fits were obtained in two dimensions. A hierarchical clustering of facilities was then formed by running a complete linkage-cluster analysis (Johnson, 1967) on the average interfacility distances.

The results for the twelfth grade (see Figure 2) can be considered on two levels. On a microlevel one notices the school–playground and fire–police pairings. On a macrolevel there are essentially three major clusters: (1) the home group comprised of home, hospital, school; (2) the business complex comprised of the factory, office, shopping, fire department; and (3) the municipal district comprised of the hotel, bus station, church, etc. These clusters are similar to those formed by college students. Comparable results for the fourth grade (see Figure 3) indicate that complexes similar to those of the twelfth grade are

---

[3] Three kinds of spatial representations are referred to in this chapter: (a) actual map—representation of the actual environment as it exists; (b) real map—representation of the environment as it was mapped by the subject when he/she was asked to reproduce the actual map; (c) ideal plan—representation of the environment as it was planned by the subject when he/she was asked to place the items where he/she would like them to be, i.e., to produce an ideal environment.

[4] In McGee's approach "work" serves the same function as "stress" in the more familiar programs of Kruskal (1964). The smaller the work, the better the fit. The values obtained indicate that excellent fits were obtained for all age groups.

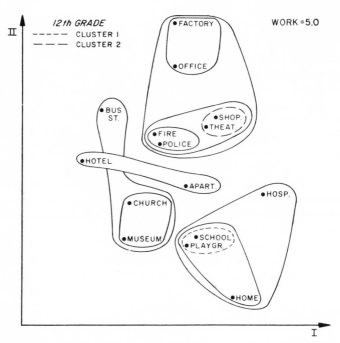

Figure 2. Composite town plan derived from applying MDS to the average interitem distances of an ideal plan: 12th grade. The enclosed contours represent the results of a hierarchical cluster analysis.

formed on the microlevel (e.g., fire–police, school–playground), but the home remains separate from the remainder of the town, as does the factory. Yet, both are relatively close to each other. School is now paired with shopping, fire and police join with church and apartment, office is placed near theater, and hospital comes together with museum. Further, the hospital is placed at the maximum distance from the home. Clearly, on the macrolevel, the plans are not the same for the two age groups.

It appears that the children's overall plan of an ideal town differs from that produced by adults, although certain subsections are similar. These results are reminiscent of findings of children's accuracy in mapping their classroom (Siegel & Schadler, 1977) or neighborhood (Ladd, 1970), in which small circumscribed areas are correctly reproduced but large macrospaces are not. The critical question is: Why does this difference occur? Do the plans represent real differences in preference for the spatial relationships among items or are they a result of developmental differences in the planning process? These two questions can be addressed in terms of task and process variables. Task variables include concerns about the nature of the task for each age group; e.g., the meaning of the items may or may not have been the same for all age groups. Process variables relate to the planning strategies of the subjects. Subjects of all ages may have the same task understanding but may differ in the cognitive processes mediating the desired end-point.

TASK VARIABLES

The Stimuli

In order to understand the way in which the children were creating their plan, it was necessary to determine empirically the psychological meaning of these items for each subject population. Presumably those items with high priority are given greater weight in a process to fix the interrelations among items. To the extent that these priorities differ

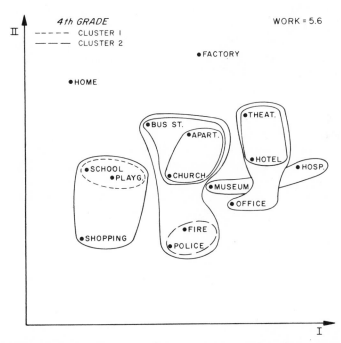

Figure 3. Composite town plan derived from applying MDS to the average interitem distances of an ideal plan: 4th grade. The enclosed contours represent the results of a hierarchical cluster analysis.

across age, different ideal plans would be expected. To obtain these data we asked each subject, after completing his design, to sequentially eliminate items from the town. Specifically, the child was asked if he/ she now had to give up an item from the town, which one would it be. That item was then removed from the board and the question was re-asked until all items were eliminated.

The results were surprisingly consistent over all age groups (4th grade through college). Within the top five rankings were: home, hospital, fire, and police. The fifth priority changed over age, generally showing a diminishing importance of church and a corresponding increase for school. In addition, playground gained in importance over age, whereas hotel dropped.

It appeared that within the highest priority range, all of our subjects perceived these items in a similar fashion. Priority was expected to be important because it was thought that the high-priority items would have the greatest weight in the planning sequence and hence be placed on the board first. Correlations of the relationships between priority and placement order indicated that all subjects placed their high priority items first (r_s ranged from .52 for 10th grade to .71 for ninth grade with no age pattern evident). Although significant, these correlations are not robust, suggesting that a priority measurement based on a process of elimination does not fully explain the mapping sequence observed. Those items maintained in the town as long as possible are generally the same items first placed in planning a town. Yet the size of the correlation suggests that other variables are also important in determining the placement order.

A more detailed look at the sequence of moves reveals that items with low priority, which are therefore removed early, may still have a role in setting spatial boundaries. For example, factory, a low-liking-priority item, is placed early in the planning scheme of the twelfth graders. One can hypothesize that factory acquires a favored stage of placement because it is at the extreme opposite end from home on the liking dimension. As such, it is placed early to afford greatest control over its location in respect to the remaining items.

Further information on this priority question is available from a study in which college students were forced to manipulate the relations of town items to partially disrupt their original ideal arrangement (Baird & Merrill, 1978). In this task undergraduates first planned their ideal towns by using a computer analog to the procedure used with the children. Then each student was asked to move items so as to achieve a criterion amount of change in their plan. The most stable spatial relationship maintained within these task constraints was the distance between home and factory (r = .64); that is, this distance seems to have a structural importance in the overall plan. Such a factor would tend to reduce the correlation between item priority and placement order.

In sum, priority of facilities remained relatively stable across age, but the final design of an ideal town changed dramatically. Thus, the differences in plans were not due to differences in the psychological meaning of the stimuli. But perhaps they were a function of different task situations. The young children may not have understood the task of creating an *ideal* space but rather replicated an existing set of spatial relationships familiar to them, in this way employing the same process as adults but to a different end. That is, children may have represented a real space rather than the ideal space adults had planned.

Instructions

To test this possibility, 4th- and 6th-grade children were asked to plan a familiar environment in both a real and ideal context. The target environment chosen was the playground adjacent to the children's school. Since the children go out to play twice a day, we were assured that this was a familiar environment. The task was similar to that described for town planning except that the planning space was not a matrix, but a piece of plain white paper. The 10 items were those actually in the playground (slide, swings, etc.). Each child was asked to plan both his real and ideal playgrounds, with order counterbalanced across subjects.

The first point considered was the level of accuracy achieved in designing the *real* playground. A quantitative measure of accuracy was obtained by using a computer program, FIT, developed by Baird *et al.* (1978). The method is similar to that proposed by Cliff (1966). The analysis centers, rotates, and adjusts the size of the configuration until it is maximally congruent with the target space. In our version the level of congruence is determined by calculating the mean distance between mapped and target items and comparing these distances with the distribution of distances generated by computer simulation of a large number of random maps.

Accuracy of the children's real maps was empirically determined by noting the size of the congruence measure compared with the random distribution. Such analysis indicated that the maps of most children were significantly more accurate than those produced randomly (see Table 1). The mean distance between mapped and target items of the simulation was 4.8 with a standard deviation of .63. Any compar-

TABLE 1
MEAN DISTANCE BETWEEN ITEMS IN THE ACTUAL, REAL, AND IDEAL
PLAYGROUNDS AS A FUNCTION OF PLANNER

Planner	Actual vs. real		Real vs. ideal				
	mean	s.d.	mean	s.d.	t	d.f.	p
Fourth grade	2.94	1.30	5.41	0.69	8.90	22	<0.0001
Sixth grade	1.97	1.29	5.22	0.80	16.45	29	<0.0001
Computer simulation	4.80	0.63					

ison yielding a mean distance of less than 3.48, two standard deviations from the mean of the random map, was considered an accurate map of the playground. A significant trend toward greater accuracy with increasing age was revealed in a comparison of the congruence measures for fourth and sixth graders [$t(50) = 2.88, p = .006$].

Consideration of the mean distances between target and mapped items for individual subjects indicated that seven fourth graders and two sixth graders did not design an accurate map of their playground. These subjects performed close to chance. This finding implies that accuracy in mapping a familiar environment is a stepwise function which for any individual child is either present or absent. Further, accuracy in planning a familiar environment is present for most children by the fourth grade, although there is some improvement by the sixth grade. Herman and Siegel (1977) have also demonstrated the ability of young children to map accurately an environment in which they have had sensorimotor experience.

The main reason for the playground study was to determine if young children understood our task requirements and created an environment different from the real one they new. The match between the real and ideal playgrounds of each child was determined by the congruence measure. Presumably, if children were reproducing the familiar environment, there should be little or no difference between their real maps and ideal plans. Examination of individual data showed that every child (in both the fourth and sixth grades) produced an ideal plan which was significantly different from his/her real map. That is, for each subject the congruence measure between the real and ideal playground was more than two standard deviations lower than the mean of the distribution of congruence measures obtained by comparing random maps.

Statistical analysis (*t*-tests) also showed that differences between the real maps and ideal plans were significantly greater than differences between the actual and real maps. This was true for both age groups (see Table 1). Thus, these children were not simply reproducing a familiar environment when asked to plan their ideal playground. It seems unlikely, therefore, that they were reproducing their familiar town when asked to design an ideal.

But what were they planning, and can it actually be called an "ideal"? That question was still open at this point in the research program, but it was now clear that the ideal plan was not a reproduction of the actual environment. Likewise, adults (college students) are very accurate in mapping a known environment (their campus) and create an ideal campus significantly different from the actual one (Baird & Merrill, 1978).

Preference

At this juncture it appeared that the children were engaged in a task similar to that of the adults. The items were perceived in a similar fashion by all age groups. The task instructions appeared to distinguish a real map from an ideal plan. To investigate whether the resulting plan was an ideal, naive groups of fourth grade children and college students were given a one-trial preference task in which the fourth-grade plan of an ideal town was paired with the respective college plan, with left–right position counterbalanced across subjects. Of the adults 81% preferred the adult plan to the children's plan. However, the children showed no clear preference for either plan. Both plans received an equal number of preference choices from the fourth graders. This finding raises a question of the role played by individual differences in this preference task. Subjects were asked to choose between the composite age-group plans. It is possible that the fourth-grade composite was too discrepant from each subject's ideal to be consistently identified as the preferred plan. However, the low variability observed in producing the composite solution for the fourth-grade plan (reflected in the work value obtained from MDS) argues against this interpretation. Rather, it appears that these young children do not have a complete cognitive representation of a hypothetical ideal space to be either created or recognized. Therefore, when asked to plan this unfamiliar, previously undeveloped conceptual space, an attempt is made but the resulting plan is not consistently perceived to be the ideal or preferred arrangement.

PROCESS VARIABLES

Planning Process

A second, but equally critical aspect of this research program was the study of *how* people placed the objects in space. What planning strategies were employed and did these strategies depend on the kind of design under consideration?

To look at planning strategies, data were collected on the manner in which items were placed on the board; that is, the pattern of placement was considered independent of the type of item. For example, the position of the first item was determined, the second, and so on. A matrix of distances between moves was tabulated and MDS was used to locate the move numbers (sequence) in a two-dimensional space. Results for the ideal town indicate a marked age difference (see Figures 4 and 5 for twelfth and fourth grade, respectively). The older subjects cluster a couple of items in one part of the space and then move to another section to cluster a few more; but the youngest subjects extend their items over the total available space on successive moves.

In order to quantify these planning strategies, the minimum, me-

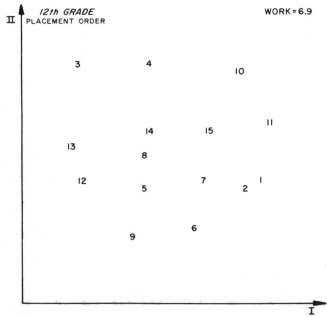

Figure 4. Placement order derived from applying MDS to the average distances between moves in planning an ideal town: 12th grade.

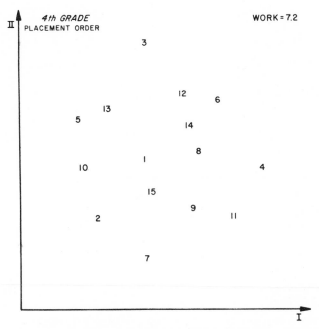

Figure 5. Placement order derived from applying MDS to the average distances between moves in planning an ideal town: 4th grade.

dian, and maximum possible distance that the subject could place each subsequent item was determined for each step in the planning task. The ratio of the number of moves less than the median to the number greater than the median is plotted in Figure 6 for each age. The smaller values, found with the younger age groups, reflect a greater tendency to place items beyond the median possible distance. Whereas older children cluster items, younger children place an item at a great distance from the previous one, thereby extending their spatial plan in an unclustered fashion. This highlights the importance of planning strategies to the understanding of spatial representations.

In planning an ideal town, young children extend items over a large space while adults form clusters. In order to determine the consistency of children's strategies, the placement orders for the ideal and real playground were analyzed. As in the town planning, data were secured on the manner in which items were placed on the board. An MDS analysis of these data yielded a satisfactory two-dimensional solution of placement location.

For each age group there were differences in placement order as a function of type of design (real or ideal). Fourth-grade children, in mapping their real playground, placed the items in a clustered fashion.

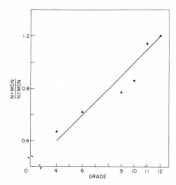

Figure 6. Relative proportion of distance moved (number less than the median divided by number greater than the median) at each step in the planning process across age groups planning an ideal town.

Basically, the first four items put on the map were clustered together, the next five items formed a second cluster and the tenth item was placed alone. However, when creating an ideal arrangement of the same space (i.e., using the same items and board specifications), clustering was absent except for one pair of moves. Similar kinds of patterns emerged from the sixth-grade data in which the real map displayed more evidence of an organized clustering strategy than the ideal plan.

An increase in clustering over age was found by comparing the placement sequence in the ideal plans of fourth- and sixth-grade children. Although neither age group displayed a lot of clustering, the sixth graders employed a more organized placement strategy than the fourth graders.

Thus, when mapping the real playground in which they have had ample experience, young children construct their design in an organized, clustered manner! However, when planning their ideal, a hypothetical concept, these same children place each item at a great distance from the last one, thereby extending the items over the total available space. Children as young as nine years do have the ability to produce a spatial arrangement in an organized fashion similar to that observed in adults. Yet when planning an ideal environment, these same children do not employ this clustering strategy.

Plan versus Process

Before delving further into the components of the planning process, it was decided to explore the relationship between the plan and the planning process. Was the strategy a result of the plan or was the plan the result of the strategy?

This issue was raised earlier in the paired preference task. The present investigation provided a different approach to the same question of preference and also allowed a closer look at the relative importance of plan preference versus plan process. The same spatial relationships should result under other conditions if the ideal plans actually represent the spatial relationships desired by the children producing them.

Fourth-grade children not involved in any of the previously described studies but from the same school (i.e., same year and school session) planned ideal towns in a manner similar to that described earlier—with one exception. Rather than choosing the item to be planned, these children were handed each item in one of two orders.

The particular order was derived from the original fourth-grade ideal-town plans in the following manner: Distance between items in the average plan was determined and two sequences of items were constructed such that each subsequent item was the closest to or farthest from the one immediately preceding. Half of the subjects received the items in order of smallest distance, while the other subjects received the items in order of greatest distance.

If the plan were guiding the process, the ideal design of these two groups would be the same (i.e., the distance between items would be maintained). On the other hand, if the process were guiding the plan, the location of facilities should be different for the two groups but the placement order would be maintained. The scaled results were consistent with the second possibility. The final plans were different, but the planning strategies were the same in both groups. Hence, planning strategy and not spatial preference for item location was the critical mediator of these children's ideal plans.

Planning Strategies

Once it was determined that the planning process was a factor to be reckoned with, we went on to investigate two components of potential relevance in the manipulation of item arrangements: (1) the association between items independent of their spatial relationships and (2) the structure of spatial relationships independent of item content (meaning).

Association Value

The relationship between items independent of a spatial context may have a strong influence in determining the resultant arrangements in a mapping task. In this case association strength is implied by the probability that one item will act as a stimulus for another. To investigate the association between items, students from each age level performed a similarity judgment task. The subject was given the 15 town items and asked to form nominal groups of those items that go together in an ordinary town. The association value between two items was the number of times they were placed together in the same group. The matrix of association values was analyzed for each age by standard MDS techniques. The results suggested that all subjects used similar dimensions in judging the association of town facilities. These dimensions[5] were identified as the two spatial coordinates characteristic of items in a town and a third semantic dimension of the functional link between items. However, there appeared to be a developmental trend in the weighting of these dimensions. For young children, item similarity was greatly influenced by the functional association between items; for adults, groupings reflected the spatial relationships between items. The most dramatic example of this difference across age appeared in the comparison of the two-dimensional solutions of 4th graders and college subjects. The fourth-grade solution showed the close association of home, apartment, and hotel, all functionally related (i.e., places to sleep or live). These same items in the college solution presented a very different configuration. Hotel was far from the home and apartment complex, joining the municipal complex.

The adult solution based on association values more closely approximated the spatial relations obtained in their town, as planned directly, than did the children's solution. For children, the association between items appeared to be more influenced by functional than by spatial relationships, and these functional association values were not consistent with the observed relationships among items in their plans.

In summary, while preliminary at this time, these data imply that developmental differences do not occur in the kind of dimensions underlying nominal groupings of town elements, but age does affect the relative weighting of these dimensions. Further, differences across age are evident in the relationship between the nonspatial association task and the direct town-planning task. For adults similar results obtained in both tasks, while for children (4th graders) no systematic relationship was apparent.

---

[5] It should be recognized that these proposed dimensions are not independent in a real sense. That is, to some degree the spatial relationship of items in a town is determined by their functional similarity.

Aesthetic Design

Association does not shed much light on the children's planning strategies. Perhaps these strategies are sensitive to the structure of spatial relationships independent of item content. We hypothesized that an aesthetic factor was relevant to the creation of a plan, especially an ideal or hypothetical plan for which the subject had no actual arrangement to reproduce. To the extent that the aesthetic design was different and/or exerted a differential influence across age, developmental differences in the created plan would occur.

First, it was necessary to determine what constitutes an aesthetically pleasing pattern. Gestalt psychologists offered the vague definition of a "good pattern" as one which "possesses such properties as regularity, symmetry and simplicity" (Koffka, 1935). This relationship was later quantified by Attneave (1954, 1955) and expanded upon by Garner (1974) in their proposition that the redundancy of information in a design can explain the goodness of a pattern. A pattern is good, then, because it is redundant or predictable from one of its sections, whereas an unpredictable pattern, lacking redundancy, is a poor one.

Another aspect of redundancy, more consistent with the planning task under discussion, is "symmetry." Symmetry is a match that occurs when reflecting complementary rows or columns of a matrix through an imaginary midline (Szilagyi & Baird, 1978). The nature of this aesthetic factor and its relationship to planning was considered both as an empirical issue and as an analytic tool. To understand its relation to the planning process we determined the aesthetically pleasing pattern(s) associated with our experimental conditions (5 × 5 matrix). Further, to investigate developmental implications, it was necessary to determine if differences across age occurred in the production strategies and/or resultant design of an aesthetically pleasing pattern. Finally, the ideal town plans created by the respective age groups were analyzed to assess the impact of aesthetics on their design.

To investigate the nature of aesthetic patterns, subjects from the fourth, sixth, tenth, and eleventh grades, and college were given 11 blank cardboard squares (2 × 2 inches) and asked to place them in a 5 × 5 matrix to form an aesthetically pleasing design. The amount and type of symmetry was analyzed for each age group. Subsequently, the amount of symmetry could be compared with the probabilities of obtaining symmetrical designs by chance alone. For example, the probability of obtaining perfect left–right or up–down symmetry by chance is .0008. Clearly, perfect symmetry is not a common event in a random world!

Contrary to such a world, however, most subjects created symmetrical patterns. Likewise, subjects displayed similar kinds of symmetrical patterns: left–right and rotational symmetry were the most prevalent. Although percentage of symmetry changed slightly over age (notably in the amount of up–down and left–right symmetry), overall, the aesthetic patterns were very similar.

Because of the dramatic differences in planning strategies previously found with content items (i.e., town or playground facilities), the strategies employed in creating aesthetic designs were examined. Inasmuch as the aesthetic patterns were quite similar, the prevailing question was whether or not these patterns were produced in similar ways by all subjects. An analysis of placement order was undertaken (similar to that described for planning strategies of towns and playgrounds). Results for the two extreme age groups (fourth grade and college) are shown in Figure 7.

Comparison of placement orders indicated a slight pattern of clustering by the youngest students while the adults showed a more organized placement strategy. At most, the young children place two sequential items near together. The adults placed at least two sequential items together, and more generally a greater number, before moving to another part of the space. It should be noted that there was a slight difference in the experimental task for college versus precollege subjects. Except for the college group, all subjects were given 11 squares to place in an aesthetically pleasing design. College students were given 15. This methodological difference is probably not significant, since, if anything, it would be expected to influence the results in the opposite direction. That is, with fewer items to place, the task should be less difficult, thereby more likely to allow for organization. Although all subjects demonstrated some organization in their placement order, the degree of organization appeared to be an increasing function of age. In addition, when compared to the strategies employed in creating an ideal town, more clustering was evident in the aesthetic designs, especially for the sixth-grade children.

The effect of the aesthetic factor on environmental planning was evaluated by reanalyzing the original town plans. It is possible that the difference in town plans across age was a function of a differential influence of an aesthetic factor in creating the ideal plan. Perhaps in creating their ideal town, children were actually creating a pleasing pattern, with little concern for the spatial relationships of town items, whereas in the same task, the adults were creating a town space with little concern for the aesthetic abstract pattern.

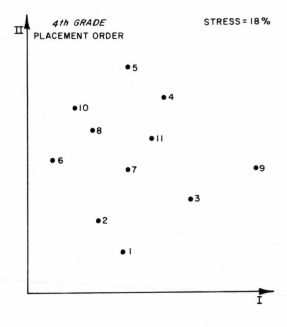

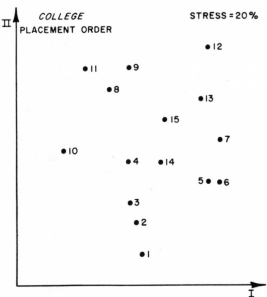

Figure 7. Placement order derived from applying MDS to the average distances between moves in planning an aesthetically pleasing design: upper, 4th grade; lower, college.

We first looked at the symmetry in the individual town plans. For all age levels only a few symmetrical patterns were found. However, visual inspection of the designs suggested an alternative measure defined as "balance" rather than symmetry. Balance was defined in the following way: Assume that each item has a fixed weight and that the board upon which items are placed is in perfect balance at the start of the task. As an item is placed on the board, it tilts to a position of imbalance, which can be corrected by adding another item in a position symmetrical to the first on the other side of the board. More specifically, balance refers to the center of gravity of the items on the board in respect to a perfectly balanced design (i.e., the board is level). By applying standard physical equations for computing center of gravity at each move in the placement order, it is possible to obtain a measure of balance in the x and y directions separately and to compare the attained balance at each step with the theoretical perfect balance. For this task, balance is a more appropriate measure than symmetry because a symmetrical design is balanced but a balanced design need not be symmetrical. If children were attempting to produce "good patterns," this approach would be revealed more clearly by balance than by symmetry. Of course, both measures derive from the same gestalt basis of pattern goodness.

Analysis of pattern goodness (i.e., balance) inherent in aesthetic designs and town plans indicated that both designs of the younger subjects were equally influenced by the aesthetic factor, but for adults the aesthetic factor differentially influenced the two patterns. The absolute mean deviation from perfect balance in the left–right direction[6] at each move (see Figure 8) resulted in identical functions for the 4th-grade aesthetic and town plans, indicating that both designs were well balanced or "good patterns." The adults had dissimilar balance functions for each design. Their aesthetic plans showed a strong influence of left–right symmetry, resulting in well-balanced designs. Yet, in creating an ideal town, evidence of balance was not so strong, implying that the aesthetic factor was significantly less important in determining the spatial relationships of items in an ideal town.

Thus, the children were more influenced by this aesthetic factor than adults. To determine the generality of this aesthetic factor, the amount of balance in real maps and ideal plans was compared. The balance analysis of the playground data indicated that young children

---

[6] Results are discussed only for the x-axis balance deviation. Degree of balance along the y-axis was similar for both designs for all age groups. This finding is thought to reflect the importance of left-right symmetry. For a full discussion of this issue, see Baird, Szilagyi, and Nagy (1977).

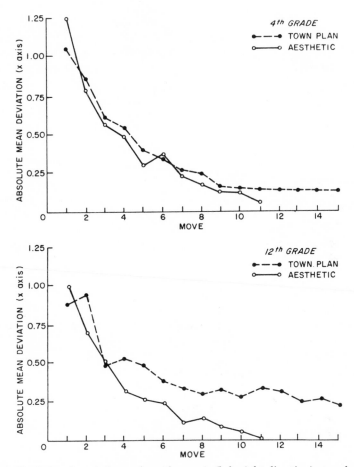

Figure 8. Deviation from balance along the x-axis (left–right direction) at each move in the planning sequence: upper, 4th grade; lower, 12th grade.

did not balance the real playground. But the results for the ideal playground parallel those of the children's ideal town; a strong tendency to balance is evident. In other words, in mapping a real, familiar environment, fourth- and sixth-grade children demonstrated significant deviation from perfect balance; but when planning a hypothetical environment no such difference from the aesthetically balanced design occurred. In this unfamiliar task, when the children were asked to produce a hypothetical environment, the influence of pattern goodness is much in evidence. When planning a real, familiar environment, the item content outweighed pattern goodness in specifying the spatial relationships.

In sum, when investigating any set of spatial relationships, it is important to consider the influence of an aesthetic factor on the spatial patterns. This can be defined in terms of symmetry or balance and is evident in aesthetically pleasing patterns of all age groups studied here. All subjects are influenced by this abstract factor of pattern goodness, but young children are more influenced by it than older ones.

SPATIAL PLANNING MODEL

As a means of summarizing the work already completed and in order to highlight questions that need to be addressed in future research, a simplified model of the planning process is proposed. The present program of research was not initiated to prove this model, but rather served as the groundwork upon which it was developed. The general characteristics of the planning model will be described first, and then each of its important components will be discussed in some detail.

It must be remembered that the model is only an approximation of the predominant characteristics of the process. Although the system is presented here in an implied temporal sequence, the nature of this temporal dimension is suggested only in its most general form. It is clear to us that several critical steps are either missing entirely or are deceptively incorporated into larger categories. If future research points to the naiveté of this model by delineating the nature and interrelation of its component parts (both as here presented and as only anticipated), this model will have served its purpose well.

General Considerations

The system begins with the task characteristics established by the experimenter. The information presented to the subject is processed into two categories: structure rules and meaning. These two components separate the input and consider individually the content of the items to be. planned and the available rules for determining the spatial relationships to be created. The content of each of these processes moves to a decision stage at which conflicts are resolved by applying differential weightings to the results of the semantic and structural analyses. The choice of desired spatial relationships then becomes input into the performance process, initiating the behavioral response: namely, placement of an item on the board.

At this point, the subject may return to the task situation to obtain the next item or may proceed to the preference component to check the output produced against the task goal. If there is a match, the process proceeds as it would have prior to the preference check. If there is a mismatch, a modification will be made, the changes in the plan executed, and the task continued. This sequence terminates after the last item is placed and the final outcome reached. The specific characteristics of each component of the process, as presently identified, are listed in Table 2.

Task Characteristics

The basis of the planning process is the framework established by the task characteristics. As currently formulated, this process is comparable to the "input stage" of Stea and Downs (1970). The requirements of the task are determined by the experimenter and have important implications for subsequent parts of the planning process.

Earlier studies with adults, using the planning technique employed in developmental studies, have found that the shape of the matrix (linear, inverted U, square, or circular) does not affect the planned towns (Baird et al., 1972). Also, several studies with different aged subjects mapping real environments have shown that different map-sketching techniques produce similar results (Lynch, 1960; Gould, 1967; Siegel & White, 1975). These data suggest that children and adults do have the conceptual framework of a large-scale environment and that it can be accommodated in the model space provided.

The number and types of items used to represent environmental facilities have not been a distinguishing force in our work, although they influence the structure rules. However, at this time neither factor has received systematic investigation. All items utilized in these tasks were very familiar to all subjects and the quantity of items was relatively small. It is thought that both the familiarity level and the number of items could tax the memory capacity of young children (as suggested by Stea & Blaut, 1973), thereby introducing a developmental effect in subsequent stages of the processing sequence.

The goal of the task differentially affects the strategies employed by various age groups. For adults, there was a slight trend toward greater clustering with the more familiar space. More dramatically, children demonstrated distinct strategies as a function of the type of environment they were planning. Their real, familiar environments were planned in a clustered fashion, but when asked to plan a hypothetical ideal, their strategies changed.

Simplified aspects of the planning process were studied in a group-

TABLE 2
ELEMENTS OF THE MODEL

Task Characteristics
1. Matrix features
2. Item features
3. Task
   a. Ideal plan
   b. Real maps
   c. Grouping

Decision Maker
1. Rank subcomponents of Meaning & Structure Rules
2. Resolve conflicts

Meaning
1. Priority
2. Ideal distance
   a. Interaction frequency
   b. Interaction importance
3. Association value

Performance
1. Physical mapping

Structure Rules
1. Pattern goodness
2. Distance between moves
3. Order of item placement
4. Number of items considered together

Preference
1. Examine item relationships and feedback to planning process.

ing task that removed spatial requirements from the planning process. Developmental differences were apparent.

MEANING

In its role in planning, meaning is a nonspatial component. It encompasses the significance of the facilities and their semantic relationships. However, this semantic component may be confounded with distance, especially for adults.

The priority of an item indicates its relative importance with respect to the facilities provided. In earlier literature, differences in cognitive representations appear to have been confounded with developmental differences in familiarity (Siegel & White, 1975). As our program of research suggests, when familiarity reaches a certain level, priorities are similar. It should be noted that familiarity here refers to the knowledge of the items being used and not to the environmental space into which these items are mapped or planned.

In placing objects in space, the distance between items is the critical endpoint. In the reproduction of a real environment, the distance is determined from the memory of that space. However, in planning an ideal space, distance between items must be created through a process of cognitive manipulation. At the moment, little is known about this process. Perhaps ideal distances are derived from a weighting of the perceived frequency of interaction between facilities and the importance of this interaction (for a full discussion of this process, see Baird & Nagy, 1977).

However, from our investigation to date, it is clear that the manipulation of ideal distances is subject to changes over age. Whereas the mapping of real distances was accomplished in a similar, clustered fashion by all of our subjects, the creation of ideal distances demonstrated a significant developmental trend in the amount of clustering—a trend evident throughout the high-school years. Why this should be so is not known. The developmental literature dealing with actual large-scale environments points to the importance of sensorimotor input to the accurate reproduction of these spaces. Ideal spaces, conceptual by nature, would have no such input. Perhaps this is a critical factor determining ideal distances. Future work should be directed toward the understanding of how sensorimotor input affects the availability, nature, and manipulation of spatial information.

Within the planning task, it is also probable that the subject considers the immediate association strength between successive items. Independent of other factors, this immediate link to an item may influence the choice of the next item to be placed. It is obvious that in a dynamic system such as that under discussion, this effect could exert considerable influence on the planning process.

Association could be triggered by many different dimensions of similarity. Nonspatial grouping is therefore included in its own right to emphasize the importance of semantic organization to the planning process. There are presently no satisfactory techniques available to study these variables without several confounds (e.g., places similar in content often are in close physical proximity). However, results from the grouping task discussed earlier suggest that children do differ from adults in their associations among town items—a difference that could influence their overall plan.

The structure rules encompass the strategies available for the production of a mapped or planned space. Several aspects of these strategies have been isolated in the research described earlier.

It has been suggested (Lynch, 1960; Siegel & White, 1975; Siegel, 1976) that in the development of a spatial map, the buildings, routes, and edges congeal to form a gestalt-like configuration. Such a configuration implies a pattern goodness that likewise may systematically influence the ideal plan. More specifically, in the studies reviewed here, the evidence suggests that all age groups agree on the kind of abstract pattern that is aesthetically pleasing. However, the influence of pattern goodness on the creation of ideal spaces was shown to be greater for children than for adults, although similar pattern goodness obtained in the mapping of real spaces by all age groups.

The distance between successive moves reflects the mapping strategies employed by different age groups. Adults employ an organized strategy evident in the clustering of successive moves for different types of environments. On the other hand, organized strategies are apparent for young children (fourth grade) only in the mapping of familiar environments. When asked to plan a hypothetical ideal space, whether with very familiar (playground) or moderately familiar (town) items, these organized strategies break down. In a simple hypothetical space (e.g., abstract design), the clustering strategy emerges, but only in its most elementary form (i.e., two successive moves). In short, the placement strategies employed by young children are affected by the type of environment they are asked to arrange.

The order in which items are placed must have an implicit effect on the planning strategy employed and on the resultant design. These studies have demonstrated that the distances between successive items varies over age in planning an ideal town, but the actual facility chosen at each step is similar for all ages. The items are placed roughly in order of priority.

Organization in planning strategies implies an overall context that exerts influence on sequential and individual moves. With the planning task, such an organization would be evident in the number of items considered on or off the board before a move was initiated. It has been proposed that the subject must view the item-to-be-placed with respect to all other facilities, both those already on the board and those to be placed later (Nagy, Szilagyi, & Baird, 1977; Siegel & White, 1975). From our data on planning hypothetical environments, it appears that in these instances young children cannot consider more than one step ahead and/or cannot relate the present item to previous or future clusters. Studies of children's reference systems within real spaces (Hart & Moore, 1973; Piaget & Inhelder, 1971; Siegel & White, 1975) suggest that an objective frame of reference is necessary for an organized spatial representation. In planning an ideal or unfamiliar environment, an entirely new reference frame is required. It is likely that young children have difficulty in developing and/or using such a hypothetical frame of reference, a difficulty reflected in the large distance between moves. The next step in this area is to determine why this difficulty occurs.

DECISION STAGE

Given the flexibility of the cognitive system and the number of component factors making up the planning process, it is necessary to incorporate an element of decision making into a model of planning behavior. In the creation of a plan, we hypothesize that each of the component processes exerts some influence—the resolution being a function of those meaning and structure rules having the greatest weight. In those instances in which the component processes are similar across age, developmental differences may still occur because of differential weighting of factors at the decision stage.

PERFORMANCE

The performance component refers to the actual production of the planned space. At this juncture in the planning sequence, it may still be important to make decisions. For example, if the placement space desired is already occupied, a modification in placement must be made. How this will be achieved is probably related to the quality of available slots. While there are no clues at this time, the hypothesis is that the subject determines a radius of indifference. If space is available within that radius, the modified placement is made. If no space is available, then more dramatic modifications must be initiated, such as shifting the weights of the structure rules or meaning factors. Potentially, developmental differences could obtain at any of these points.

It appears that the ideal towns created by young children do not represent their preferred spatial relationships. On the other hand, such preferred distances are established in the ideal plans of adults.

Theoretically, some kind of preference check should be incorporated into the planning scheme. In the event that a subject perceives a mismatch between the desired goal and the produced plan, there are several possibilities for modification: through changes in goal state, meaning relationships, structure rules, and/or the decision stage. Each of these possibilities, as well as the points at which a preference check would be made, has the potential for important developmental differences in the planning process. From the available data, this stage of the planning sequence is not evident in the children's responses.

GENERAL CONCLUSIONS

In this final section, the more general relevance of this research to the understanding of the development of environmental cognition will be discussed. Until the present investigation of the planning process, little attention has been given to the manipulation of spatial information. Rather, studies of large-scale environments have focused on the accuracy of their reproduction. In addition, the usual approach has provided little or no specification of the psychological processes that contribute to either the nature or development of mapping or planning. The present model is a first attempt to specify the actual processes underlying the development of the planning of spatial configurations.

Planning is a more sophisticated (i.e., complex) form of mapping. Spatial information that has been encoded can be reproduced, but this information may also be manipulated to produce new representations. Therefore, the present model provides a useful framework within which to view the general issue of the creation of spatial representations, whether actual or hypothetical. Likewise, since the spatial dimension has been found to be a useful mediator in problem solving, the model also has relevance to that area of research. And by proposing specific processes within the planning sequence, the model is a sensitive tool for the investigation of developmental changes.

Whether or not differences between young children and adults are obtained depends on the task characteristics. The greater the complexity of the task, the more the process is affected. Complexity may derive from a number of factors. The principal focus of our research has been on the production of environmental spaces, real and ideal. In this work few differences over age were found in either the accuracy or production strategies of real spaces. However, significant developmental differences were obtained in the creation of ideal spaces. Furthermore, the ideal plans created by young children did not appear to reflect their preferences. This was not so for adults. Clearly, for young children, planning an ideal space was a more complex task than mapping a real environment. Complexity in this case affected the use or weighting of structure rules within the planning process. Why this should be so is unclear. Several investigators have pointed to the importance of sensorimotor input to the development of cognitive representations of large-scale environments. Perhaps this is a clue to the difficulty young children encounter in creating ideal spaces, which require cognitive manipulation of spatial information. If so, it will be important to determine what it is about sensorimotor input that affects the ultimate use of spatial information and to understand its developmental implications.

This focus, however, represents but one approach to complexity. Theoretically, other manipulations (e.g., number of items to be placed) could also affect the complexity of the task and hence the planning process. This line of reasoning suggests that developmental differences are linked to capacity limitations that affect the components of the planning sequence. Within the study of cognition, processing capacity has been hypothesized to be a determinant of the effectiveness of each stage of information processing (Kahneman, 1973). A similar hypothesis is proposed here for planning: that is, if the required capacity is unavailable, the sequence will break down, the point at or fashion in which it changes being a function of the task demands and the level of cognitive development attained by the planner. It is not possible at this time to state whether development involves a change in capacity amount or in capacity requirements. Further, it is not possible from our data to know whether or not the limitations observed are a function of the component processes or if the differences lie in the weightings applied to the component factors at the point of decision making. We favor the latter view; we believe that the planning components are the same for people of all ages (studied thus far) but that the relative importance of these components is not fixed over age.

Clearly, there is much to be learned about the planning process in both children and adults. In our opinion, future work in this area must focus more on the delineation of the strategies employed in creating spatial configurations, their development, restrictions, and control. In this way we hope to extend our understanding of the nature of environmental information, its acquisition, and its use in spatial planning.

ACKNOWLEDGMENTS

We wish to express our appreciation to D. Carver, A. Pease, A. Coulture, S. Riggall, and all the teachers and students of the Lebanon school system, who so generously gave their time and support to this project.

REFERENCES

Acredolo, L. P. Frames of reference used by children for orientation in unfamiliar spaces. *In* G. Moore & R. Golledge (Eds.), *Environmental knowing.* Stroudsburg, Penn.: Dowden, Hutchinson & Ross, 1976.

Acredolo, L. P., Pick, H. L., & Olsen, M. G. Environmental differentiation and familiarity as determinants of children's memory for spatial location. *Developmental Psychology,* 1975, *11,* 495–501.

Attneave, F. Some informational aspects of visual perception. *Psychological Review,* 1954, *61,* 183–193.

Attneave, F. Symmetry, information and memory for patterns. *American Journal of Psychology,* 1955, *68,* 209–222.

Baird, J. C. *Psychophysical Analysis of Visual Space.* Oxford: Pergamon Press, 1970.

Baird, J. C., & Merrill, A. A. Cognitive maps and the computer. *Proceedings of EDRA 8,* 1978.

Baird, J. C., & Nagy, J. N. Preference and process in the cognitive development of spatial representations: VI. Theory and models. Unpublished manuscript, Dartmouth College, 1977.

Baird, J. C., Degerman, R., Paris, R., & Noma, E. Student planning of town configuration. *Environment and Behavior,* 1972, *4,* 159–188.

Baird, J. C., Szilagyi, P., & Nagy, J. N. Preference and process in the cognitive development of spatial representations: IV. Aesthetics. Unpublished manuscript, Dartmouth College, 1977.

Baird, J. C., Merrill, A. A., & Tannenbaum, J. Cognitive representation of spatial relations: II. A familiar environment. *Journal of Experimental Psychology-General,* in press, 1978.

Borke, H. Piaget's mountains revisited. Changes in the egocentric landscape. *Developmental Psychology,* 1975, *11,* 240–243.

Briggs, R. Urban cognitive distance. In R. M. Downs & D. Stea (Eds.), Image and environment. Chicago: Aldine, 1973.

Cadwallader, M. T. A methodological analysis of cognitive distance. In W. F. E. Preiser (Ed.), Environmental design research. Vol. 2. Stroudsburg, Penn: Dowden, Hutchinson & Ross, 1973.

Canter, D., & Tagg, S. Distance estimation in cities. Environment and Behavior, 1975, 7, 59–80.

Cliff, N. Orthogonal rotation to congruence. Psychometrika, 1966, 31, 33–42.

Ekman, G., & Bratfisch, G. Subjective distance and emotional involvement; a psychological mechanism. Acta Psychologica, 1965, 24, 446–453.

Fishbein, H., Lewis, S., & Keiffer, K. Children's understanding of spatial relations: Coordination of perspectives. Developmental Psychology, 1972, 7, 21–33.

Garner, W. R. The processing information and structure. New York: Halsted Press, 1974.

Golledge, R. G., & Zannaras, G. Cognitive approaches to the analysis of human spatial behavior. In W. H. Ittelson (Ed.), Environment and cognition. New York: Seminar Press, 1973.

Gould, P. Structuring information on spacio-temporal preferences. Journal of Regional Science, 1967, 7, 2–16.

Hardwick, D. A., McIntyre, C. W., & Pick, H. L. The content and manipulation of cognitive maps in children and adults. Monographs for the Society for Research in Child Development 1976, 41, Serial No. 166, 1–55.

Hart, R. A., & Moore, G. T. The development of spatial cognition: A review. In R. M. Downs & D. Stea (Eds.), Image and environment. Chicago: Aldine, 1973.

Herman, J. F., & Siegel, A. W. The development of spatial representations of large-scale environments. Paper presented to the Society for Research in Child Development, 1977.

Huttenlocher, J. Children's ability to order and orient objects. Child Development, 1967, 38, 1169–1176.

Ives, S. W. Children's ability to coordinate spatial perspectives through linguistic description. Paper presented to the Society for Research in Child Development, 1977.

Johnson, S. C. Hierarchical clustering schemes. Psychometrika, 1967, 32, 241–254.

Kahneman, D. Attention and effort. Englewood Cliff, N.J.: Prentice-Hall, 1973.

Keogh, B. K. Pattern walking under 3 conditions of available cues. American Journal of Mental Deficiency, 1969, 74, 376–381.

Keogh, B. K. Pattern copying under 3 conditions of an expanded visual field. Developmental Psychology, 1971, 4, 25–31.

Koffka, H. Principles of Gestalt psychology. London: Kegan Paul, 1935.

Kosslyn, S. M., Pick, H. L., & Fariello, G. R. Cognitive maps in children and men. Child Development, 1974, 45, 707–716.

Kruskal, J. B. Nonmetric multidimensional scaling: A numerical method. Psychometrika, 1964, 29, 115–129.

Ladd, F. C. Black youths view their environment: neighborhood maps. Environment and Behavior, 1970, 2, 64–79.

Lee, T. R. Psychology and living space. Transactions of the Bartlett Society, 1963–1964, 2, 9–36.

Lord, F. E. A study of spatial orientation of children. Journal of Educational Research, 1941, 34, 481–505.

Lynch, K. The image of the city. Cambridge, Mass.: MIT Press, 1960.

MacKay, D. B. The effect of spatial stimuli on the estimation of cognitive maps. Geographical Analysis, 1976, 3, 439–452.

McGee, V. The multidimensional analysis of "elastic" distances. *British Journal of Mathematics and Statistical Psychology*, 1966, *19*, 181–196.

Merrill, A. A., & Baird, J. C. Cognitive representation of spatial relations: III. A hypothetical environment. *Journal of Experimental Psychology-General*, in press, 1978.

Nagy, J. N., & Baird, J. C. A developmental look at town configuration. Paper presented to the Eastern Psychological Association, 1974.

Nagy, J. N., Szilagyi, P. G., & Baird, J. C. Children's planning strategies in environmental design. Paper presented to the Eastern Psychological Association, 1977.

Piaget, J., & Inhelder, B. *Mental imagery in the child*. New York: Basic, 1971.

Piaget, J., Inhelder, B., & Szeminaka, A. *The child's conception of geometry*. New York: Basic Books, 1960.

Potts, G. R. Information processing strategies used in the encoding of linear orderings. *Journal of Verbal Learning and Verbal Behavior*, 1972, *11*, 727–740.

Potts, G. R. Bringing order to cognitive structures. In F. Restle, R. M. Shriffin, N. J. Castellan, H. R. Lindman, & D. B. Pisoni (Eds.), *Cognitive Theory*. Vol. 1. Hillsdale, N.J.: Erlbaum Associates, 1975.

Saarinen, T. F. *Environmental planning; Perception and behavior*. Boston: Houghton Mifflin, 1976.

Shantz, C., & Watson, J. S. Spatial abilities and spatial egocentrism in the young child. *Child Development*, 1971, *42*, 171–181.

Shemyakin, F. N. Orientation in space. In B. G. Anan'yev et al. (Eds.), *Psychological science in the U.S.S.R.*. Vol. 1 (Report No. 11466). Washington, D.C.: U.S. Office of Technical Reports, 1962, Pp. 186–255.

Siegel, A. W. The place of environmental cognition in psychology (or vice versa). Paper presented to the Eastern Psychological Association, 1976.

Siegel, A. W., & Schadler, M. The development of young children's spatial representation of their classroom. *Child Development*, 1977, *48*, 388–394.

Siegel, A. W., & White, S. H. The development of spatial representations of large-scale environments. In H. W. Reese (Ed.) *Advances in child development and behavior*. Vol. 10. New York: Academic Press, 1975.

Smothergill, D. W. Accuracy and variability in the localization of spatial targets at three age levels. *Developmental Psychology*, 1973, *8*, 62–66.

Stea, D., & Blaut, J. M. Toward a developmental theory of spatial learning. In R. M. Downs & D. Stea (Eds.), *Image and environment*. Chicago: Aldine, 1973, Pp. 51–62.

Stea, D., & Downs, R. M. From the outside looking in at the inside looking out. *Environment and Behavior*, 1970, *2*, 3–13.

Szilagyi, P. G., & Baird, J. C. A quantitative approach to the study of visual symmetry. *Perception & Psychophysics*. In press, 1978.

Trabasso, T., & Riley, C. A. An information processing analysis of transitive inferences. Paper presented to the Eastern Psychological Association, 1973.

Trabasso, T., Riley, C. A., & Wilson, E. Spatial strategies in reasoning: A developmental study. In R. Falmagne (Ed.), *Psychological studies of logic and its development*. Hillsdale, N.J.: Erlbaum Associates, 1975.

Trowbridge, C. C. On fundamental methods of orientation and imaginary maps. *Science*, 1913, *38*, 888–897.

Index